OVER THE HEDGE

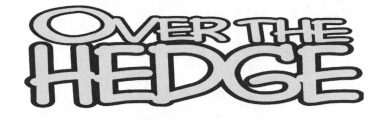

Stuffed Animals

Other Books by Michael Fry and T Lewis

Over the Hedge

Over the Hedge 2

Over the Hedge 3: Knights of the Picnic Table

OVER THE HEDGE

Stuffed Animals

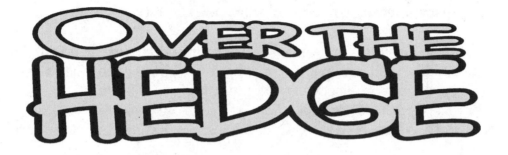

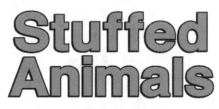

by Michael Fry
and T Lewis

Andrews McMeel
Publishing

Kansas City

Over the Hedge is distributed by United Feature Syndicate, Inc.

06 07 08 09 10 BBG 10 9 8 7 6 5 4

ISBN-13: 978-0-7407-5701-3
ISBN-10: 0-7407-5701-6

Library of Congress Control Number: 2005935604

www.andrewsmcmeel.com

To Jim Cox

Jim was the first to see that *Over the Hedge*
could reach beyond the funny pages. We thank him
for his passion, persistence, patience,
and—most of all—his friendship.

Foreword

The book you now hold is more than a mere collection of hysterical comic strips. It's about the timeless battle between living for the moment and planning for the future. Between immediate gratification and inner fulfillment. Between the id and the superego. Between RJ and Verne.

I've been reading the strip for a decade, and now I view the world through RJ- and Verne-colored glasses, especially since I began the job of bringing *Over the Hedge* to the big screen as an animated feature film. Nowadays, everyone I see is either a raccoon or a turtle. A simple trip to one of my umpteen local coffee hawkers becomes an involuntary exercise in personality sorting.

That guy over there dumping five white sugar packets into his triple giga-latte? He's an RJ. The woman with the decaf and the low-fat bran muffin? A Verne. The boy with the game system in his hands, the MP3 player in his ears, and the fudge brownie in his mouth? He's a major raccoon. And the slightly damp-looking character reading Baudelaire in the cardigan sweater? He's got turtle written all over him.

Me? I'm mostly a Verne. Except when I'm an RJ. The truth is, of course, that we're all a bit of both. And that is Mike and T's genius. Verne and RJ need each other. And we need them. This outdoor odd couple holds up a fun-house mirror to our contemporary obsessions. From the safety of their wilderness vantage point, they show us humans as we really are: a race of navel-gazing, pop-culture-enslaved hedonists encroaching on their pristine habitat.

But Verne and RJ are nothing if not forgiving. The suburbs took half their forest away from them, but they love us all the same. After all, if we didn't provide them with a constant stream of high-fructose munchies they'd have to go back to eating . . . whatever little woodland creatures eat in the wild. I don't know—bark? Roots? Ugh. Makes me shudder.

So grab a caffeinated sugar soda, snag some BHT-preserved snacks, park your behind in an electric shiatsu massage recliner, and read on. Dare to find out—are you an RJ or a Verne?

Tim Johnson
Codirector, *Over the Hedge* motion picture,
DreamWorks

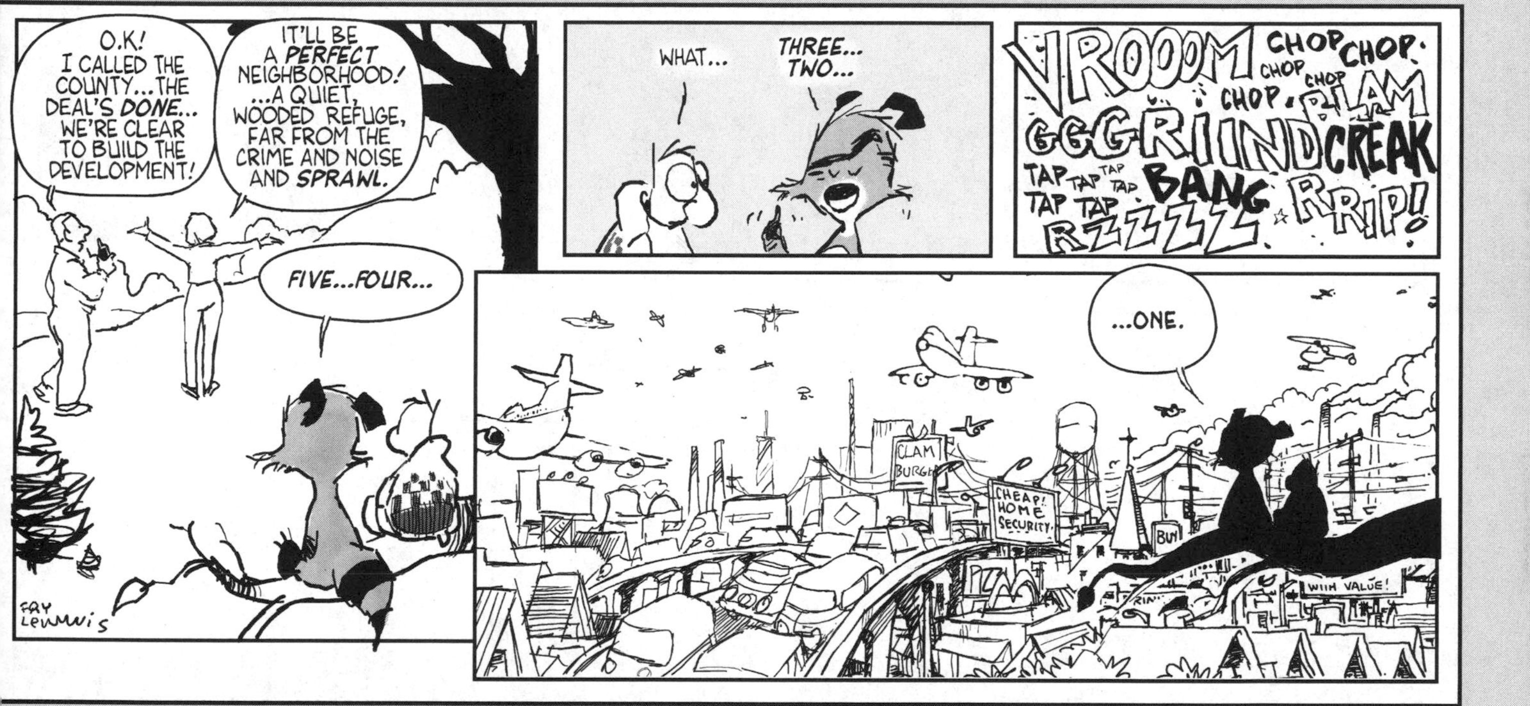
O.K! I CALLED THE COUNTY...THE DEAL'S DONE... WE'RE CLEAR TO BUILD THE DEVELOPMENT!
IT'LL BE A PERFECT NEIGHBORHOOD! ...A QUIET, WOODED REFUGE, FAR FROM THE CRIME AND NOISE AND SPRAWL.
FIVE...FOUR...
FRY LEWIS
WHAT...
THREE... TWO...
VROOOM CHOP CHOP CHOP CHOP CHOP BLAM
GGGRIIND CREAK
TAP TAP TAP TAP TAP TAP BANG RRIP!
RZZZZZ
...ONE.
CLAM BURG
CHEAP! HOME SECURITY.
BUY!
WITH VALUE!

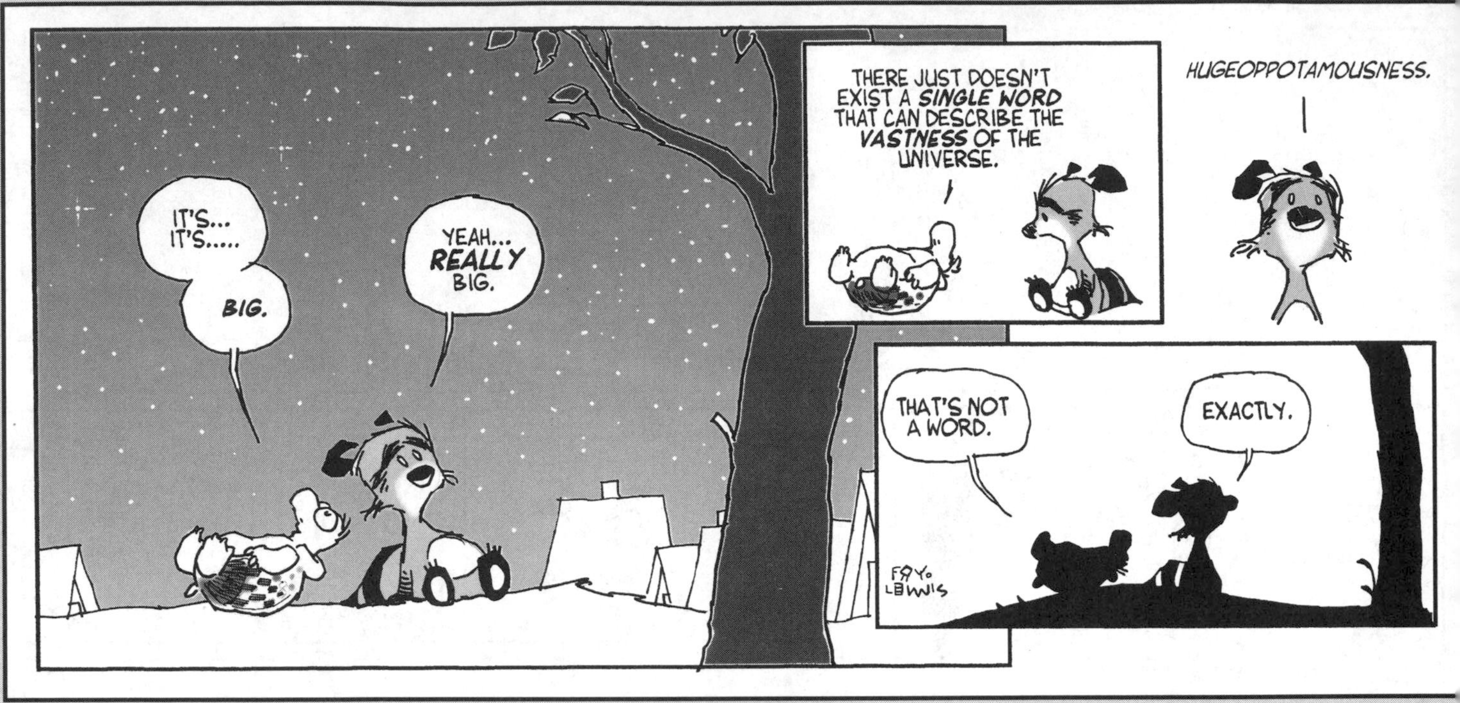
IT'S... IT'S.....
BIG.
YEAH... REALLY BIG.
THERE JUST DOESN'T EXIST A SINGLE WORD THAT CAN DESCRIBE THE VASTNESS OF THE UNIVERSE.
HUGEOPPOTAMOUSNESS.
THAT'S NOT A WORD.
EXACTLY.

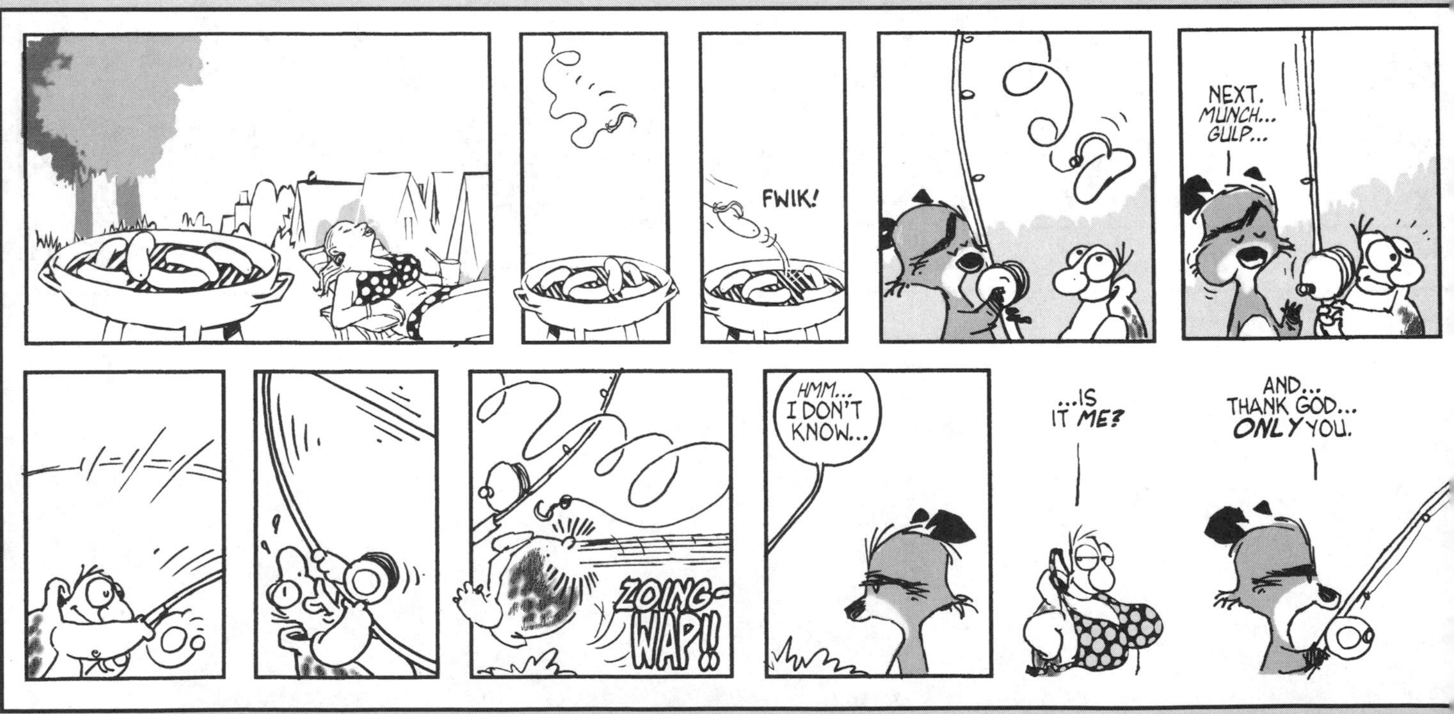
FWIK!
NEXT.
MUNCH... GULP...
ZOING-WAP!!
HMM... I DON'T KNOW...
...IS IT ME?
AND... THANK GOD... ONLY YOU.

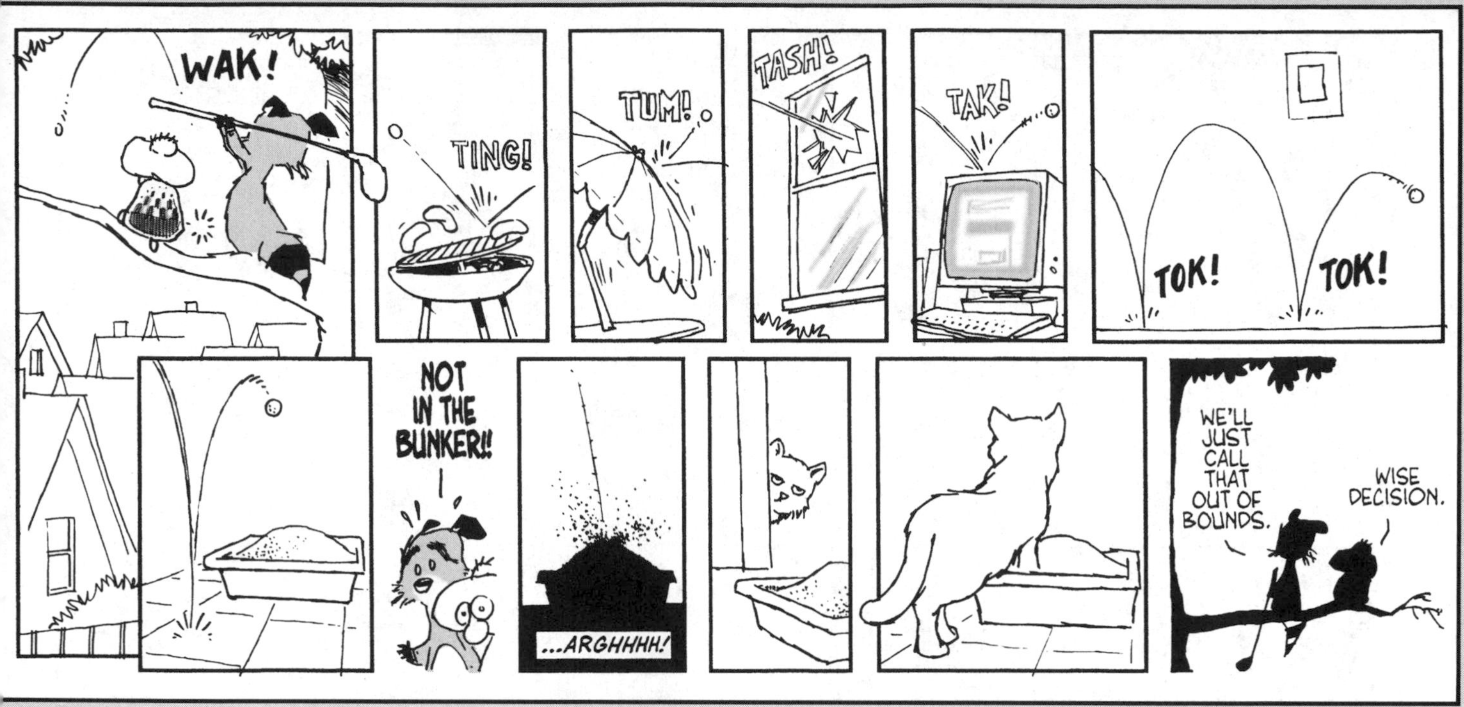
WAK!
TING!
TUM!
TASH!
TAK!
TOK!
TOK!
NOT IN THE BUNKER!!
...ARGHHHH!
WE'LL JUST CALL THAT OUT OF BOUNDS.
WISE DECISION.

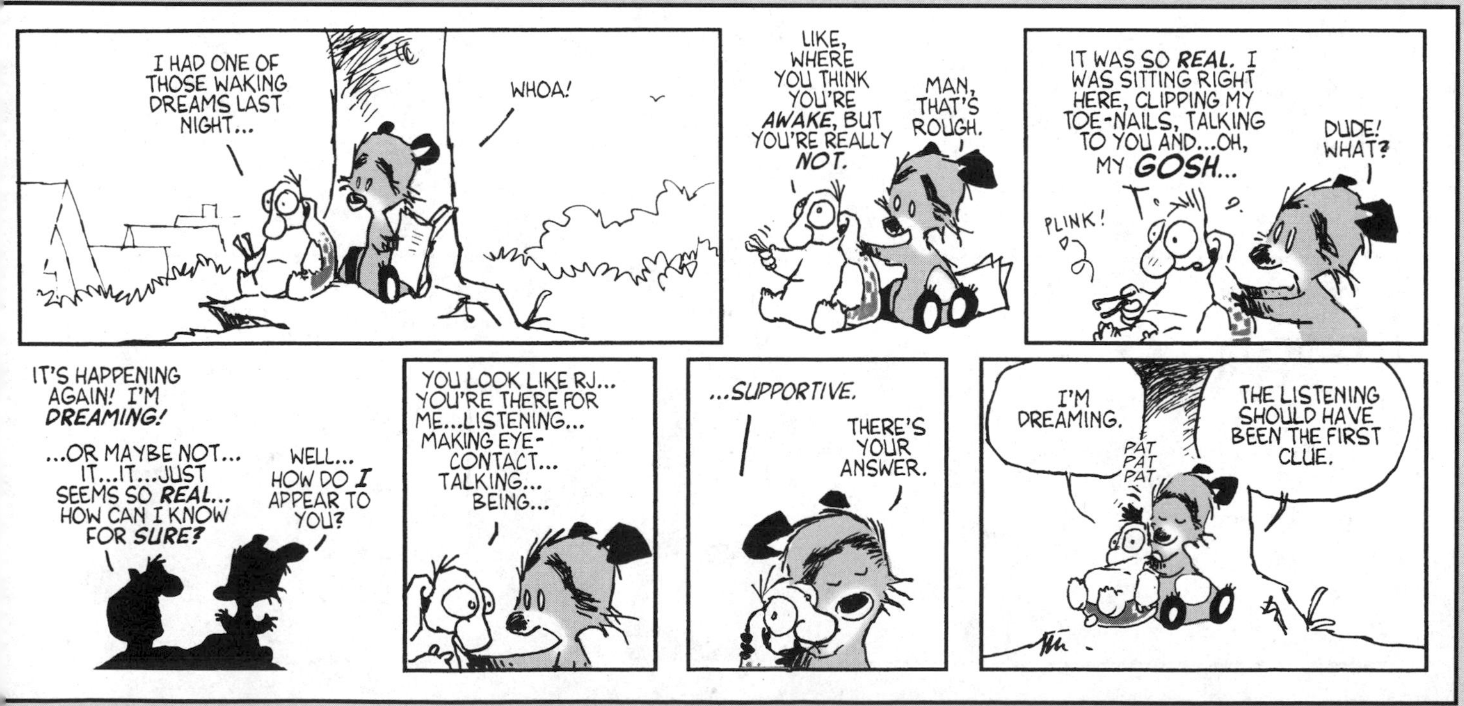
I HAD ONE OF THOSE WAKING DREAMS LAST NIGHT...
WHOA!
LIKE, WHERE YOU THINK YOU'RE AWAKE, BUT YOU'RE REALLY NOT.
MAN, THAT'S ROUGH.
IT WAS SO REAL. I WAS SITTING RIGHT HERE, CLIPPING MY TOE-NAILS, TALKING TO YOU AND...OH, MY GOSH...
PLINK!
DUDE! WHAT?
IT'S HAPPENING AGAIN! I'M DREAMING!
...OR MAYBE NOT... IT...IT...JUST SEEMS SO REAL... HOW CAN I KNOW FOR SURE?
WELL... HOW DO I APPEAR TO YOU?
YOU LOOK LIKE RJ... YOU'RE THERE FOR ME...LISTENING... MAKING EYE-CONTACT... TALKING... BEING...
...SUPPORTIVE.
THERE'S YOUR ANSWER.
I'M DREAMING.
PAT PAT PAT
THE LISTENING SHOULD HAVE BEEN THE FIRST CLUE.

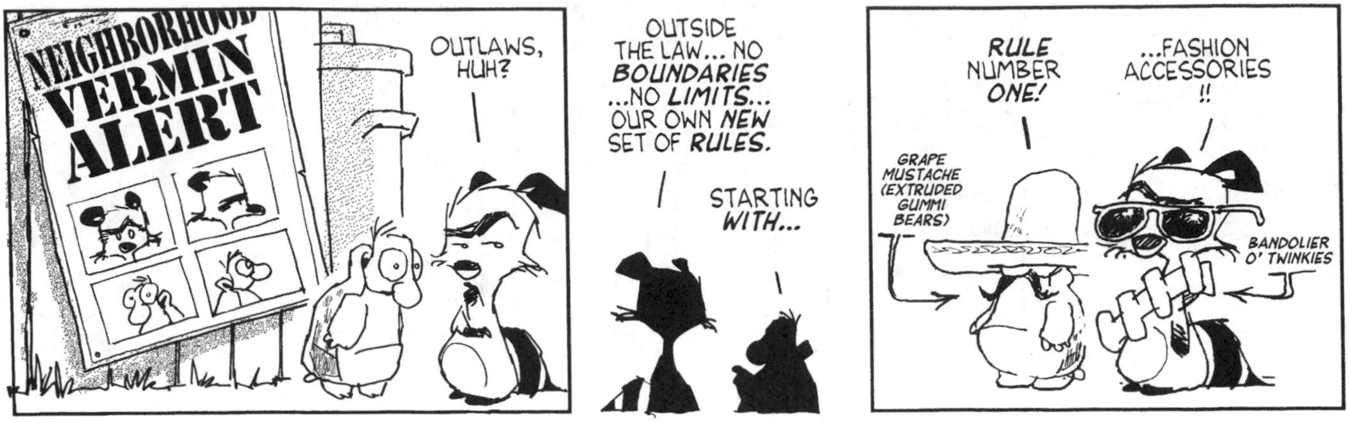
NEIGHBORHOOD VERMIN ALERT
OUTLAWS, HUH?
OUTSIDE THE LAW... NO *BOUNDARIES* ...NO *LIMITS*... OUR OWN *NEW* SET OF *RULES.*
STARTING *WITH...*
RULE NUMBER *ONE!*
...FASHION ACCESSORIES !!
GRAPE MUSTACHE (EXTRUDED GUMMI BEARS)
BANDOLIER O' TWINKIES

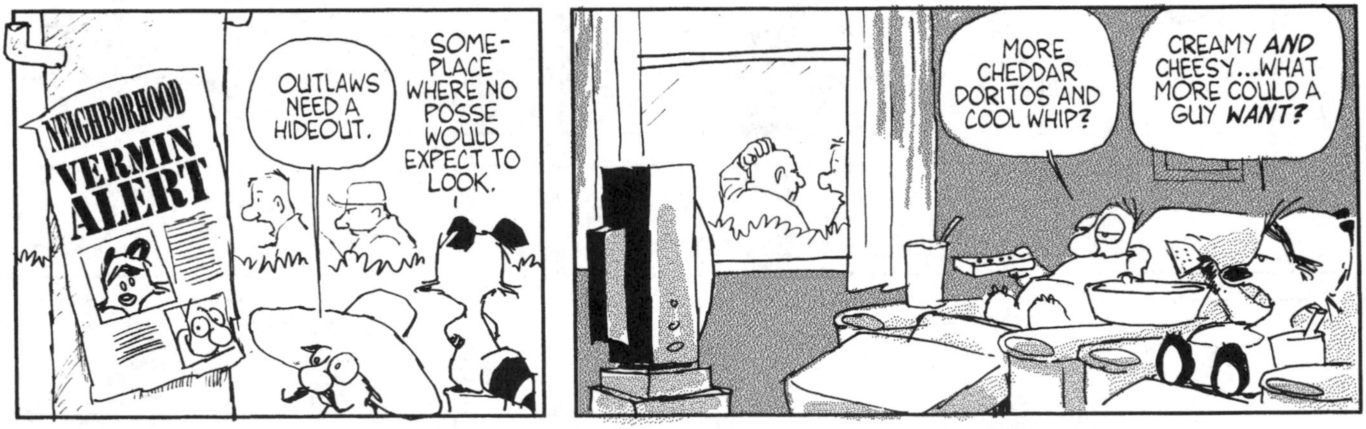
NEIGHBORHOOD VERMIN ALERT
OUTLAWS NEED A HIDEOUT.
SOME-PLACE WHERE NO POSSE WOULD EXPECT TO LOOK.
MORE CHEDDAR DORITOS AND COOL WHIP?
CREAMY *AND* CHEESY...WHAT MORE COULD A GUY *WANT?*

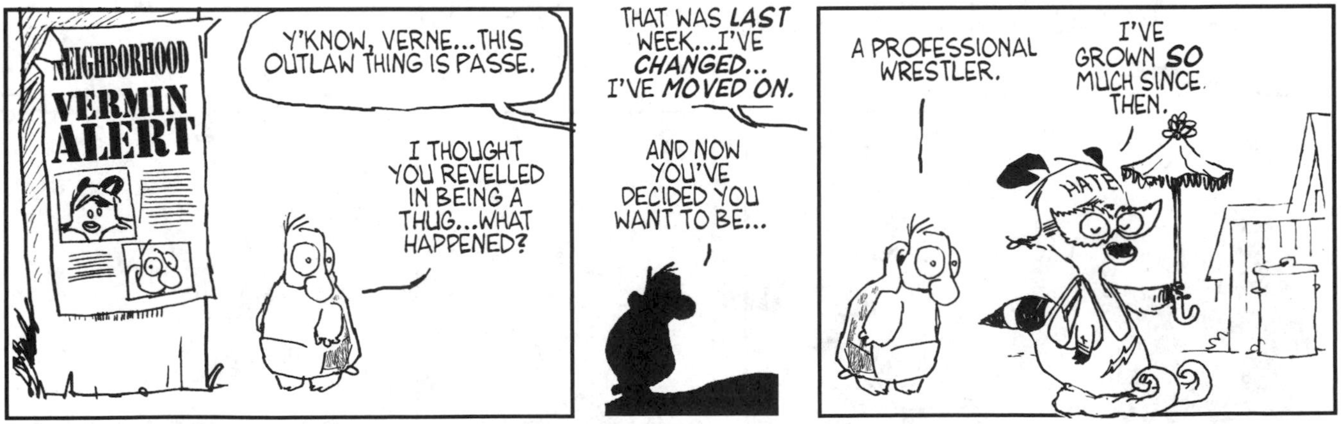
NEIGHBORHOOD VERMIN ALERT
Y'KNOW, VERNE...THIS OUTLAW THING IS PASSE.
I THOUGHT YOU REVELLED IN BEING A THUG...WHAT HAPPENED?
THAT WAS *LAST* WEEK...I'VE *CHANGED...* I'VE *MOVED ON.*
AND NOW YOU'VE DECIDED YOU WANT TO BE...
A PROFESSIONAL WRESTLER.
I'VE GROWN *SO* MUCH SINCE THEN.
HATE

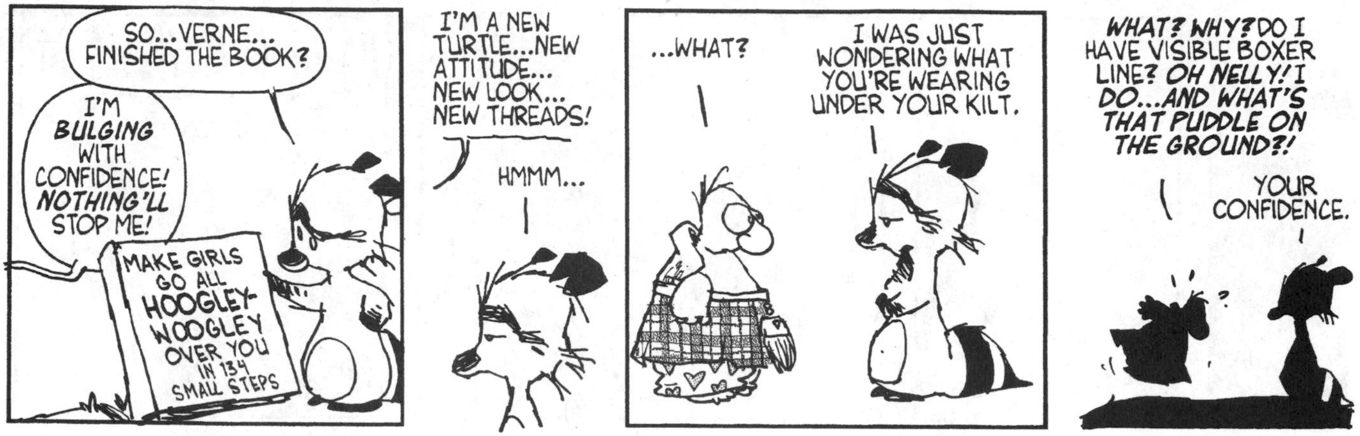
SO...VERNE... FINISHED THE BOOK?
I'M BULGING WITH CONFIDENCE! NOTHING'LL STOP ME!
MAKE GIRLS GO ALL HOOGLEY-WOOGLEY OVER YOU IN 134 SMALL STEPS
I'M A NEW TURTLE...NEW ATTITUDE... NEW LOOK... NEW THREADS!
HMMM...
...WHAT?
I WAS JUST WONDERING WHAT YOU'RE WEARING UNDER YOUR KILT.
WHAT? WHY? DO I HAVE VISIBLE BOXER LINE? OH NELLY! I DO...AND WHAT'S THAT PUDDLE ON THE GROUND?!
YOUR CONFIDENCE.

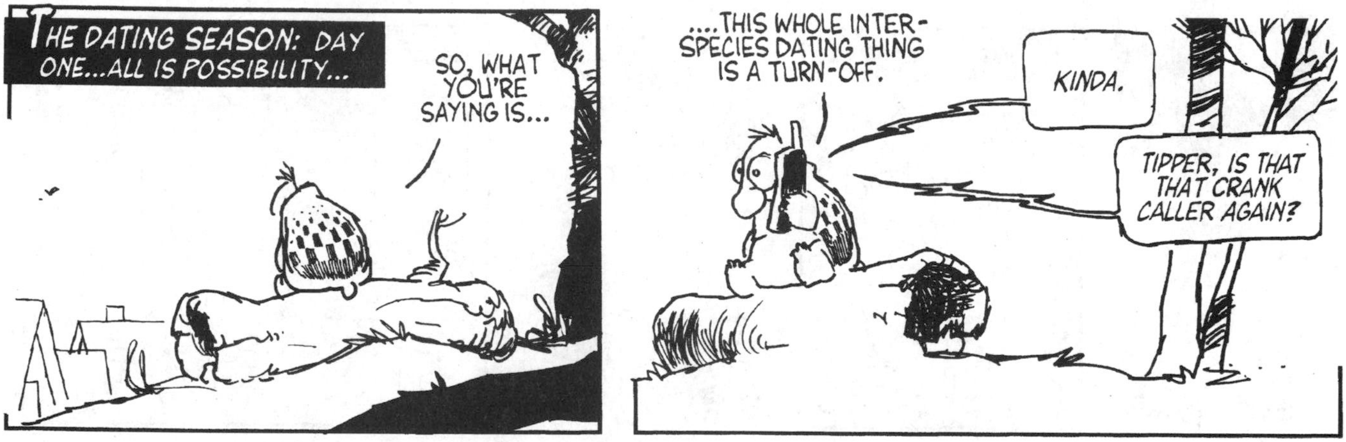
THE DATING SEASON: DAY ONE...ALL IS POSSIBILITY...
SO, WHAT YOU'RE SAYING IS...
....THIS WHOLE INTER-SPECIES DATING THING IS A TURN-OFF.
KINDA.
TIPPER, IS THAT THAT CRANK CALLER AGAIN?

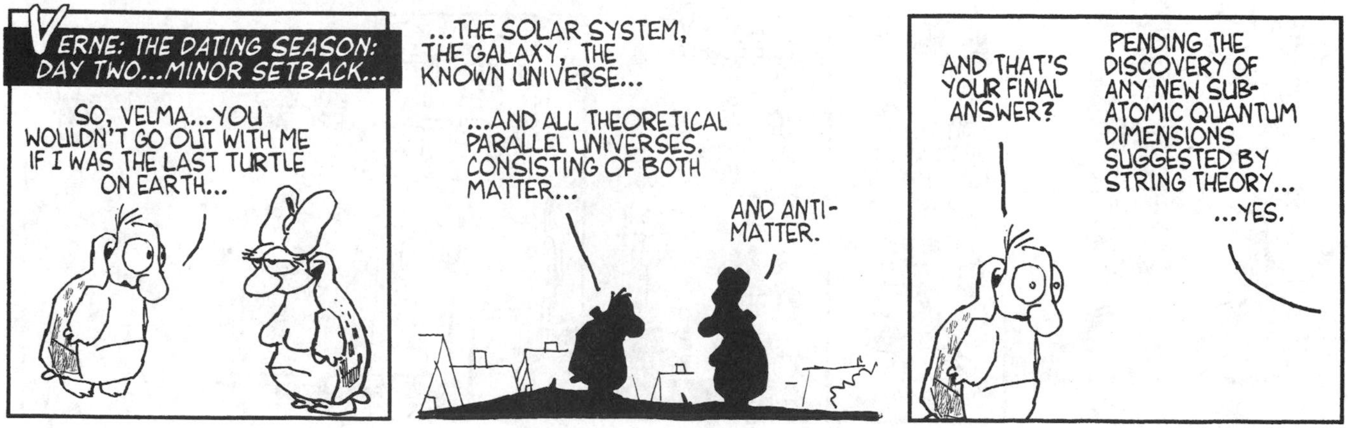
VERNE: THE DATING SEASON: DAY TWO...MINOR SETBACK...
SO, VELMA...YOU WOULDN'T GO OUT WITH ME IF I WAS THE LAST TURTLE ON EARTH...
...THE SOLAR SYSTEM, THE GALAXY, THE KNOWN UNIVERSE...
...AND ALL THEORETICAL PARALLEL UNIVERSES. CONSISTING OF BOTH MATTER...
AND ANTI-MATTER.
AND THAT'S YOUR FINAL ANSWER?
PENDING THE DISCOVERY OF ANY NEW SUB-ATOMIC QUANTUM DIMENSIONS SUGGESTED BY STRING THEORY...
...YES.

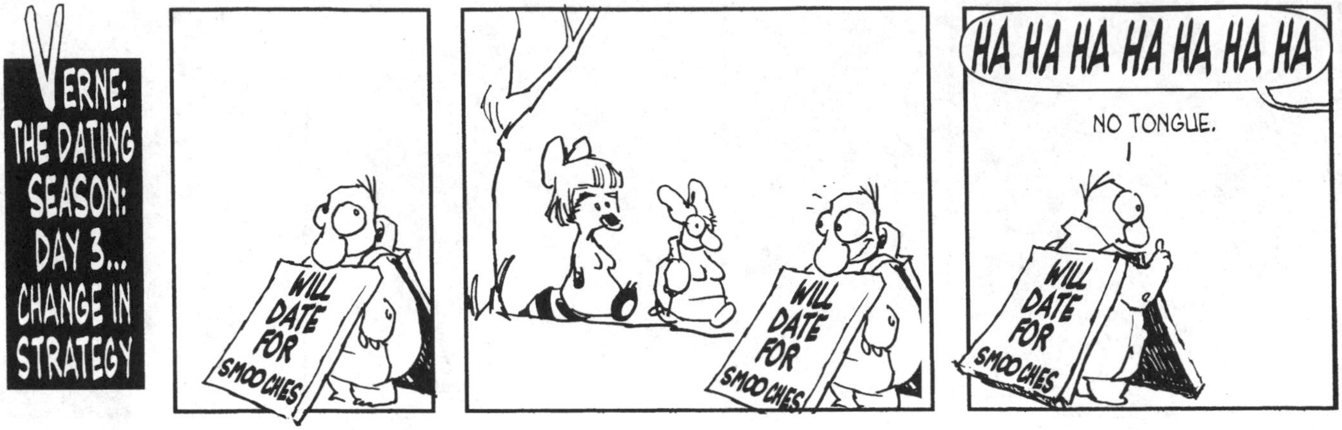
VERNE: THE DATING SEASON: DAY 3... CHANGE IN STRATEGY
WILL DATE FOR SMOOCHES
WILL DATE FOR SMOOCHES
HA HA HA HA HA HA HA
NO TONGUE.
WILL DATE FOR SMOOCHES

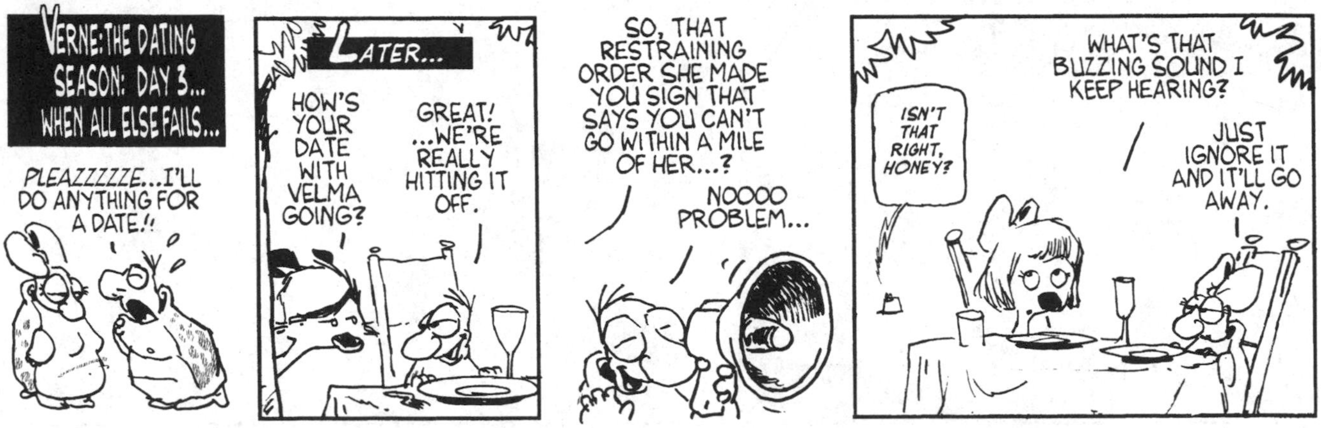
VERNE: THE DATING SEASON: DAY 3... WHEN ALL ELSE FAILS...
PLEAZZZZZE...I'LL DO ANYTHING FOR A DATE!!
LATER...
HOW'S YOUR DATE WITH VELMA GOING?
GREAT! ...WE'RE REALLY HITTING IT OFF.
SO, THAT RESTRAINING ORDER SHE MADE YOU SIGN THAT SAYS YOU CAN'T GO WITHIN A MILE OF HER...?
NOOOO PROBLEM...
ISN'T THAT RIGHT, HONEY?
WHAT'S THAT BUZZING SOUND I KEEP HEARING?
JUST IGNORE IT AND IT'LL GO AWAY.

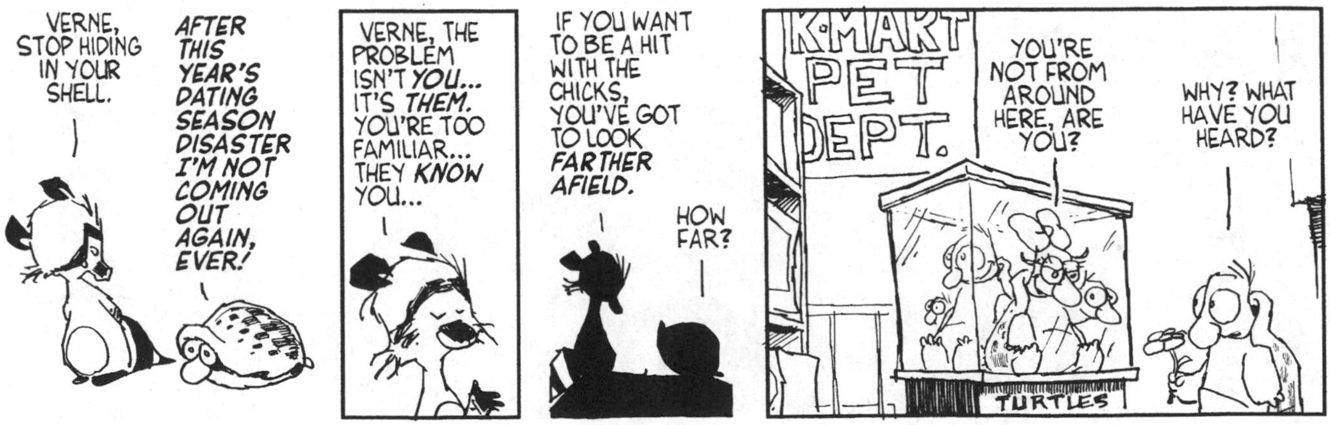
VERNE, STOP HIDING IN YOUR SHELL.
AFTER THIS YEAR'S DATING SEASON DISASTER I'M NOT COMING OUT AGAIN, EVER!
VERNE, THE PROBLEM ISN'T YOU... IT'S THEM. YOU'RE TOO FAMILIAR... THEY KNOW YOU...
IF YOU WANT TO BE A HIT WITH THE CHICKS, YOU'VE GOT TO LOOK FARTHER AFIELD.
HOW FAR?
K-MART PET DEPT.
YOU'RE NOT FROM AROUND HERE, ARE YOU?
WHY? WHAT HAVE YOU HEARD?
TURTLES

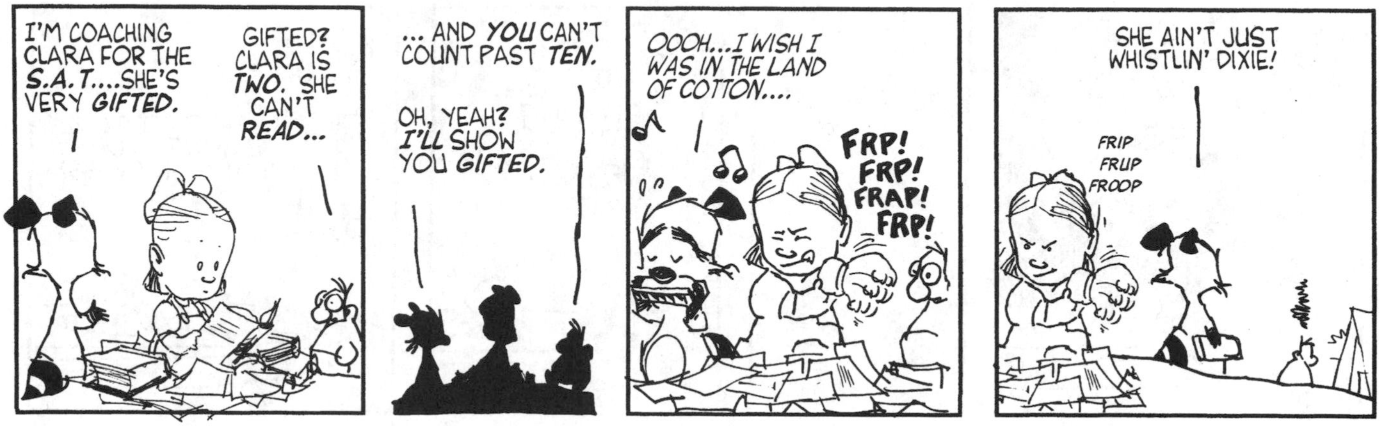
I'M COACHING CLARA FOR THE S.A.T....SHE'S VERY GIFTED.
GIFTED? CLARA IS TWO. SHE CAN'T READ...
... AND YOU CAN'T COUNT PAST TEN.
OH, YEAH? I'LL SHOW YOU GIFTED.
OOOH...I WISH I WAS IN THE LAND OF COTTON....
FRP! FRP! FRAP! FRP!
SHE AIN'T JUST WHISTLIN' DIXIE!
FRIP FRUP FROOP

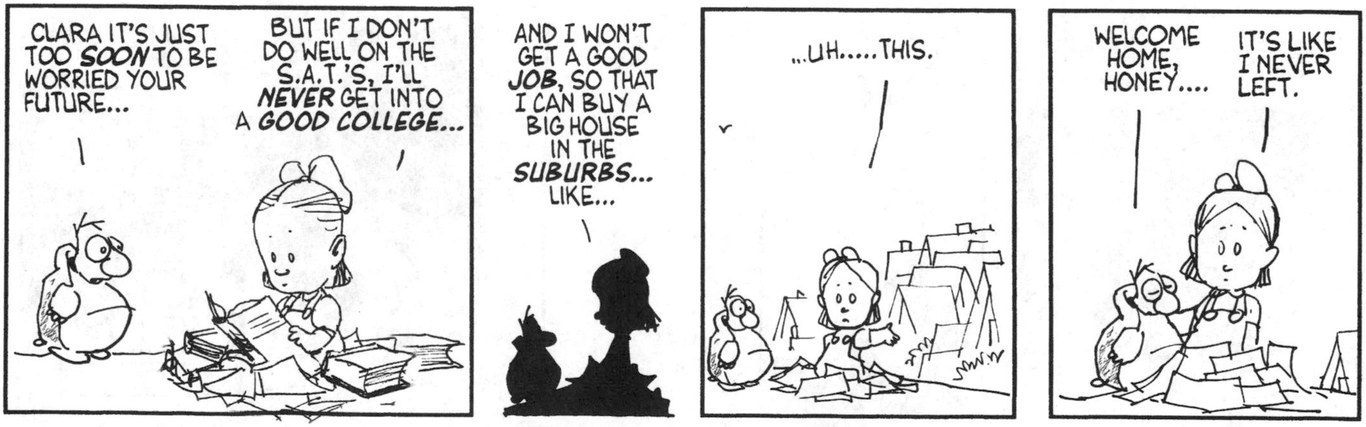
CLARA IT'S JUST TOO SOON TO BE WORRIED YOUR FUTURE...
BUT IF I DON'T DO WELL ON THE S.A.T.'S, I'LL NEVER GET INTO A GOOD COLLEGE...
AND I WON'T GET A GOOD JOB, SO THAT I CAN BUY A BIG HOUSE IN THE SUBURBS... LIKE...
...UH.....THIS.
WELCOME HOME, HONEY....
IT'S LIKE I NEVER LEFT.

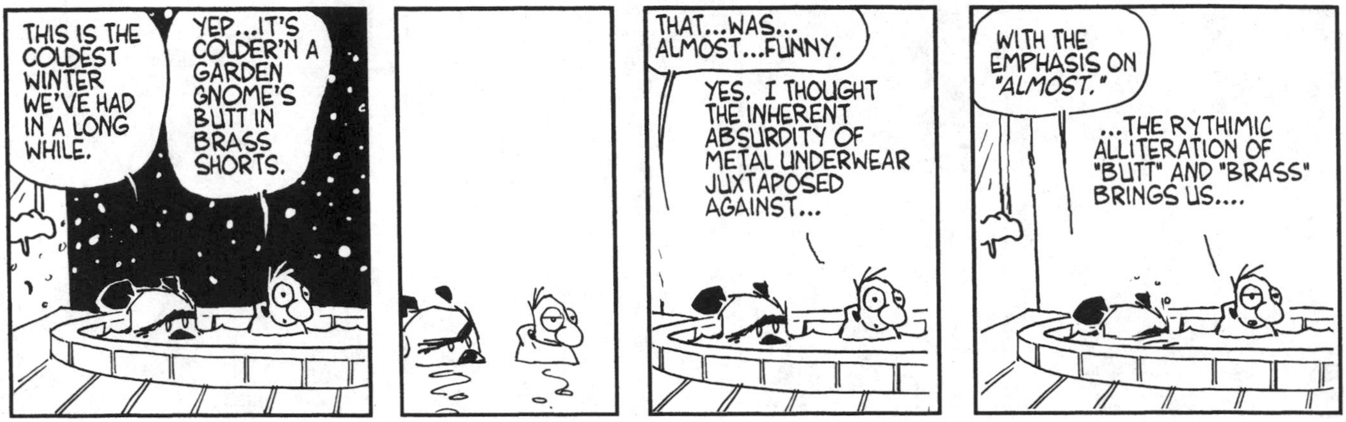
THIS IS THE COLDEST WINTER WE'VE HAD IN A LONG WHILE.
YEP...IT'S COLDER'N A GARDEN GNOME'S BUTT IN BRASS SHORTS.
THAT...WAS... ALMOST...FUNNY.
YES. I THOUGHT THE INHERENT ABSURDITY OF METAL UNDERWEAR JUXTAPOSED AGAINST...
WITH THE EMPHASIS ON "ALMOST."
...THE RYTHIMIC ALLITERATION OF "BUTT" AND "BRASS" BRINGS US....

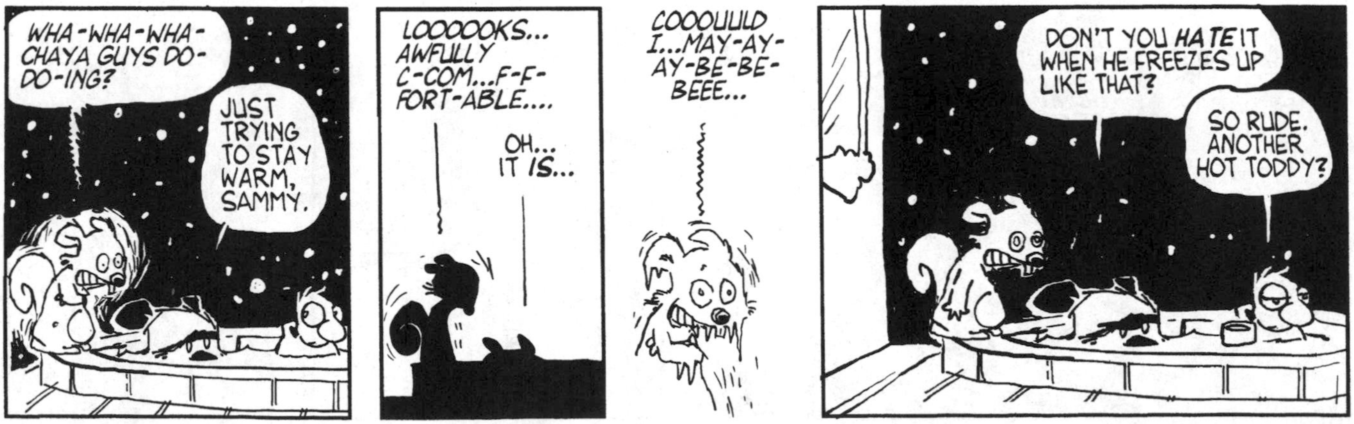
WHA-WHA-WHA-CHAYA GUYS DO-DO-ING?
JUST TRYING TO STAY WARM, SAMMY.
LOOOOOKS... AWFULLY C-COM...F-F-FORT-ABLE....
OH... IT IS...
COOOUULD I...MAY-AY-AY-BE-BE-BEEE...
DON'T YOU HATE IT WHEN HE FREEZES UP LIKE THAT?
SO RUDE. ANOTHER HOT TODDY?

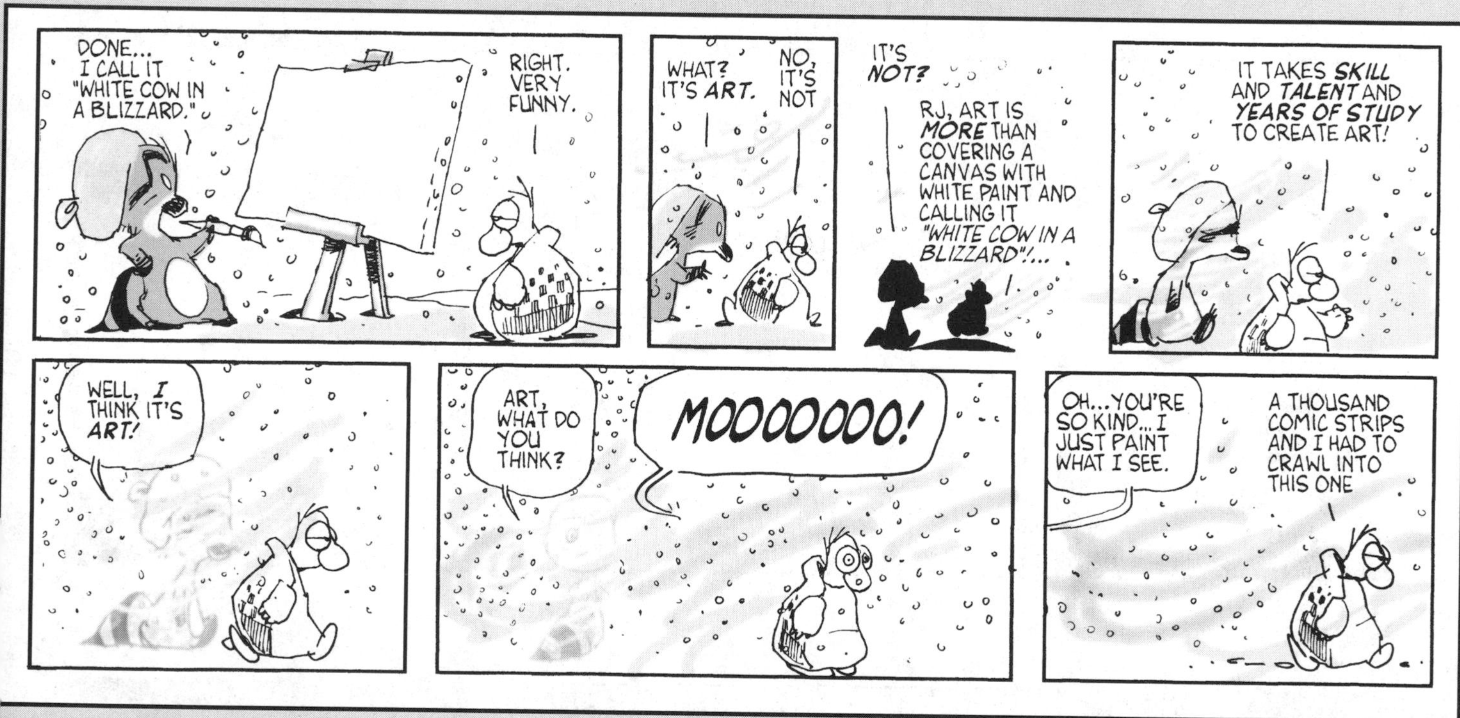
DONE... I CALL IT "WHITE COW IN A BLIZZARD."
RIGHT. VERY FUNNY.
WHAT? IT'S ART.
NO, IT'S NOT
IT'S NOT?
RJ, ART IS MORE THAN COVERING A CANVAS WITH WHITE PAINT AND CALLING IT "WHITE COW IN A BLIZZARD"!...
IT TAKES SKILL AND TALENT AND YEARS OF STUDY TO CREATE ART!
WELL, I THINK IT'S ART!
ART, WHAT DO YOU THINK?
MOOOOOOO!
OH...YOU'RE SO KIND... I JUST PAINT WHAT I SEE.
A THOUSAND COMIC STRIPS AND I HAD TO CRAWL INTO THIS ONE

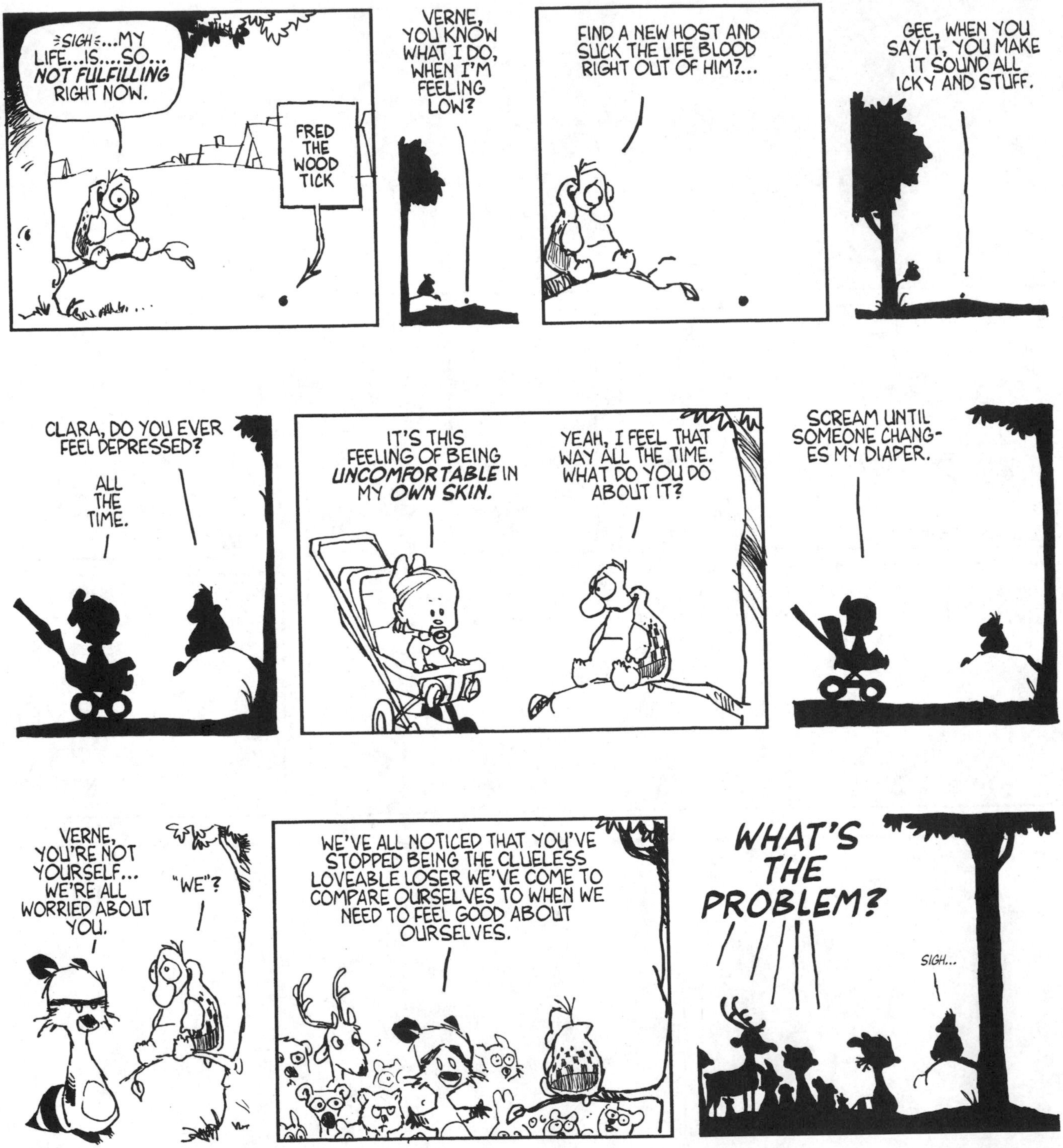

SIGH...MY LIFE...IS....SO... NOT FULFILLING RIGHT NOW.
FRED THE WOOD TICK
VERNE, YOU KNOW WHAT I DO, WHEN I'M FEELING LOW?
FIND A NEW HOST AND SUCK THE LIFE BLOOD RIGHT OUT OF HIM?...
GEE, WHEN YOU SAY IT, YOU MAKE IT SOUND ALL ICKY AND STUFF.
CLARA, DO YOU EVER FEEL DEPRESSED?
ALL THE TIME.
IT'S THIS FEELING OF BEING UNCOMFORTABLE IN MY OWN SKIN.
YEAH, I FEEL THAT WAY ALL THE TIME. WHAT DO YOU DO ABOUT IT?
SCREAM UNTIL SOMEONE CHANGES MY DIAPER.
VERNE, YOU'RE NOT YOURSELF... WE'RE ALL WORRIED ABOUT YOU.
"WE"?
WE'VE ALL NOTICED THAT YOU'VE STOPPED BEING THE CLUELESS LOVEABLE LOSER WE'VE COME TO COMPARE OURSELVES TO WHEN WE NEED TO FEEL GOOD ABOUT OURSELVES.
WHAT'S THE PROBLEM?
SIGH...

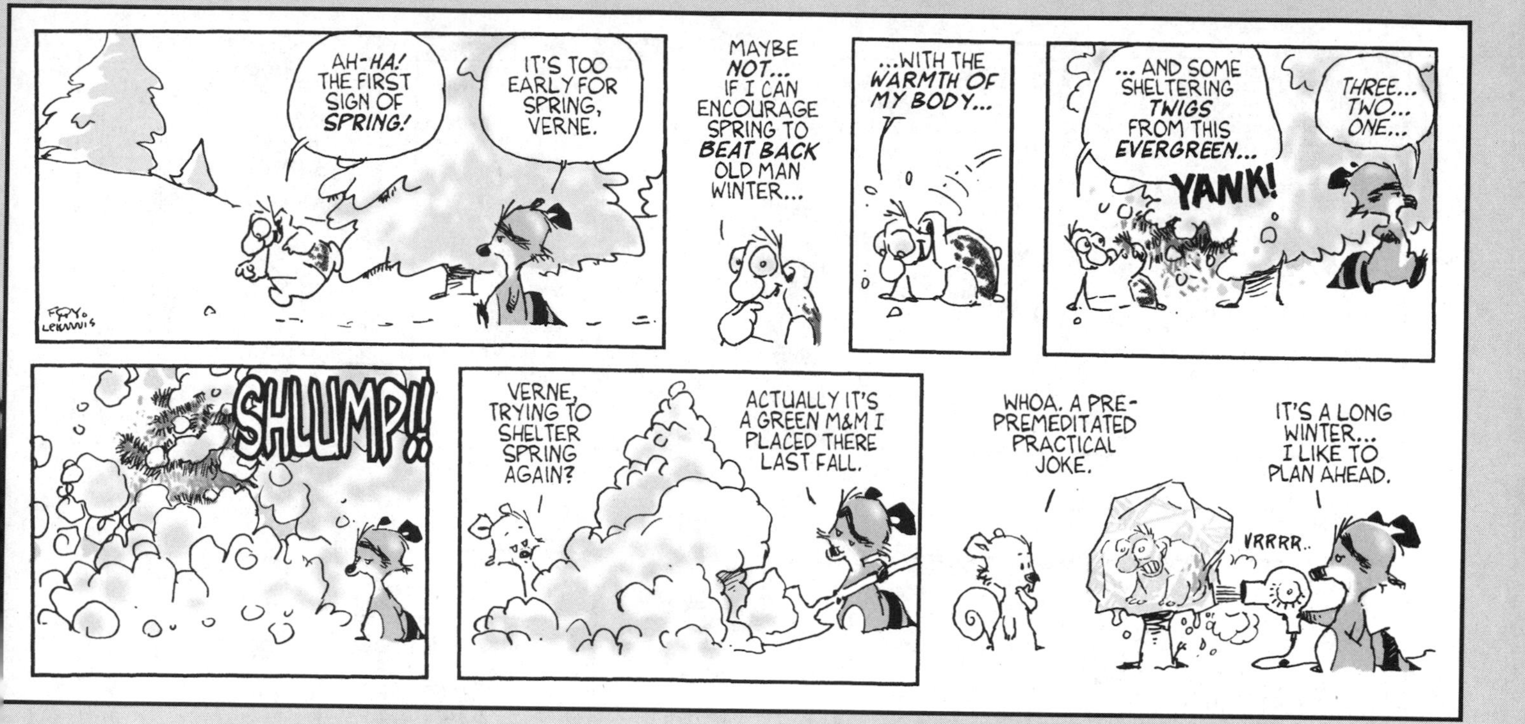
AH-*HA!* THE FIRST SIGN OF *SPRING!*
IT'S TOO EARLY FOR SPRING, VERNE.
MAYBE *NOT*... IF I CAN ENCOURAGE SPRING TO *BEAT BACK* OLD MAN WINTER...
...WITH THE *WARMTH OF MY BODY*...
... AND SOME SHELTERING *TWIGS* FROM THIS *EVERGREEN*...
YANK!
THREE... TWO... ONE...
SHLUMP!!
VERNE, TRYING TO SHELTER SPRING AGAIN?
ACTUALLY IT'S A GREEN M&M I PLACED THERE LAST FALL.
WHOA. A PRE-PREMEDITATED PRACTICAL JOKE.
IT'S A LONG WINTER... I LIKE TO PLAN AHEAD.
VRRRR..

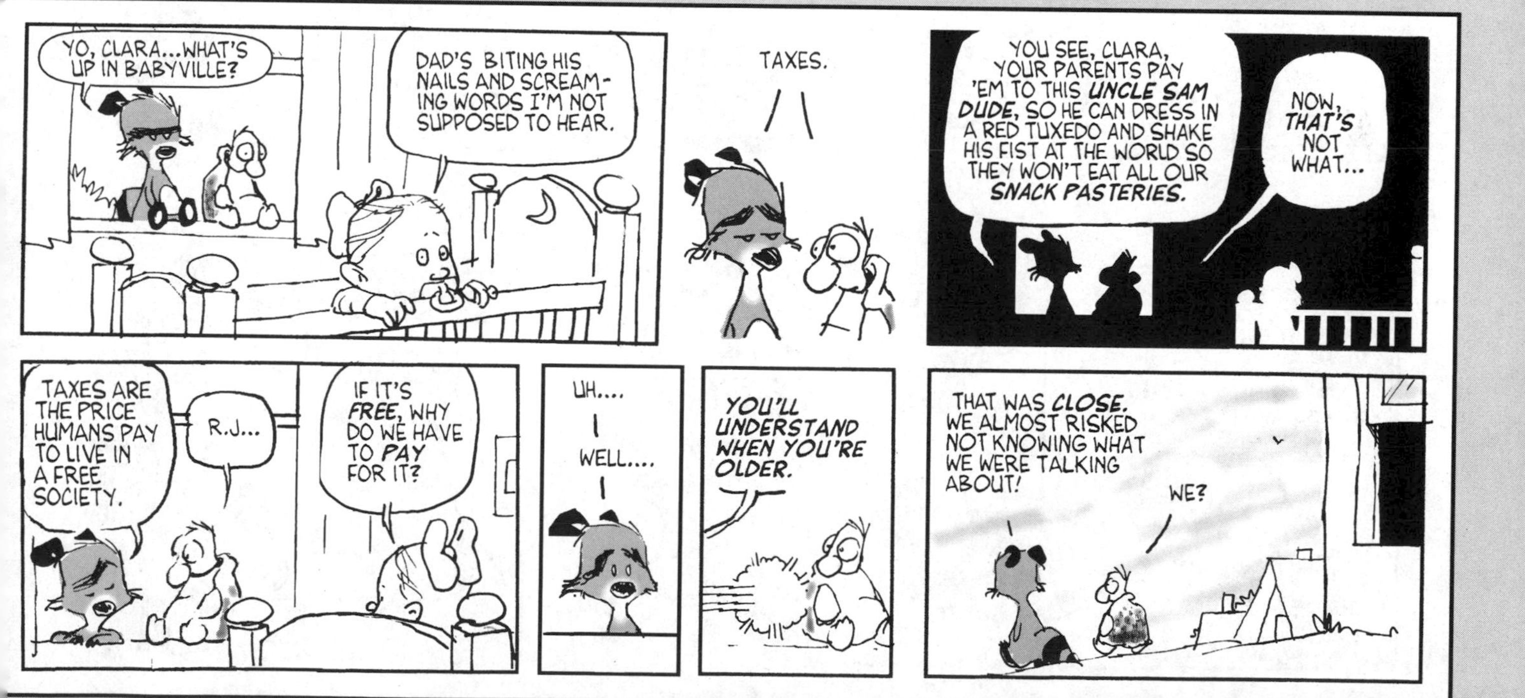
YO, CLARA...WHAT'S UP IN BABYVILLE?
DAD'S BITING HIS NAILS AND SCREAMING WORDS I'M NOT SUPPOSED TO HEAR.
TAXES.
YOU SEE, CLARA, YOUR PARENTS PAY 'EM TO THIS *UNCLE SAM DUDE*, SO HE CAN DRESS IN A RED TUXEDO AND SHAKE HIS FIST AT THE WORLD SO THEY WON'T EAT ALL OUR *SNACK PASTERIES.*
NOW, *THAT'S* NOT WHAT...
TAXES ARE THE PRICE HUMANS PAY TO LIVE IN A FREE SOCIETY.
R.J...
IF IT'S *FREE*, WHY DO WE HAVE TO *PAY* FOR IT?
UH....
WELL....
YOU'LL UNDERSTAND WHEN YOU'RE OLDER.
THAT WAS *CLOSE.* WE ALMOST RISKED NOT KNOWING WHAT WE WERE TALKING ABOUT!
WE?

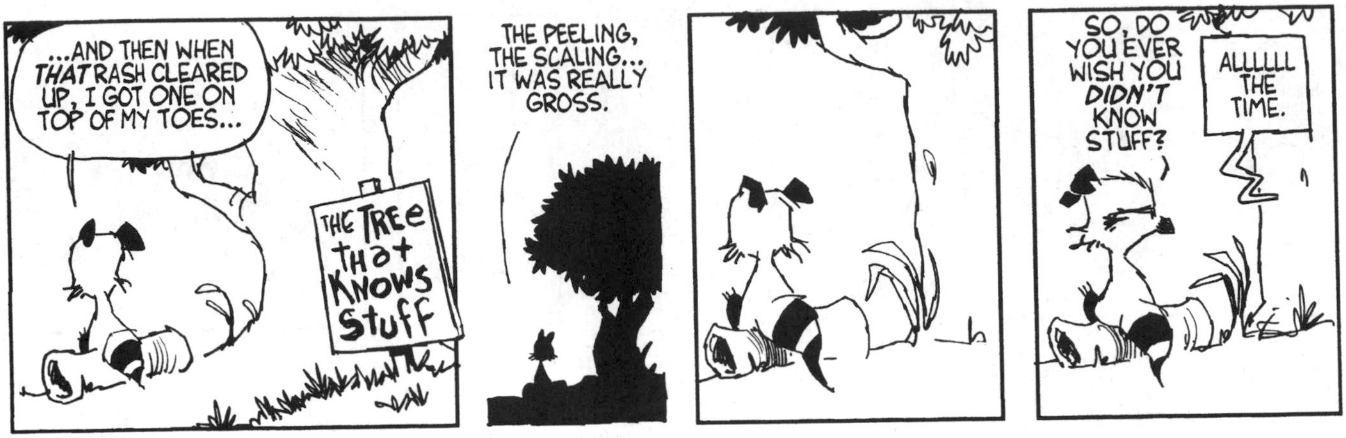
...AND THEN WHEN *THAT* RASH CLEARED UP, I GOT ONE ON TOP OF MY TOES...
THE TREE THAT KNOWS STUFF
THE PEELING, THE SCALING... IT WAS REALLY GROSS.
SO, DO YOU EVER WISH YOU *DIDN'T* KNOW STUFF?
ALLLLLL THE TIME.

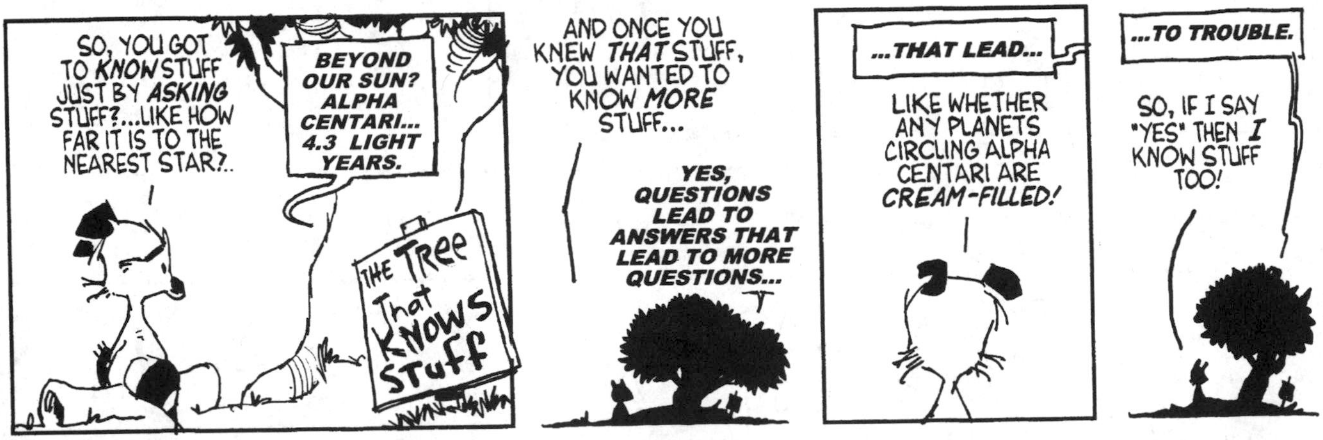
SO, YOU GOT TO *KNOW* STUFF JUST BY *ASKING* STUFF?...LIKE HOW FAR IT IS TO THE NEAREST STAR?..
BEYOND OUR SUN? ALPHA CENTARI... 4.3 LIGHT YEARS.
THE TREE THAT KNOWS STUFF
AND ONCE YOU KNEW *THAT* STUFF, YOU WANTED TO KNOW *MORE* STUFF...
YES, QUESTIONS LEAD TO ANSWERS THAT LEAD TO MORE QUESTIONS...
...THAT LEAD...
LIKE WHETHER ANY PLANETS CIRCLING ALPHA CENTARI ARE *CREAM-FILLED!*
...TO TROUBLE.
SO, IF I SAY "YES" THEN *I* KNOW STUFF TOO!

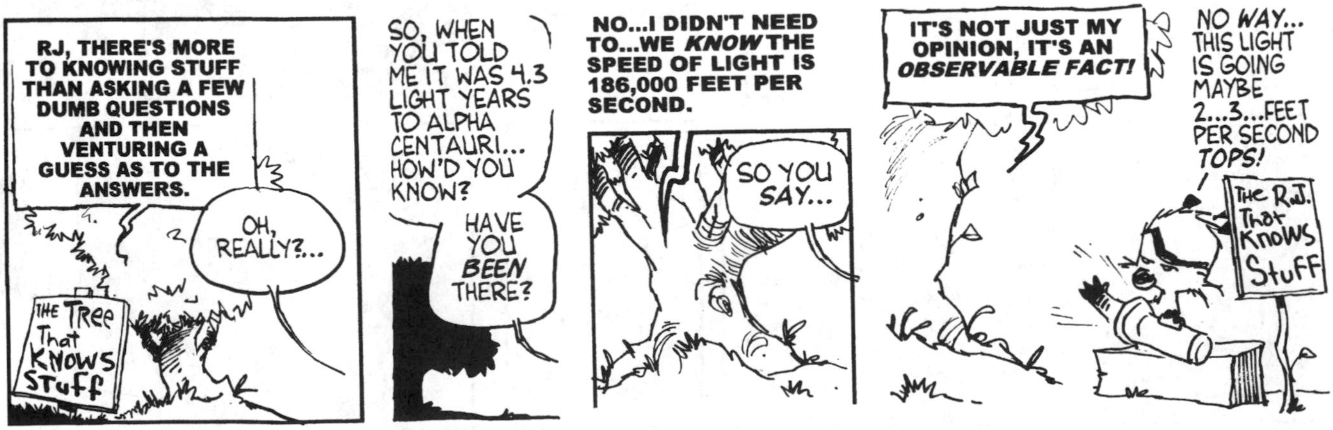
RJ, THERE'S MORE TO KNOWING STUFF THAN ASKING A FEW DUMB QUESTIONS AND THEN VENTURING A GUESS AS TO THE ANSWERS.
OH, REALLY?...
THE TREE THAT KNOWS STUFF
SO, WHEN YOU TOLD ME IT WAS 4.3 LIGHT YEARS TO ALPHA CENTAURI... HOW'D YOU KNOW?
HAVE YOU *BEEN* THERE?
NO...I DIDN'T NEED TO...WE *KNOW* THE SPEED OF LIGHT IS 186,000 FEET PER SECOND.
SO YOU SAY...
IT'S NOT JUST MY OPINION, IT'S AN *OBSERVABLE FACT!*
NO *WAY*... THIS LIGHT IS GOING MAYBE 2...3...FEET PER SECOND *TOPS!*
THE R.J. THAT KNOWS STUFF

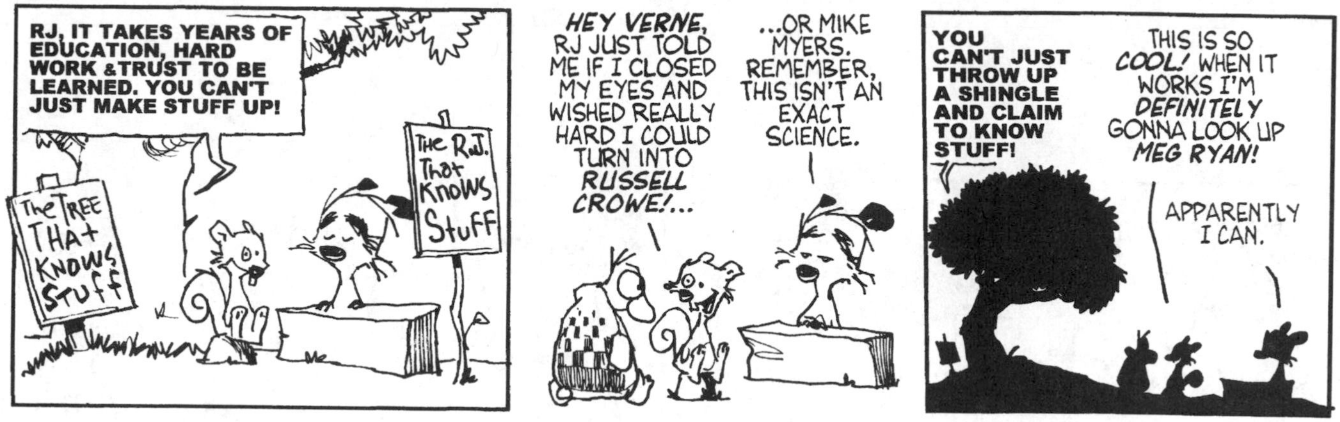
RJ, IT TAKES YEARS OF EDUCATION, HARD WORK &TRUST TO BE LEARNED. YOU CAN'T JUST MAKE STUFF UP!
The TREE THAT KNOWS Stuff
The R.J. That Knows Stuff
HEY VERNE, RJ JUST TOLD ME IF I CLOSED MY EYES AND WISHED REALLY HARD I COULD TURN INTO RUSSELL CROWE!...
...OR MIKE MYERS. REMEMBER, THIS ISN'T AN EXACT SCIENCE.
YOU CAN'T JUST THROW UP A SHINGLE AND CLAIM TO KNOW STUFF!
THIS IS SO COOL! WHEN IT WORKS I'M DEFINITELY GONNA LOOK UP MEG RYAN!
APPARENTLY I CAN.

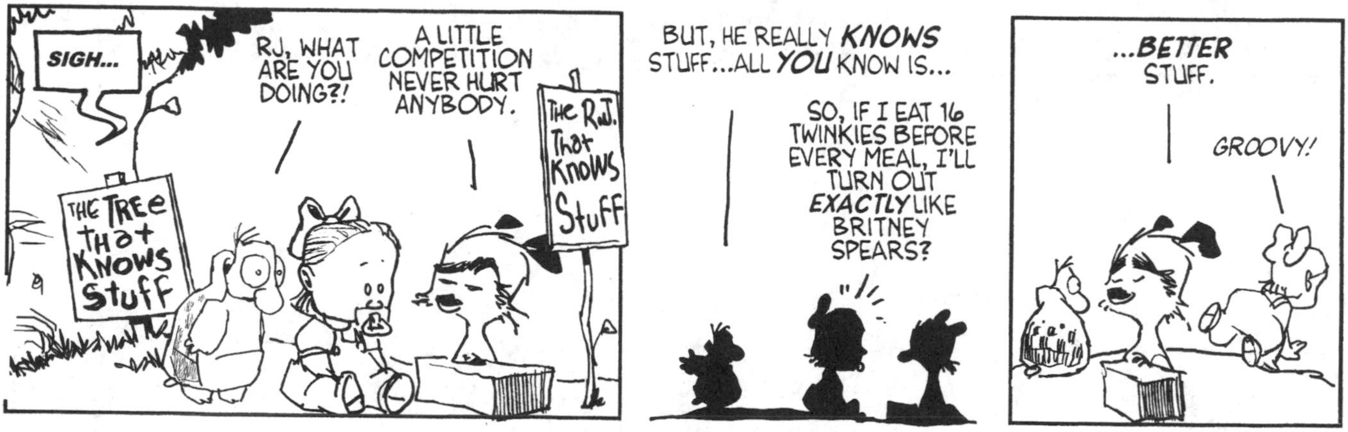
SIGH...
RJ, WHAT ARE YOU DOING?!
A LITTLE COMPETITION NEVER HURT ANYBODY.
THE TREE that KNOWS Stuff
The R.J. That Knows Stuff
BUT, HE REALLY KNOWS STUFF...ALL YOU KNOW IS...
SO, IF I EAT 16 TWINKIES BEFORE EVERY MEAL, I'LL TURN OUT EXACTLY LIKE BRITNEY SPEARS?
...BETTER STUFF.
GROOVY!

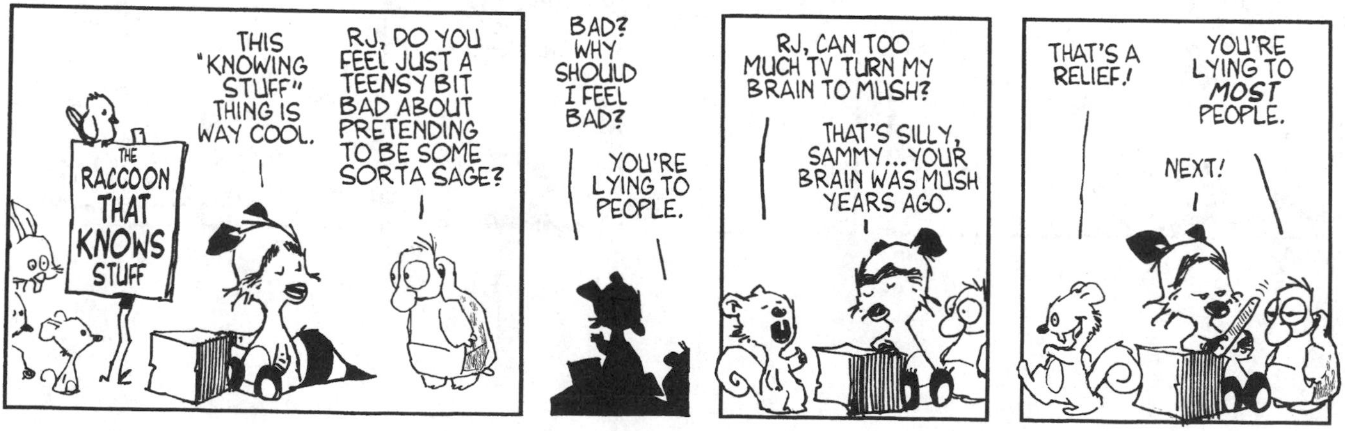
THE RACCOON THAT KNOWS STUFF
THIS "KNOWING STUFF" THING IS WAY COOL.
RJ, DO YOU FEEL JUST A TEENSY BIT BAD ABOUT PRETENDING TO BE SOME SORTA SAGE?
BAD? WHY SHOULD I FEEL BAD?
YOU'RE LYING TO PEOPLE.
RJ, CAN TOO MUCH TV TURN MY BRAIN TO MUSH?
THAT'S SILLY, SAMMY...YOUR BRAIN WAS MUSH YEARS AGO.
THAT'S A RELIEF!
YOU'RE LYING TO MOST PEOPLE.
NEXT!

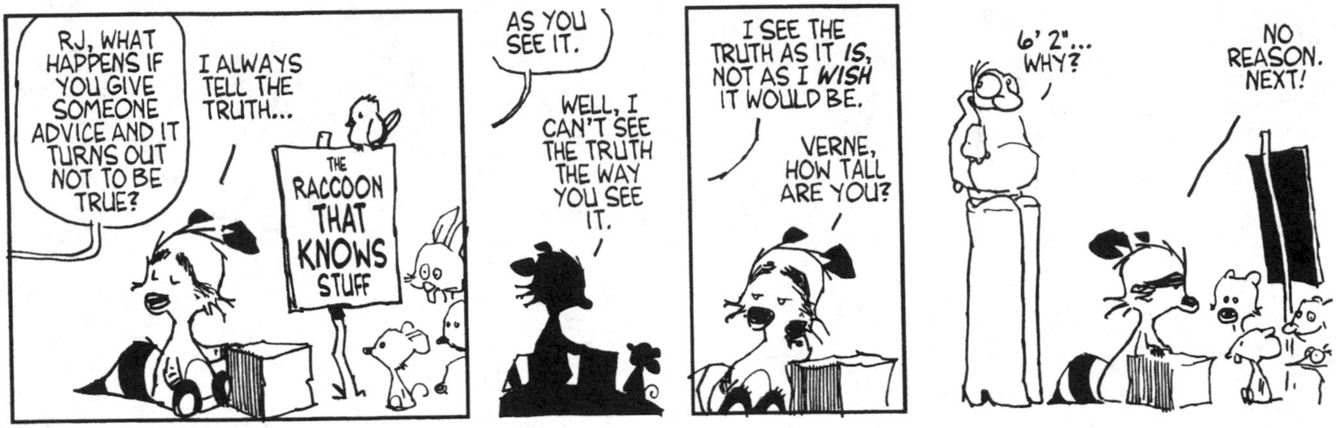
RJ, WHAT HAPPENS IF YOU GIVE SOMEONE ADVICE AND IT TURNS OUT NOT TO BE TRUE?
I ALWAYS TELL THE TRUTH...
THE RACCOON THAT KNOWS STUFF
AS YOU SEE IT.
WELL, I CAN'T SEE THE TRUTH THE WAY YOU SEE IT.
I SEE THE TRUTH AS IT *IS*, NOT AS I *WISH* IT WOULD BE.
VERNE, HOW TALL ARE YOU?
6' 2"... WHY?
NO REASON. NEXT!

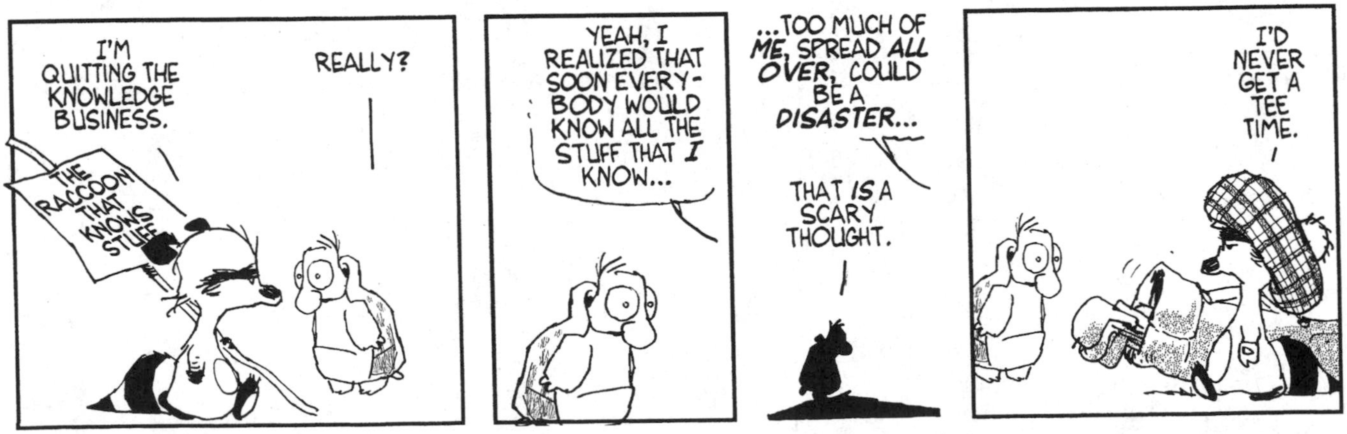
I'M QUITTING THE KNOWLEDGE BUSINESS.
REALLY?
THE RACCOON THAT KNOWS STUFF
YEAH, I REALIZED THAT SOON EVERY-BODY WOULD KNOW ALL THE STUFF THAT *I* KNOW...
...TOO MUCH OF *ME*, SPREAD *ALL OVER*, COULD BE A *DISASTER*...
THAT *IS* A SCARY THOUGHT.
I'D NEVER GET A TEE TIME.

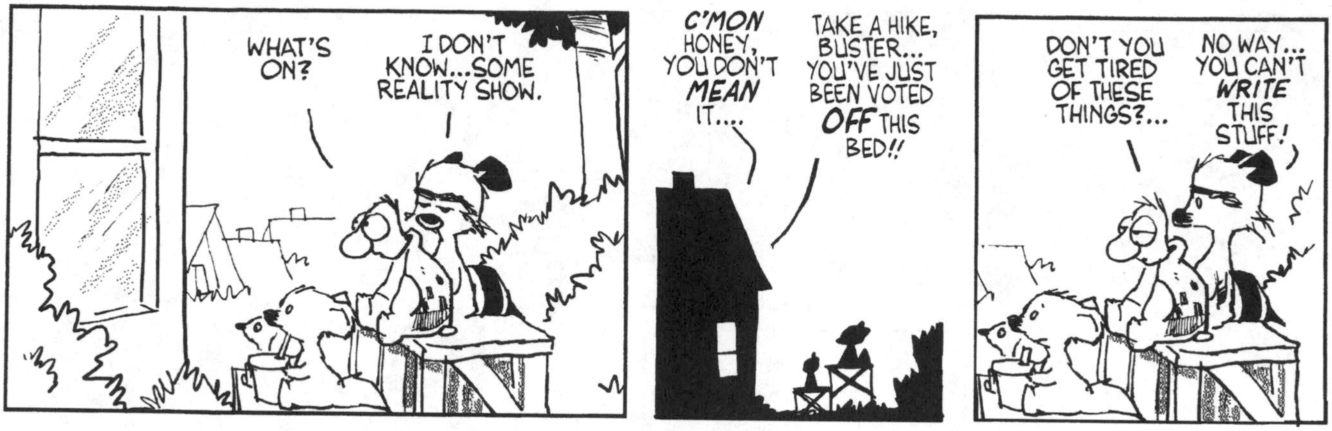
WHAT'S ON?
I DON'T KNOW...SOME REALITY SHOW.
C'MON HONEY, YOU DON'T MEAN IT....
TAKE A HIKE, BUSTER... YOU'VE JUST BEEN VOTED OFF THIS BED!!
DON'T YOU GET TIRED OF THESE THINGS?...
NO WAY... YOU CAN'T WRITE THIS STUFF!

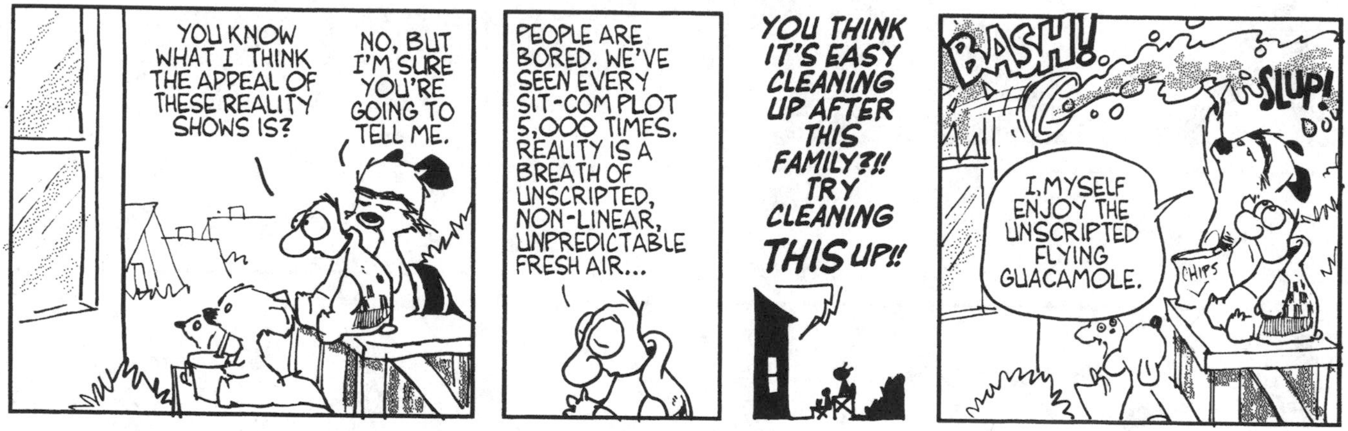
YOU KNOW WHAT I THINK THE APPEAL OF THESE REALITY SHOWS IS?
NO, BUT I'M SURE YOU'RE GOING TO TELL ME.
PEOPLE ARE BORED. WE'VE SEEN EVERY SIT-COM PLOT 5,000 TIMES. REALITY IS A BREATH OF UNSCRIPTED, NON-LINEAR, UNPREDICTABLE FRESH AIR...
YOU THINK IT'S EASY CLEANING UP AFTER THIS FAMILY?!! TRY CLEANING THIS UP!!
BASH!
SLUP!
I, MYSELF ENJOY THE UNSCRIPTED FLYING GUACAMOLE.
CHIPS

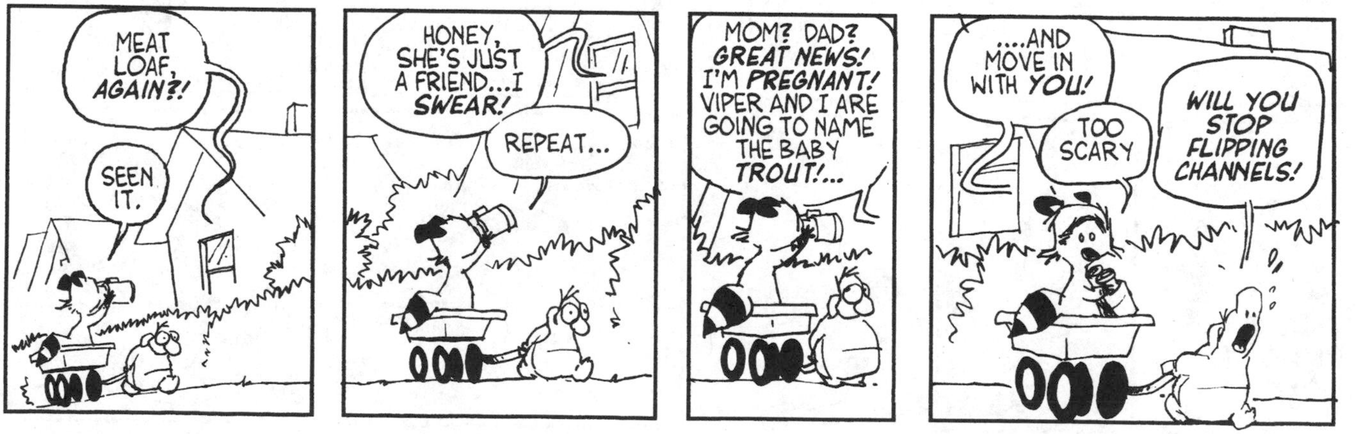
MEAT LOAF, AGAIN?!
SEEN IT.
HONEY, SHE'S JUST A FRIEND...I SWEAR!
REPEAT...
MOM? DAD? GREAT NEWS! I'M PREGNANT! VIPER AND I ARE GOING TO NAME THE BABY TROUT!...
....AND MOVE IN WITH YOU!
TOO SCARY
WILL YOU STOP FLIPPING CHANNELS!

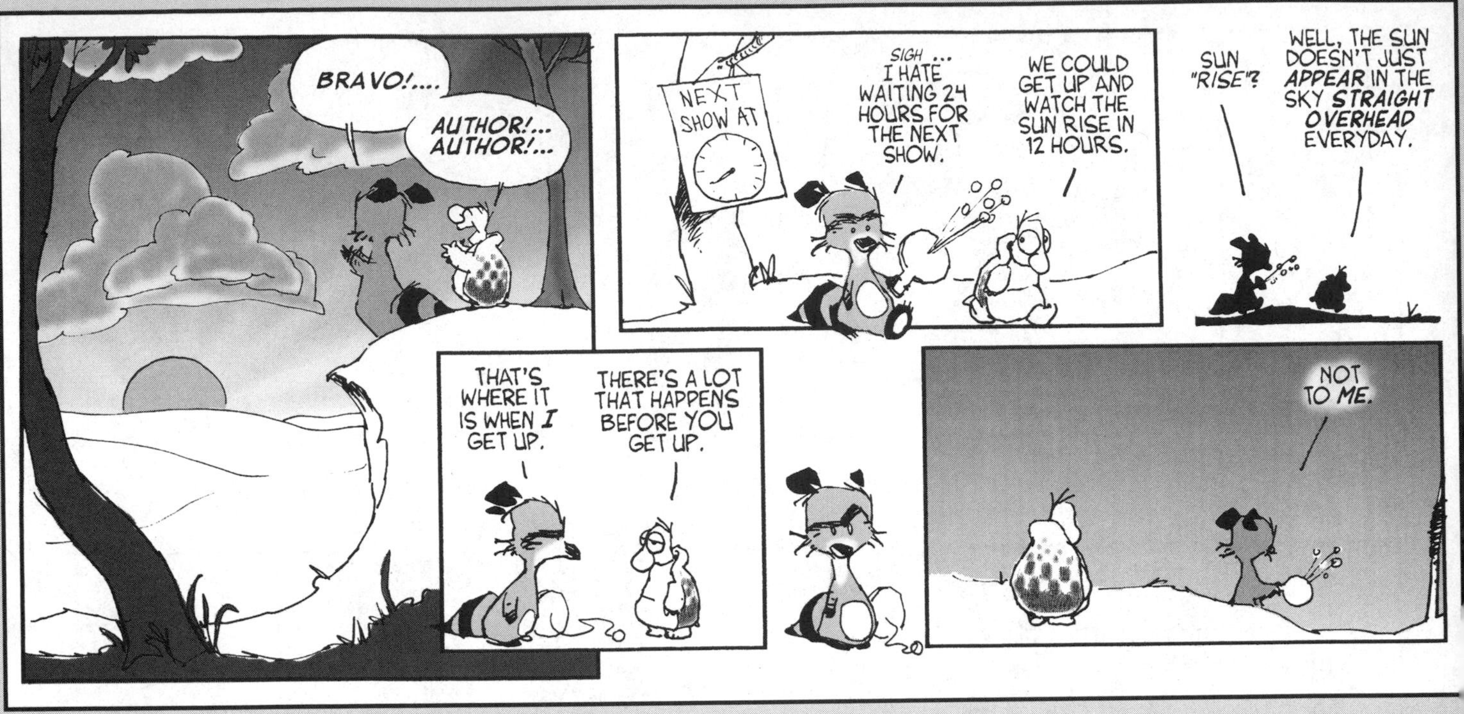
BRAVO!....
AUTHOR!... AUTHOR!...
NEXT SHOW AT
SIGH ... I HATE WAITING 24 HOURS FOR THE NEXT SHOW.
WE COULD GET UP AND WATCH THE SUN RISE IN 12 HOURS.
SUN "RISE"?
WELL, THE SUN DOESN'T JUST APPEAR IN THE SKY STRAIGHT OVERHEAD EVERYDAY.
THAT'S WHERE IT IS WHEN I GET UP.
THERE'S A LOT THAT HAPPENS BEFORE YOU GET UP.
NOT TO ME.

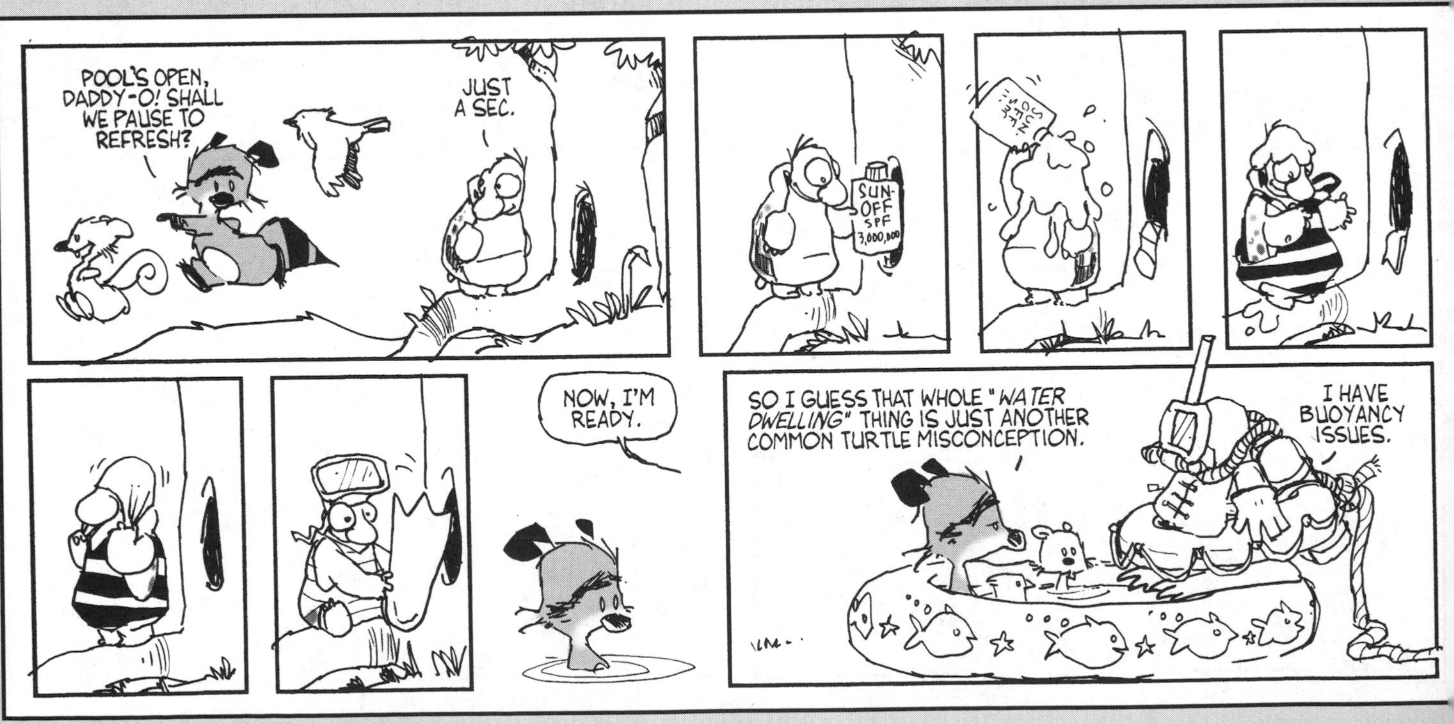
POOL'S OPEN, DADDY-O! SHALL WE PAUSE TO REFRESH?
JUST A SEC.
SUN-OFF SPF 3,000,000
NOW, I'M READY.
SO I GUESS THAT WHOLE "WATER DWELLING" THING IS JUST ANOTHER COMMON TURTLE MISCONCEPTION.
I HAVE BUOYANCY ISSUES.

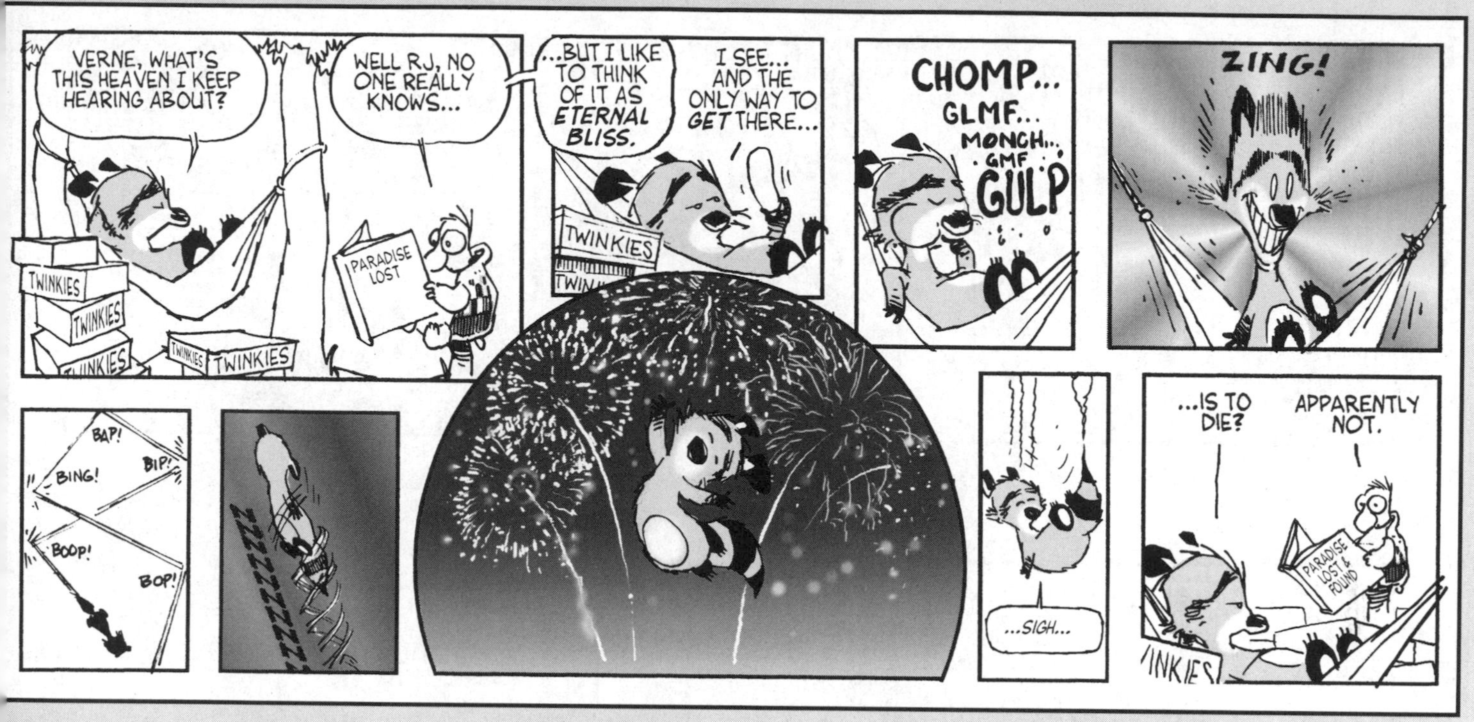
VERNE, WHAT'S THIS HEAVEN I KEEP HEARING ABOUT?
TWINKIES
WELL RJ, NO ONE REALLY KNOWS...
PARADISE LOST
...BUT I LIKE TO THINK OF IT AS ETERNAL BLISS.
I SEE... AND THE ONLY WAY TO GET THERE...
CHOMP... GLMF... MONCH... GMF GULP
ZING!
BAP! BING! BIP! BOOP! BOP!
...SIGH...
...IS TO DIE?
APPARENTLY NOT.
PARADISE LOST & FOUND

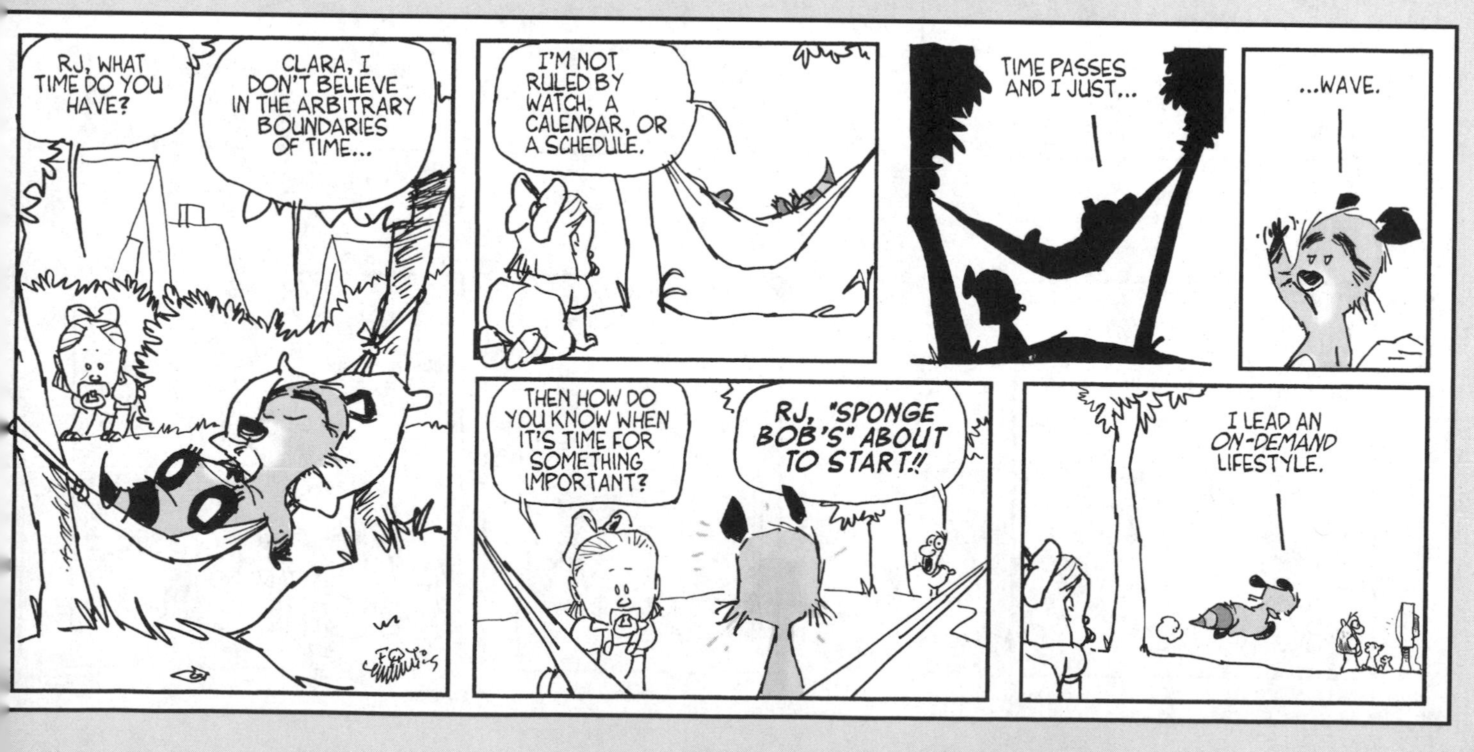
RJ, WHAT TIME DO YOU HAVE?
CLARA, I DON'T BELIEVE IN THE ARBITRARY BOUNDARIES OF TIME...
I'M NOT RULED BY WATCH, A CALENDAR, OR A SCHEDULE.
TIME PASSES AND I JUST...
...WAVE.
THEN HOW DO YOU KNOW WHEN IT'S TIME FOR SOMETHING IMPORTANT?
RJ, "SPONGE BOB'S" ABOUT TO START!!
I LEAD AN ON-DEMAND LIFESTYLE.

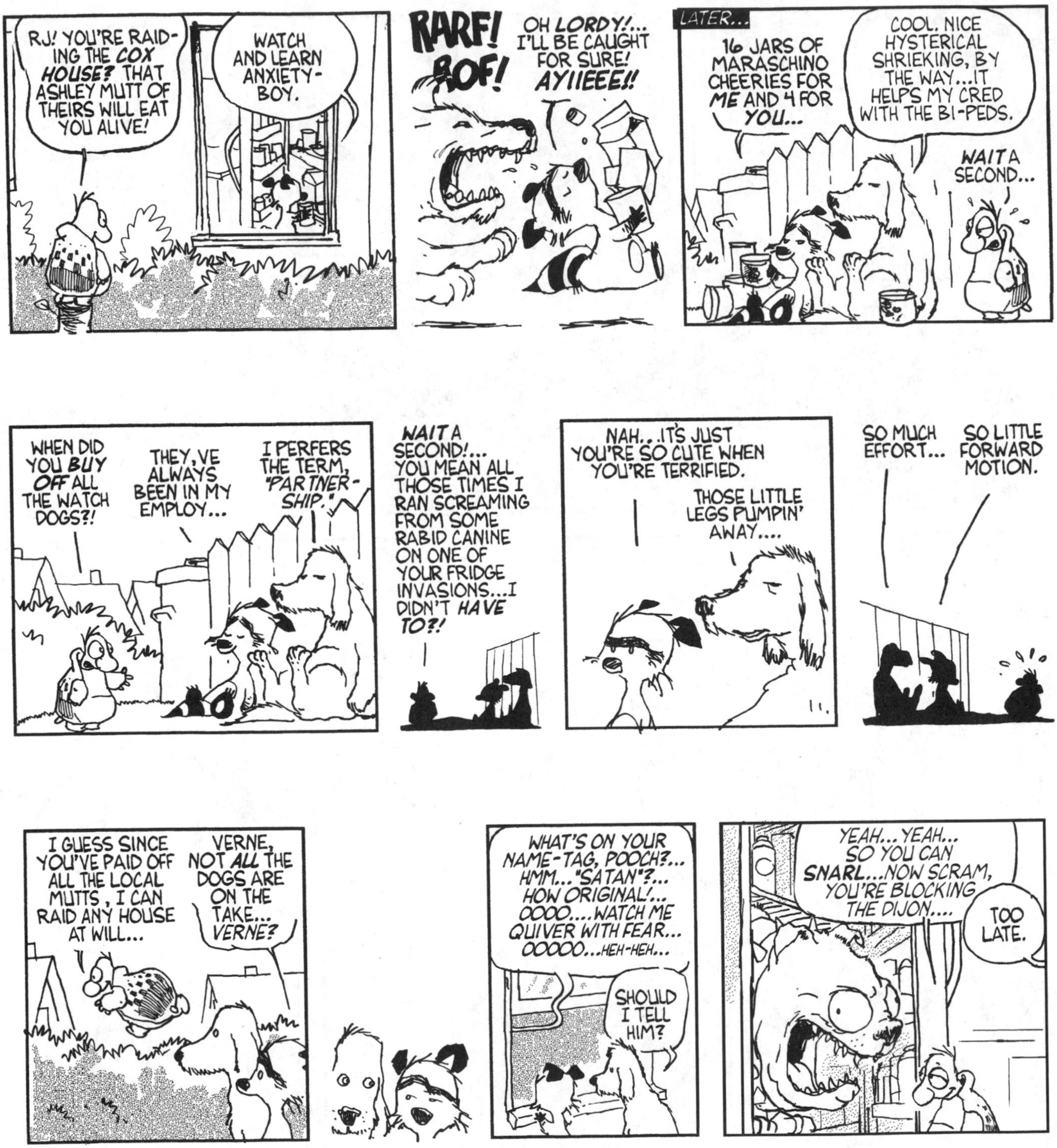
RJ! YOU'RE RAIDING THE COX HOUSE? THAT ASHLEY MUTT OF THEIRS WILL EAT YOU ALIVE!
WATCH AND LEARN ANXIETY-BOY.
RARF! ROF!
OH LORDY!... I'LL BE CAUGHT FOR SURE! AYIIEEE!!
LATER...
16 JARS OF MARASCHINO CHEERIES FOR ME AND 4 FOR YOU...
COOL. NICE HYSTERICAL SHRIEKING, BY THE WAY...IT HELPS MY CRED WITH THE BI-PEDS.
WAIT A SECOND...
WHEN DID YOU BUY OFF ALL THE WATCH DOGS?!
THEY,VE ALWAYS BEEN IN MY EMPLOY...
I PERFERS THE TERM, "PARTNERSHIP."
WAIT A SECOND!... YOU MEAN ALL THOSE TIMES I RAN SCREAMING FROM SOME RABID CANINE ON ONE OF YOUR FRIDGE INVASIONS...I DIDN'T HAVE TO?!
NAH...IT'S JUST YOU'RE SO CUTE WHEN YOU'RE TERRIFIED.
THOSE LITTLE LEGS PUMPIN' AWAY....
SO MUCH EFFORT...
SO LITTLE FORWARD MOTION.
I GUESS SINCE YOU'VE PAID OFF ALL THE LOCAL MUTTS, I CAN RAID ANY HOUSE AT WILL...
VERNE, NOT ALL THE DOGS ARE ON THE TAKE... VERNE?
WHAT'S ON YOUR NAME-TAG, POOCH?... HMM..."SATAN"?... HOW ORIGINAL!... OOOO....WATCH ME QUIVER WITH FEAR... OOOOO...HEH-HEH...
SHOULD I TELL HIM?
YEAH...YEAH... SO YOU CAN SNARL...NOW SCRAM, YOU'RE BLOCKING THE DIJON....
TOO LATE.

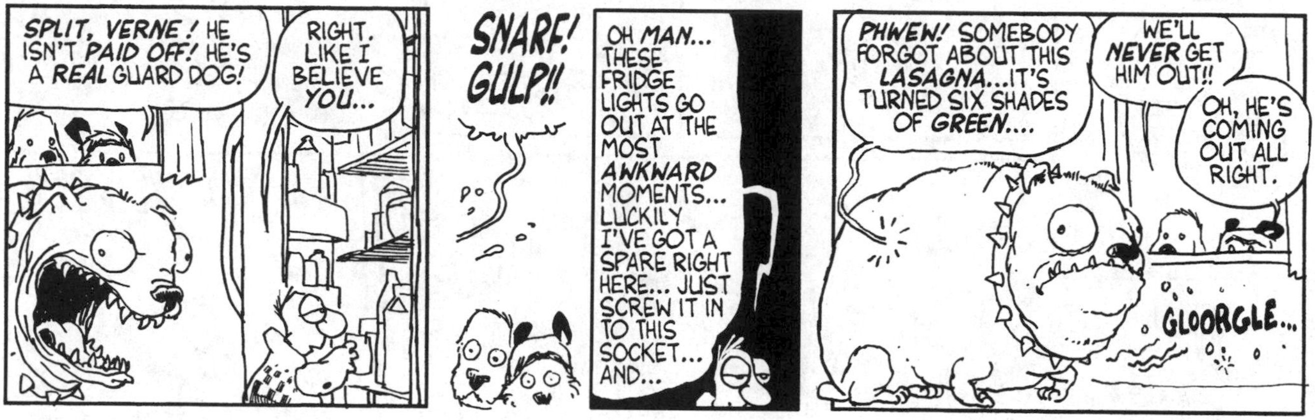
SPLIT, VERNE! HE ISN'T PAID OFF! HE'S A REAL GUARD DOG!
RIGHT. LIKE I BELIEVE YOU...
SNARF! GULP!!
OH MAN... THESE FRIDGE LIGHTS GO OUT AT THE MOST AWKWARD MOMENTS... LUCKILY I'VE GOT A SPARE RIGHT HERE... JUST SCREW IT IN TO THIS SOCKET... AND...
PHWEW! SOMEBODY FORGOT ABOUT THIS LASAGNA...IT'S TURNED SIX SHADES OF GREEN....
WE'LL NEVER GET HIM OUT!!
OH, HE'S COMING OUT ALL RIGHT.
GLOORGLE...

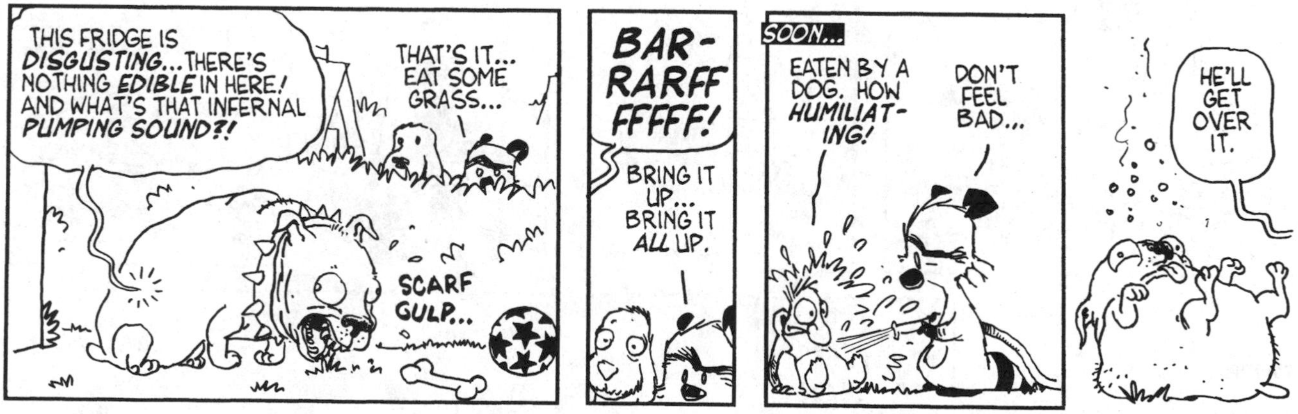
THIS FRIDGE IS DISGUSTING...THERE'S NOTHING EDIBLE IN HERE! AND WHAT'S THAT INFERNAL PUMPING SOUND?!
THAT'S IT... EAT SOME GRASS...
SCARF GULP...
BAR-RARFF FFFFF!
BRING IT UP... BRING IT ALL UP.
SOON...
EATEN BY A DOG. HOW HUMILIAT-ING!
DON'T FEEL BAD...
HE'LL GET OVER IT.

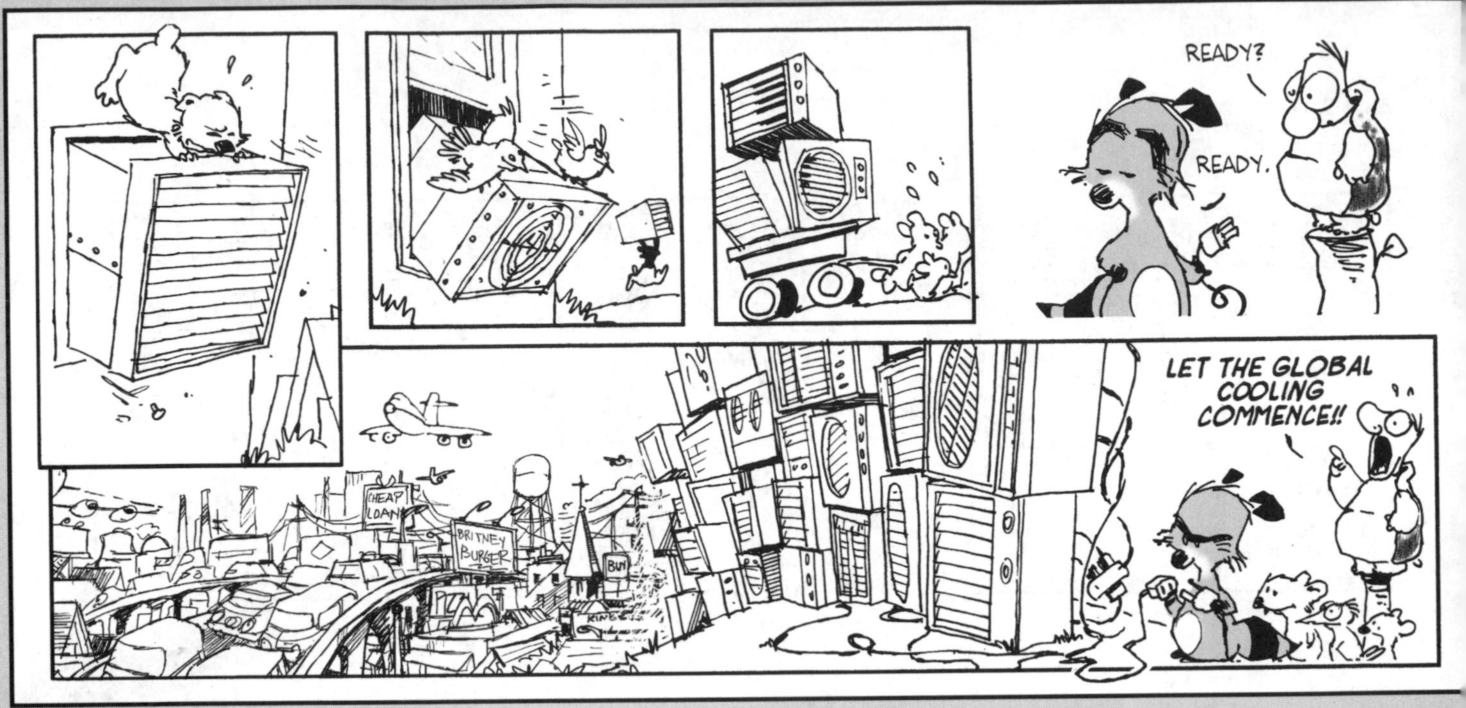
READY?
READY.
CHEAP LOAN
BRITNEY BURGER
LET THE GLOBAL COOLING COMMENCE!!

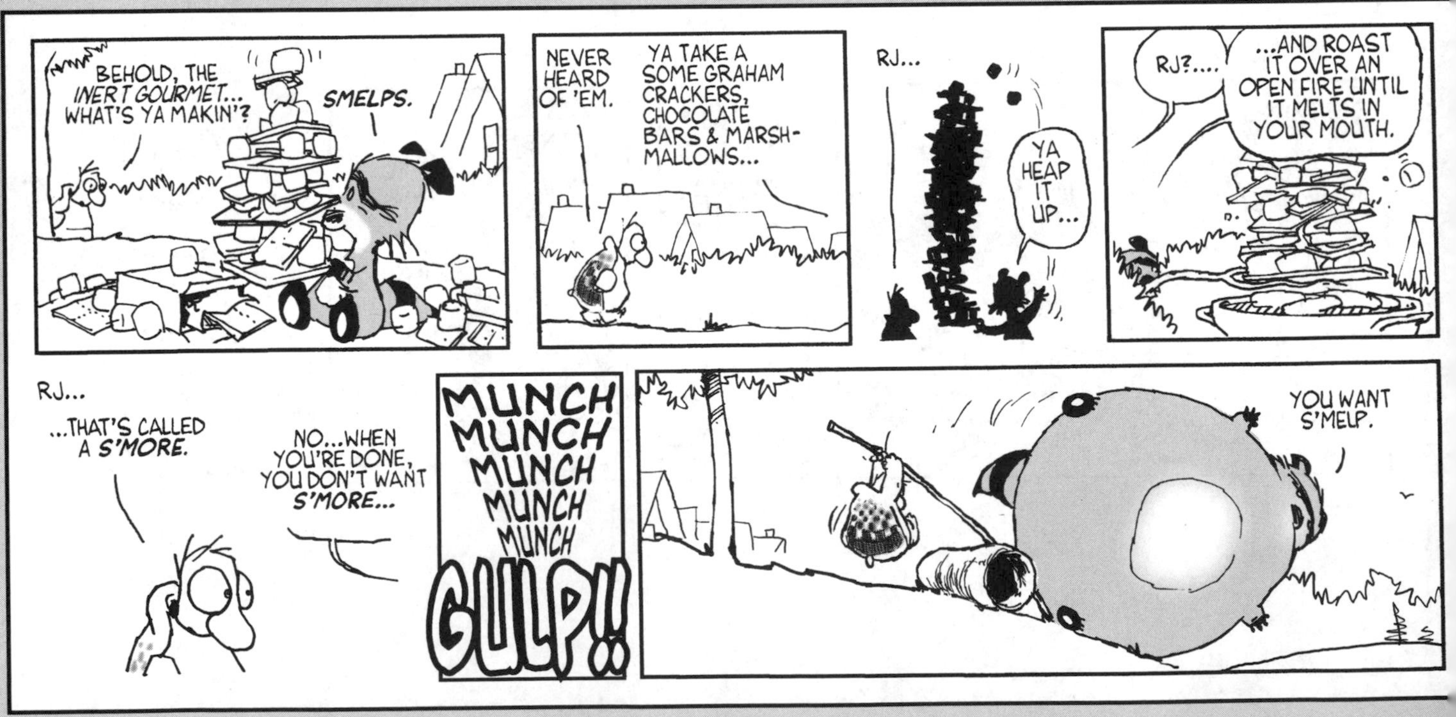
BEHOLD, THE *INERT GOURMET*... WHAT'S YA MAKIN'?
SMELPS.
NEVER HEARD OF 'EM.
YA TAKE A SOME GRAHAM CRACKERS, CHOCOLATE BARS & MARSHMALLOWS...
RJ...
YA HEAP IT UP...
RJ?....
...AND ROAST IT OVER AN OPEN FIRE UNTIL IT MELTS IN YOUR MOUTH.
RJ...
...THAT'S CALLED A ***S'MORE***.
NO...WHEN YOU'RE DONE, YOU DON'T WANT ***S'MORE***...
MUNCH
MUNCH
MUNCH
MUNCH
MUNCH
GULP!!
YOU WANT S'MELP.

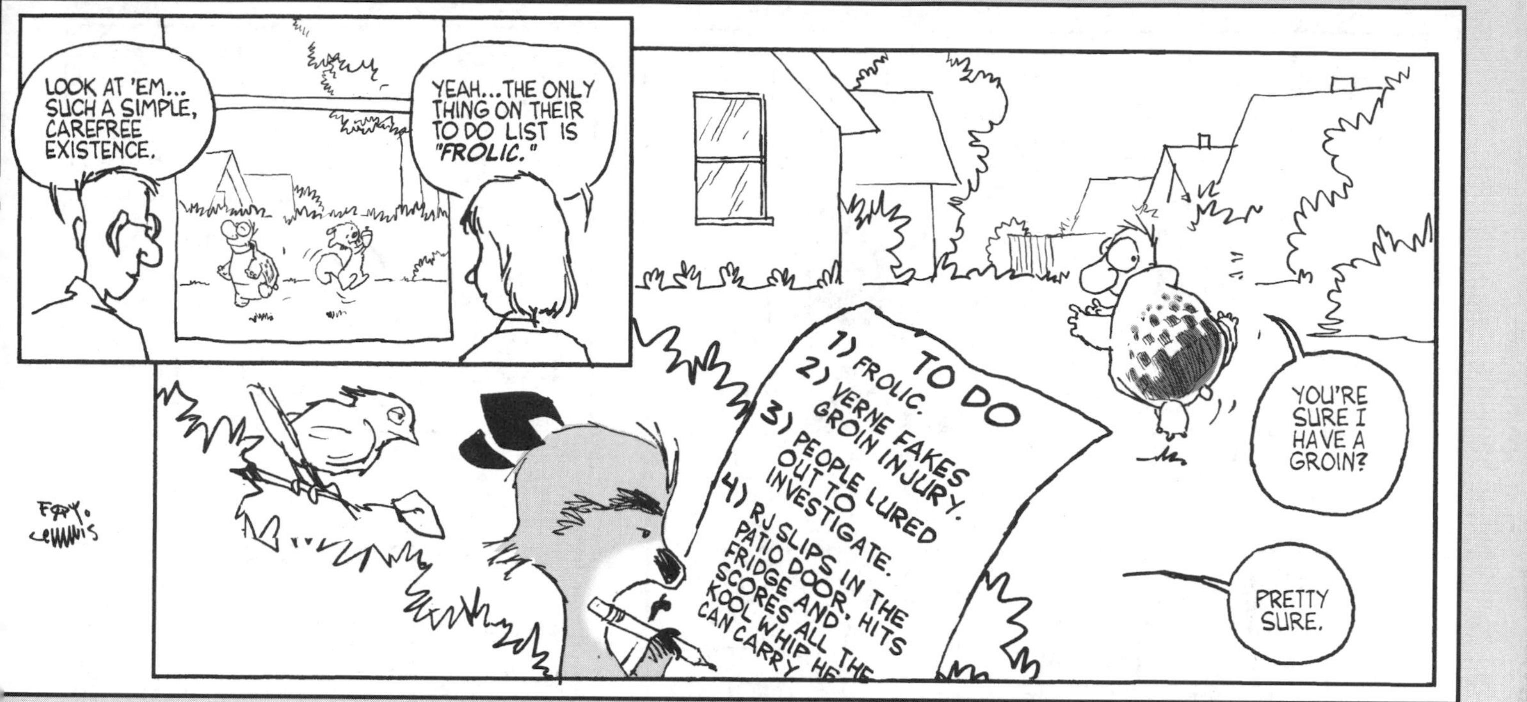
LOOK AT 'EM... SUCH A SIMPLE, CAREFREE EXISTENCE.
YEAH...THE ONLY THING ON THEIR TO DO LIST IS "FROLIC."
TO DO
1) FROLIC.
2) VERNE FAKES GROIN INJURY.
3) PEOPLE LURED OUT TO INVESTIGATE.
4) RJ SLIPS IN THE PATIO DOOR, HITS FRIDGE AND SCORES ALL THE KOOL WHIP HE CAN CARRY
YOU'RE SURE I HAVE A GROIN?
PRETTY SURE.

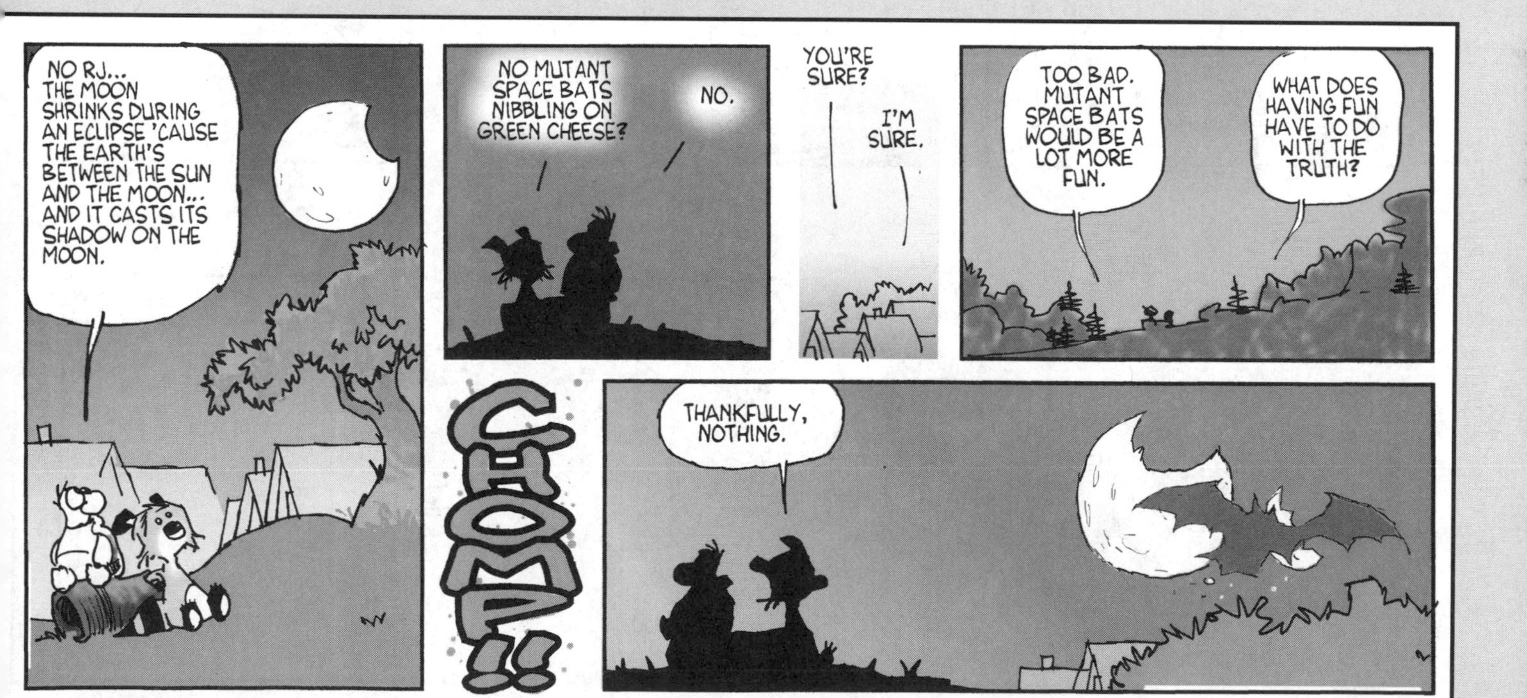
NO RJ... THE MOON SHRINKS DURING AN ECLIPSE 'CAUSE THE EARTH'S BETWEEN THE SUN AND THE MOON... AND IT CASTS ITS SHADOW ON THE MOON.
NO MUTANT SPACE BATS NIBBLING ON GREEN CHEESE?
NO.
YOU'RE SURE?
I'M SURE.
TOO BAD. MUTANT SPACE BATS WOULD BE A LOT MORE FUN.
WHAT DOES HAVING FUN HAVE TO DO WITH THE TRUTH?
CHOMP!!
THANKFULLY, NOTHING.

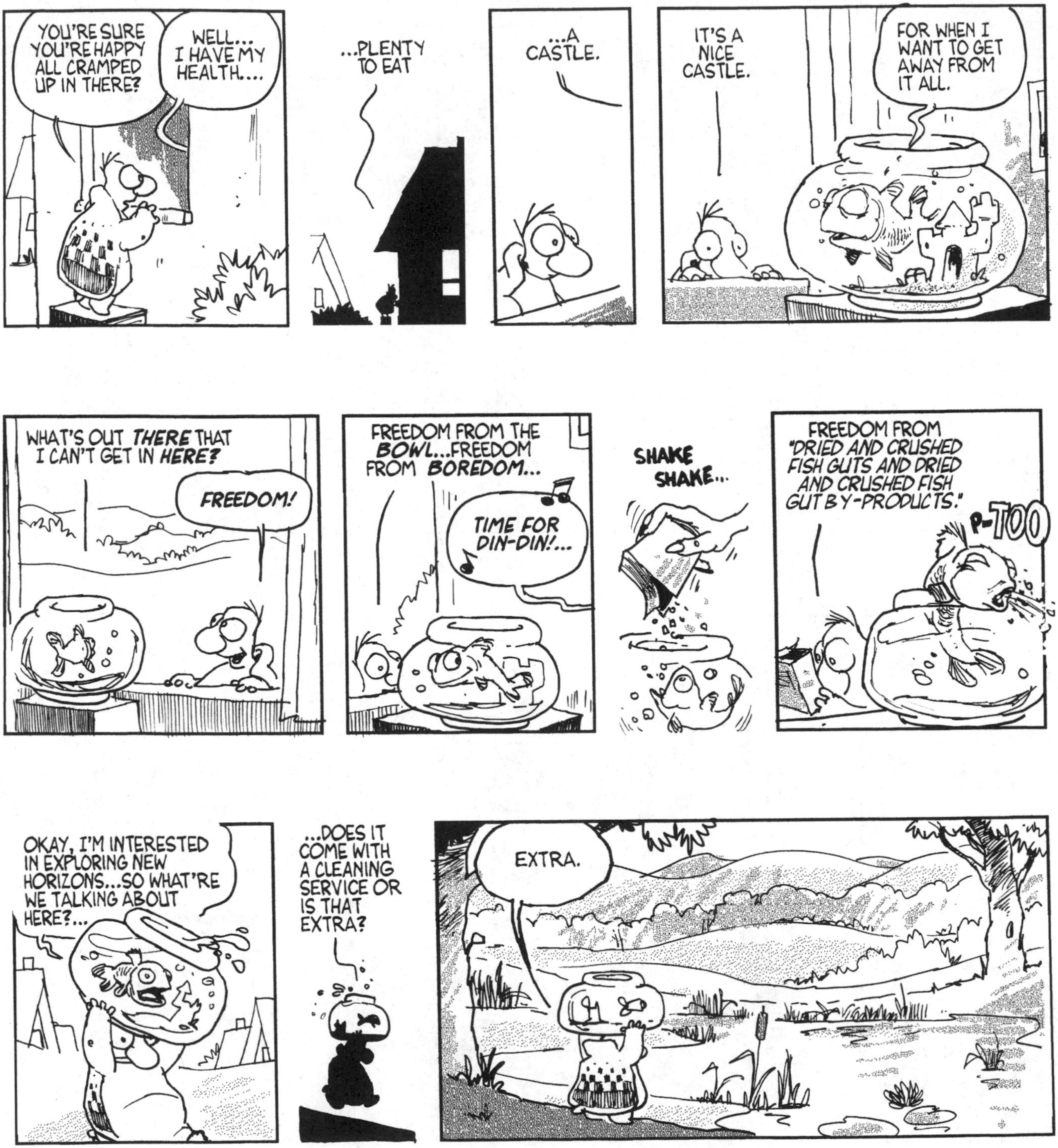
YOU'RE SURE YOU'RE HAPPY ALL CRAMPED UP IN THERE?
WELL... I HAVE MY HEALTH....
...PLENTY TO EAT
...A CASTLE.
IT'S A NICE CASTLE.
FOR WHEN I WANT TO GET AWAY FROM IT ALL.
WHAT'S OUT THERE THAT I CAN'T GET IN HERE?
FREEDOM!
FREEDOM FROM THE BOWL...FREEDOM FROM BOREDOM...
TIME FOR DIN-DIN!...
SHAKE SHAKE...
FREEDOM FROM "DRIED AND CRUSHED FISH GUTS AND DRIED AND CRUSHED FISH GUT BY-PRODUCTS."
P-TOO
OKAY, I'M INTERESTED IN EXPLORING NEW HORIZONS...SO WHAT'RE WE TALKING ABOUT HERE?...
...DOES IT COME WITH A CLEANING SERVICE OR IS THAT EXTRA?
EXTRA.

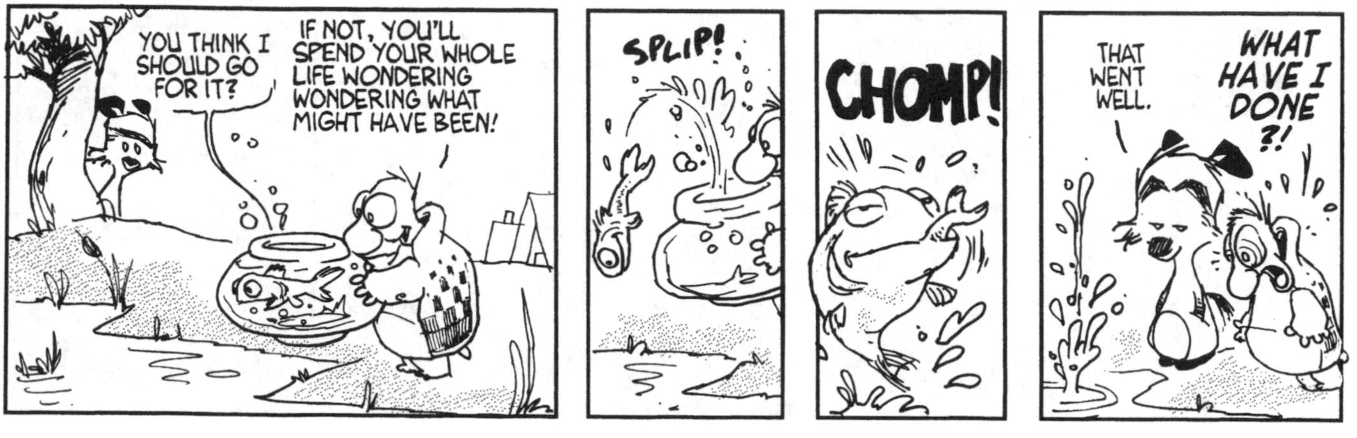
YOU THINK I SHOULD GO FOR IT?
IF NOT, YOU'LL SPEND YOUR WHOLE LIFE WONDERING WONDERING WHAT MIGHT HAVE BEEN!
SPLIP!
CHOMP!
THAT WENT WELL.
WHAT HAVE I DONE ?!

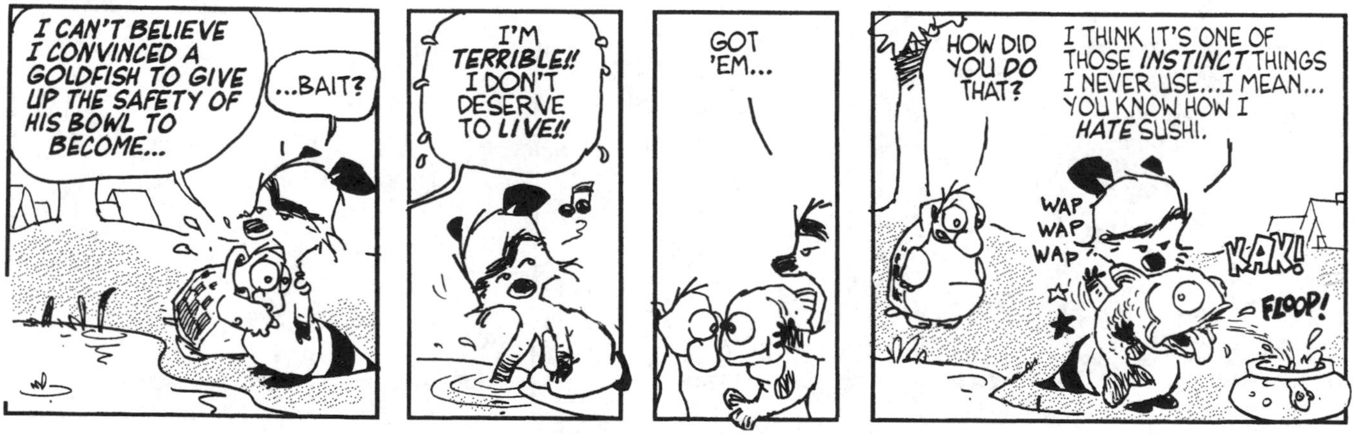
I CAN'T BELIEVE I CONVINCED A GOLDFISH TO GIVE UP THE SAFETY OF HIS BOWL TO BECOME...
...BAIT?
I'M TERRIBLE!! I DON'T DESERVE TO LIVE!!
GOT 'EM...
HOW DID YOU DO THAT?
I THINK IT'S ONE OF THOSE INSTINCT THINGS I NEVER USE...I MEAN... YOU KNOW HOW I HATE SUSHI.
WAP
WAP
WAP
KAK!
FLOOP!

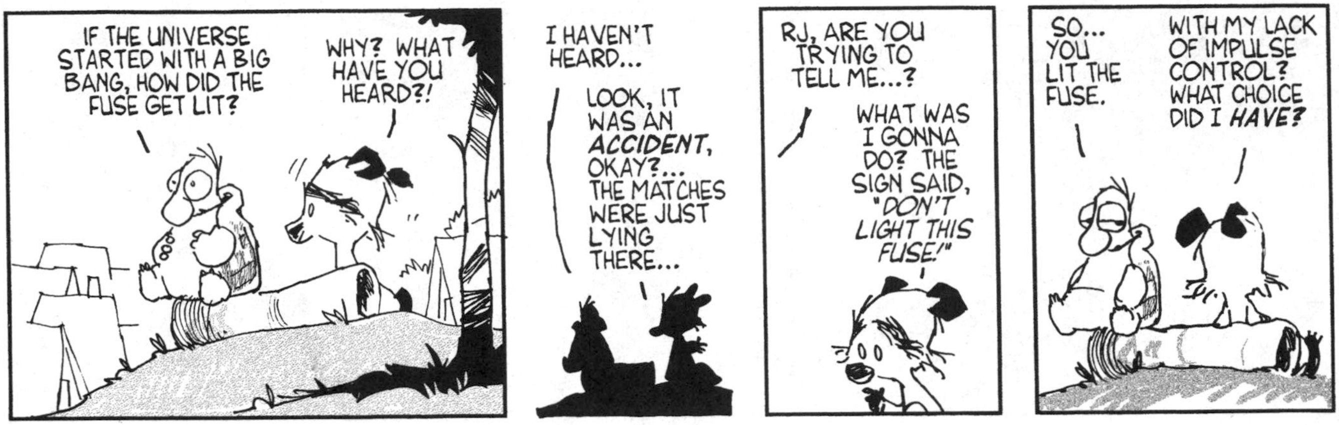
IF THE UNIVERSE STARTED WITH A BIG BANG, HOW DID THE FUSE GET LIT?
WHY? WHAT HAVE YOU HEARD?!
I HAVEN'T HEARD...
LOOK, IT WAS AN *ACCIDENT*, OKAY?... THE MATCHES WERE JUST LYING THERE...
RJ, ARE YOU TRYING TO TELL ME...?
WHAT WAS I GONNA DO? THE SIGN SAID, *"DON'T LIGHT THIS FUSE!"*
SO... YOU LIT THE FUSE.
WITH MY LACK OF IMPULSE CONTROL? WHAT CHOICE DID I ***HAVE?***

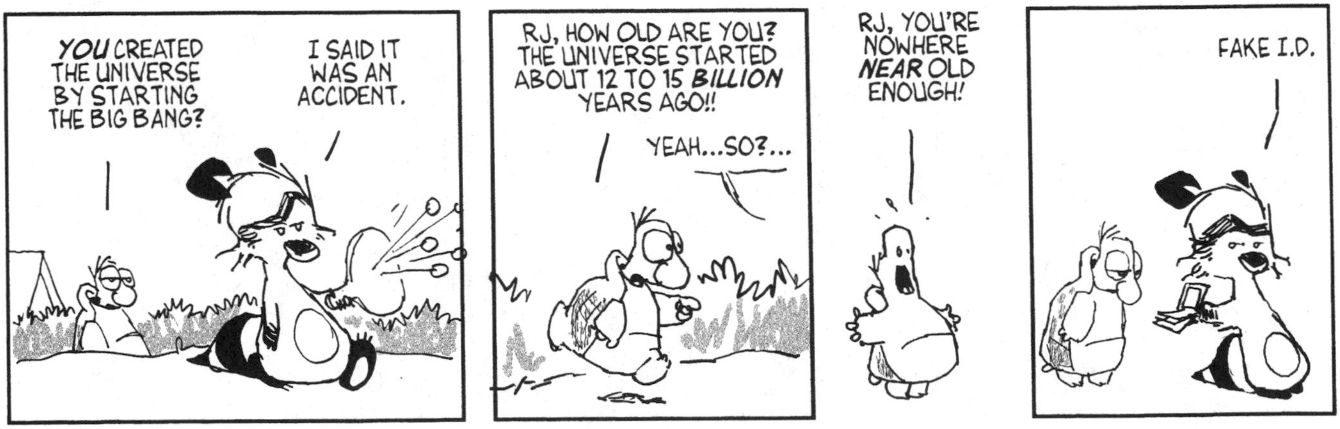
YOU CREATED THE UNIVERSE BY STARTING THE BIG BANG?
I SAID IT WAS AN ACCIDENT.
RJ, HOW OLD ARE YOU? THE UNIVERSE STARTED ABOUT 12 TO 15 ***BILLION*** YEARS AGO!!
YEAH...SO?...
RJ, YOU'RE NOWHERE ***NEAR*** OLD ENOUGH!
FAKE I.D.

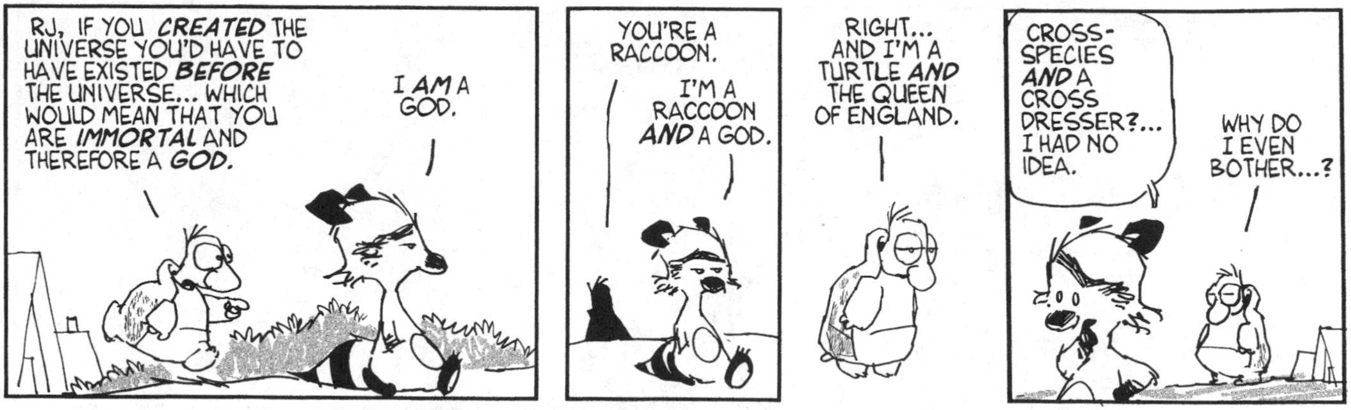
RJ, IF YOU CREATED THE UNIVERSE YOU'D HAVE TO HAVE EXISTED BEFORE THE UNIVERSE... WHICH WOULD MEAN THAT YOU ARE IMMORTAL AND THEREFORE A GOD.
I AM A GOD.
YOU'RE A RACCOON.
I'M A RACCOON AND A GOD.
RIGHT... AND I'M A TURTLE AND THE QUEEN OF ENGLAND.
CROSS-SPECIES AND A CROSS DRESSER?... I HAD NO IDEA.
WHY DO I EVEN BOTHER...?

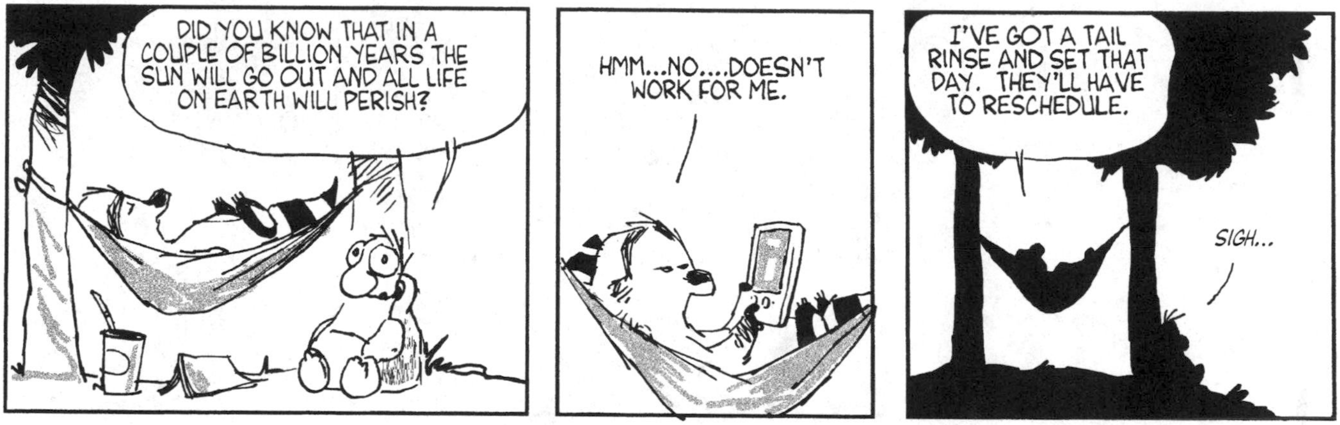
DID YOU KNOW THAT IN A COUPLE OF BILLION YEARS THE SUN WILL GO OUT AND ALL LIFE ON EARTH WILL PERISH?
HMM...NO....DOESN'T WORK FOR ME.
I'VE GOT A TAIL RINSE AND SET THAT DAY. THEY'LL HAVE TO RESCHEDULE.
SIGH...

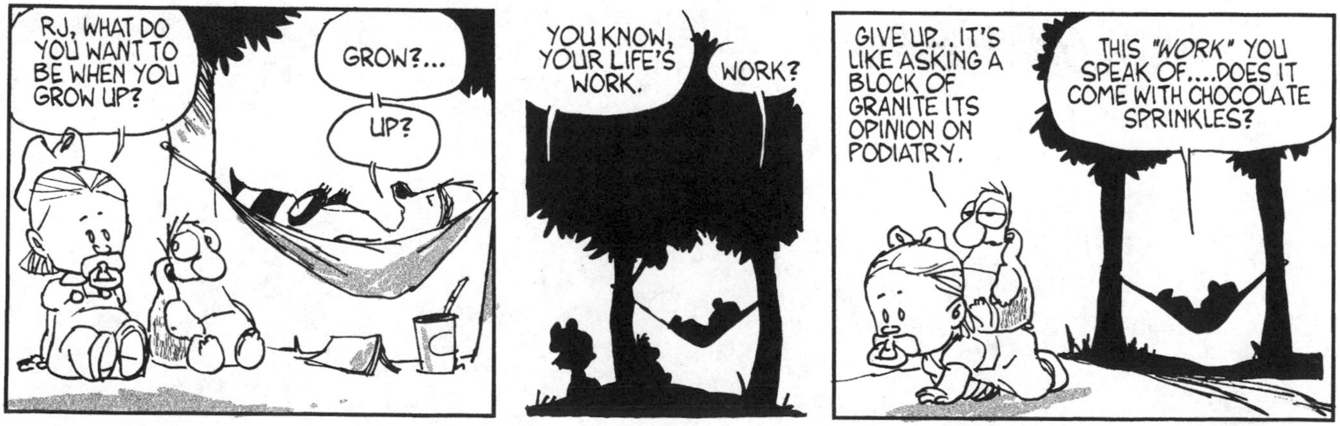
RJ, WHAT DO YOU WANT TO BE WHEN YOU GROW UP?
GROW?...
UP?
YOU KNOW, YOUR LIFE'S WORK.
WORK?
GIVE UP... IT'S LIKE ASKING A BLOCK OF GRANITE ITS OPINION ON PODIATRY.
THIS "WORK" YOU SPEAK OF....DOES IT COME WITH CHOCOLATE SPRINKLES?

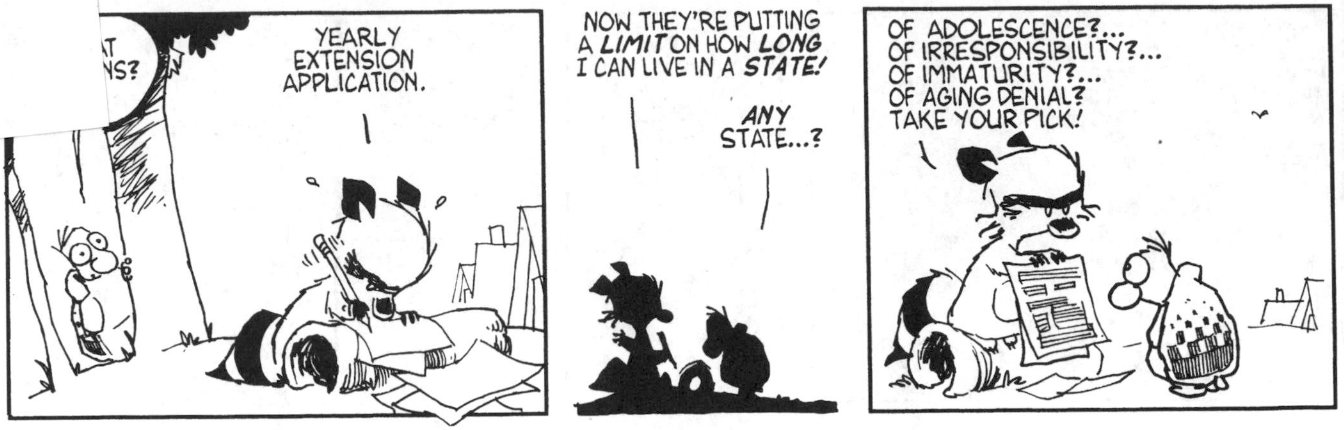

YEARLY EXTENSION APPLICATION.
NOW THEY'RE PUTTING A **LIMIT** ON HOW **LONG** I CAN LIVE IN A **STATE!**
ANY STATE...?
OF ADOLESCENCE?... OF IRRESPONSIBILITY?... OF IMMATURITY?... OF AGING DENIAL? TAKE YOUR PICK!

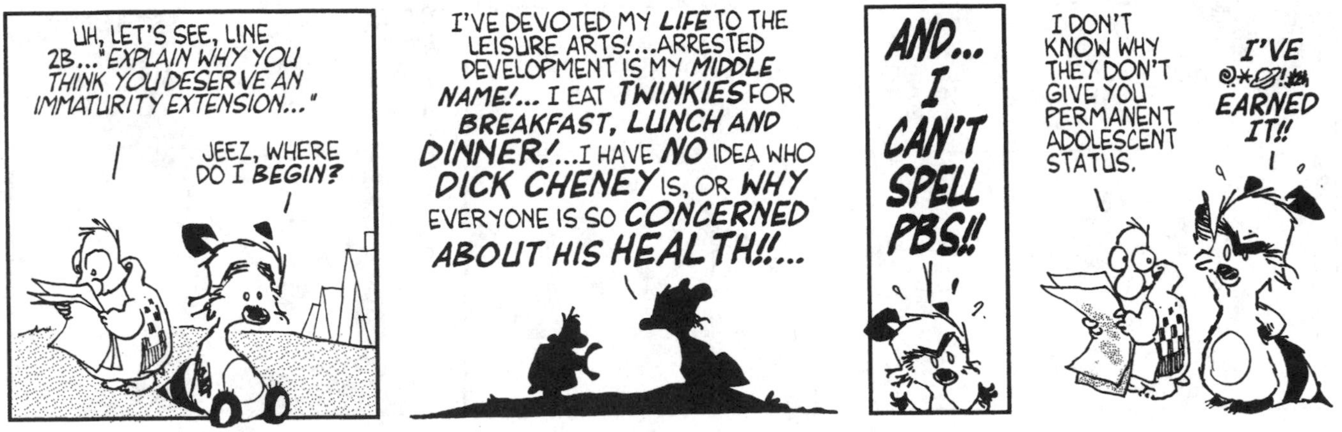

UH, LET'S SEE, LINE 2B..."*EXPLAIN WHY YOU THINK YOU DESERVE AN IMMATURITY EXTENSION...*"
JEEZ, WHERE DO I **BEGIN?**
I'VE DEVOTED MY **LIFE** TO THE LEISURE ARTS!...ARRESTED DEVELOPMENT IS MY **MIDDLE NAME!**... I EAT **TWINKIES** FOR **BREAKFAST, LUNCH AND DINNER!**...I HAVE **NO** IDEA WHO **DICK CHENEY** IS, OR **WHY** EVERYONE IS SO **CONCERNED ABOUT HIS HEALTH!!**...
AND... I CAN'T SPELL PBS!!
I DON'T KNOW WHY THEY DON'T GIVE YOU PERMANENT ADOLESCENT STATUS.
I'VE EARNED IT!!

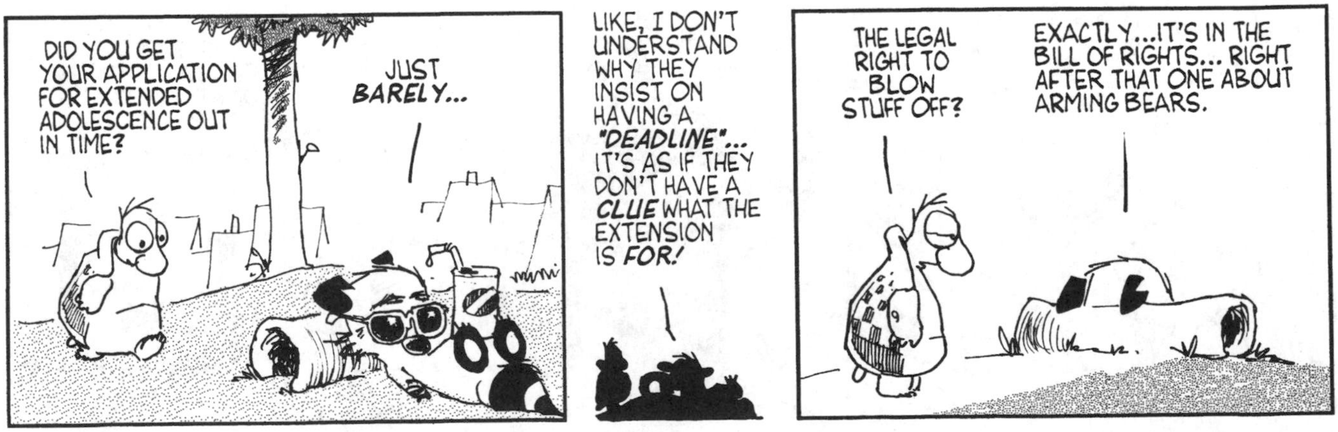

DID YOU GET YOUR APPLICATION FOR EXTENDED ADOLESCENCE OUT IN TIME?
JUST **BARELY...**
LIKE, I DON'T UNDERSTAND WHY THEY INSIST ON HAVING A **"DEADLINE"**... IT'S AS IF THEY DON'T HAVE A **CLUE** WHAT THE EXTENSION IS **FOR!**
THE LEGAL RIGHT TO BLOW STUFF OFF?
EXACTLY...IT'S IN THE BILL OF RIGHTS... RIGHT AFTER THAT ONE ABOUT ARMING BEARS.

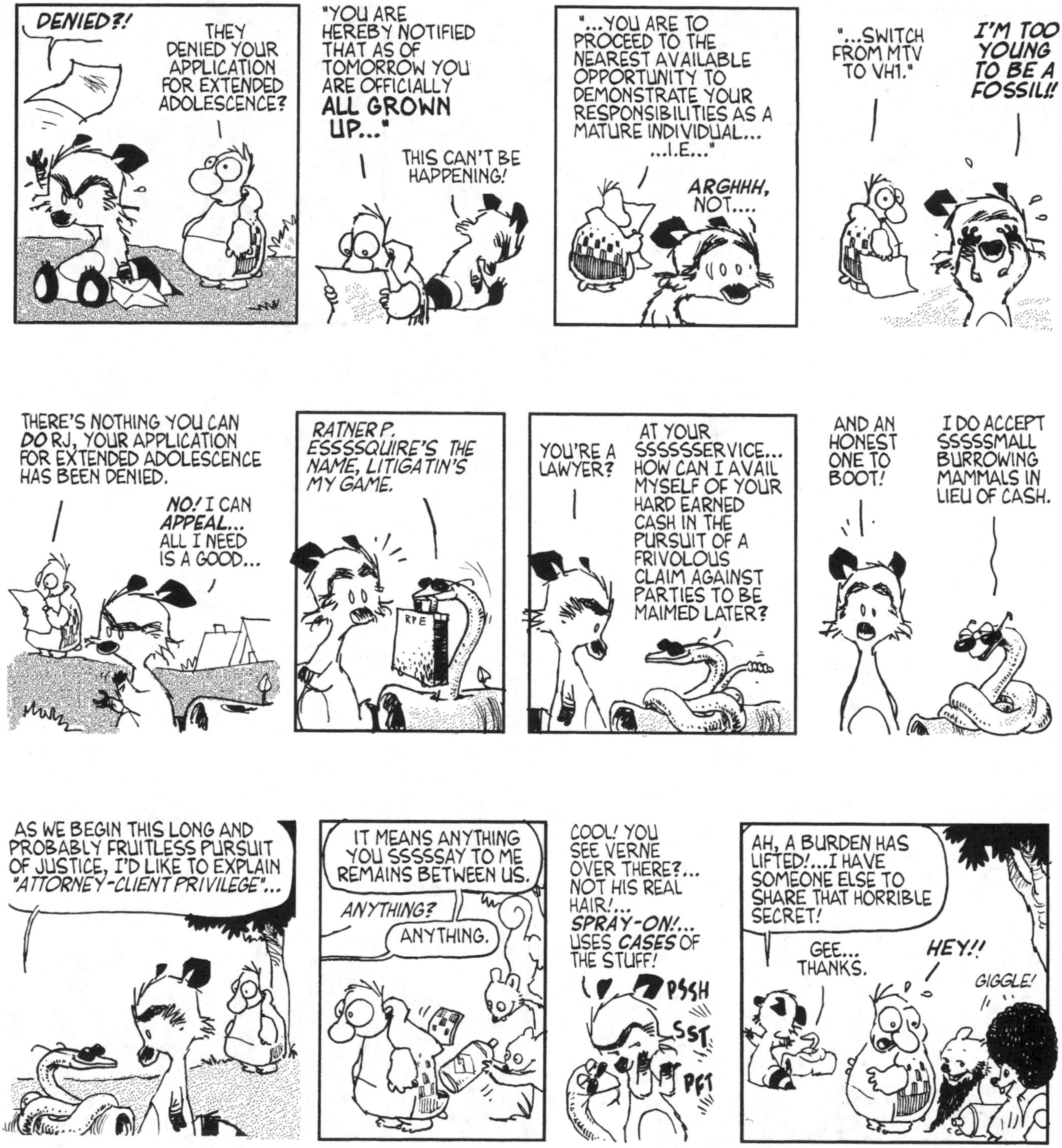
DENIED?!
THEY DENIED YOUR APPLICATION FOR EXTENDED ADOLESCENCE?
"YOU ARE HEREBY NOTIFIED THAT AS OF TOMORROW YOU ARE OFFICIALLY ALL GROWN UP..."
THIS CAN'T BE HAPPENING!
"...YOU ARE TO PROCEED TO THE NEAREST AVAILABLE OPPORTUNITY TO DEMONSTRATE YOUR RESPONSIBILITIES AS A MATURE INDIVIDUAL... ...I.E..."
ARGHHH, NOT....
"...SWITCH FROM MTV TO VH1."
I'M TOO YOUNG TO BE A FOSSIL!!
THERE'S NOTHING YOU CAN DO RJ, YOUR APPLICATION FOR EXTENDED ADOLESCENCE HAS BEEN DENIED.
NO! I CAN APPEAL... ALL I NEED IS A GOOD...
RATNER P. ESSSSQUIRE'S THE NAME, LITIGATIN'S MY GAME.
RPE
YOU'RE A LAWYER?
AT YOUR SSSSSSERVICE... HOW CAN I AVAIL MYSELF OF YOUR HARD EARNED CASH IN THE PURSUIT OF A FRIVOLOUS CLAIM AGAINST PARTIES TO BE MAIMED LATER?
AND AN HONEST ONE TO BOOT!
I DO ACCEPT SSSSSMALL BURROWING MAMMALS IN LIEU OF CASH.
AS WE BEGIN THIS LONG AND PROBABLY FRUITLESS PURSUIT OF JUSTICE, I'D LIKE TO EXPLAIN "ATTORNEY-CLIENT PRIVILEGE"...
IT MEANS ANYTHING YOU SSSSSAY TO ME REMAINS BETWEEN US.
ANYTHING?
ANYTHING.
COOL! YOU SEE VERNE OVER THERE?... NOT HIS REAL HAIR!... SPRAY-ON!... USES CASES OF THE STUFF!
PSSH
SST
PFT
AH, A BURDEN HAS LIFTED!...I HAVE SOMEONE ELSE TO SHARE THAT HORRIBLE SECRET!
GEE... THANKS.
HEY!!
GIGGLE!

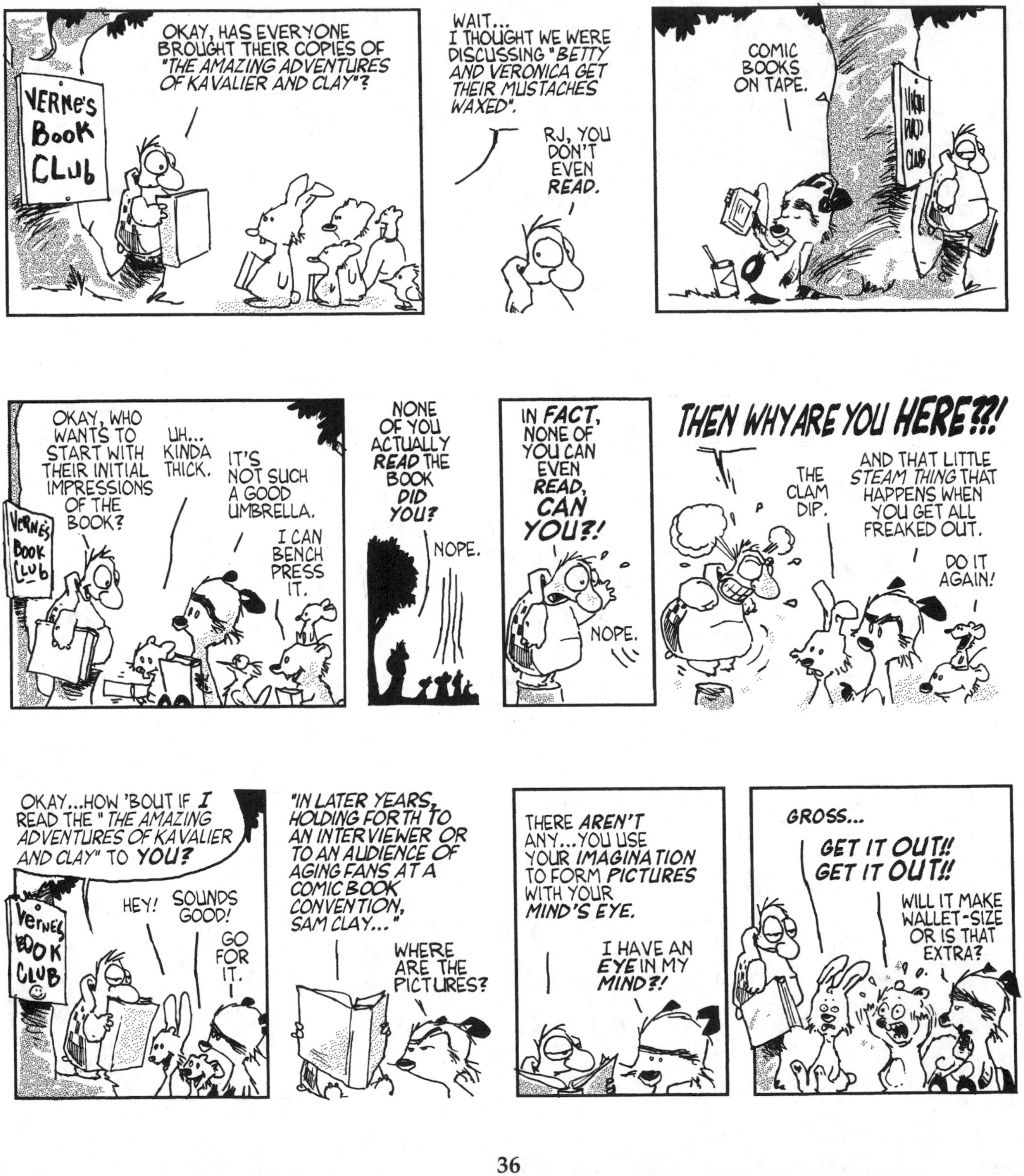
VERNE'S BOOK CLUB
OKAY, HAS EVERYONE BROUGHT THEIR COPIES OF "THE AMAZING ADVENTURES OF KAVALIER AND CLAY"?
WAIT... I THOUGHT WE WERE DISCUSSING "BETTY AND VERONICA GET THEIR MUSTACHES WAXED".
RJ, YOU DON'T EVEN READ.
COMIC BOOKS ON TAPE.
VERNE'S BOOK CLUB
OKAY, WHO WANTS TO START WITH THEIR INITIAL IMPRESSIONS OF THE BOOK?
UH... KINDA THICK.
IT'S NOT SUCH A GOOD UMBRELLA.
I CAN BENCH PRESS IT.
NONE OF YOU ACTUALLY READ THE BOOK DID YOU?
NOPE.
IN FACT, NONE OF YOU CAN EVEN READ, CAN YOU?!
NOPE.
THEN WHY ARE YOU HERE??!
THE CLAM DIP.
AND THAT LITTLE STEAM THING THAT HAPPENS WHEN YOU GET ALL FREAKED OUT.
DO IT AGAIN!
OKAY...HOW 'BOUT IF I READ THE "THE AMAZING ADVENTURES OF KAVALIER AND CLAY" TO YOU?
VERNE'S BOOK CLUB
HEY!
SOUNDS GOOD!
GO FOR IT.
"IN LATER YEARS, HOLDING FORTH TO AN INTERVIEWER OR TO AN AUDIENCE OF AGING FANS AT A COMIC BOOK CONVENTION, SAM CLAY..."
WHERE ARE THE PICTURES?
THERE AREN'T ANY...YOU USE YOUR IMAGINATION TO FORM PICTURES WITH YOUR MIND'S EYE.
I HAVE AN EYE IN MY MIND?!
GROSS...
GET IT OUT!! GET IT OUT!!
WILL IT MAKE WALLET-SIZE OR IS THAT EXTRA?

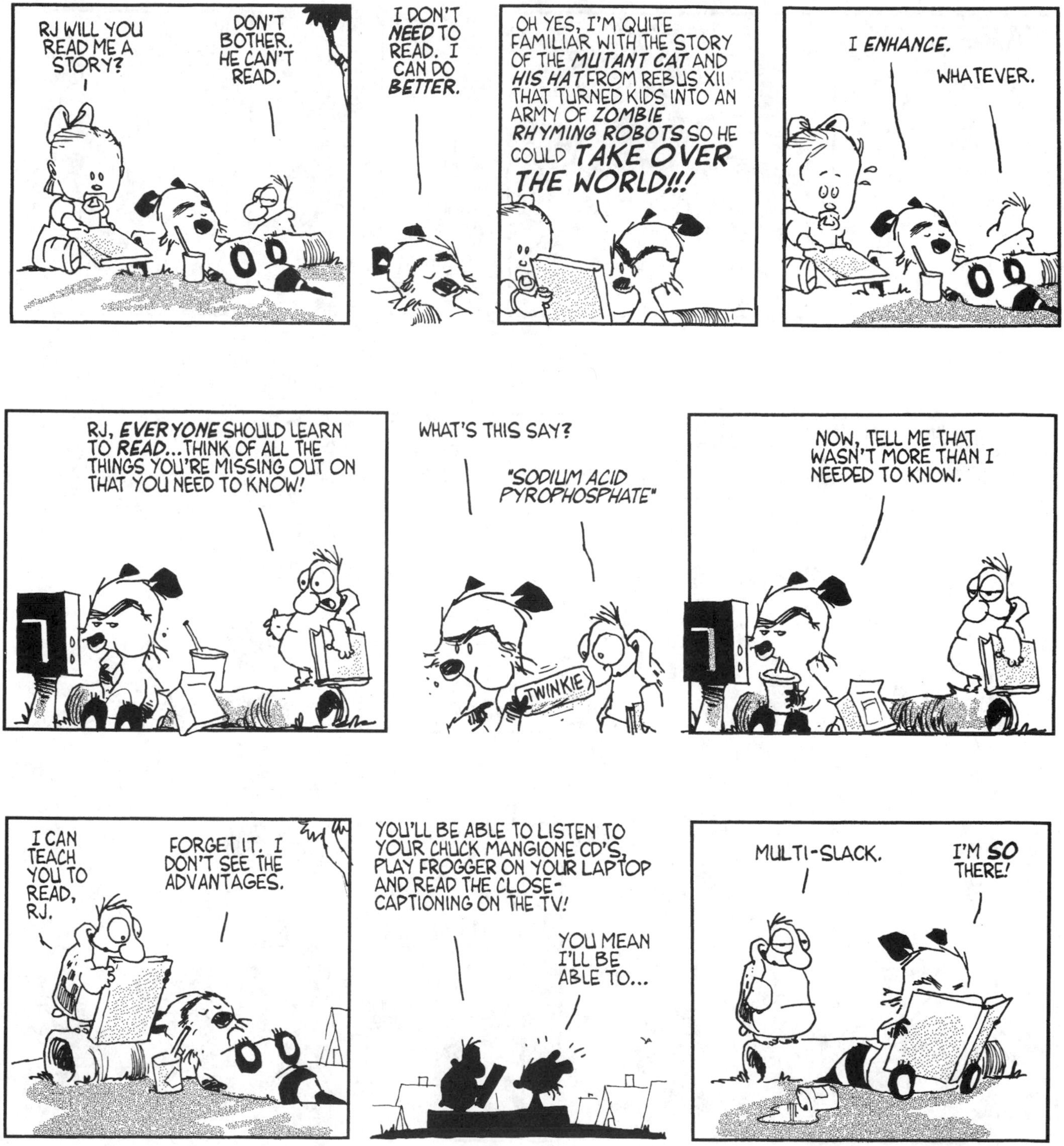
RJ WILL YOU READ ME A STORY?
DON'T BOTHER. HE CAN'T READ.
I DON'T NEED TO READ. I CAN DO BETTER.
OH YES, I'M QUITE FAMILIAR WITH THE STORY OF THE MUTANT CAT AND HIS HAT FROM REBUS XII THAT TURNED KIDS INTO AN ARMY OF ZOMBIE RHYMING ROBOTS SO HE COULD TAKE OVER THE WORLD!!!
I ENHANCE.
WHATEVER.
RJ, EVERYONE SHOULD LEARN TO READ... THINK OF ALL THE THINGS YOU'RE MISSING OUT ON THAT YOU NEED TO KNOW!
WHAT'S THIS SAY?
"SODIUM ACID PYROPHOSPHATE"
TWINKIE
NOW, TELL ME THAT WASN'T MORE THAN I NEEDED TO KNOW.
I CAN TEACH YOU TO READ, RJ.
FORGET IT. I DON'T SEE THE ADVANTAGES.
YOU'LL BE ABLE TO LISTEN TO YOUR CHUCK MANGIONE CD'S, PLAY FROGGER ON YOUR LAPTOP AND READ THE CLOSE-CAPTIONING ON THE TV!
YOU MEAN I'LL BE ABLE TO...
MULTI-SLACK.
I'M SO THERE!

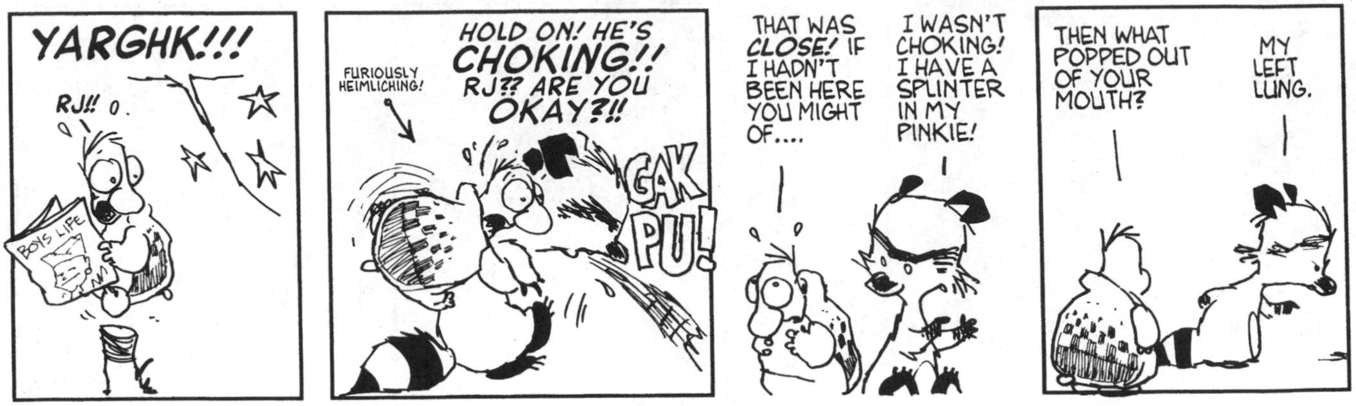
YARGHK!!!
RJ!!
BOYS LIFE
FURIOUSLY HEIMLICHING!
HOLD ON! HE'S CHOKING!! RJ?? ARE YOU OKAY?!!
GAK PU!
THAT WAS CLOSE! IF I HADN'T BEEN HERE YOU MIGHT OF....
I WASN'T CHOKING! I HAVE A SPLINTER IN MY PINKIE!
THEN WHAT POPPED OUT OF YOUR MOUTH?
MY LEFT LUNG.

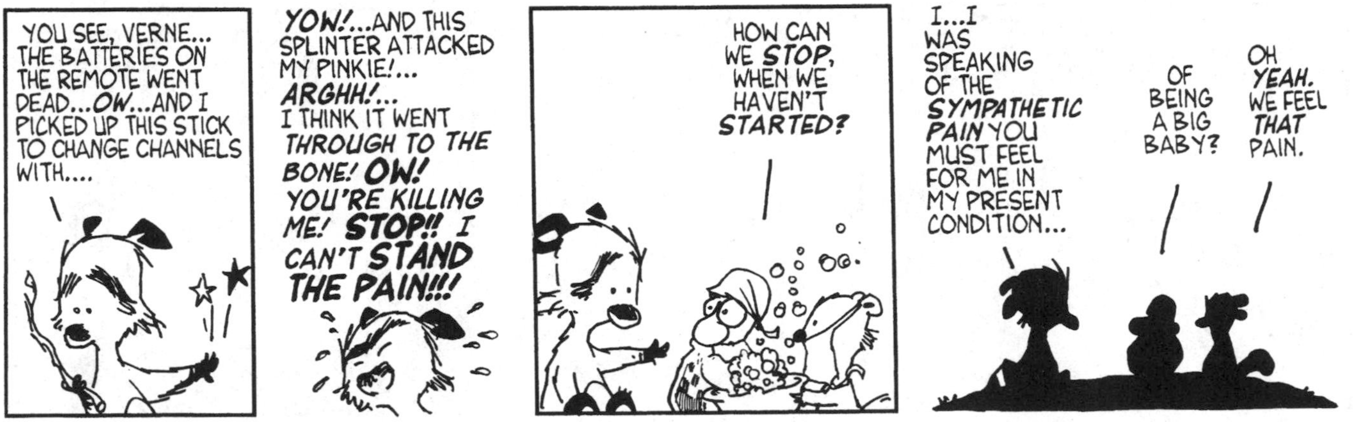
YOU SEE, VERNE... THE BATTERIES ON THE REMOTE WENT DEAD...OW...AND I PICKED UP THIS STICK TO CHANGE CHANNELS WITH....
YOW!...AND THIS SPLINTER ATTACKED MY PINKIE!... ARGHH!... I THINK IT WENT THROUGH TO THE BONE! OW! YOU'RE KILLING ME! STOP!! I CAN'T STAND THE PAIN!!!
HOW CAN WE STOP, WHEN WE HAVEN'T STARTED?
I...I WAS SPEAKING OF THE SYMPATHETIC PAIN YOU MUST FEEL FOR ME IN MY PRESENT CONDITION...
OF BEING A BIG BABY?
OH YEAH. WE FEEL THAT PAIN.

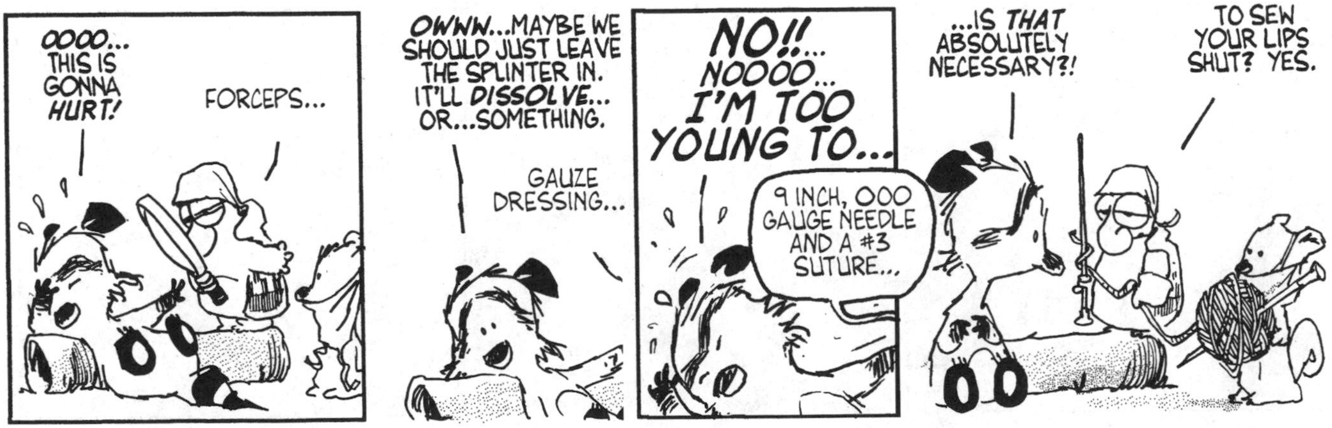
OOOO... THIS IS GONNA HURT!
FORCEPS...
OWNW...MAYBE WE SHOULD JUST LEAVE THE SPLINTER IN. IT'LL DISSOLVE... OR...SOMETHING.
GAUZE DRESSING...
NO!!... NOOOO... I'M TOO YOUNG TO...
9 INCH, OOO GAUGE NEEDLE AND A #3 SUTURE...
...IS THAT ABSOLUTELY NECESSARY?!
TO SEW YOUR LIPS SHUT? YES.

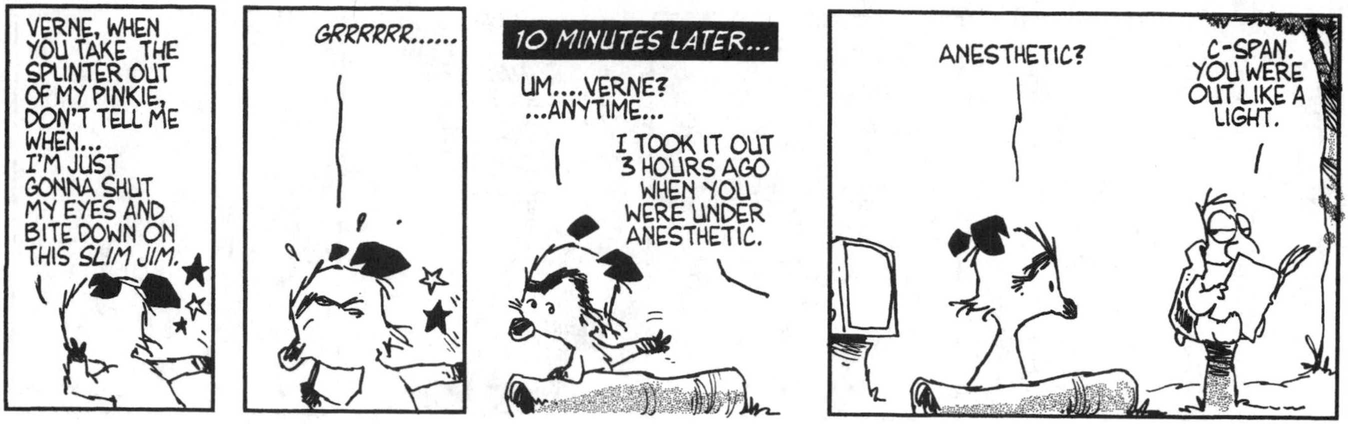
VERNE, WHEN YOU TAKE THE SPLINTER OUT OF MY PINKIE, DON'T TELL ME WHEN... I'M JUST GONNA SHUT MY EYES AND BITE DOWN ON THIS *SLIM JIM.*
GRRRRRR......
10 MINUTES LATER...
UM....VERNE? ...ANYTIME...
I TOOK IT OUT 3 HOURS AGO WHEN YOU WERE UNDER ANESTHETIC.
ANESTHETIC?
C-SPAN. YOU WERE OUT LIKE A LIGHT.

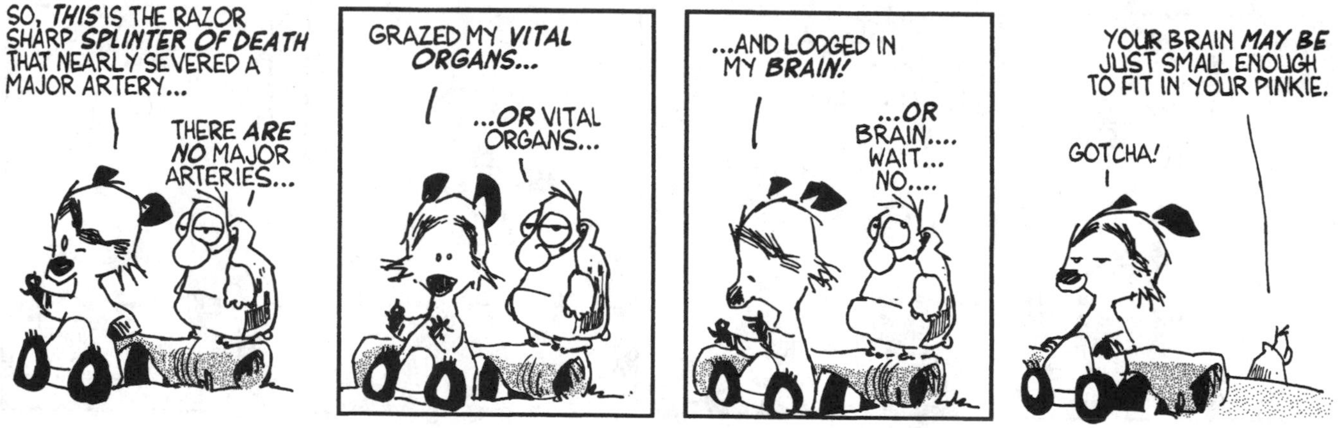
SO, ***THIS*** IS THE RAZOR SHARP ***SPLINTER OF DEATH*** THAT NEARLY SEVERED A MAJOR ARTERY...
THERE ***ARE NO*** MAJOR ARTERIES...
GRAZED MY ***VITAL ORGANS...***
...OR VITAL ORGANS...
...AND LODGED IN MY ***BRAIN!***
...OR BRAIN.... WAIT... NO....
GOTCHA!
YOUR BRAIN ***MAY BE*** JUST SMALL ENOUGH TO FIT IN YOUR PINKIE.

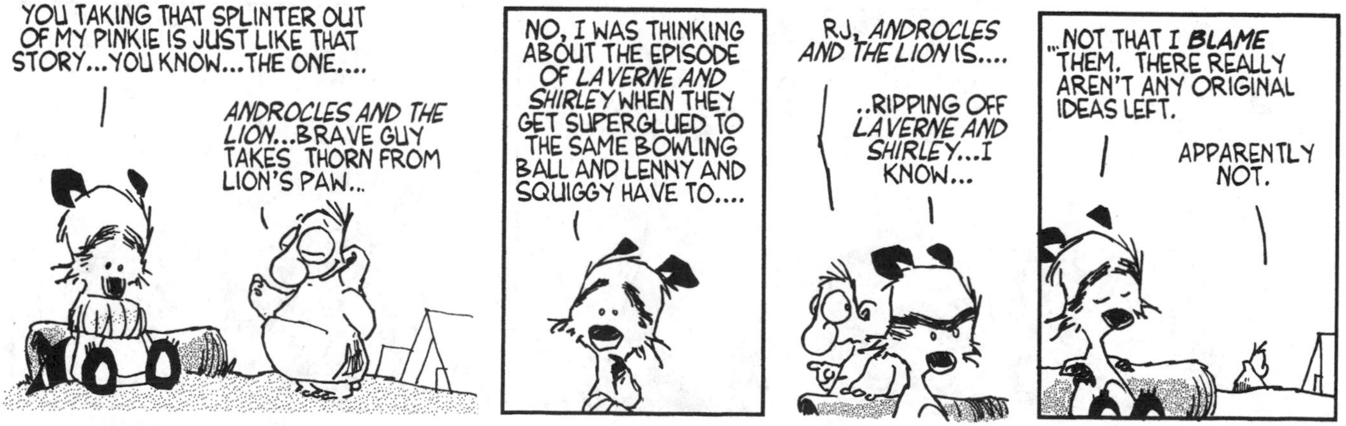
YOU TAKING THAT SPLINTER OUT OF MY PINKIE IS JUST LIKE THAT STORY...YOU KNOW...THE ONE....
ANDROCLES AND THE LION...BRAVE GUY TAKES THORN FROM LION'S PAW...
NO, I WAS THINKING ABOUT THE EPISODE OF *LAVERNE AND SHIRLEY* WHEN THEY GET SUPERGLUED TO THE SAME BOWLING BALL AND LENNY AND SQUIGGY HAVE TO....
RJ, *ANDROCLES AND THE LION* IS....
..RIPPING OFF *LAVERNE AND SHIRLEY*...I KNOW...
...NOT THAT I ***BLAME*** THEM. THERE REALLY AREN'T ANY ORIGINAL IDEAS LEFT.
APPARENTLY NOT.

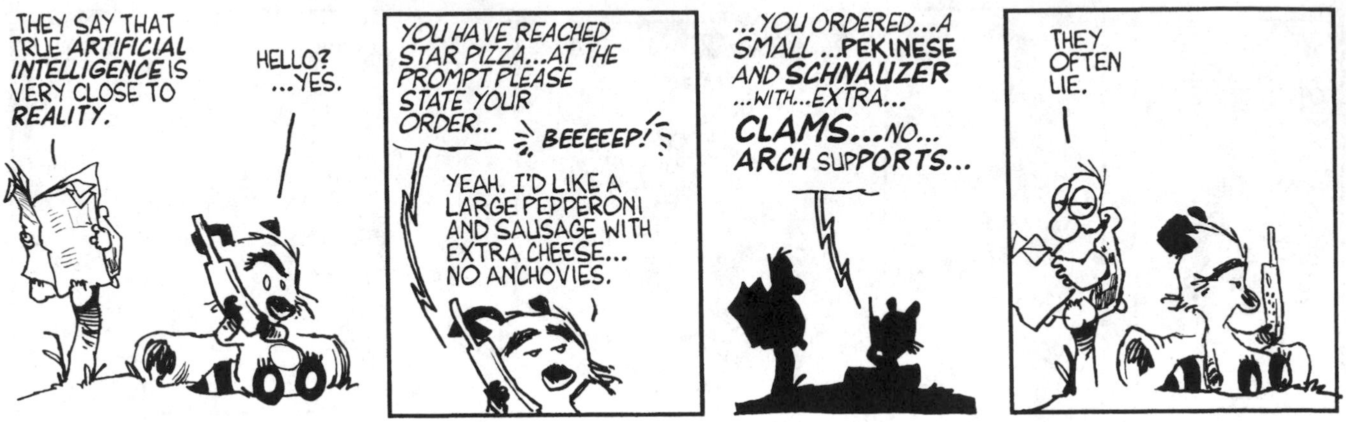
THEY SAY THAT TRUE **ARTIFICIAL INTELLIGENCE** IS VERY CLOSE TO **REALITY**.
HELLO? ...YES.
YOU HAVE REACHED STAR PIZZA...AT THE PROMPT PLEASE STATE YOUR ORDER...
BEEEEEP!
YEAH. I'D LIKE A LARGE PEPPERONI AND SAUSAGE WITH EXTRA CHEESE... NO ANCHOVIES.
...YOU ORDERED...A SMALL ...**PEKINESE** AND **SCHNAUZER** ...WITH...EXTRA... **CLAMS...**NO... **ARCH** SUPPORTS...
THEY OFTEN LIE.

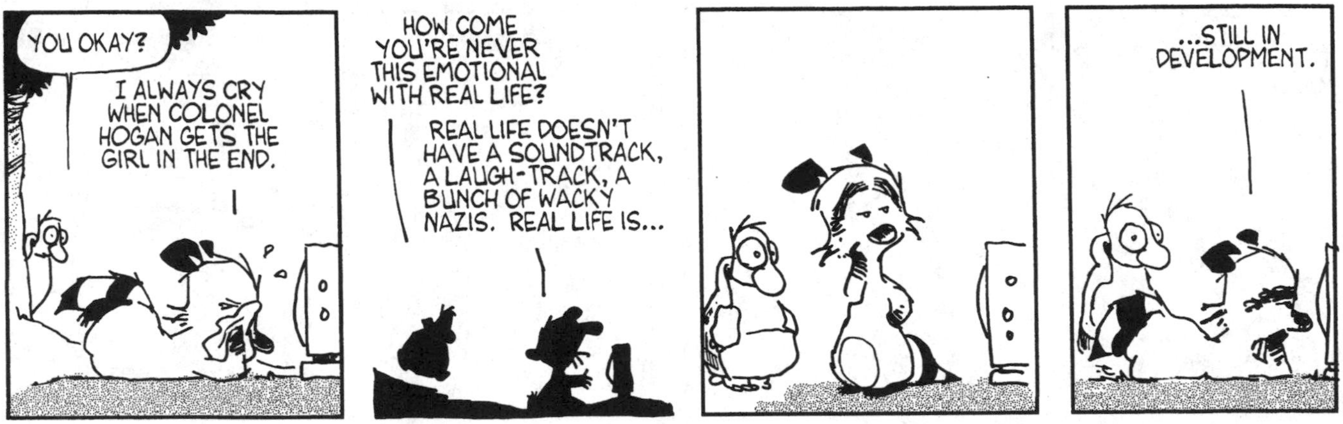
YOU OKAY?
I ALWAYS CRY WHEN COLONEL HOGAN GETS THE GIRL IN THE END.
HOW COME YOU'RE NEVER THIS EMOTIONAL WITH REAL LIFE?
REAL LIFE DOESN'T HAVE A SOUNDTRACK, A LAUGH-TRACK, A BUNCH OF WACKY NAZIS. REAL LIFE IS...
...STILL IN DEVELOPMENT.

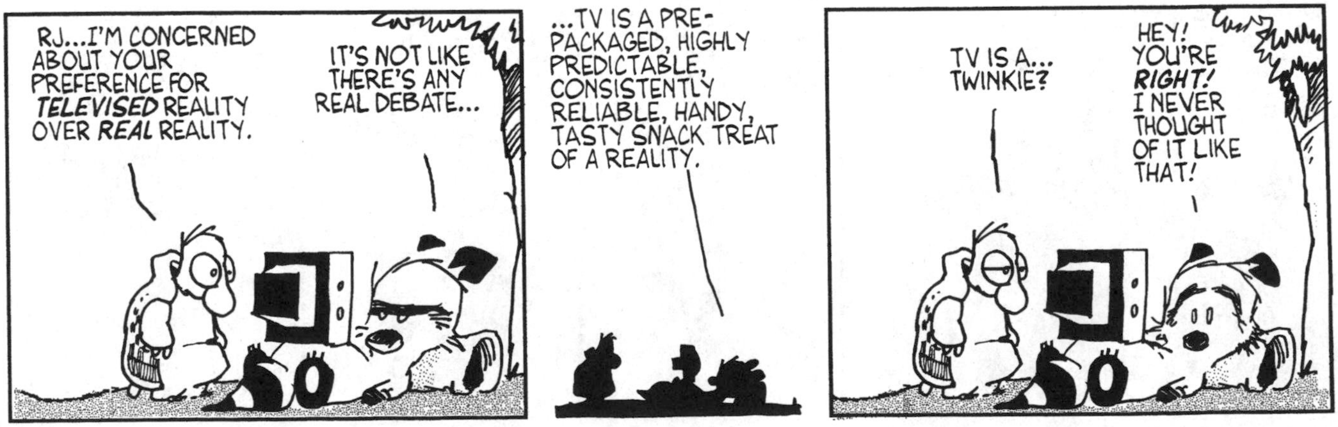
RJ...I'M CONCERNED ABOUT YOUR PREFERENCE FOR **TELEVISED** REALITY OVER **REAL** REALITY.
IT'S NOT LIKE THERE'S ANY REAL DEBATE...
...TV IS A PRE-PACKAGED, HIGHLY PREDICTABLE, CONSISTENTLY RELIABLE, HANDY, TASTY SNACK TREAT OF A REALITY.
TV IS A... TWINKIE?
HEY! YOU'RE **RIGHT!** I NEVER THOUGHT OF IT LIKE THAT!

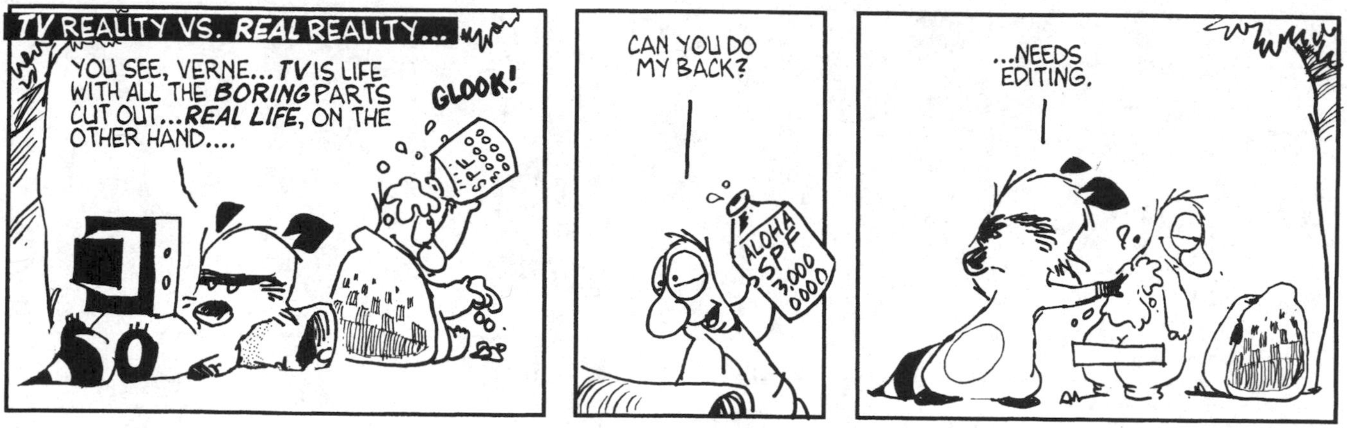
TV REALITY VS. REAL REALITY...
YOU SEE, VERNE... TV IS LIFE WITH ALL THE BORING PARTS CUT OUT... REAL LIFE, ON THE OTHER HAND....
GLOOK!
CAN YOU DO MY BACK?
ALOHA SPF
...NEEDS EDITING.

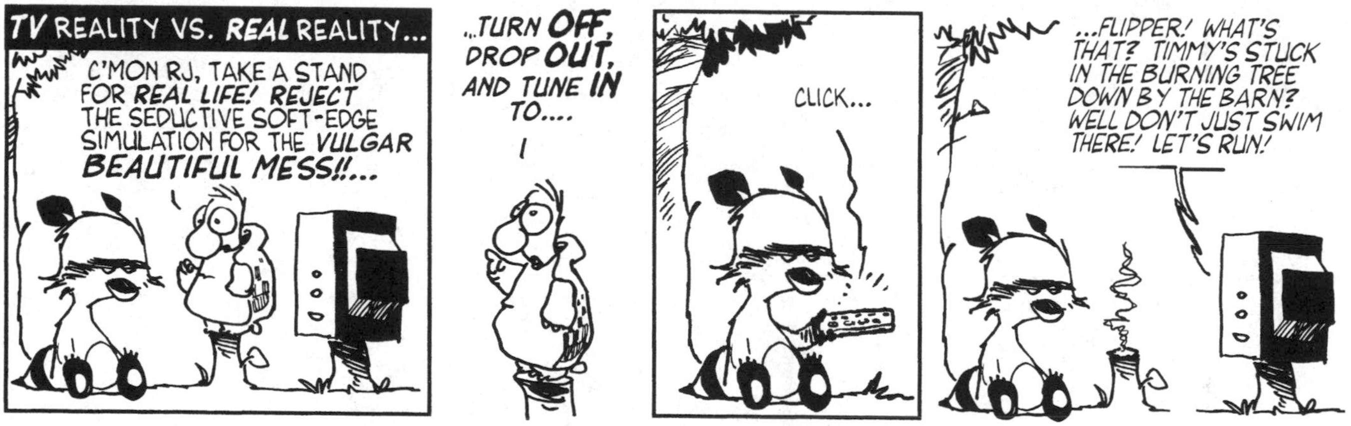
TV REALITY VS. REAL REALITY...
C'MON RJ, TAKE A STAND FOR REAL LIFE! REJECT THE SEDUCTIVE SOFT-EDGE SIMULATION FOR THE VULGAR BEAUTIFUL MESS!!...
...TURN OFF, DROP OUT, AND TUNE IN TO....
CLICK...
...FLIPPER! WHAT'S THAT? TIMMY'S STUCK IN THE BURNING TREE DOWN BY THE BARN? WELL DON'T JUST SWIM THERE! LET'S RUN!

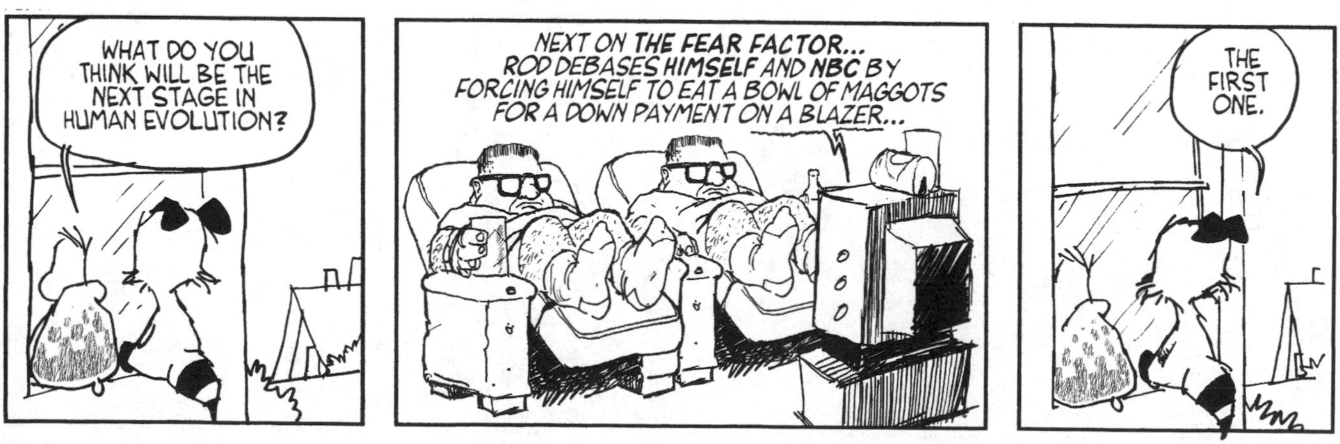
WHAT DO YOU THINK WILL BE THE NEXT STAGE IN HUMAN EVOLUTION?
NEXT ON THE FEAR FACTOR... ROD DEBASES HIMSELF AND NBC BY FORCING HIMSELF TO EAT A BOWL OF MAGGOTS FOR A DOWN PAYMENT ON A BLAZER...
THE FIRST ONE.

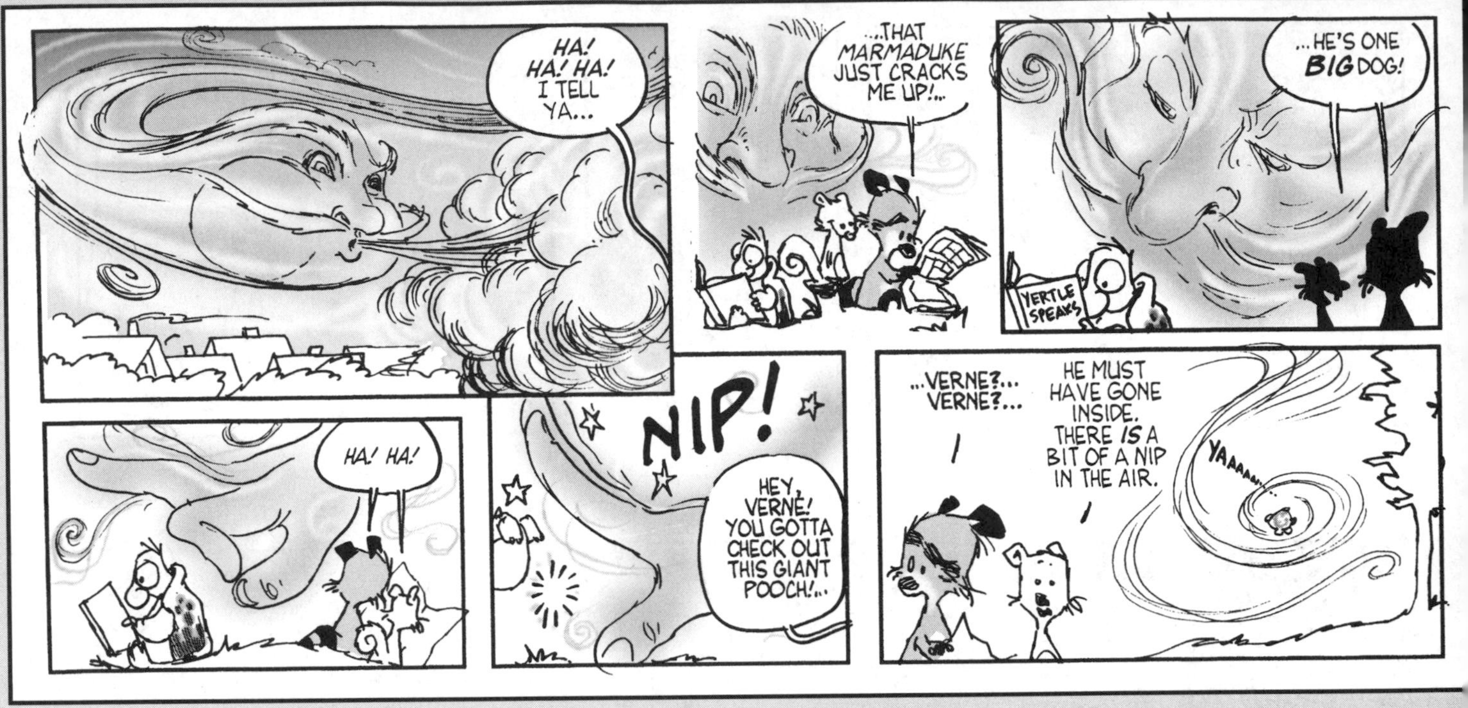
HA! HA! HA! I TELL YA...
...THAT MARMADUKE JUST CRACKS ME UP!...
...HE'S ONE BIG DOG!
YERTLE SPEAKS
HA! HA!
NIP!
HEY, VERNE! YOU GOTTA CHECK OUT THIS GIANT POOCH!...
...VERNE?... VERNE?...
HE MUST HAVE GONE INSIDE. THERE IS A BIT OF A NIP IN THE AIR.
YAAAAA...

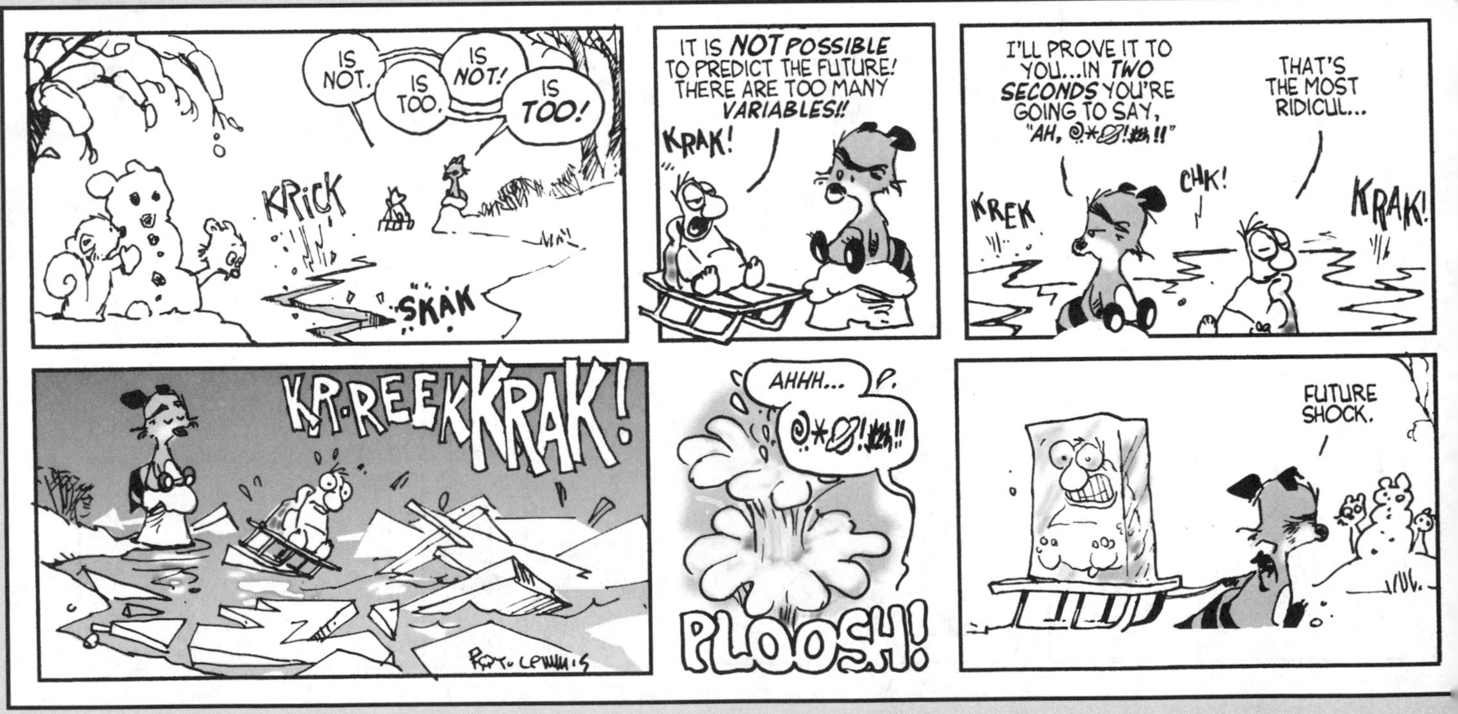
IS NOT.
IS TOO.
IS NOT!
IS TOO!
KRICK
SKAK
IT IS NOT POSSIBLE TO PREDICT THE FUTURE! THERE ARE TOO MANY VARIABLES!!
KRAK!
I'LL PROVE IT TO YOU...IN TWO SECONDS YOU'RE GOING TO SAY, "AH, @*!#!!"
THAT'S THE MOST RIDICUL...
KREK
CHK!
KRAK!
KR-REEKKRAK!
AHHH... @*!#!!
PLOOSH!
FUTURE SHOCK.

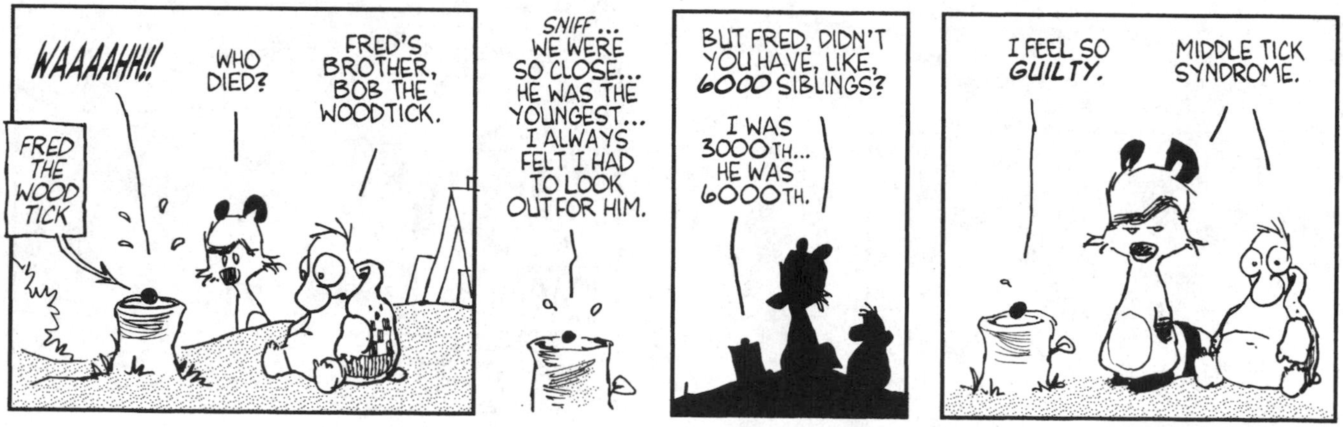
WAAAAHH!!
WHO DIED?
FRED'S BROTHER, BOB THE WOODTICK.
FRED THE WOOD TICK
SNIFF... WE WERE SO CLOSE... HE WAS THE YOUNGEST... I ALWAYS FELT I HAD TO LOOK OUT FOR HIM.
BUT FRED, DIDN'T YOU HAVE, LIKE, 6000 SIBLINGS?
I WAS 3000TH... HE WAS 6000TH.
I FEEL SO GUILTY.
MIDDLE TICK SYNDROME.

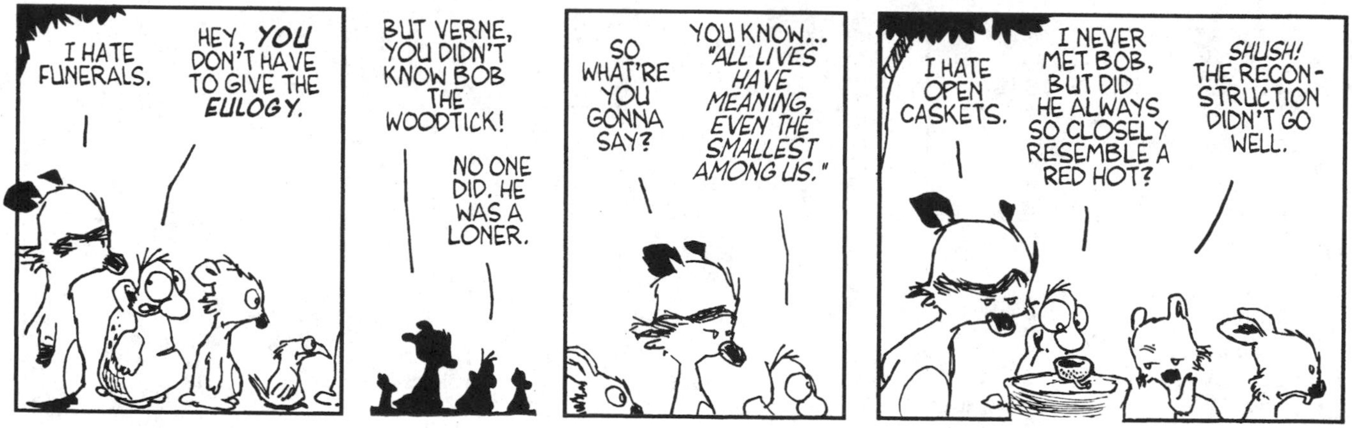
I HATE FUNERALS.
HEY, YOU DON'T HAVE TO GIVE THE EULOGY.
BUT VERNE, YOU DIDN'T KNOW BOB THE WOODTICK!
NO ONE DID. HE WAS A LONER.
SO WHAT'RE YOU GONNA SAY?
YOU KNOW... "ALL LIVES HAVE MEANING, EVEN THE SMALLEST AMONG US."
I HATE OPEN CASKETS.
I NEVER MET BOB, BUT DID HE ALWAYS SO CLOSELY RESEMBLE A RED HOT?
SHUSH! THE RECON-STRUCTION DIDN'T GO WELL.

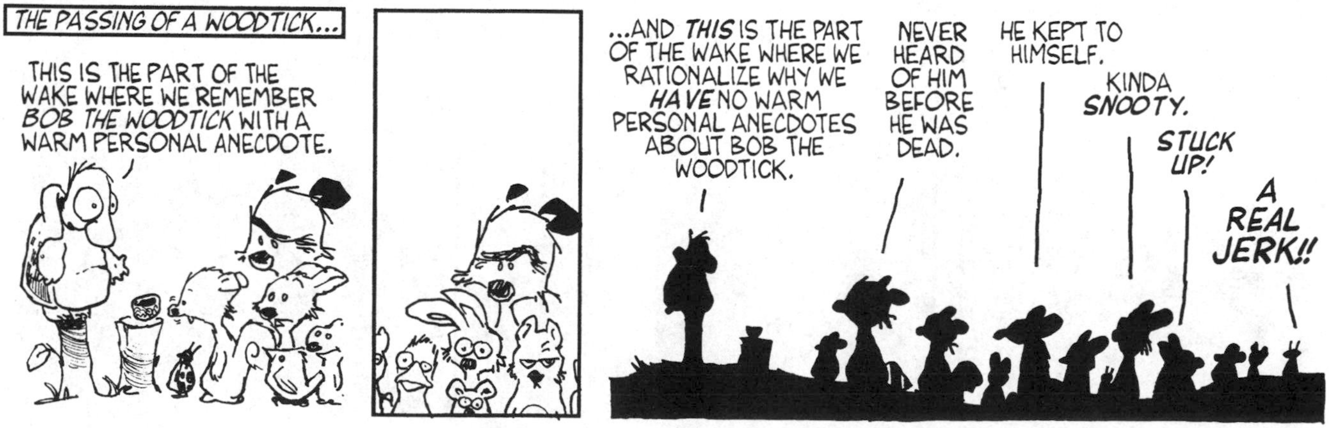
THE PASSING OF A WOODTICK...
THIS IS THE PART OF THE WAKE WHERE WE REMEMBER BOB THE WOODTICK WITH A WARM PERSONAL ANECDOTE.
...AND THIS IS THE PART OF THE WAKE WHERE WE RATIONALIZE WHY WE HAVE NO WARM PERSONAL ANECDOTES ABOUT BOB THE WOODTICK.
NEVER HEARD OF HIM BEFORE HE WAS DEAD.
HE KEPT TO HIMSELF.
KINDA SNOOTY.
STUCK UP!
A REAL JERK!!

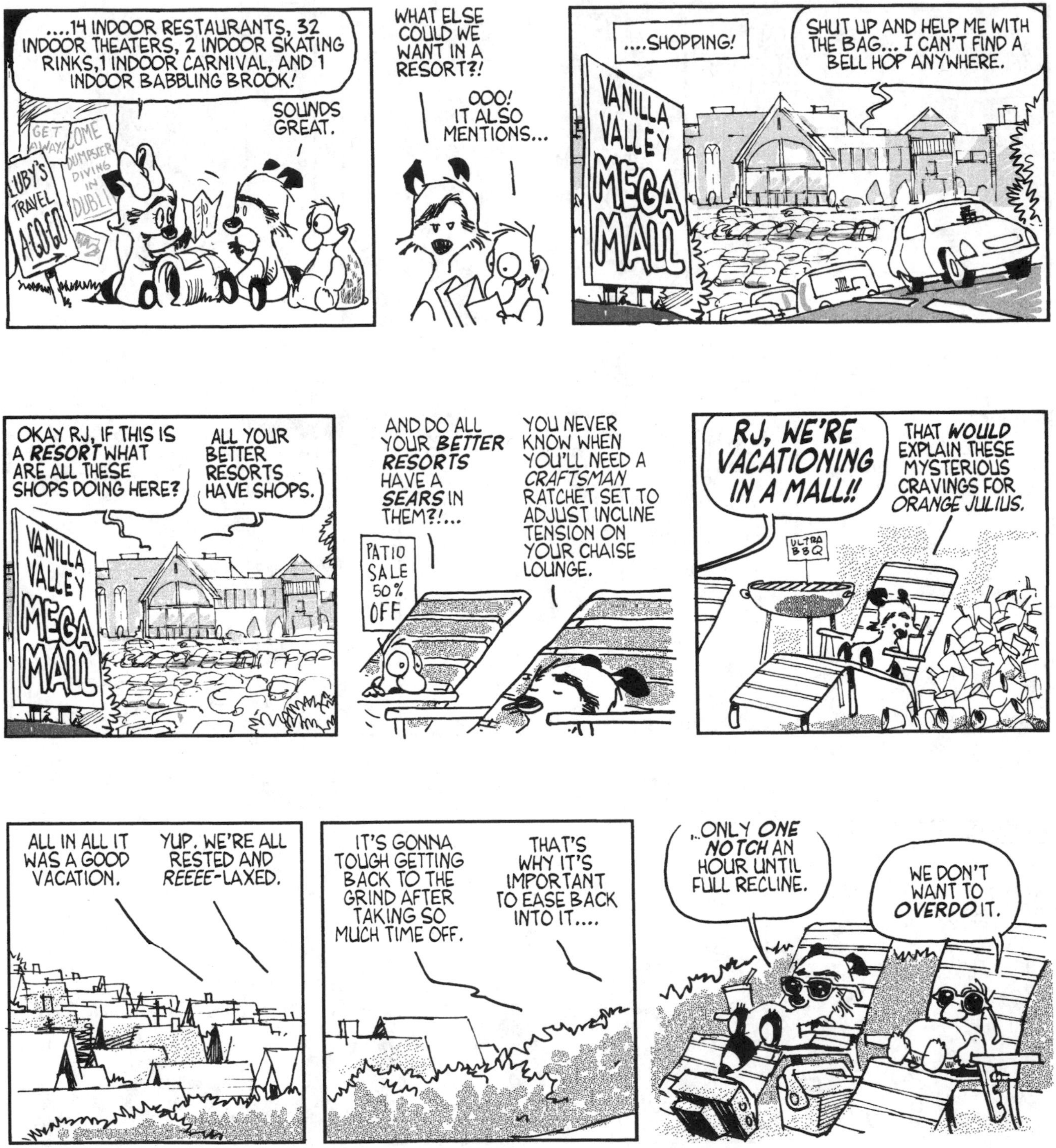
....14 INDOOR RESTAURANTS, 32 INDOOR THEATERS, 2 INDOOR SKATING RINKS, 1 INDOOR CARNIVAL, AND 1 INDOOR BABBLING BROOK!
GET AWAY!
COME DUMPSTER DIVING IN DUBLI
LUBY'S TRAVEL A-GO-GO
SOUNDS GREAT.
WHAT ELSE COULD WE WANT IN A RESORT?!
OOO! IT ALSO MENTIONS...
....SHOPPING!
SHUT UP AND HELP ME WITH THE BAG... I CAN'T FIND A BELL HOP ANYWHERE.
VANILLA VALLEY MEGA MALL
OKAY RJ, IF THIS IS A **RESORT** WHAT ARE ALL THESE SHOPS DOING HERE?
ALL YOUR BETTER RESORTS HAVE SHOPS.
VANILLA VALLEY MEGA MALL
AND DO ALL YOUR ***BETTER RESORTS*** HAVE A ***SEARS*** IN THEM?!...
PATIO SALE 50% OFF
YOU NEVER KNOW WHEN YOU'LL NEED A *CRAFTSMAN* RATCHET SET TO ADJUST INCLINE TENSION ON YOUR CHAISE LOUNGE.
RJ, WE'RE VACATIONING IN A MALL!!
ULTRA BBQ
THAT ***WOULD*** EXPLAIN THESE MYSTERIOUS CRAVINGS FOR *ORANGE JULIUS.*
ALL IN ALL IT WAS A GOOD VACATION.
YUP. WE'RE ALL RESTED AND *REEEE*-LAXED.
IT'S GONNA TOUGH GETTING BACK TO THE GRIND AFTER TAKING SO MUCH TIME OFF.
THAT'S WHY IT'S IMPORTANT TO EASE BACK INTO IT....
..ONLY ***ONE NOTCH*** AN HOUR UNTIL FULL RECLINE.
WE DON'T WANT TO ***OVERDO*** IT.

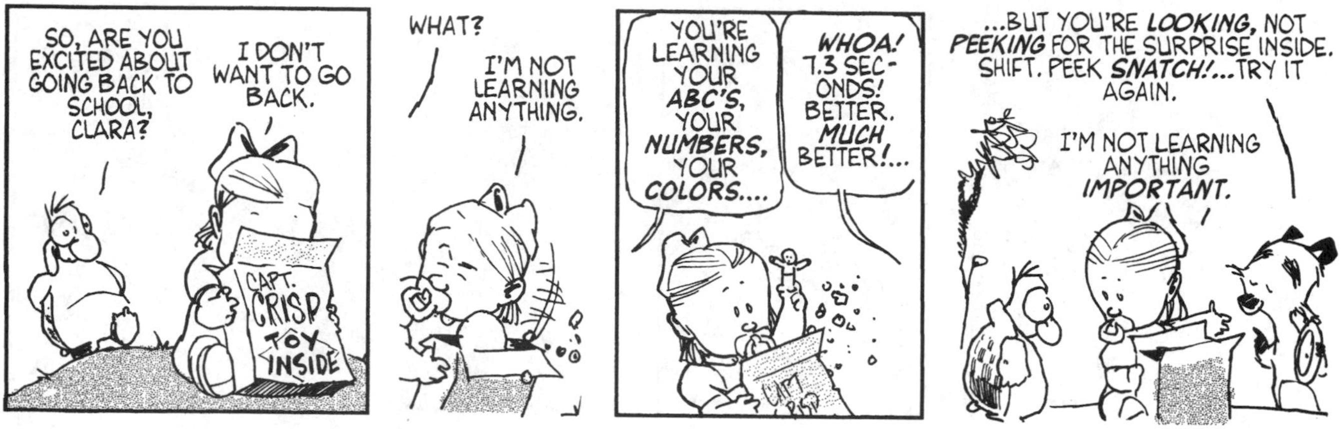
SO, ARE YOU EXCITED ABOUT GOING BACK TO SCHOOL, CLARA?
I DON'T WANT TO GO BACK.
CAPT. CRISP TOY INSIDE
WHAT?
I'M NOT LEARNING ANYTHING.
YOU'RE LEARNING YOUR ABC'S, YOUR NUMBERS, YOUR COLORS....
WHOA! 7.3 SECONDS! BETTER. MUCH BETTER!...
...BUT YOU'RE LOOKING, NOT PEEKING FOR THE SURPRISE INSIDE. SHIFT. PEEK SNATCH!...TRY IT AGAIN.
I'M NOT LEARNING ANYTHING IMPORTANT.

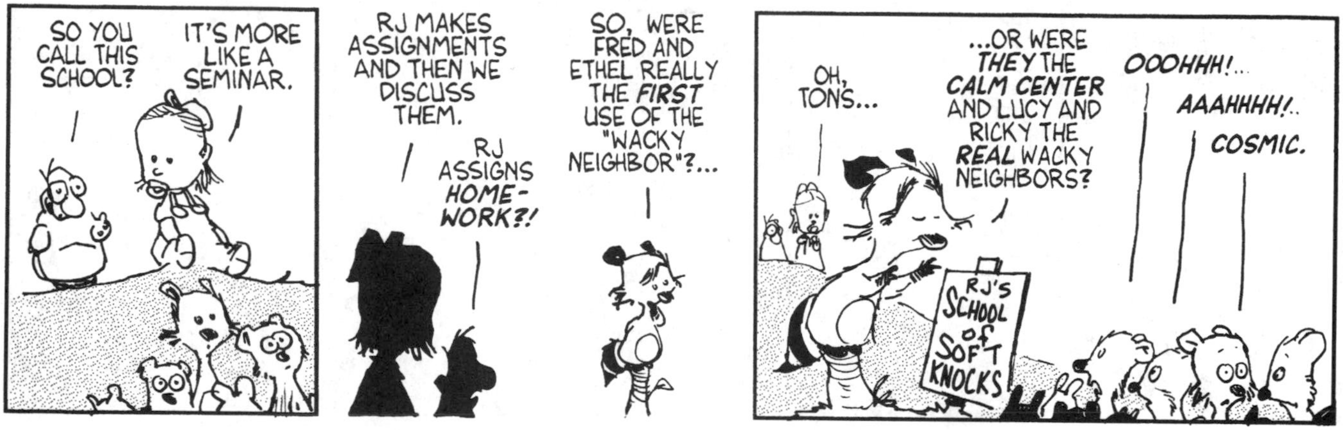
SO YOU CALL THIS SCHOOL?
IT'S MORE LIKE A SEMINAR.
RJ MAKES ASSIGNMENTS AND THEN WE DISCUSS THEM.
RJ ASSIGNS HOME-WORK?!
SO, WERE FRED AND ETHEL REALLY THE FIRST USE OF THE "WACKY NEIGHBOR"?...
OH, TONS...
...OR WERE THEY THE CALM CENTER AND LUCY AND RICKY THE REAL WACKY NEIGHBORS?
OOOHHH!...
AAAHHHH!...
COSMIC.
RJ'S SCHOOL of SOFT KNOCKS

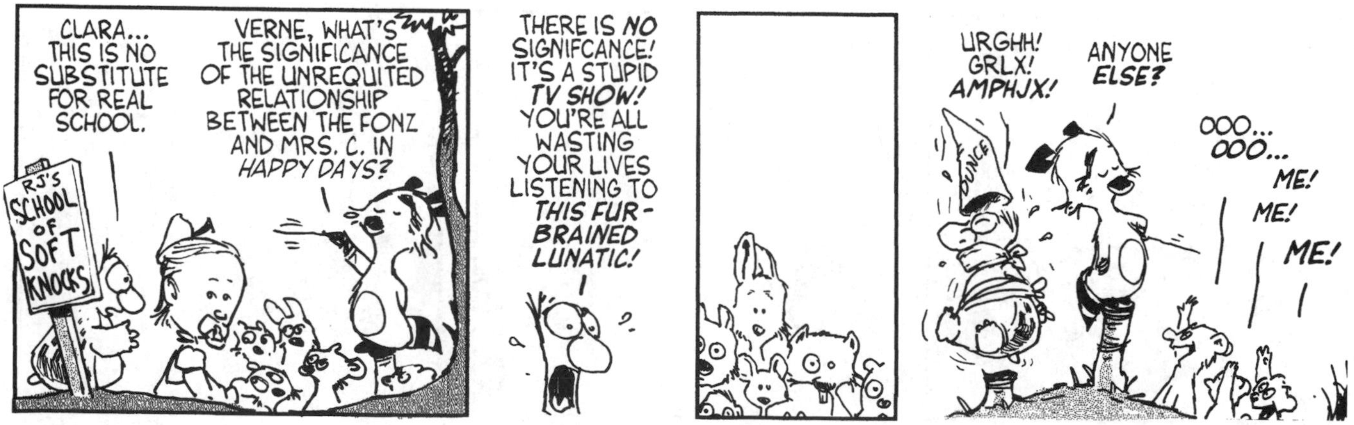
CLARA... THIS IS NO SUBSTITUTE FOR REAL SCHOOL.
VERNE, WHAT'S THE SIGNIFICANCE OF THE UNREQUITED RELATIONSHIP BETWEEN THE FONZ AND MRS. C. IN HAPPY DAYS?
RJ'S SCHOOL OF SOFT KNOCKS
THERE IS NO SIGNIFCANCE! IT'S A STUPID TV SHOW! YOU'RE ALL WASTING YOUR LIVES LISTENING TO THIS FUR-BRAINED LUNATIC!
URGHH! GRLX! AMPHJX!
DUNCE
ANYONE ELSE?
OOO... OOO...
ME!
ME!
ME!

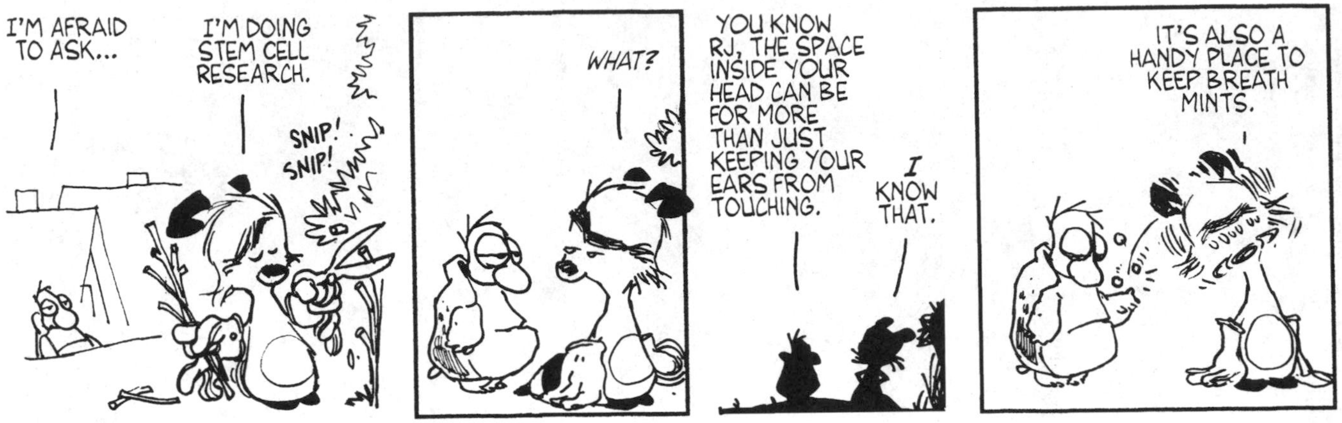
I'M AFRAID TO ASK...
I'M DOING STEM CELL RESEARCH.
SNIP! SNIP!
WHAT?
YOU KNOW RJ, THE SPACE INSIDE YOUR HEAD CAN BE FOR MORE THAN JUST KEEPING YOUR EARS FROM TOUCHING.
I KNOW THAT.
IT'S ALSO A HANDY PLACE TO KEEP BREATH MINTS.

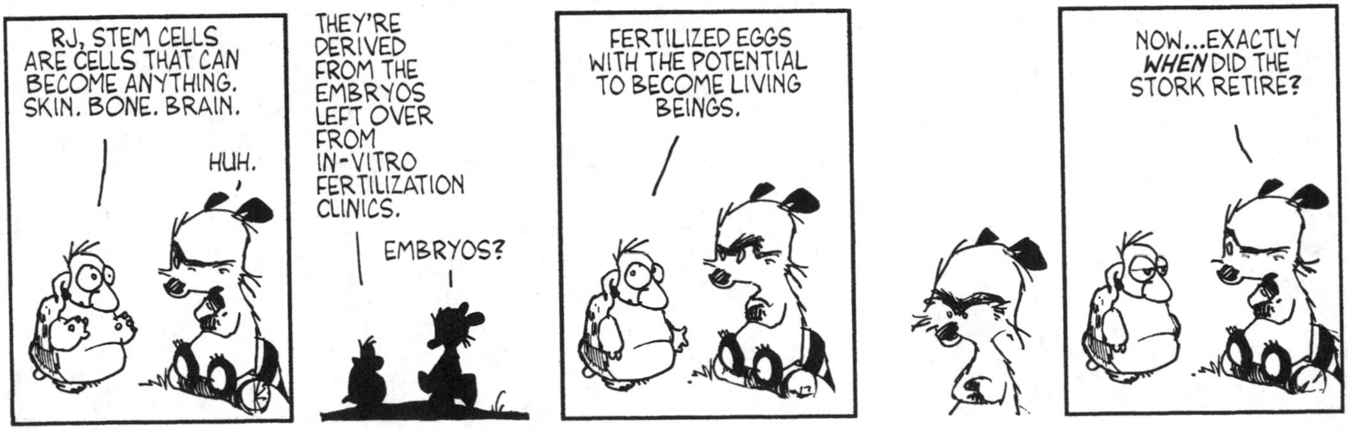
RJ, STEM CELLS ARE CELLS THAT CAN BECOME ANYTHING. SKIN. BONE. BRAIN.
HUH.
THEY'RE DERIVED FROM THE EMBRYOS LEFT OVER FROM IN-VITRO FERTILIZATION CLINICS.
EMBRYOS?
FERTILIZED EGGS WITH THE POTENTIAL TO BECOME LIVING BEINGS.
NOW...EXACTLY *WHEN* DID THE STORK RETIRE?

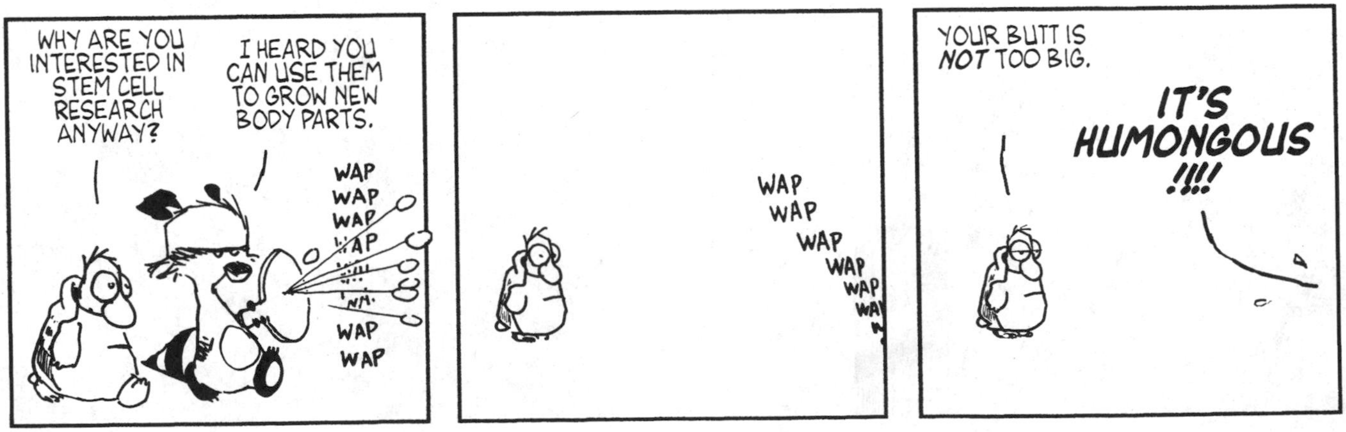
WHY ARE YOU INTERESTED IN STEM CELL RESEARCH ANYWAY?
I HEARD YOU CAN USE THEM TO GROW NEW BODY PARTS.
WAP WAP WAP WAP WAP WAP
WAP WAP WAP WAP WAP
YOUR BUTT IS *NOT* TOO BIG.
IT'S HUMONGOUS !!!!

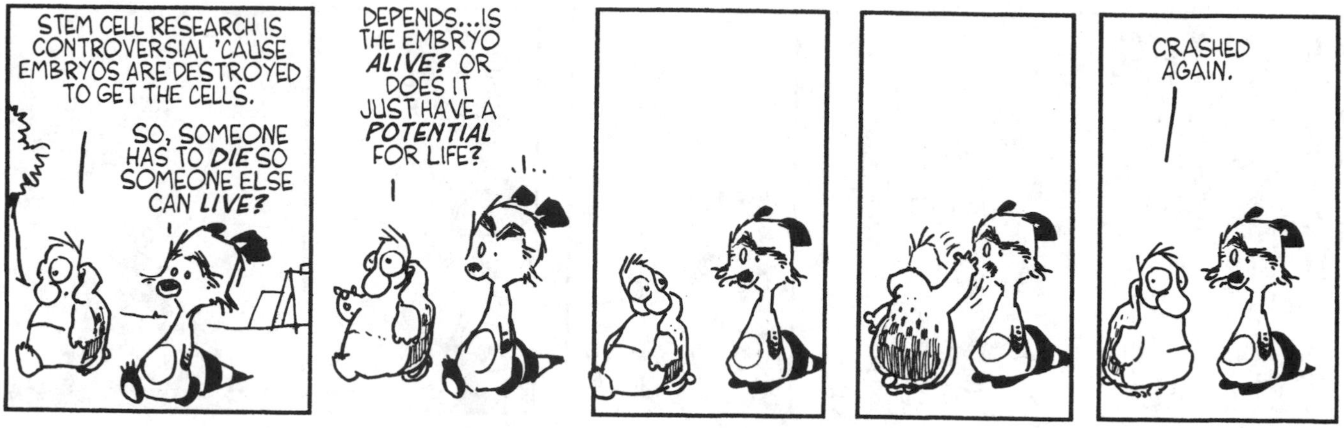
STEM CELL RESEARCH IS CONTROVERSIAL 'CAUSE EMBRYOS ARE DESTROYED TO GET THE CELLS.
SO, SOMEONE HAS TO DIE SO SOMEONE ELSE CAN LIVE?
DEPENDS...IS THE EMBRYO ALIVE? OR DOES IT JUST HAVE A POTENTIAL FOR LIFE?
CRASHED AGAIN.

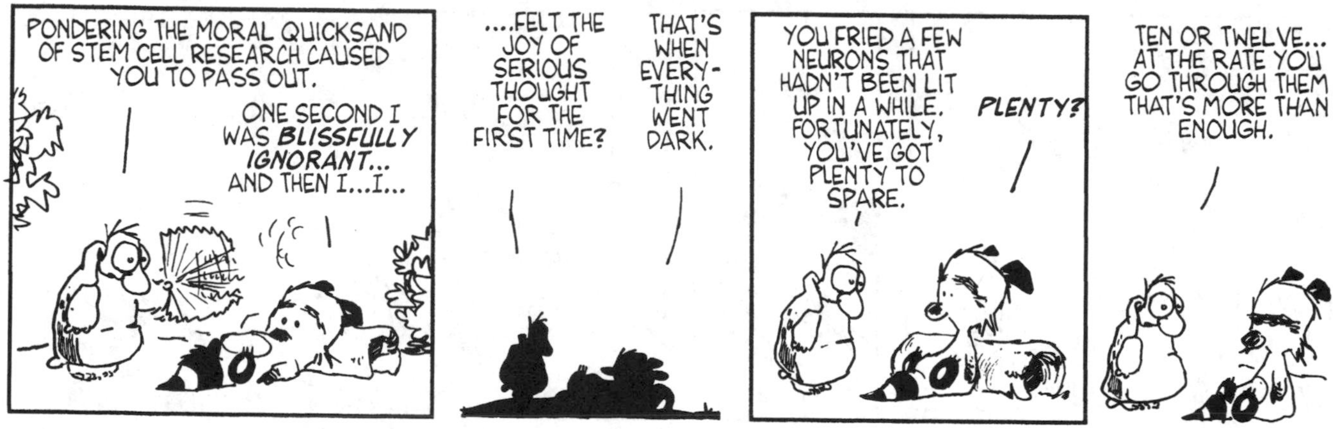
PONDERING THE MORAL QUICKSAND OF STEM CELL RESEARCH CAUSED YOU TO PASS OUT.
ONE SECOND I WAS BLISSFULLY IGNORANT... AND THEN I...I...
....FELT THE JOY OF SERIOUS THOUGHT FOR THE FIRST TIME?
THAT'S WHEN EVERY-THING WENT DARK.
YOU FRIED A FEW NEURONS THAT HADN'T BEEN LIT UP IN A WHILE. FORTUNATELY, YOU'VE GOT PLENTY TO SPARE.
PLENTY?
TEN OR TWELVE... AT THE RATE YOU GO THROUGH THEM THAT'S MORE THAN ENOUGH.

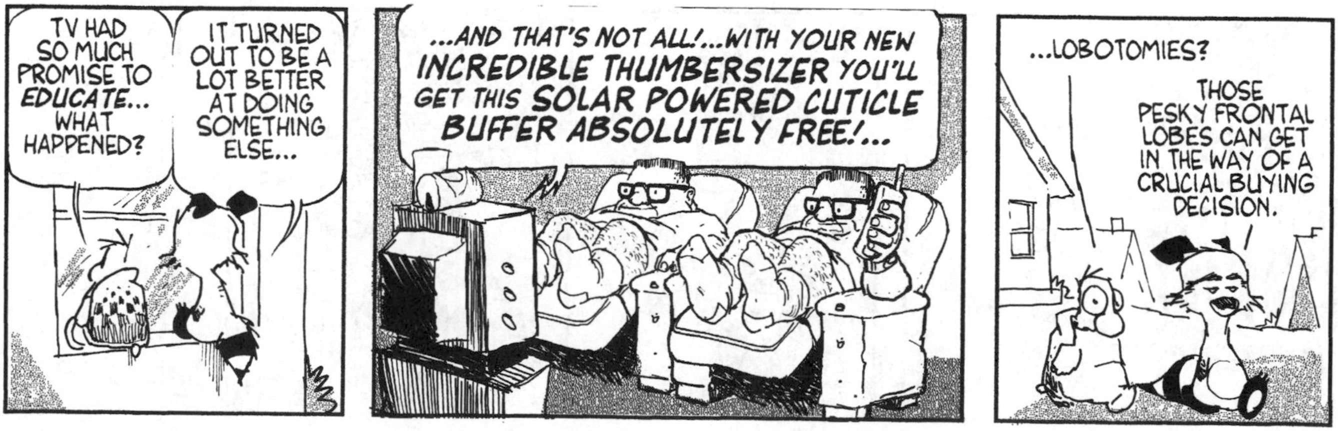
TV HAD SO MUCH PROMISE TO EDUCATE... WHAT HAPPENED?
IT TURNED OUT TO BE A LOT BETTER AT DOING SOMETHING ELSE...
...AND THAT'S NOT ALL!...WITH YOUR NEW INCREDIBLE THUMBERSIZER YOU'LL GET THIS SOLAR POWERED CUTICLE BUFFER ABSOLUTELY FREE!...
...LOBOTOMIES?
THOSE PESKY FRONTAL LOBES CAN GET IN THE WAY OF A CRUCIAL BUYING DECISION.

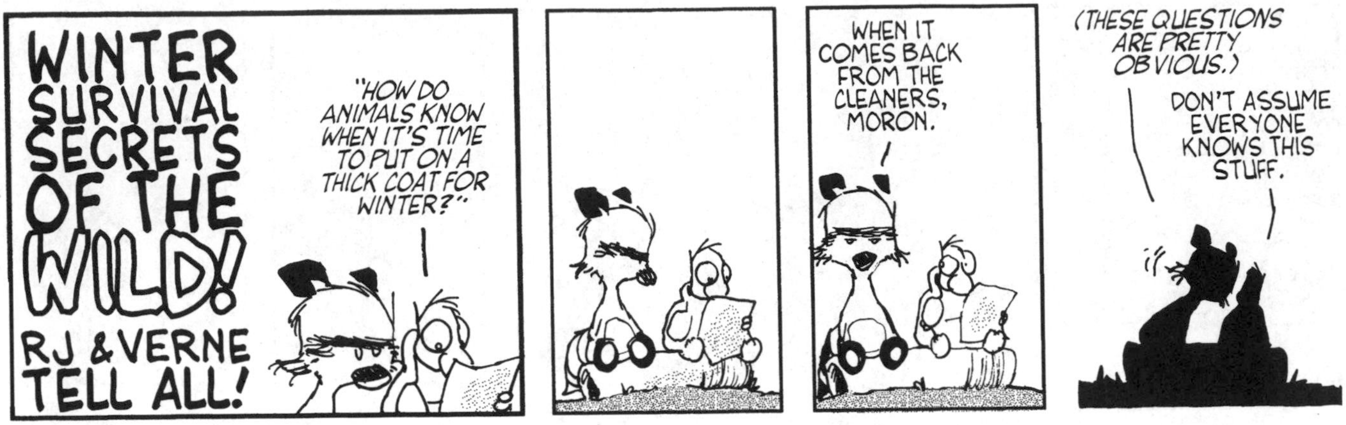
WINTER SURVIVAL SECRETS OF THE WILD!
RJ & VERNE TELL ALL!
"HOW DO ANIMALS KNOW WHEN IT'S TIME TO PUT ON A THICK COAT FOR WINTER?"
WHEN IT COMES BACK FROM THE CLEANERS, MORON.
(THESE QUESTIONS ARE PRETTY OBVIOUS.)
DON'T ASSUME EVERYONE KNOWS THIS STUFF.

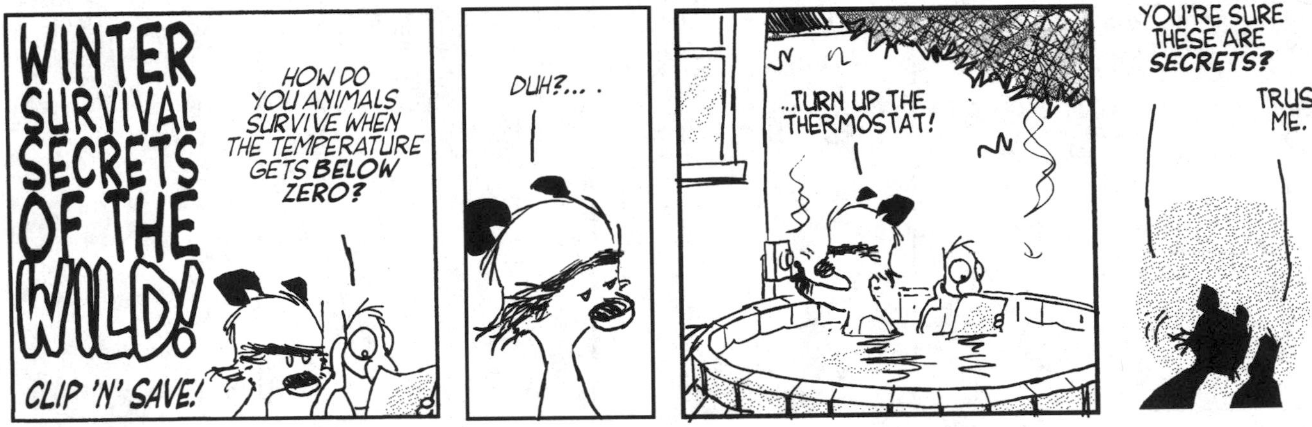
WINTER SURVIVAL SECRETS OF THE WILD!
CLIP 'N' SAVE!
HOW DO YOU ANIMALS SURVIVE WHEN THE TEMPERATURE GETS BELOW ZERO?
DUH?. . .
..TURN UP THE THERMOSTAT!
YOU'RE SURE THESE ARE SECRETS?
TRUST ME.

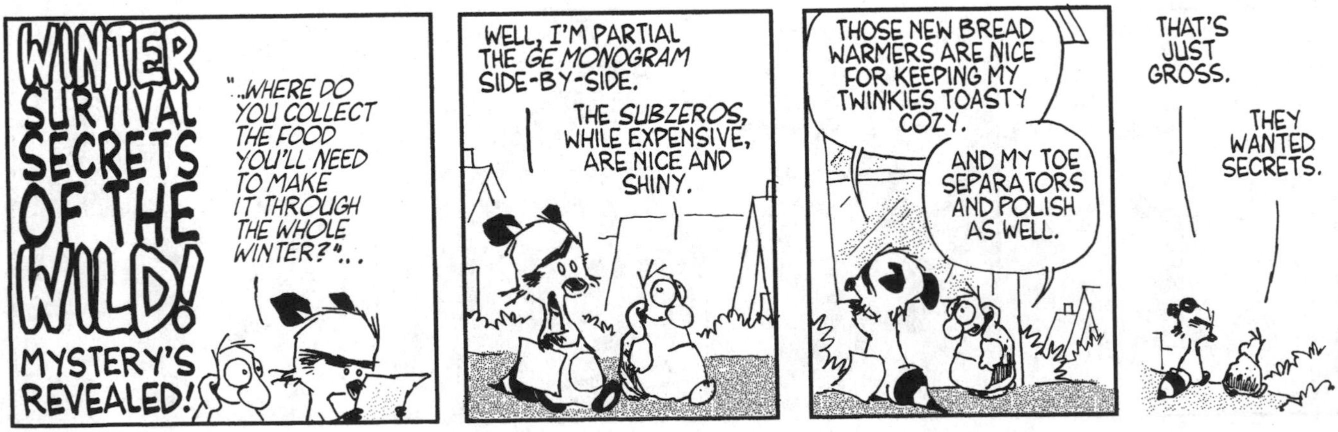
WINTER SURVIVAL SECRETS OF THE WILD!
MYSTERY'S REVEALED!
"..WHERE DO YOU COLLECT THE FOOD YOU'LL NEED TO MAKE IT THROUGH THE WHOLE WINTER?"...
WELL, I'M PARTIAL THE GE MONOGRAM SIDE-BY-SIDE.
THE SUBZEROS, WHILE EXPENSIVE, ARE NICE AND SHINY.
THOSE NEW BREAD WARMERS ARE NICE FOR KEEPING MY TWINKIES TOASTY COZY.
AND MY TOE SEPARATORS AND POLISH AS WELL.
THAT'S JUST GROSS.
THEY WANTED SECRETS.

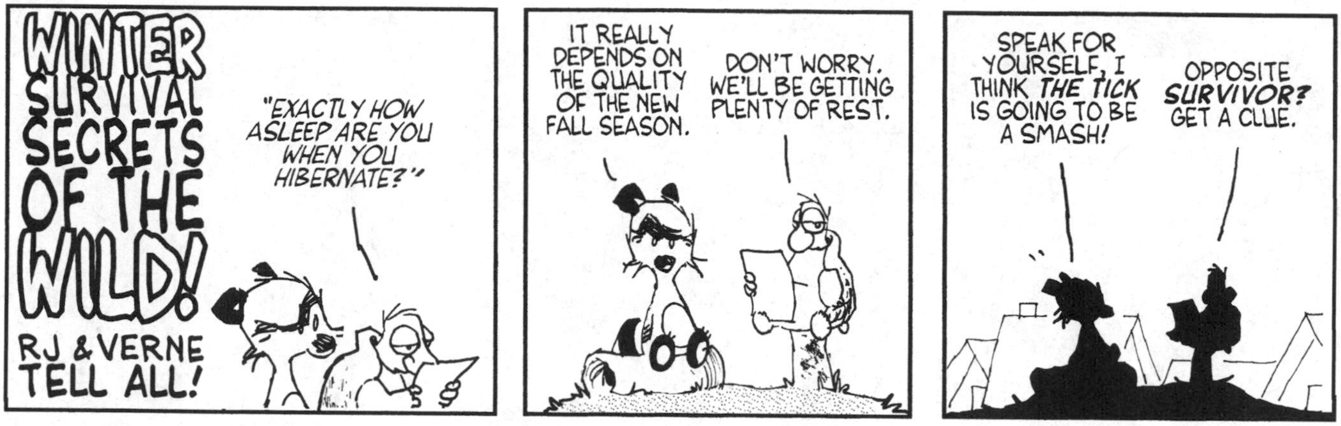
WINTER SURVIVAL SECRETS OF THE WILD!
RJ & VERNE TELL ALL!
"EXACTLY HOW ASLEEP ARE YOU WHEN YOU HIBERNATE?"
IT REALLY DEPENDS ON THE QUALITY OF THE NEW FALL SEASON.
DON'T WORRY. WE'LL BE GETTING PLENTY OF REST.
SPEAK FOR YOURSELF, I THINK THE TICK IS GOING TO BE A SMASH!
OPPOSITE SURVIVOR? GET A CLUE.

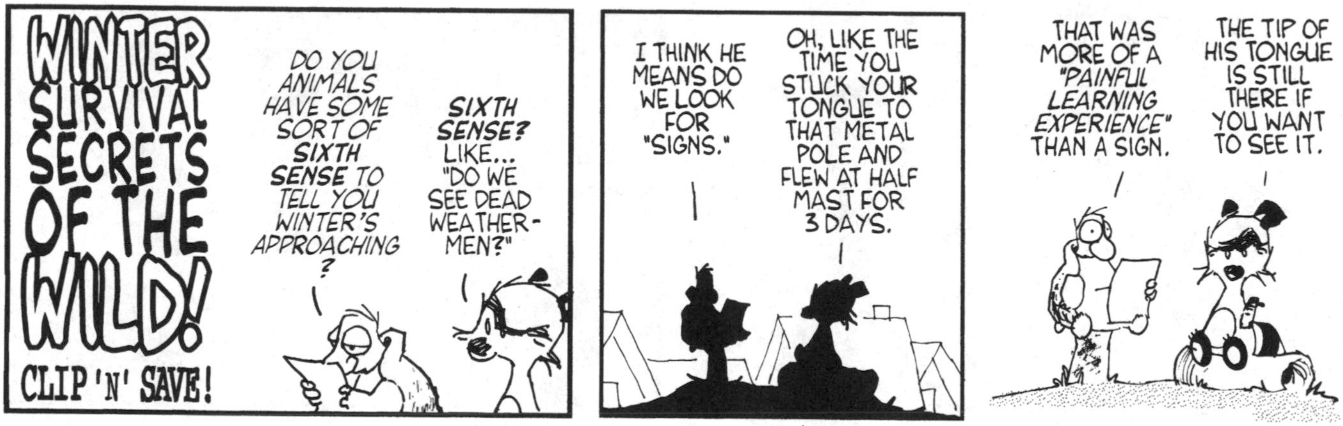
WINTER SURVIVAL SECRETS OF THE WILD!
CLIP 'N' SAVE!
DO YOU ANIMALS HAVE SOME SORT OF SIXTH SENSE TO TELL YOU WINTER'S APPROACHING?
SIXTH SENSE? LIKE... "DO WE SEE DEAD WEATHER-MEN?"
I THINK HE MEANS DO WE LOOK FOR "SIGNS."
OH, LIKE THE TIME YOU STUCK YOUR TONGUE TO THAT METAL POLE AND FLEW AT HALF MAST FOR 3 DAYS.
THAT WAS MORE OF A "PAINFUL LEARNING EXPERIENCE" THAN A SIGN.
THE TIP OF HIS TONGUE IS STILL THERE IF YOU WANT TO SEE IT.

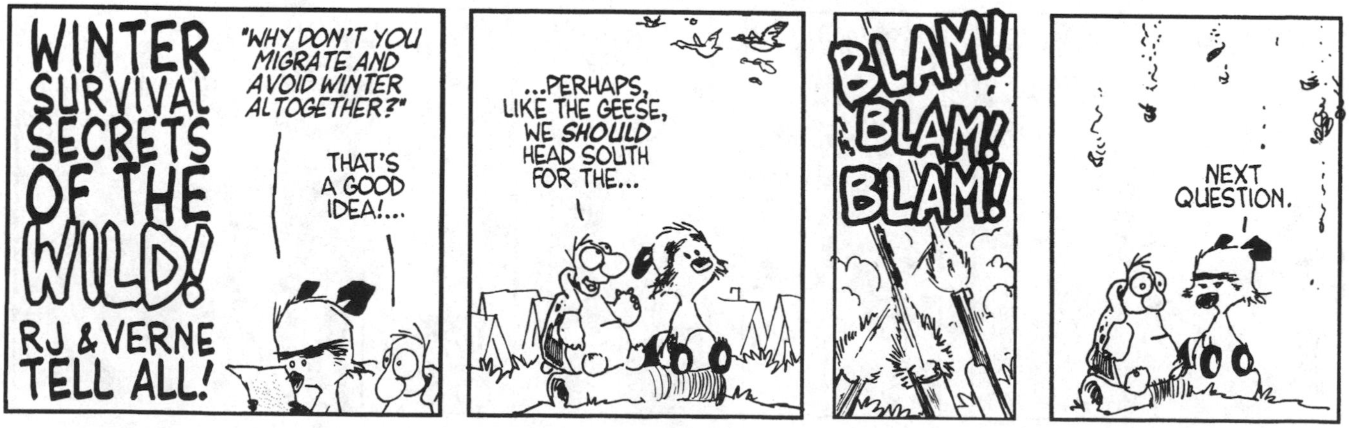
WINTER SURVIVAL SECRETS OF THE WILD!
RJ & VERNE TELL ALL!
"WHY DON'T YOU MIGRATE AND AVOID WINTER ALTOGETHER?"
THAT'S A GOOD IDEA!...
...PERHAPS, LIKE THE GEESE, WE SHOULD HEAD SOUTH FOR THE...
BLAM! BLAM! BLAM!
NEXT QUESTION.

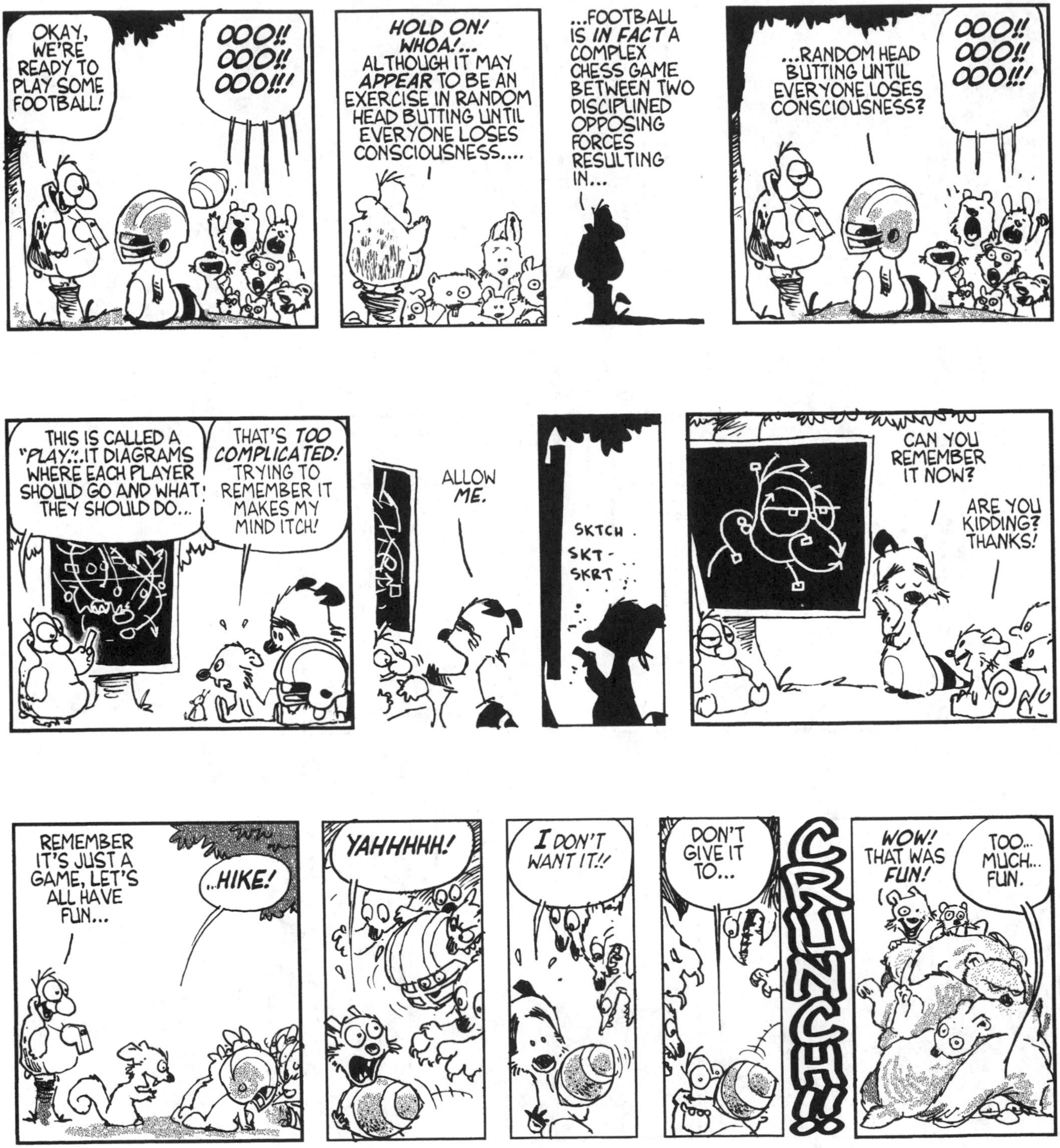
OKAY, WE'RE READY TO PLAY SOME FOOTBALL!
OOO!! OOO!! OOO!!!
HOLD ON! WHOA!... ALTHOUGH IT MAY APPEAR TO BE AN EXERCISE IN RANDOM HEAD BUTTING UNTIL EVERYONE LOSES CONSCIOUSNESS....
...FOOTBALL IS IN FACT A COMPLEX CHESS GAME BETWEEN TWO DISCIPLINED OPPOSING FORCES RESULTING IN...
...RANDOM HEAD BUTTING UNTIL EVERYONE LOSES CONSCIOUSNESS?
OOO!! OOO!! OOO!!!
THIS IS CALLED A "PLAY."..IT DIAGRAMS WHERE EACH PLAYER SHOULD GO AND WHAT THEY SHOULD DO...
THAT'S TOO COMPLICATED! TRYING TO REMEMBER IT MAKES MY MIND ITCH!
ALLOW ME.
SKTCH
SKT-
SKRT
CAN YOU REMEMBER IT NOW?
ARE YOU KIDDING? THANKS!
REMEMBER IT'S JUST A GAME, LET'S ALL HAVE FUN...
...HIKE!
YAHHHHH!
I DON'T WANT IT!!
DON'T GIVE IT TO...
CRUNCH!!
WOW! THAT WAS FUN!
TOO... MUCH... FUN.

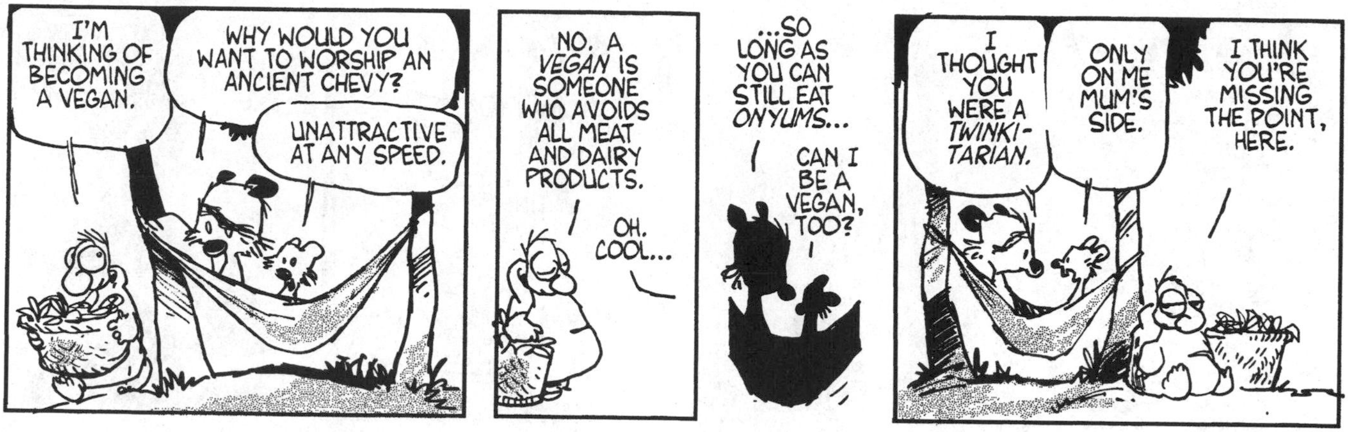
I'M THINKING OF BECOMING A VEGAN.
WHY WOULD YOU WANT TO WORSHIP AN ANCIENT CHEVY?
UNATTRACTIVE AT ANY SPEED.
NO. A VEGAN IS SOMEONE WHO AVOIDS ALL MEAT AND DAIRY PRODUCTS.
OH. COOL...
...SO LONG AS YOU CAN STILL EAT ONYUMS...
CAN I BE A VEGAN, TOO?
I THOUGHT YOU WERE A TWINKI-TARIAN.
ONLY ON ME MUM'S SIDE.
I THINK YOU'RE MISSING THE POINT, HERE.

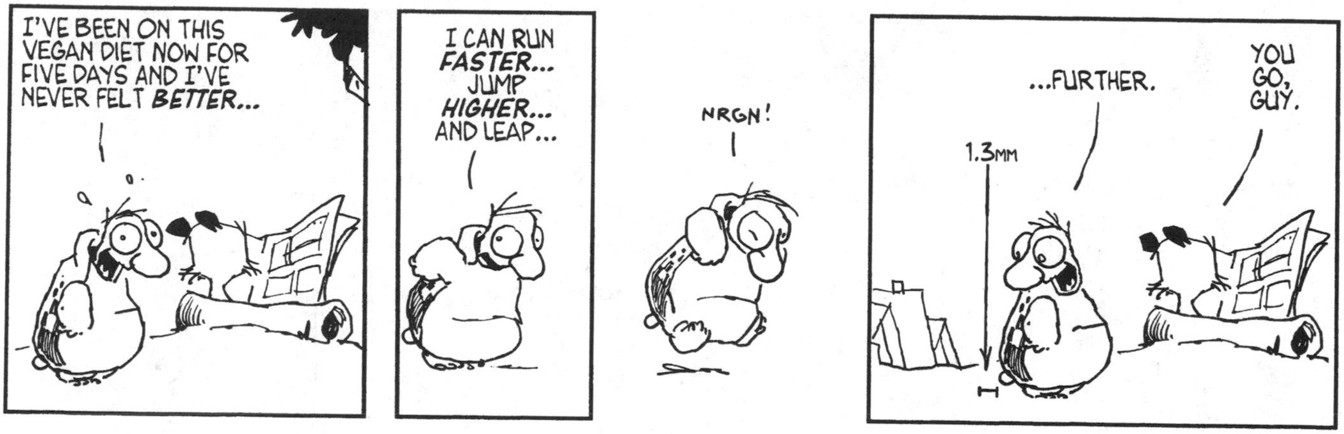
I'VE BEEN ON THIS VEGAN DIET NOW FOR FIVE DAYS AND I'VE NEVER FELT BETTER...
I CAN RUN FASTER... JUMP HIGHER... AND LEAP...
NRGN!
1.3MM
...FURTHER.
YOU GO, GUY.

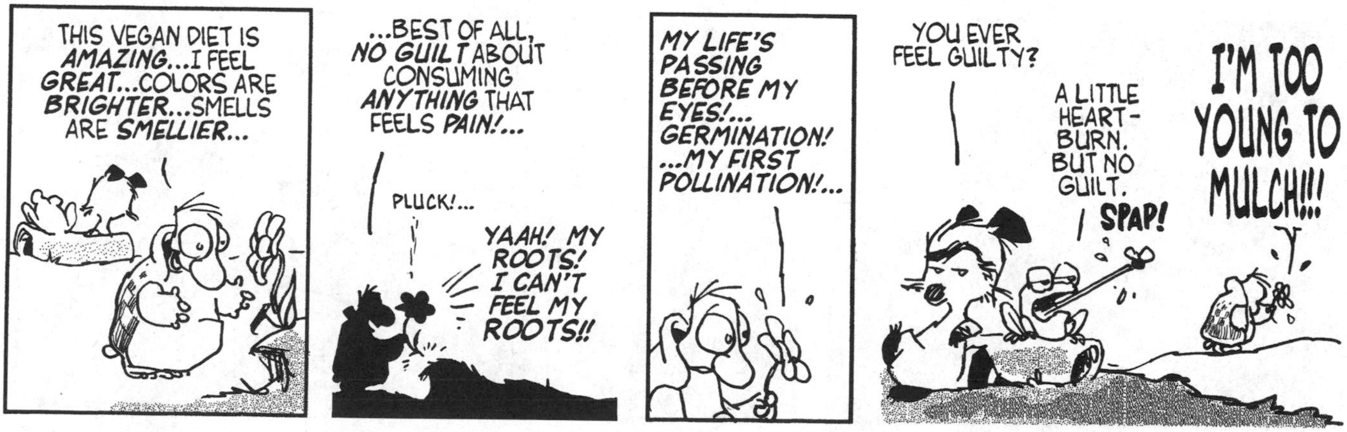
THIS VEGAN DIET IS AMAZING...I FEEL GREAT...COLORS ARE BRIGHTER...SMELLS ARE SMELLIER...
...BEST OF ALL, NO GUILT ABOUT CONSUMING ANYTHING THAT FEELS PAIN!...
PLUCK!...
YAAH! MY ROOTS! I CAN'T FEEL MY ROOTS!!
MY LIFE'S PASSING BEFORE MY EYES!... GERMINATION! ...MY FIRST POLLINATION!...
YOU EVER FEEL GUILTY?
A LITTLE HEART-BURN. BUT NO GUILT.
SPAP!
I'M TOO YOUNG TO MULCH!!!

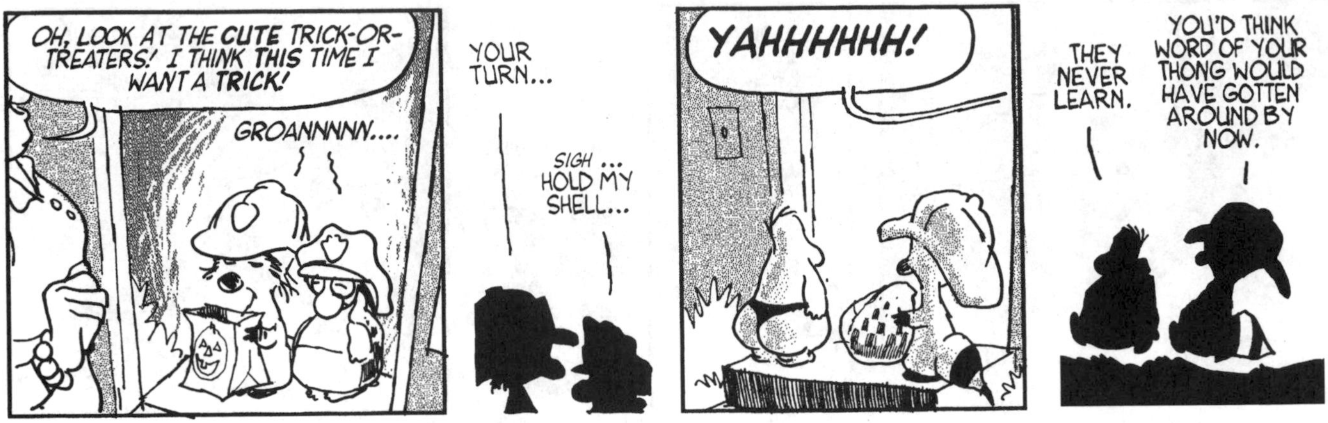
OH, LOOK AT THE CUTE TRICK-OR-TREATERS! I THINK THIS TIME I WANT A TRICK!
GROANNNNN....
YOUR TURN...
SIGH ... HOLD MY SHELL...
YAHHHHHH!
THEY NEVER LEARN.
YOU'D THINK WORD OF YOUR THONG WOULD HAVE GOTTEN AROUND BY NOW.

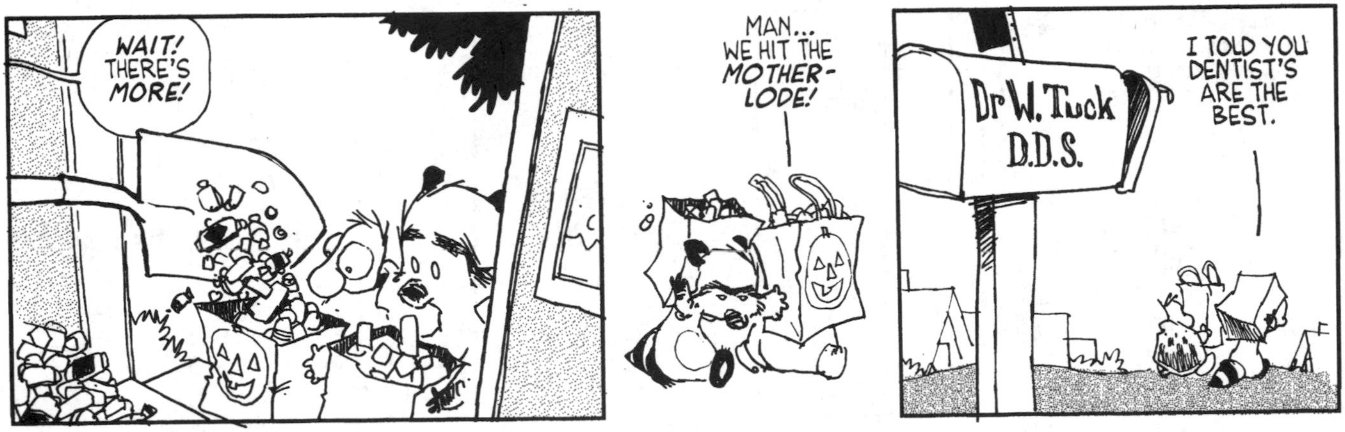
WAIT! THERE'S MORE!
MAN... WE HIT THE MOTHER-LODE!
Dr W. Tuck D.D.S.
I TOLD YOU DENTIST'S ARE THE BEST.

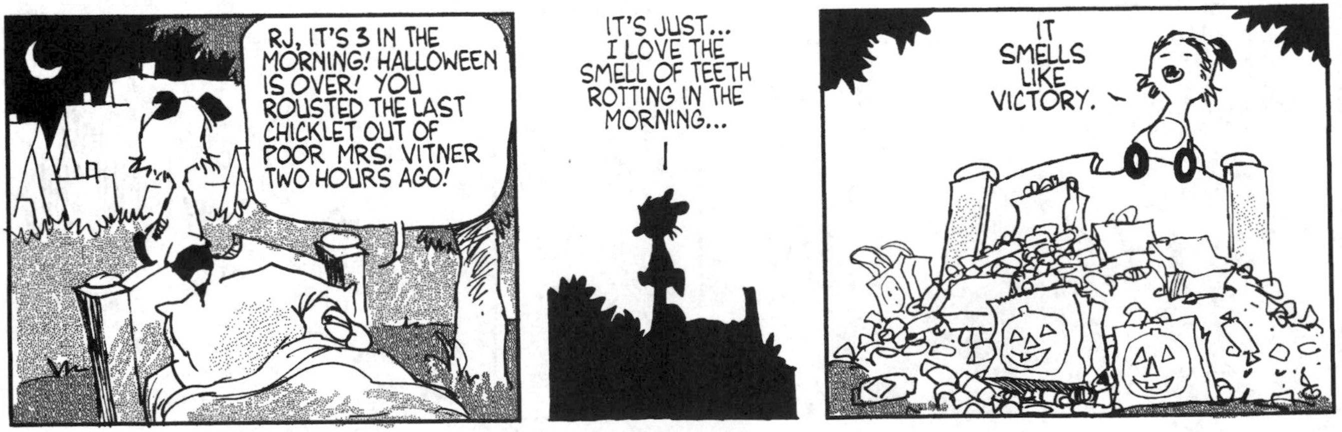
RJ, IT'S 3 IN THE MORNING! HALLOWEEN IS OVER! YOU ROUSTED THE LAST CHICKLET OUT OF POOR MRS. VITNER TWO HOURS AGO!
IT'S JUST... I LOVE THE SMELL OF TEETH ROTTING IN THE MORNING...
IT SMELLS LIKE VICTORY.

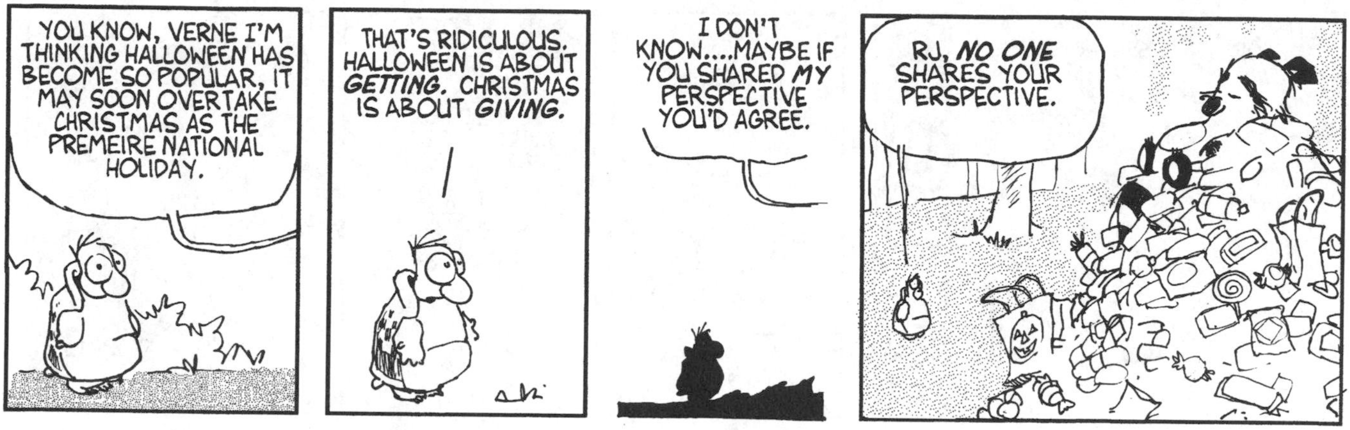
YOU KNOW, VERNE I'M THINKING HALLOWEEN HAS BECOME SO POPULAR, IT MAY SOON OVERTAKE CHRISTMAS AS THE PREMEIRE NATIONAL HOLIDAY.
THAT'S RIDICULOUS. HALLOWEEN IS ABOUT GETTING. CHRISTMAS IS ABOUT GIVING.
I DON'T KNOW....MAYBE IF YOU SHARED MY PERSPECTIVE YOU'D AGREE.
RJ, NO ONE SHARES YOUR PERSPECTIVE.

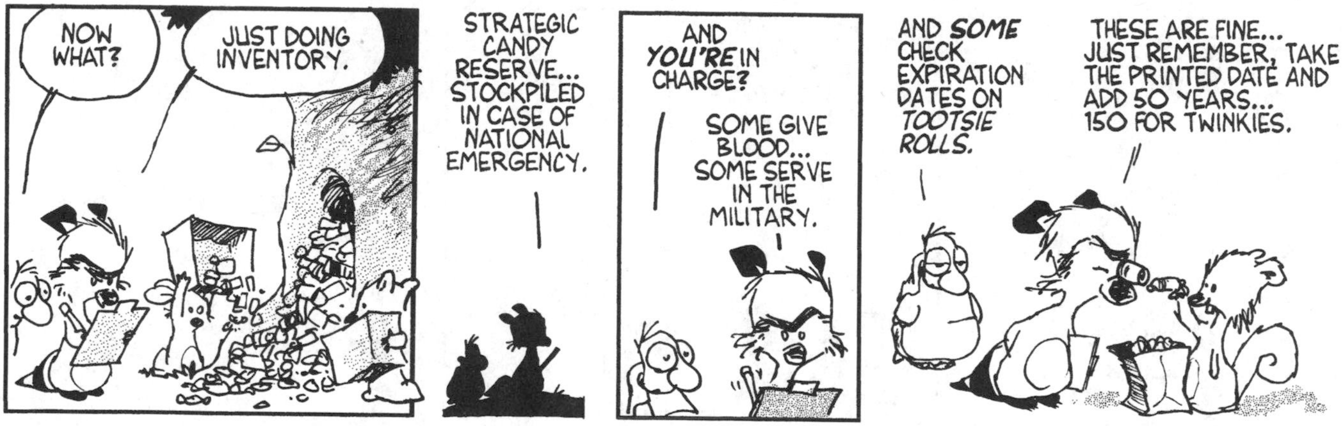
NOW WHAT?
JUST DOING INVENTORY.
STRATEGIC CANDY RESERVE... STOCKPILED IN CASE OF NATIONAL EMERGENCY.
AND YOU'RE IN CHARGE?
SOME GIVE BLOOD... SOME SERVE IN THE MILITARY.
AND SOME CHECK EXPIRATION DATES ON TOOTSIE ROLLS.
THESE ARE FINE... JUST REMEMBER, TAKE THE PRINTED DATE AND ADD 50 YEARS... 150 FOR TWINKIES.

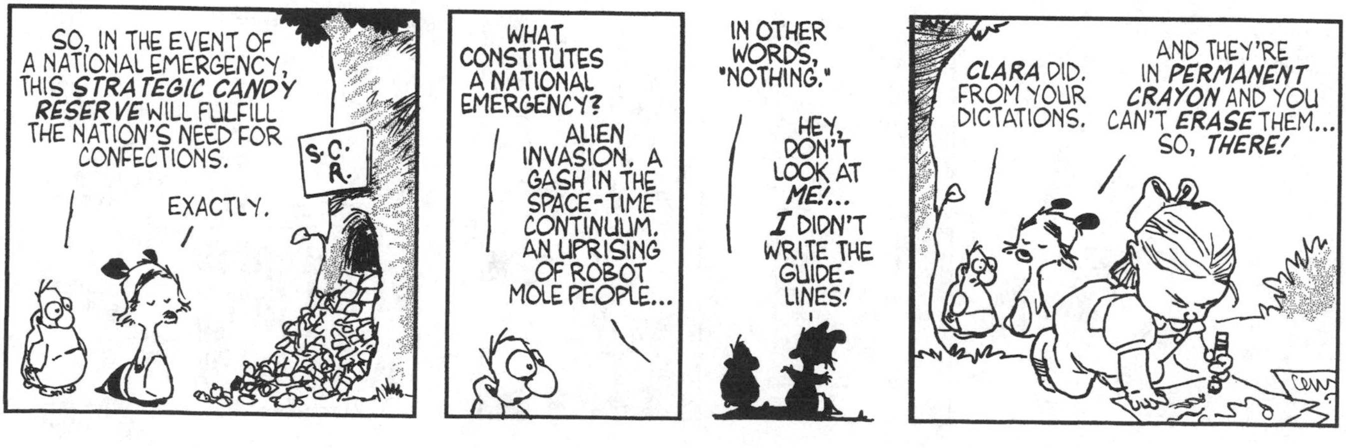
SO, IN THE EVENT OF A NATIONAL EMERGENCY, THIS STRATEGIC CANDY RESERVE WILL FULFILL THE NATION'S NEED FOR CONFECTIONS.
EXACTLY.
S.C.R.
WHAT CONSTITUTES A NATIONAL EMERGENCY?
ALIEN INVASION. A GASH IN THE SPACE-TIME CONTINUUM. AN UPRISING OF ROBOT MOLE PEOPLE...
IN OTHER WORDS, "NOTHING."
HEY, DON'T LOOK AT ME!... I DIDN'T WRITE THE GUIDE-LINES!
CLARA DID. FROM YOUR DICTATIONS.
AND THEY'RE IN PERMANENT CRAYON AND YOU CAN'T ERASE THEM... SO, THERE!

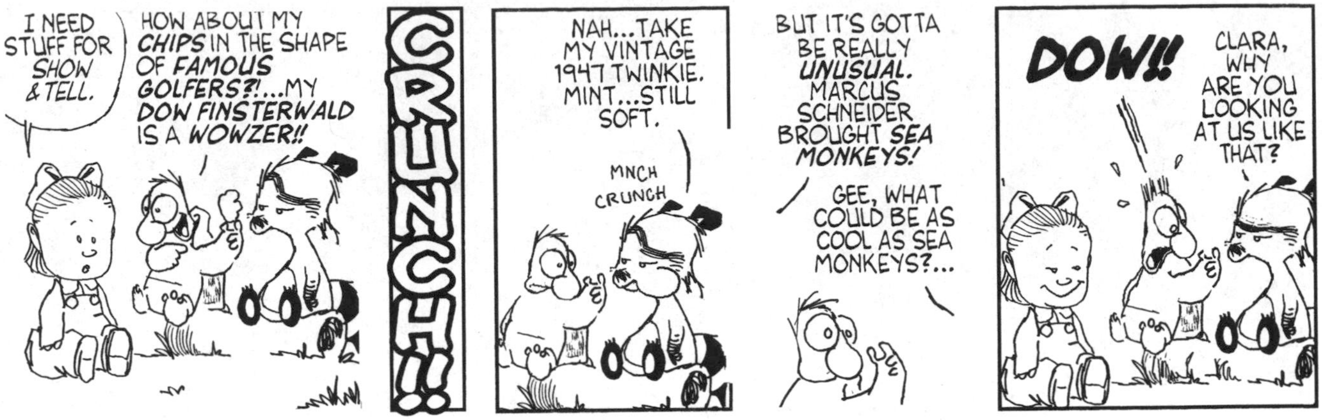
I NEED STUFF FOR SHOW & TELL.
HOW ABOUT MY CHIPS IN THE SHAPE OF FAMOUS GOLFERS?!...MY DOW FINSTERWALD IS A WOWZER!!
CRUNCH!!
NAH...TAKE MY VINTAGE 1947 TWINKIE. MINT...STILL SOFT.
MNCH CRUNCH
BUT IT'S GOTTA BE REALLY UNUSUAL. MARCUS SCHNEIDER BROUGHT SEA MONKEYS!
GEE, WHAT COULD BE AS COOL AS SEA MONKEYS?...
DOW!!
CLARA, WHY ARE YOU LOOKING AT US LIKE THAT?

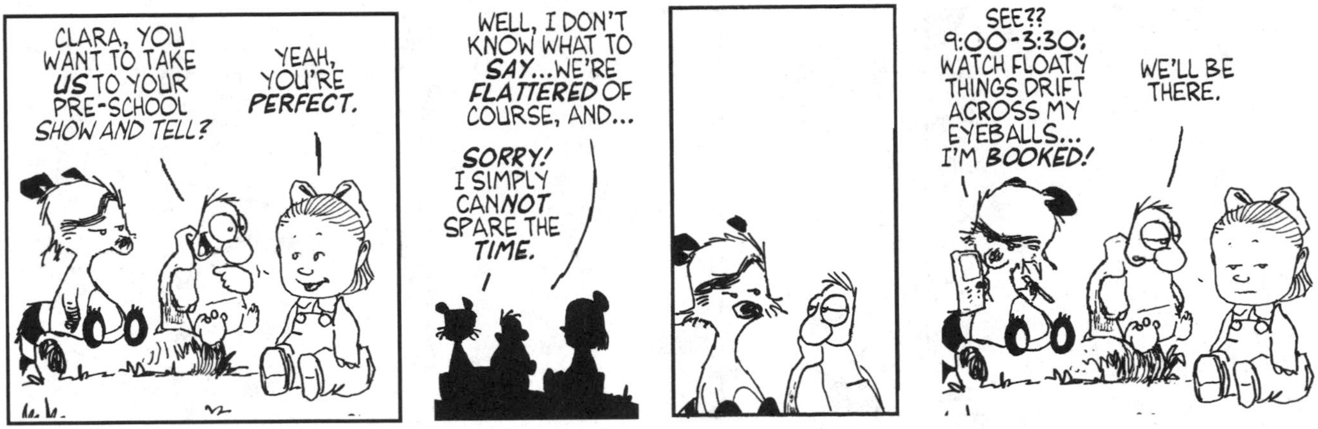
CLARA, YOU WANT TO TAKE US TO YOUR PRE-SCHOOL SHOW AND TELL?
YEAH, YOU'RE PERFECT.
WELL, I DON'T KNOW WHAT TO SAY...WE'RE FLATTERED OF COURSE, AND...
SORRY! I SIMPLY CANNOT SPARE THE TIME.
SEE?? 9:00-3:30: WATCH FLOATY THINGS DRIFT ACROSS MY EYEBALLS... I'M BOOKED!
WE'LL BE THERE.

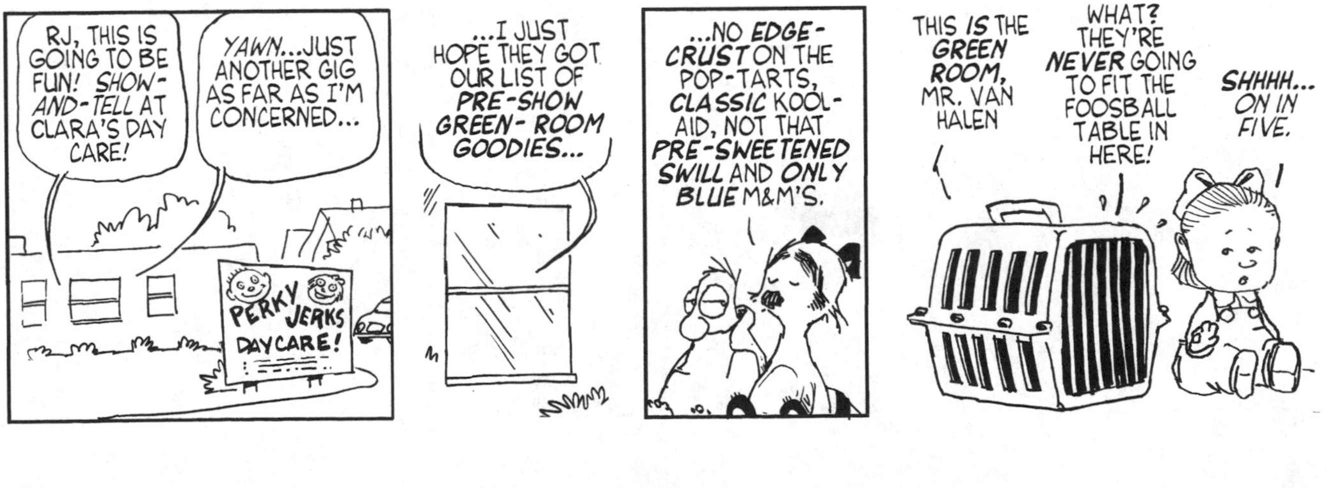
RJ, THIS IS GOING TO BE FUN! SHOW-AND-TELL AT CLARA'S DAY CARE!
YAWN...JUST ANOTHER GIG AS FAR AS I'M CONCERNED...
PERKY JERKS DAYCARE!
...I JUST HOPE THEY GOT OUR LIST OF PRE-SHOW GREEN-ROOM GOODIES...
...NO EDGE-CRUST ON THE POP-TARTS, CLASSIC KOOL-AID, NOT THAT PRE-SWEETENED SWILL AND ONLY BLUE M&M'S.
THIS IS THE GREEN ROOM, MR. VAN HALEN
WHAT? THEY'RE NEVER GOING TO FIT THE FOOSBALL TABLE IN HERE!
SHHHH... ON IN FIVE.

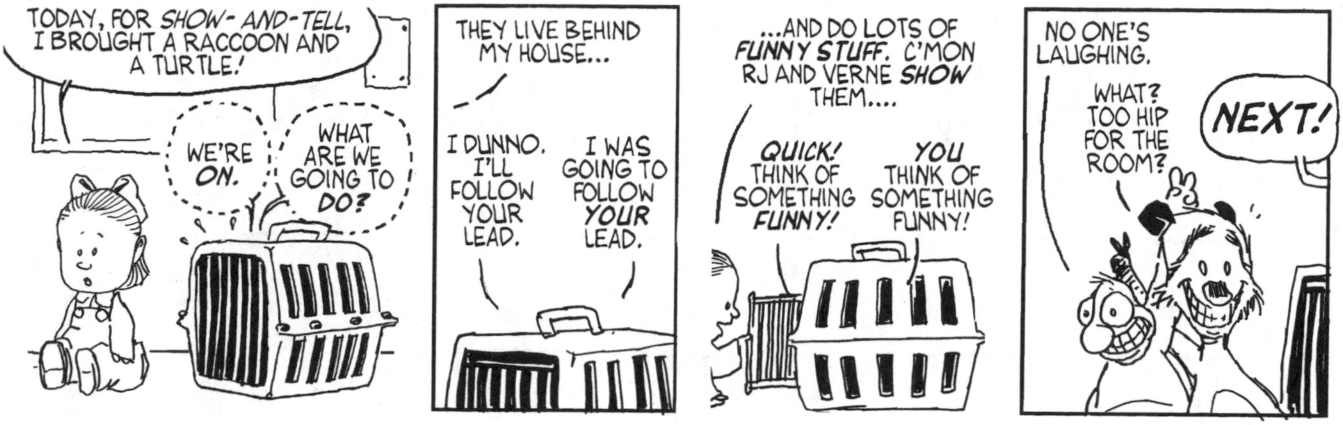
TODAY, FOR SHOW-AND-TELL, I BROUGHT A RACCOON AND A TURTLE!
WE'RE ON.
WHAT ARE WE GOING TO DO?
THEY LIVE BEHIND MY HOUSE...
I DUNNO. I'LL FOLLOW YOUR LEAD.
I WAS GOING TO FOLLOW YOUR LEAD.
...AND DO LOTS OF FUNNY STUFF. C'MON RJ AND VERNE SHOW THEM....
QUICK! THINK OF SOMETHING FUNNY!
YOU THINK OF SOMETHING FUNNY!
NO ONE'S LAUGHING.
WHAT? TOO HIP FOR THE ROOM?
NEXT!

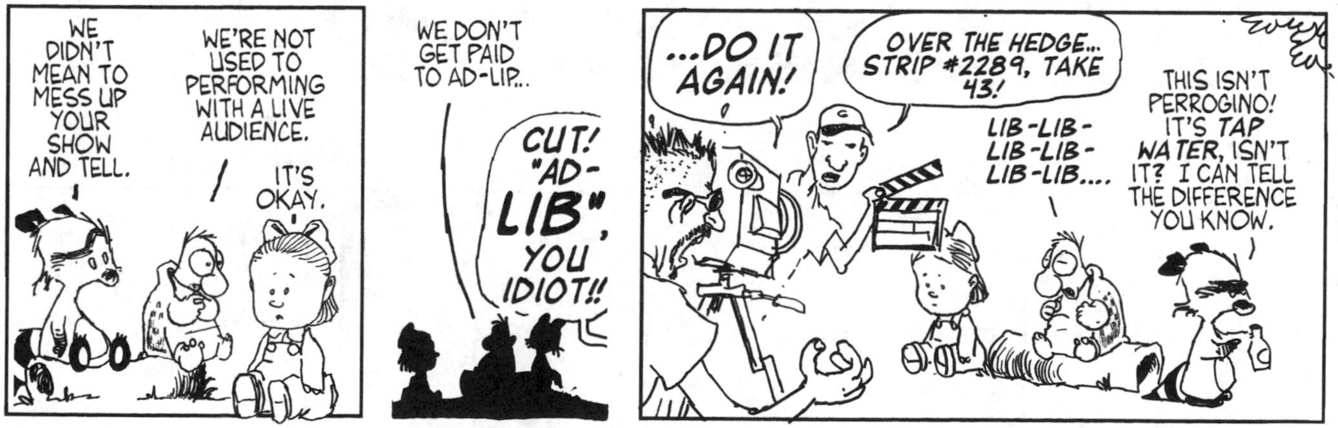
WE DIDN'T MEAN TO MESS UP YOUR SHOW AND TELL.
WE'RE NOT USED TO PERFORMING WITH A LIVE AUDIENCE.
IT'S OKAY.
WE DON'T GET PAID TO AD-LIP...
CUT! "AD-LIB", YOU IDIOT!!
...DO IT AGAIN!
OVER THE HEDGE... STRIP #2289, TAKE 43!
LIB-LIB-LIB-LIB-LIB-LIB....
THIS ISN'T PERROGINO! IT'S TAP WATER, ISN'T IT? I CAN TELL THE DIFFERENCE YOU KNOW.

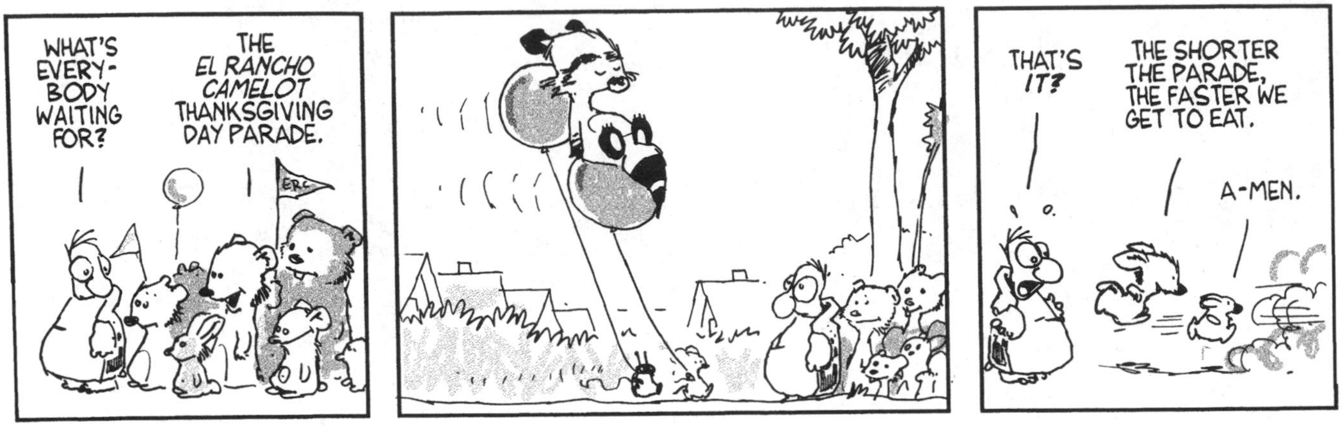
WHAT'S EVERYBODY WAITING FOR?
THE EL RANCHO CAMELOT THANKSGIVING DAY PARADE.
ERC
THAT'S IT?
THE SHORTER THE PARADE, THE FASTER WE GET TO EAT.
A-MEN.

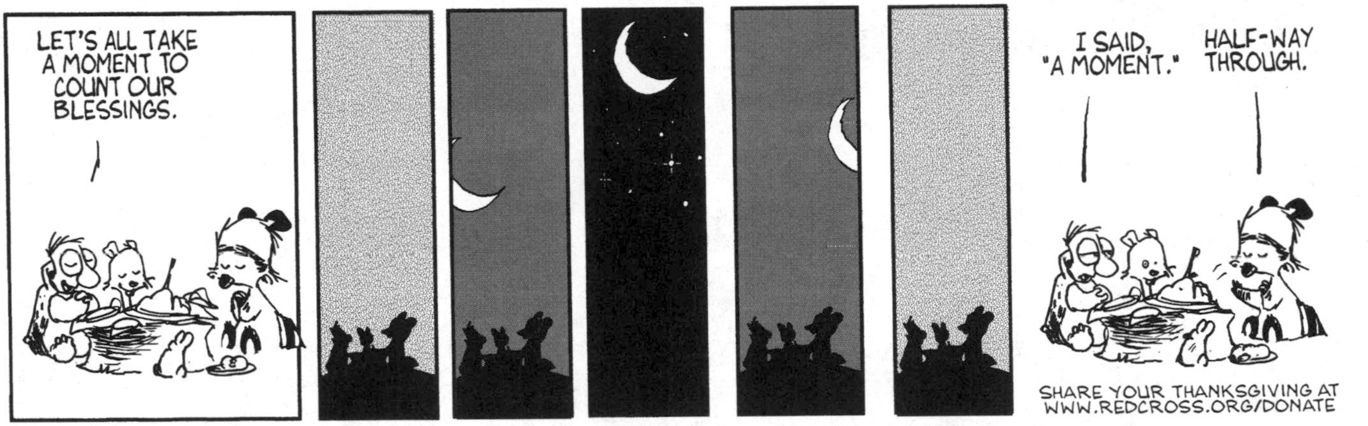
LET'S ALL TAKE A MOMENT TO COUNT OUR BLESSINGS.
I SAID, "A MOMENT."
HALF-WAY THROUGH.
SHARE YOUR THANKSGIVING AT WWW.REDCROSS.ORG/DONATE

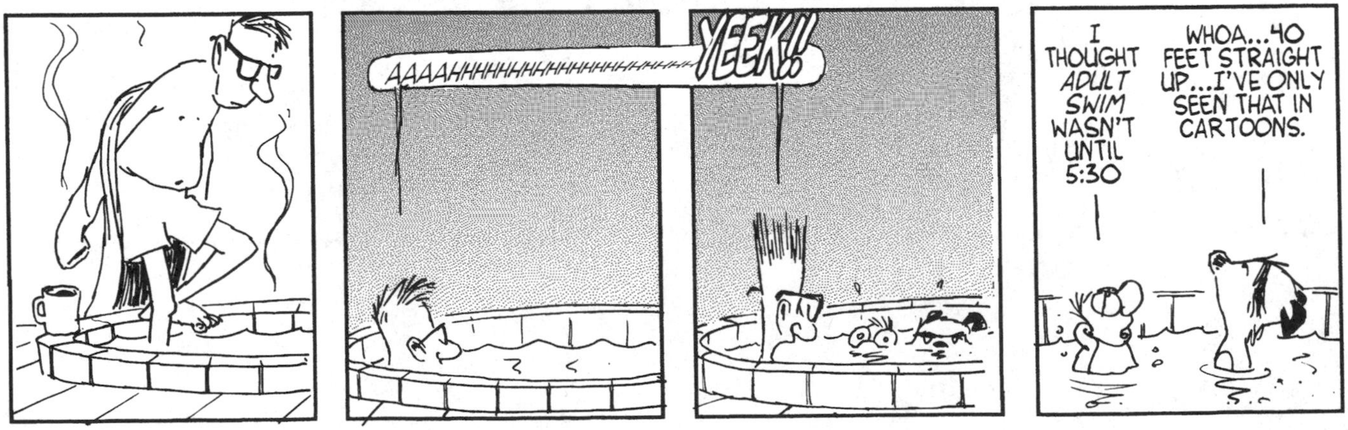
AAAAHHHHHHHHHHHHHHHHHHHHHHHHhhhhhh YEEK!!
I THOUGHT ADULT SWIM WASN'T UNTIL 5:30
WHOA...40 FEET STRAIGHT UP...I'VE ONLY SEEN THAT IN CARTOONS.

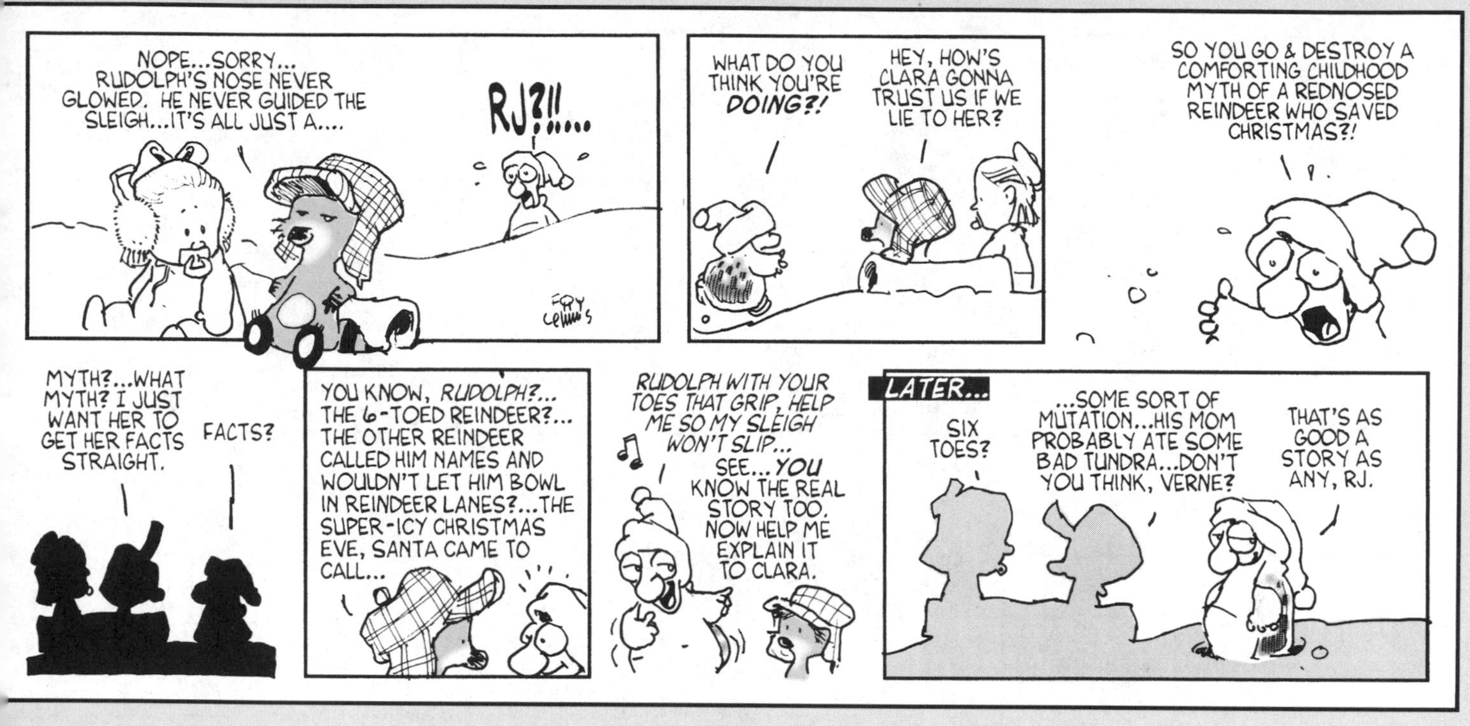
NOPE...SORRY... RUDOLPH'S NOSE NEVER GLOWED. HE NEVER GUIDED THE SLEIGH...IT'S ALL JUST A....
RJ?!!.....
WHAT DO YOU THINK YOU'RE DOING?!
HEY, HOW'S CLARA GONNA TRUST US IF WE LIE TO HER?
SO YOU GO & DESTROY A COMFORTING CHILDHOOD MYTH OF A REDNOSED REINDEER WHO SAVED CHRISTMAS?!
MYTH?...WHAT MYTH? I JUST WANT HER TO GET HER FACTS STRAIGHT.
FACTS?
YOU KNOW, RUDOLPH?... THE 6-TOED REINDEER?... THE OTHER REINDEER CALLED HIM NAMES AND WOULDN'T LET HIM BOWL IN REINDEER LANES?...THE SUPER-ICY CHRISTMAS EVE, SANTA CAME TO CALL...
RUDOLPH WITH YOUR TOES THAT GRIP, HELP ME SO MY SLEIGH WON'T SLIP...
SEE...YOU KNOW THE REAL STORY TOO. NOW HELP ME EXPLAIN IT TO CLARA.
LATER...
SIX TOES?
...SOME SORT OF MUTATION...HIS MOM PROBABLY ATE SOME BAD TUNDRA...DON'T YOU THINK, VERNE?
THAT'S AS GOOD A STORY AS ANY, RJ.

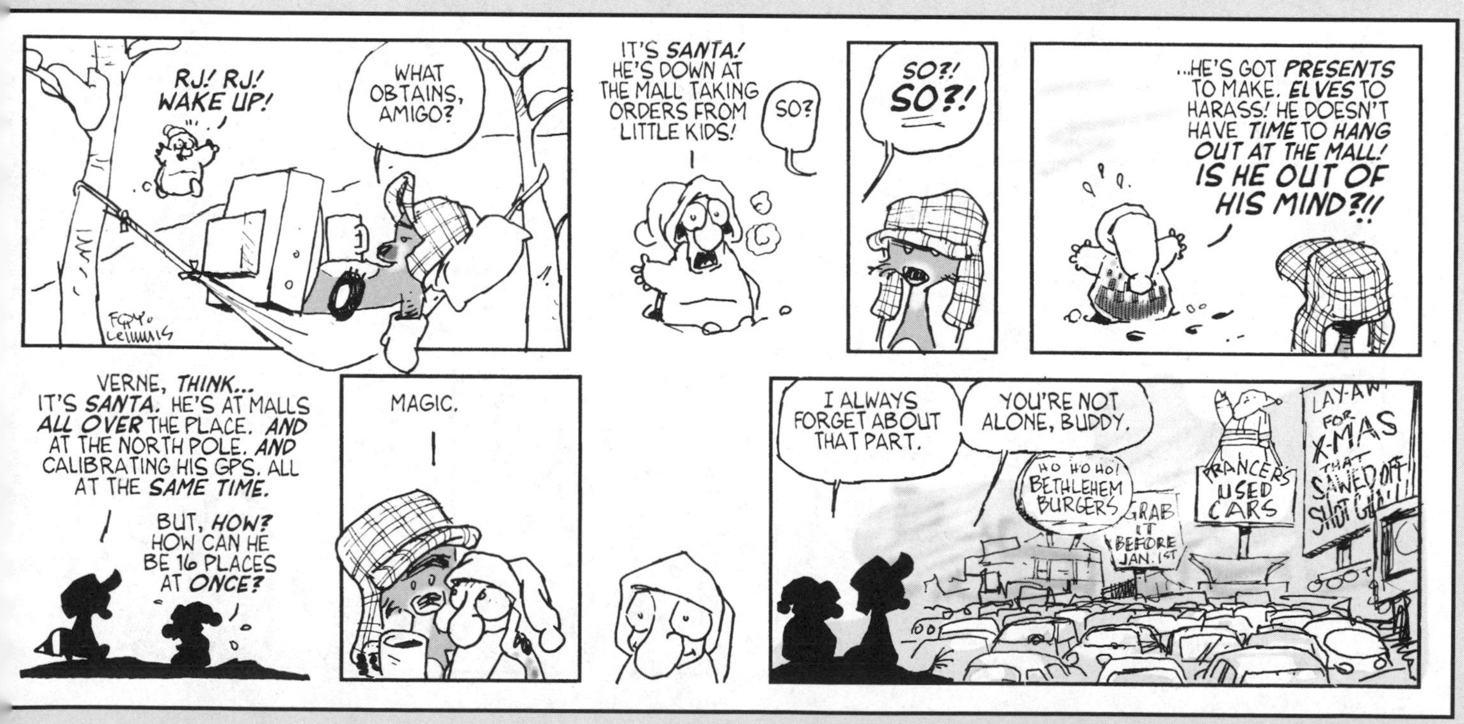
RJ! RJ! WAKE UP!
WHAT OBTAINS, AMIGO?
IT'S SANTA! HE'S DOWN AT THE MALL TAKING ORDERS FROM LITTLE KIDS!
SO?
SO?! SO?!
...HE'S GOT PRESENTS TO MAKE. ELVES TO HARASS! HE DOESN'T HAVE TIME TO HANG OUT AT THE MALL! IS HE OUT OF HIS MIND?!!
VERNE, THINK... IT'S SANTA. HE'S AT MALLS ALL OVER THE PLACE. AND AT THE NORTH POLE. AND CALIBRATING HIS GPS. ALL AT THE SAME TIME.
BUT, HOW? HOW CAN HE BE 16 PLACES AT ONCE?
MAGIC.
I ALWAYS FORGET ABOUT THAT PART.
YOU'RE NOT ALONE, BUDDY.
HO HO HO! BETHLEHEM BURGERS
GRAB IT BEFORE JAN. 1ST
PRANCER'S USED CARS
FOR X-MAS THAT SAWED OFF SHOTGUN

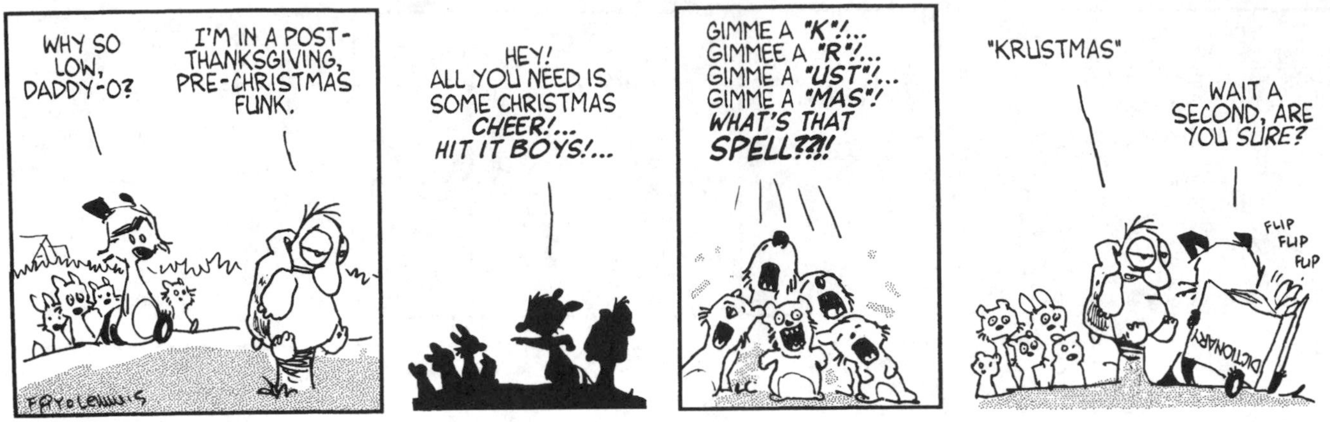
WHY SO LOW, DADDY-O?
I'M IN A POST-THANKSGIVING, PRE-CHRISTMAS FUNK.
HEY! ALL YOU NEED IS SOME CHRISTMAS CHEER!... HIT IT BOYS!...
GIMME A "K"!... GIMMEE A "R"!... GIMME A "UST"!... GIMME A "MAS"! WHAT'S THAT SPELL??!!
"KRUSTMAS"
WAIT A SECOND, ARE YOU SURE?
FLIP FLIP FLIP
DICTIONARY

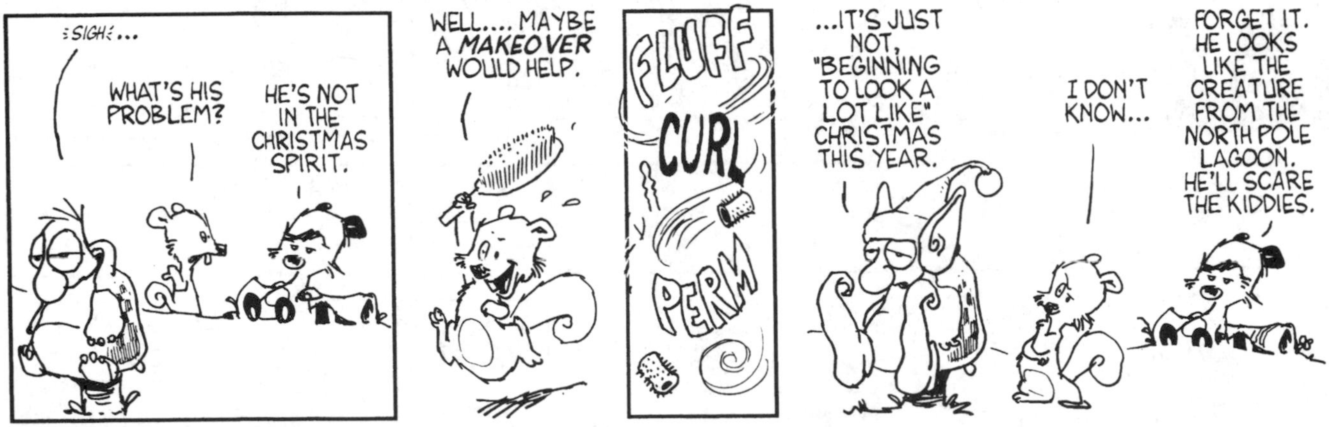
SIGH...
WHAT'S HIS PROBLEM?
HE'S NOT IN THE CHRISTMAS SPIRIT.
WELL.... MAYBE A MAKEOVER WOULD HELP.
FLUFF
CURL
PERM
...IT'S JUST NOT, "BEGINNING TO LOOK A LOT LIKE" CHRISTMAS THIS YEAR.
I DON'T KNOW...
FORGET IT. HE LOOKS LIKE THE CREATURE FROM THE NORTH POLE LAGOON. HE'LL SCARE THE KIDDIES.

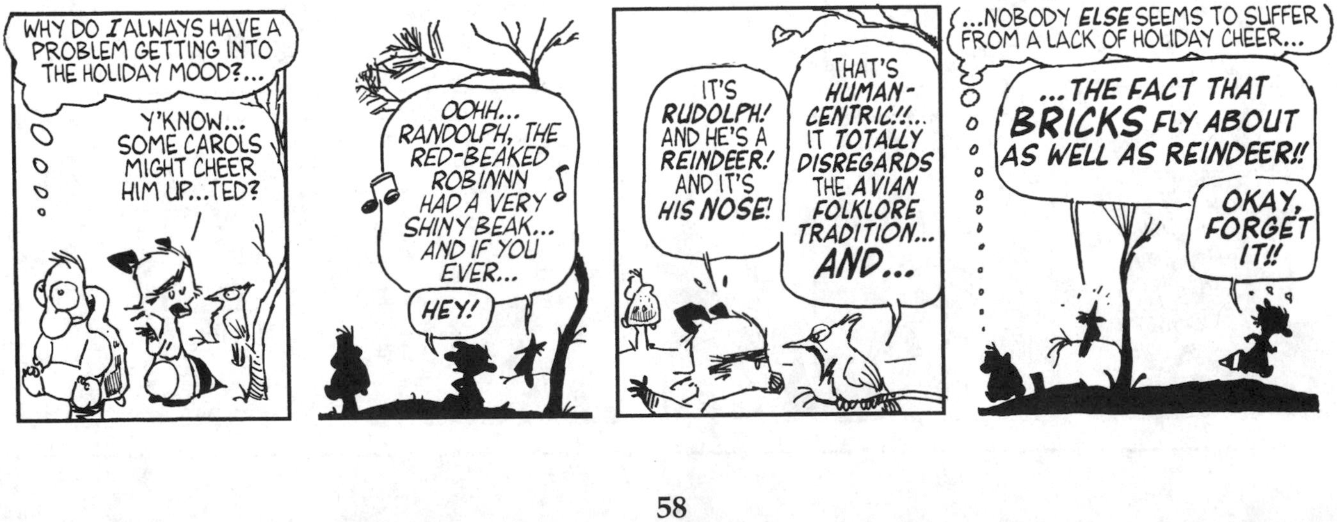
WHY DO I ALWAYS HAVE A PROBLEM GETTING INTO THE HOLIDAY MOOD?...
Y'KNOW... SOME CAROLS MIGHT CHEER HIM UP...TED?
OOHH... RANDOLPH, THE RED-BEAKED ROBINNN HAD A VERY SHINY BEAK... AND IF YOU EVER...
HEY!
IT'S RUDOLPH! AND HE'S A REINDEER! AND IT'S HIS NOSE!
THAT'S HUMAN-CENTRIC!!... IT TOTALLY DISREGARDS THE AVIAN FOLKLORE TRADITION... AND...
...NOBODY ELSE SEEMS TO SUFFER FROM A LACK OF HOLIDAY CHEER...
...THE FACT THAT BRICKS FLY ABOUT AS WELL AS REINDEER!!
OKAY, FORGET IT!!

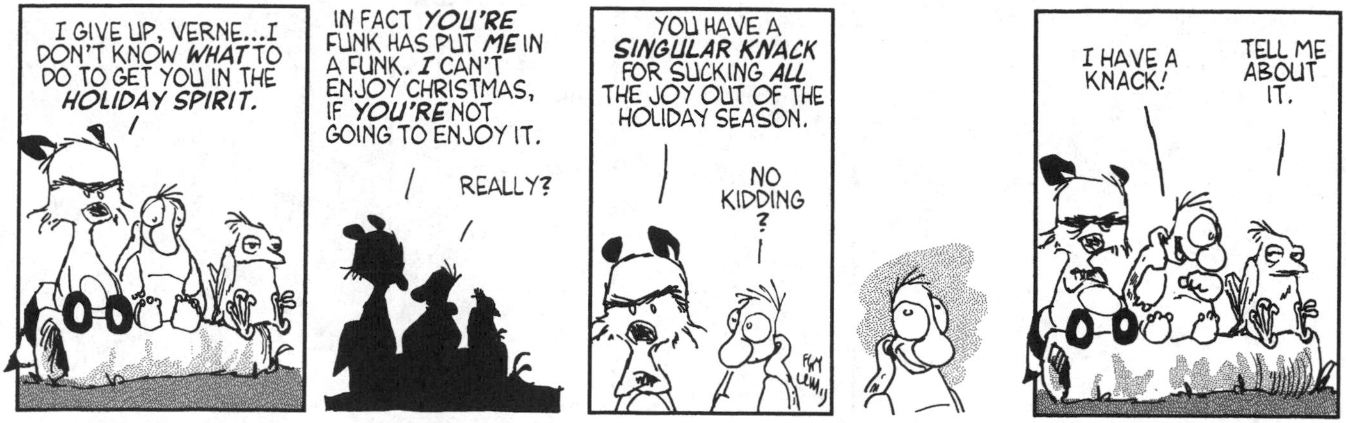
I GIVE UP, VERNE...I DON'T KNOW WHAT TO DO TO GET YOU IN THE HOLIDAY SPIRIT.
IN FACT YOU'RE FUNK HAS PUT ME IN A FUNK. I CAN'T ENJOY CHRISTMAS, IF YOU'RE NOT GOING TO ENJOY IT.
REALLY?
YOU HAVE A SINGULAR KNACK FOR SUCKING ALL THE JOY OUT OF THE HOLIDAY SEASON.
NO KIDDING ?
I HAVE A KNACK!
TELL ME ABOUT IT.

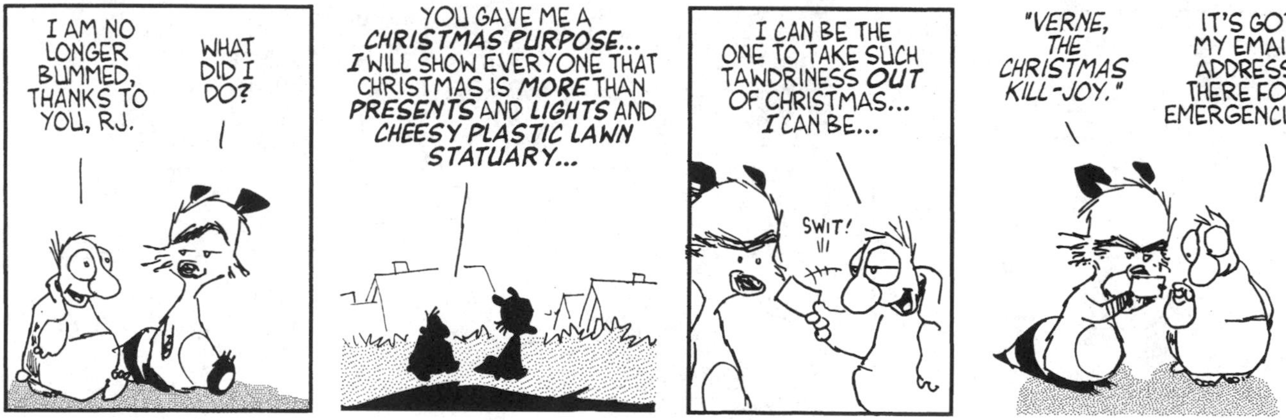
I AM NO LONGER BUMMED, THANKS TO YOU, RJ.
WHAT DID I DO?
YOU GAVE ME A CHRISTMAS PURPOSE... I WILL SHOW EVERYONE THAT CHRISTMAS IS MORE THAN PRESENTS AND LIGHTS AND CHEESY PLASTIC LAWN STATUARY...
I CAN BE THE ONE TO TAKE SUCH TAWDRINESS OUT OF CHRISTMAS... I CAN BE...
SWIT!
"VERNE, THE CHRISTMAS KILL-JOY."
IT'S GOT MY EMAIL ADDRESS THERE FOR EMERGENCIES.

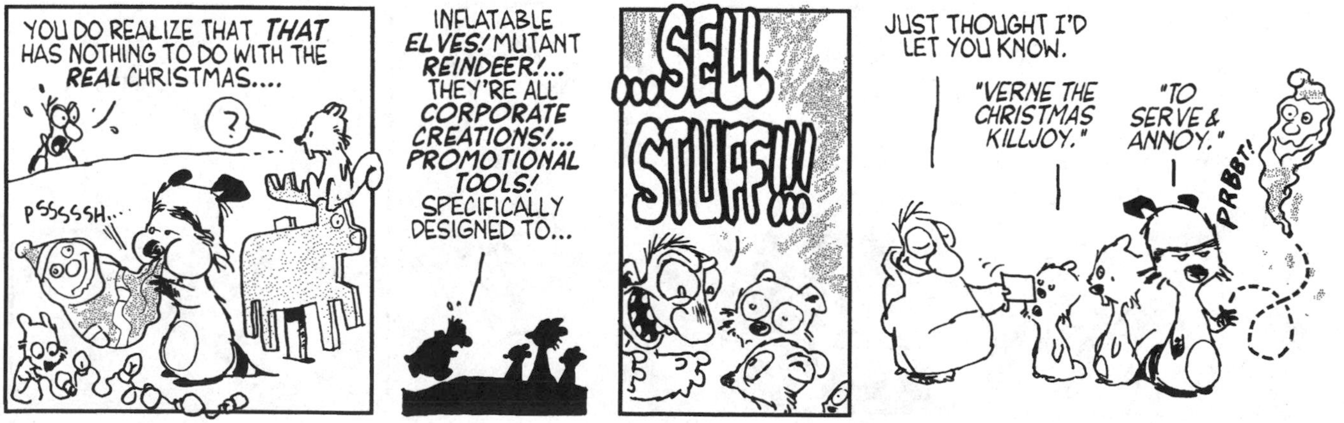
YOU DO REALIZE THAT THAT HAS NOTHING TO DO WITH THE REAL CHRISTMAS....
?
PSSSSSH...
INFLATABLE ELVES! MUTANT REINDEER!... THEY'RE ALL CORPORATE CREATIONS!... PROMOTIONAL TOOLS! SPECIFICALLY DESIGNED TO...
...SELL STUFF!!!
JUST THOUGHT I'D LET YOU KNOW.
"VERNE THE CHRISTMAS KILLJOY."
"TO SERVE & ANNOY."
PRBBT!

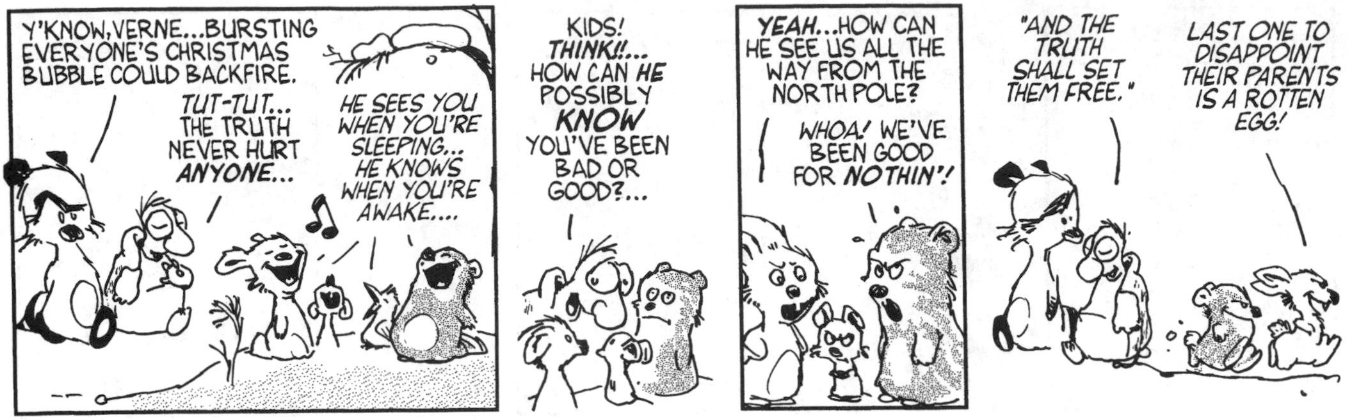
Y'KNOW, VERNE...BURSTING EVERYONE'S CHRISTMAS BUBBLE COULD BACKFIRE.
TUT-TUT... THE TRUTH NEVER HURT ANYONE...
HE SEES YOU WHEN YOU'RE SLEEPING... HE KNOWS WHEN YOU'RE AWAKE....
KIDS! THINK!!... HOW CAN HE POSSIBLY KNOW YOU'VE BEEN BAD OR GOOD?...
YEAH...HOW CAN HE SEE US ALL THE WAY FROM THE NORTH POLE?
WHOA! WE'VE BEEN GOOD FOR NOTHIN'!
"AND THE TRUTH SHALL SET THEM FREE."
LAST ONE TO DISAPPOINT THEIR PARENTS IS A ROTTEN EGG!

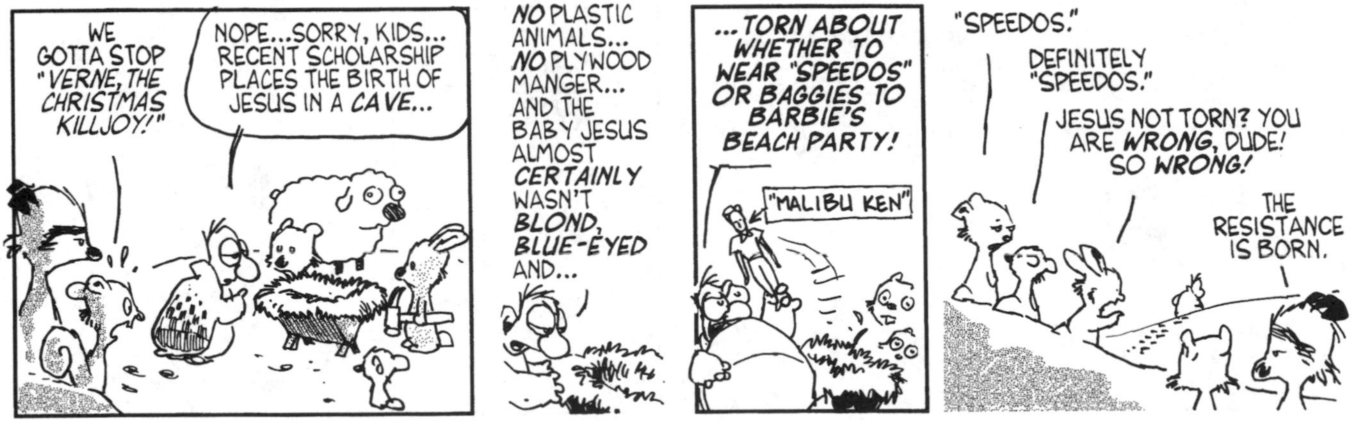
WE GOTTA STOP "VERNE, THE CHRISTMAS KILLJOY!"
NOPE...SORRY, KIDS... RECENT SCHOLARSHIP PLACES THE BIRTH OF JESUS IN A CAVE...
NO PLASTIC ANIMALS... NO PLYWOOD MANGER... AND THE BABY JESUS ALMOST CERTAINLY WASN'T BLOND, BLUE-EYED AND...
...TORN ABOUT WHETHER TO WEAR "SPEEDOS" OR BAGGIES TO BARBIE'S BEACH PARTY!
"MALIBU KEN"
"SPEEDOS."
DEFINITELY "SPEEDOS."
JESUS NOT TORN? YOU ARE WRONG, DUDE! SO WRONG!
THE RESISTANCE IS BORN.

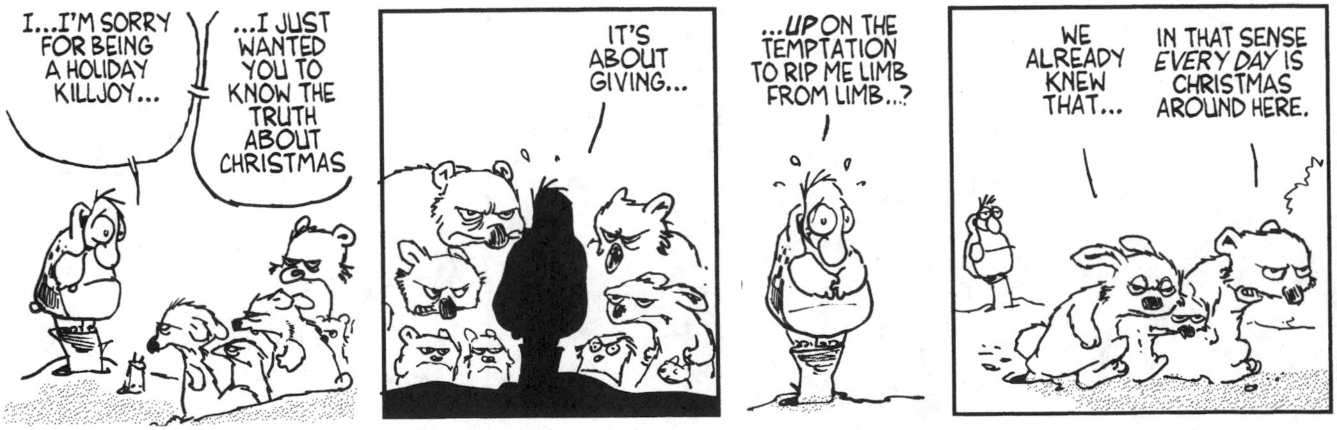
I...I'M SORRY FOR BEING A HOLIDAY KILLJOY...
...I JUST WANTED YOU TO KNOW THE TRUTH ABOUT CHRISTMAS
IT'S ABOUT GIVING...
...UP ON THE TEMPTATION TO RIP ME LIMB FROM LIMB...?
WE ALREADY KNEW THAT...
IN THAT SENSE EVERY DAY IS CHRISTMAS AROUND HERE.

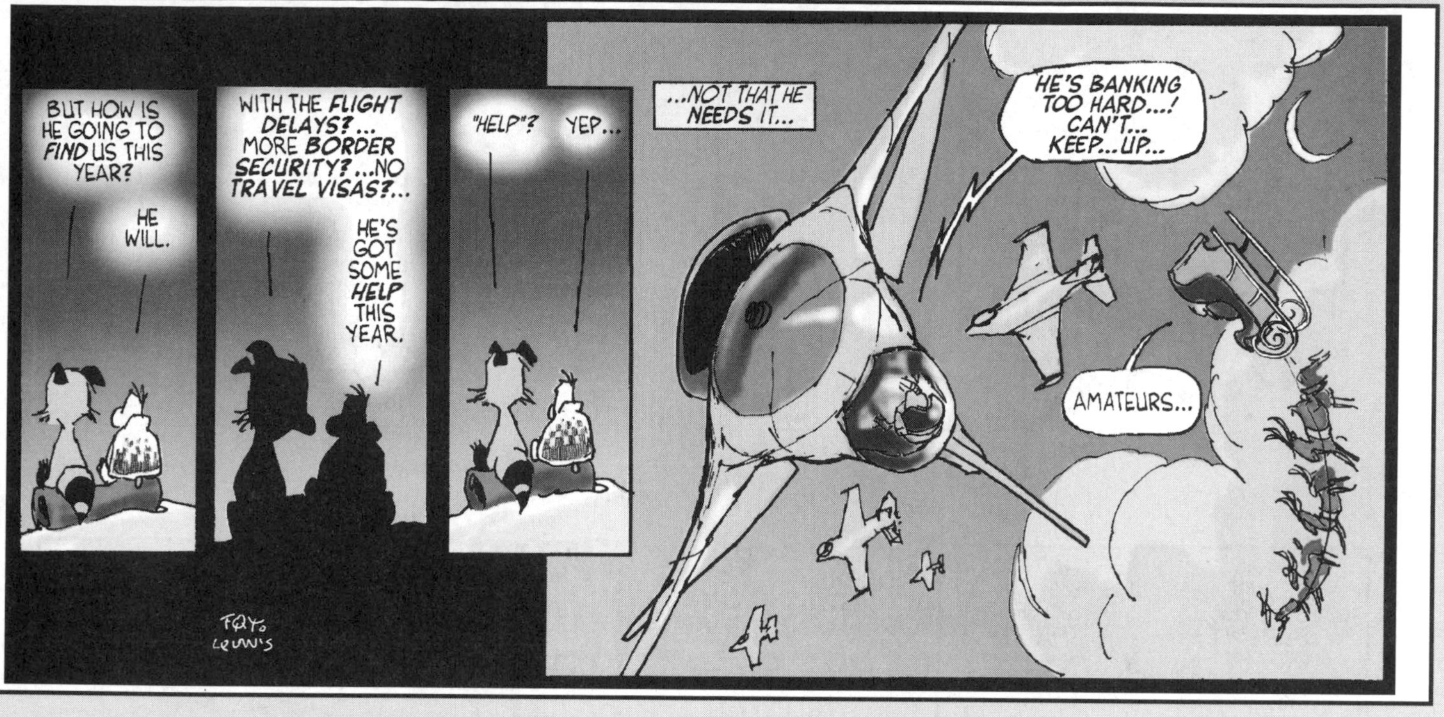
BUT HOW IS HE GOING TO FIND US THIS YEAR?
HE WILL.
WITH THE FLIGHT DELAYS?... MORE BORDER SECURITY?...NO TRAVEL VISAS?...
HE'S GOT SOME HELP THIS YEAR.
"HELP"?
YEP...
...NOT THAT HE NEEDS IT...
HE'S BANKING TOO HARD...! CAN'T... KEEP...UP...
AMATEURS...

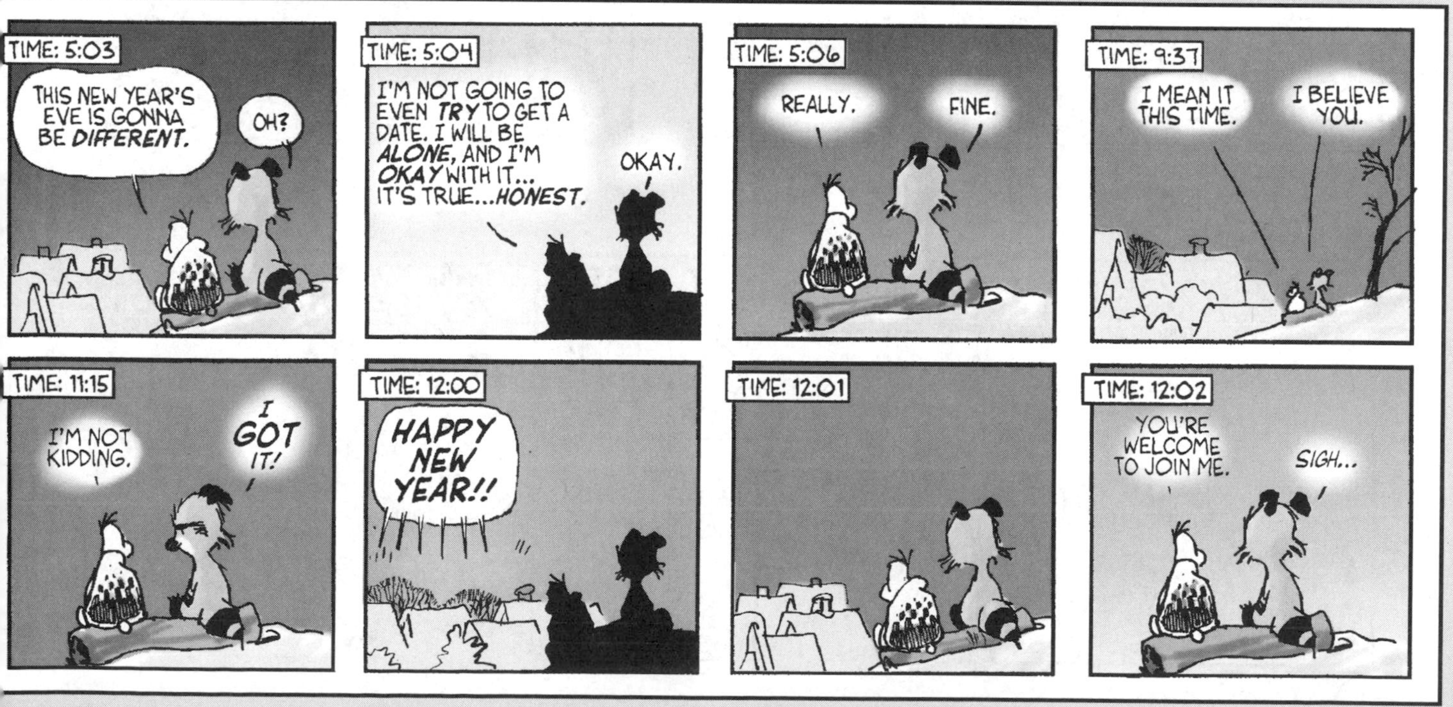
TIME: 5:03
THIS NEW YEAR'S EVE IS GONNA BE DIFFERENT.
OH?
TIME: 5:04
I'M NOT GOING TO EVEN TRY TO GET A DATE. I WILL BE ALONE, AND I'M OKAY WITH IT... IT'S TRUE...HONEST.
OKAY.
TIME: 5:06
REALLY.
FINE.
TIME: 9:37
I MEAN IT THIS TIME.
I BELIEVE YOU.
TIME: 11:15
I'M NOT KIDDING.
I GOT IT!
TIME: 12:00
HAPPY NEW YEAR!!
TIME: 12:01
TIME: 12:02
YOU'RE WELCOME TO JOIN ME.
SIGH...

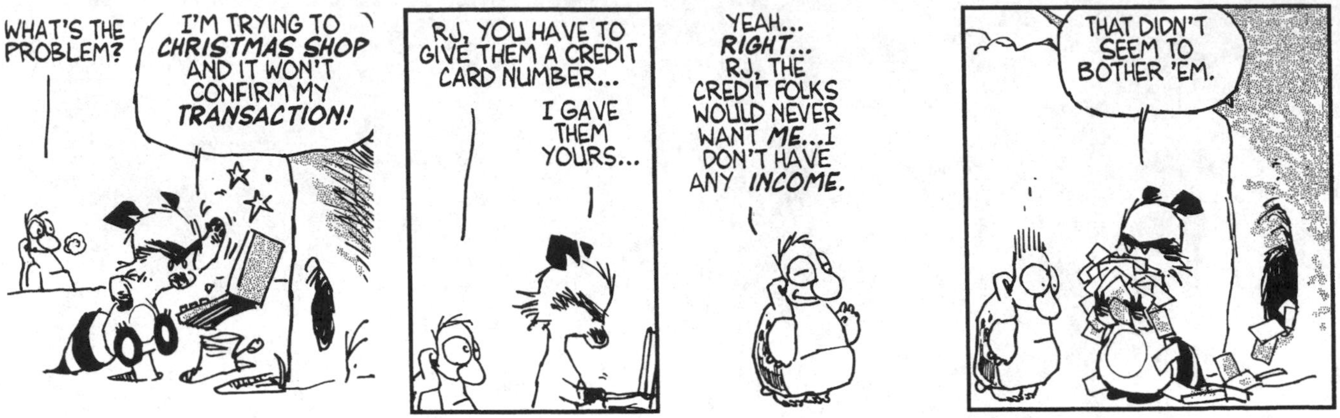
WHAT'S THE PROBLEM?
I'M TRYING TO CHRISTMAS SHOP AND IT WON'T CONFIRM MY TRANSACTION!
RJ, YOU HAVE TO GIVE THEM A CREDIT CARD NUMBER...
I GAVE THEM YOURS...
YEAH... RIGHT... RJ, THE CREDIT FOLKS WOULD NEVER WANT ME...I DON'T HAVE ANY INCOME.
THAT DIDN'T SEEM TO BOTHER 'EM.

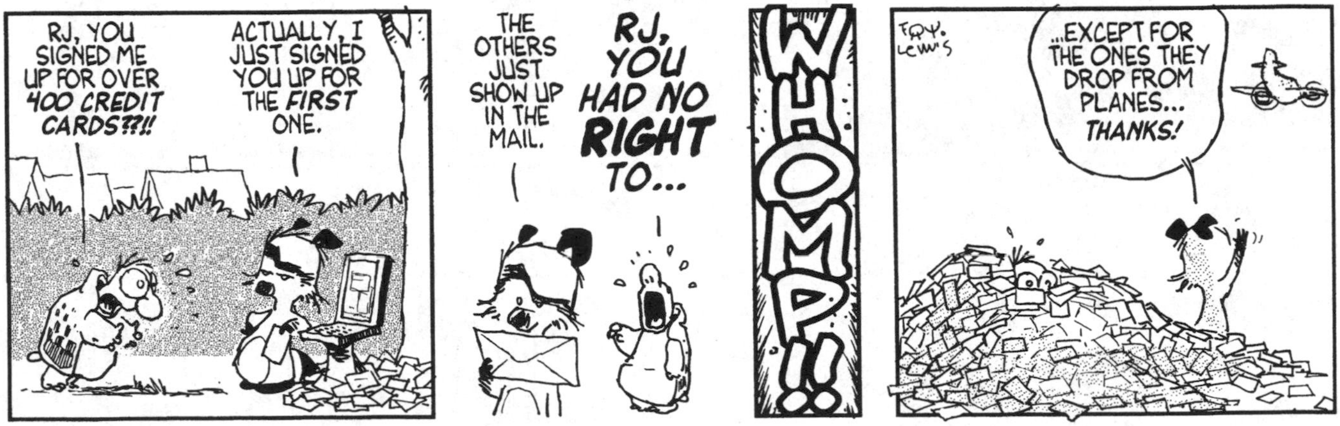
RJ, YOU SIGNED ME UP FOR OVER 400 CREDIT CARDS??!!
ACTUALLY, I JUST SIGNED YOU UP FOR THE FIRST ONE.
THE OTHERS JUST SHOW UP IN THE MAIL.
RJ, YOU HAD NO RIGHT TO...
WHOMP!!
...EXCEPT FOR THE ONES THEY DROP FROM PLANES... THANKS!

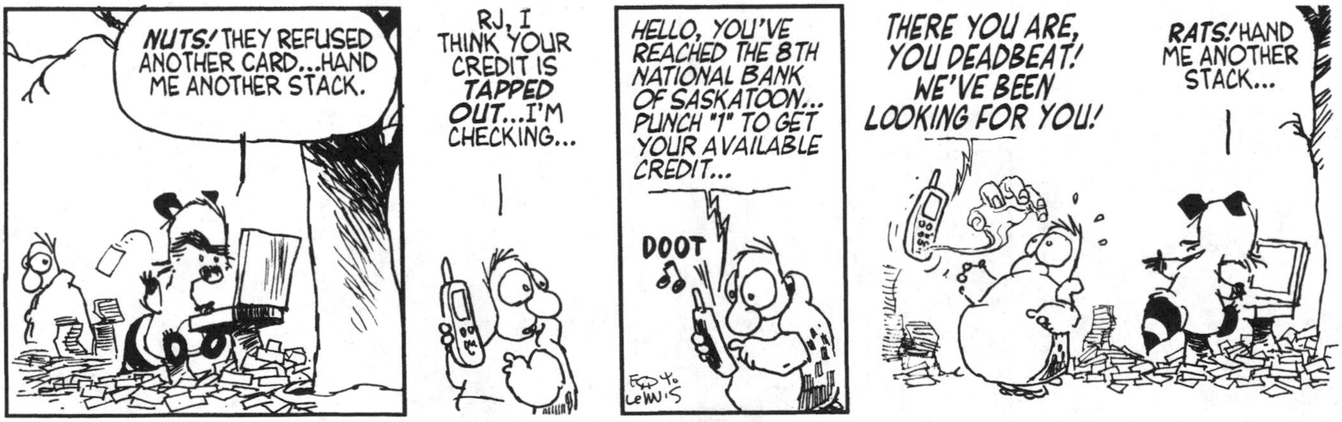
NUTS! THEY REFUSED ANOTHER CARD...HAND ME ANOTHER STACK.
RJ, I THINK YOUR CREDIT IS TAPPED OUT...I'M CHECKING...
HELLO, YOU'VE REACHED THE 8TH NATIONAL BANK OF SASKATOON... PUNCH "1" TO GET YOUR AVAILABLE CREDIT...
DOOT
THERE YOU ARE, YOU DEADBEAT! WE'VE BEEN LOOKING FOR YOU!
RATS! HAND ME ANOTHER STACK...

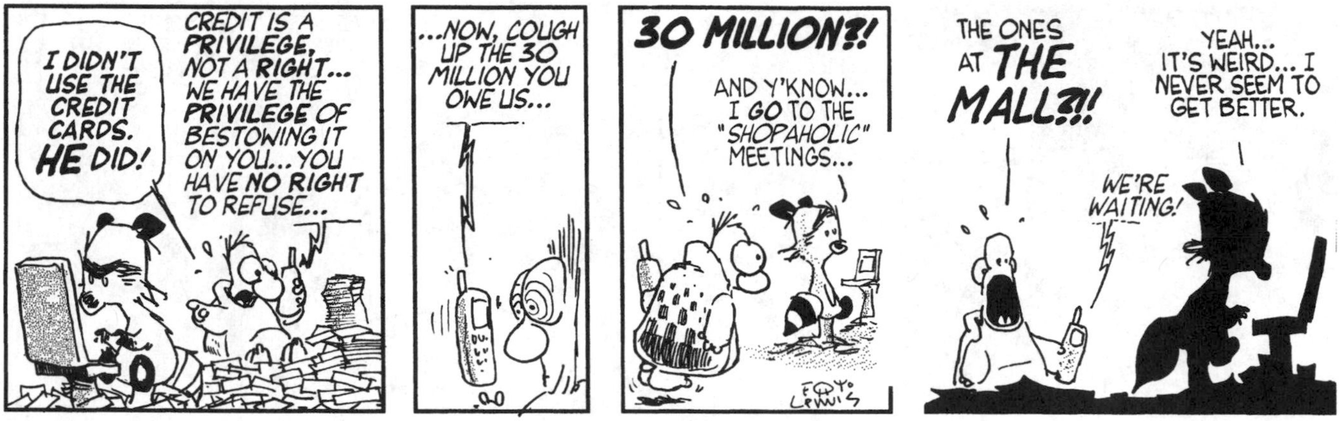
I DIDN'T USE THE CREDIT CARDS. HE DID!
CREDIT IS A PRIVILEGE, NOT A RIGHT... WE HAVE THE PRIVILEGE OF BESTOWING IT ON YOU... YOU HAVE NO RIGHT TO REFUSE...
...NOW, COUGH UP THE 30 MILLION YOU OWE US...
30 MILLION?!
AND Y'KNOW... I GO TO THE "SHOPAHOLIC" MEETINGS...
THE ONES AT THE MALL?!!
WE'RE WAITING!
YEAH... IT'S WEIRD... I NEVER SEEM TO GET BETTER.

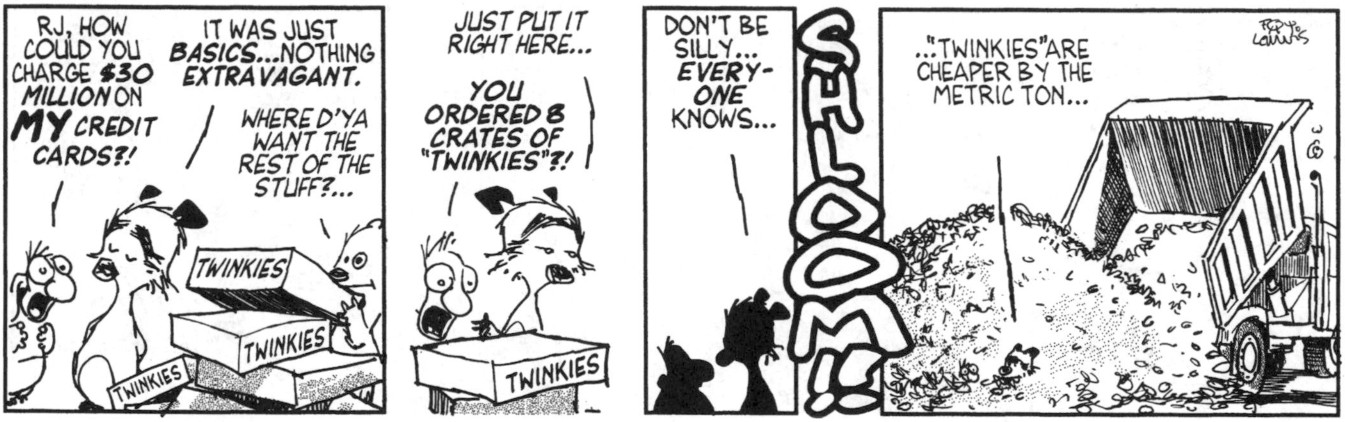
RJ, HOW COULD YOU CHARGE $30 MILLION ON MY CREDIT CARDS?!
IT WAS JUST BASICS...NOTHING EXTRAVAGANT.
WHERE D'YA WANT THE REST OF THE STUFF?...
TWINKIES
TWINKIES
TWINKIES
JUST PUT IT RIGHT HERE...
YOU ORDERED 8 CRATES OF "TWINKIES"?!
TWINKIES
DON'T BE SILLY... EVERY-ONE KNOWS...
SHLOOM
..."TWINKIES" ARE CHEAPER BY THE METRIC TON...

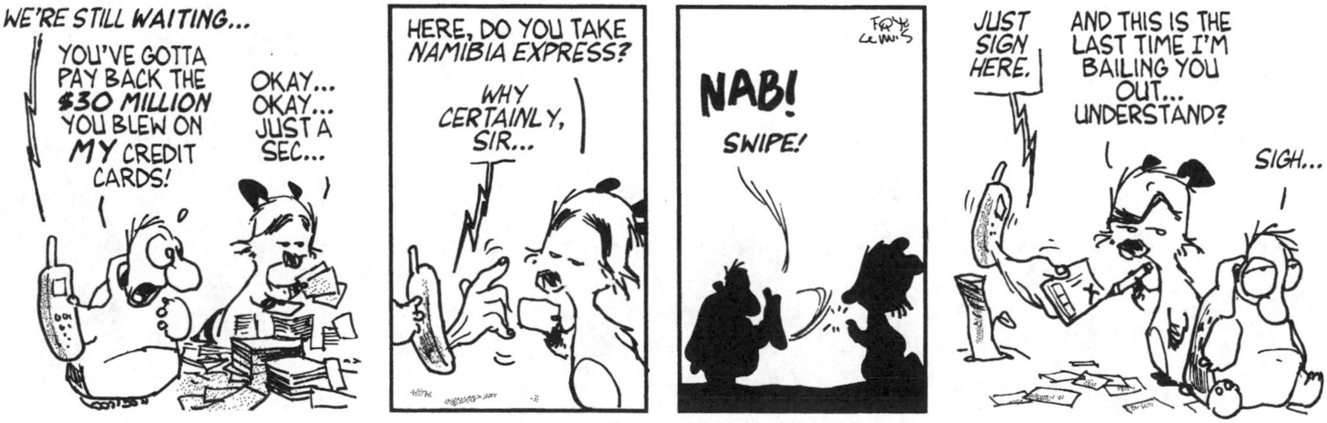
WE'RE STILL WAITING...
YOU'VE GOTTA PAY BACK THE $30 MILLION YOU BLEW ON MY CREDIT CARDS!
OKAY... OKAY... JUST A SEC...
HERE, DO YOU TAKE NAMIBIA EXPRESS?
WHY CERTAINLY, SIR...
NAB!
SWIPE!
JUST SIGN HERE.
AND THIS IS THE LAST TIME I'M BAILING YOU OUT... UNDERSTAND?
SIGH...

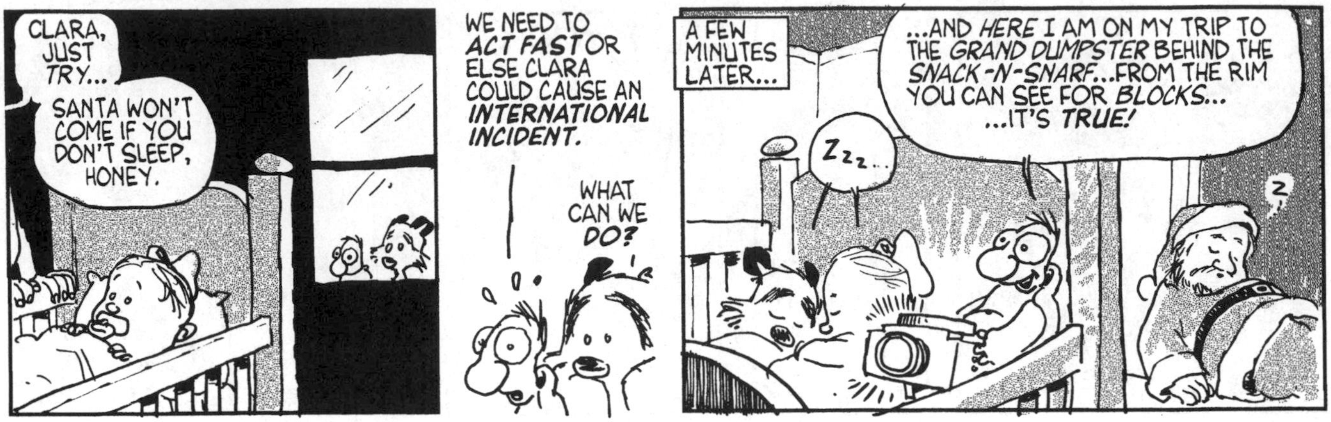
CLARA, JUST TRY...
SANTA WON'T COME IF YOU DON'T SLEEP, HONEY.
WE NEED TO ACT FAST OR ELSE CLARA COULD CAUSE AN INTERNATIONAL INCIDENT.
WHAT CAN WE DO?
A FEW MINUTES LATER...
ZZZ...
...AND HERE I AM ON MY TRIP TO THE GRAND DUMPSTER BEHIND THE SNACK-N-SNARF...FROM THE RIM YOU CAN SEE FOR BLOCKS... ...IT'S TRUE!
Z

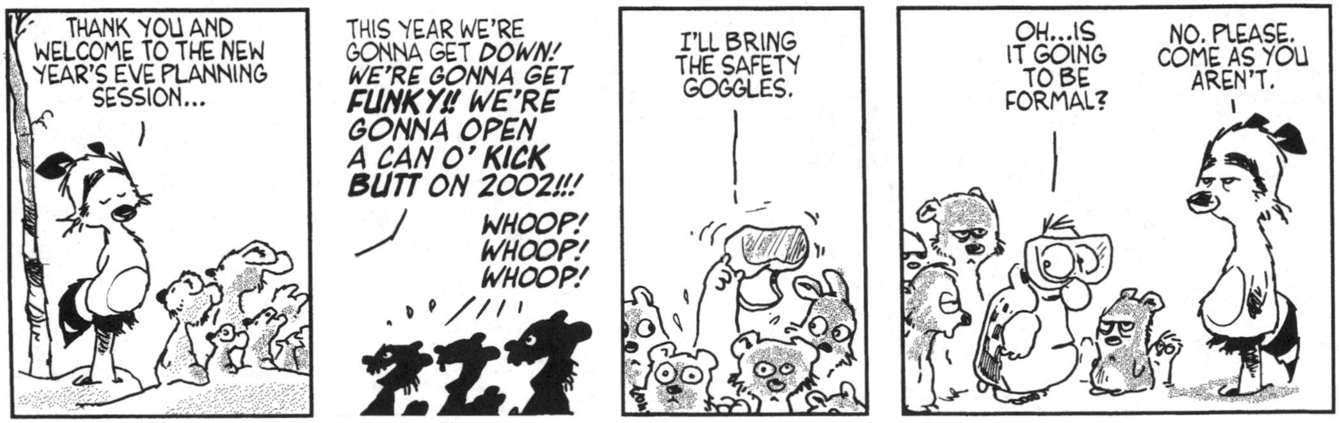
THANK YOU AND WELCOME TO THE NEW YEAR'S EVE PLANNING SESSION...
THIS YEAR WE'RE GONNA GET DOWN! WE'RE GONNA GET FUNKY!! WE'RE GONNA OPEN A CAN O' KICK BUTT ON 2002!!!
WHOOP! WHOOP! WHOOP!
I'LL BRING THE SAFETY GOGGLES.
OH...IS IT GOING TO BE FORMAL?
NO. PLEASE. COME AS YOU AREN'T.

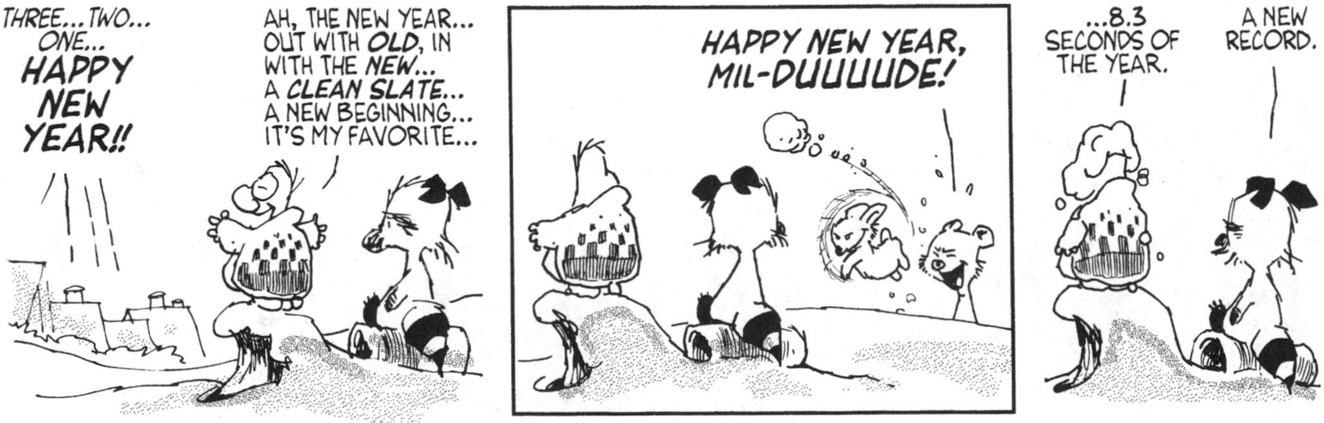
THREE...TWO... ONE... HAPPY NEW YEAR!!
AH, THE NEW YEAR... OUT WITH OLD, IN WITH THE NEW... A CLEAN SLATE... A NEW BEGINNING... IT'S MY FAVORITE...
HAPPY NEW YEAR, MIL-DUUUUDE!
...8.3 SECONDS OF THE YEAR.
A NEW RECORD.

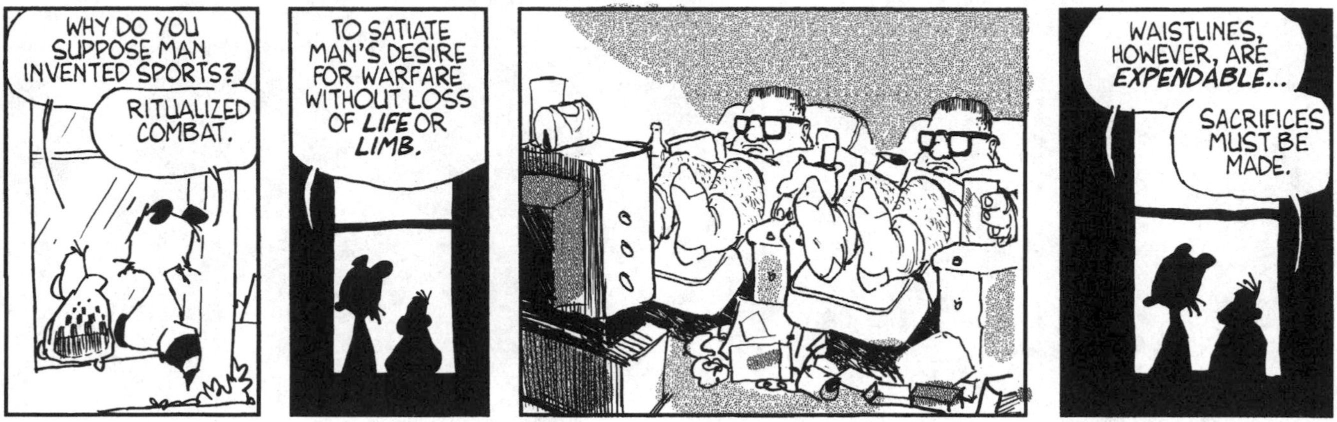
WHY DO YOU SUPPOSE MAN INVENTED SPORTS?
RITUALIZED COMBAT.
TO SATIATE MAN'S DESIRE FOR WARFARE WITHOUT LOSS OF *LIFE* OR *LIMB.*
WAISTLINES, HOWEVER, ARE *EXPENDABLE...*
SACRIFICES MUST BE MADE.

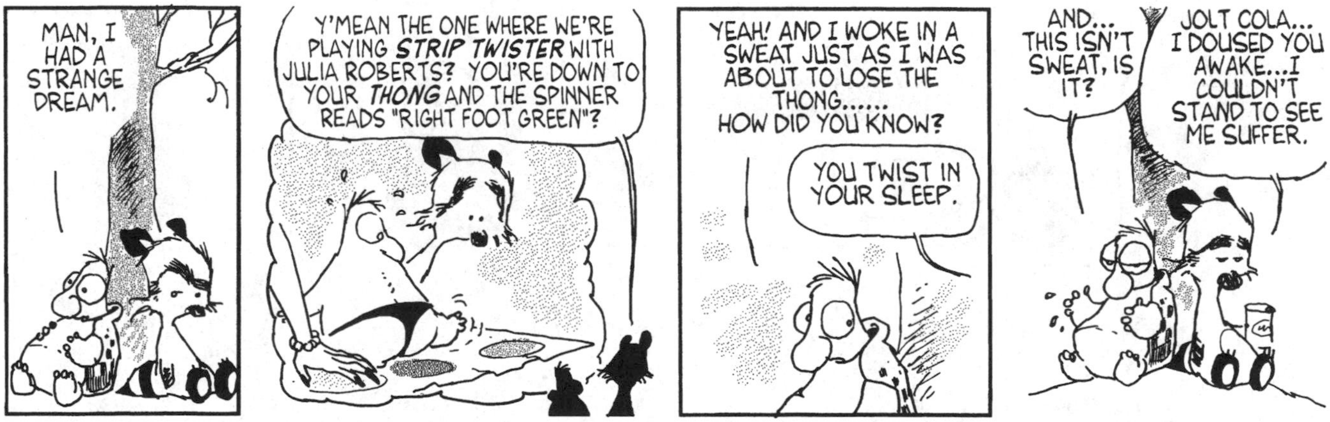
MAN, I HAD A STRANGE DREAM.
Y'MEAN THE ONE WHERE WE'RE PLAYING *STRIP TWISTER* WITH JULIA ROBERTS? YOU'RE DOWN TO YOUR *THONG* AND THE SPINNER READS "RIGHT FOOT GREEN"?
YEAH! AND I WOKE IN A SWEAT JUST AS I WAS ABOUT TO LOSE THE THONG...... HOW DID YOU KNOW?
YOU TWIST IN YOUR SLEEP.
AND... THIS ISN'T SWEAT, IS IT?
JOLT COLA... I DOUSED YOU AWAKE...I COULDN'T STAND TO SEE ME SUFFER.

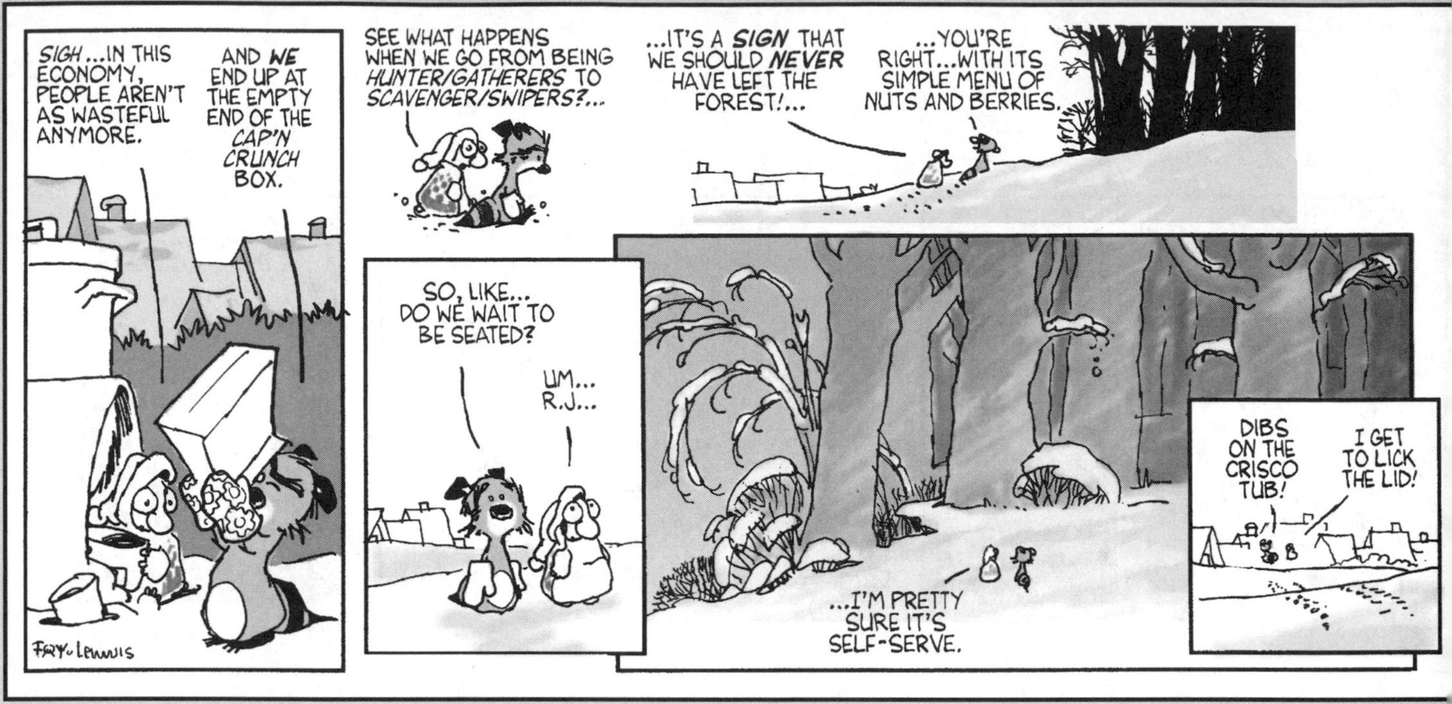
SIGH...IN THIS ECONOMY, PEOPLE AREN'T AS WASTEFUL ANYMORE.
AND WE END UP AT THE EMPTY END OF THE CAP'N CRUNCH BOX.
SEE WHAT HAPPENS WHEN WE GO FROM BEING HUNTER/GATHERERS TO SCAVENGER/SWIPERS?...
...IT'S A SIGN THAT WE SHOULD NEVER HAVE LEFT THE FOREST!...
...YOU'RE RIGHT...WITH ITS SIMPLE MENU OF NUTS AND BERRIES.
SO, LIKE... DO WE WAIT TO BE SEATED?
UM... R.J...
...I'M PRETTY SURE IT'S SELF-SERVE.
DIBS ON THE CRISCO TUB!
I GET TO LICK THE LID!

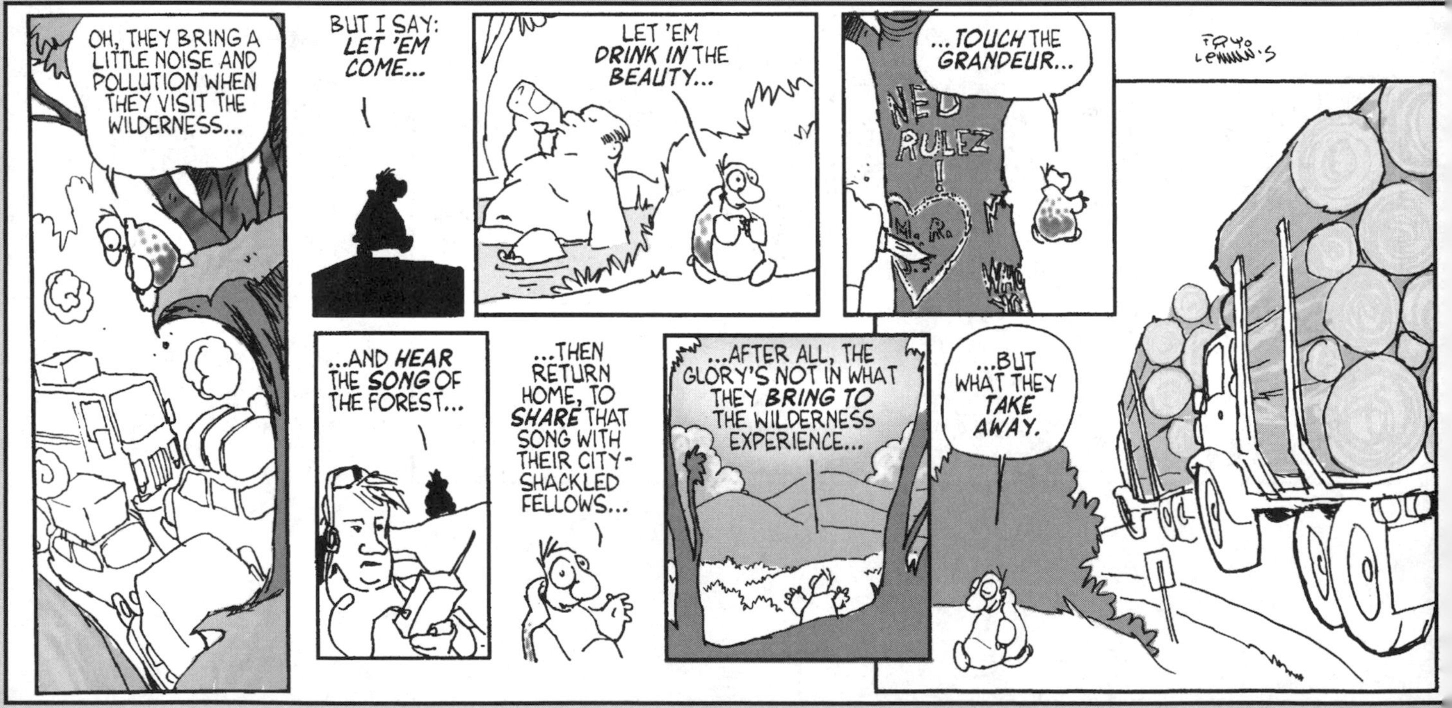
OH, THEY BRING A LITTLE NOISE AND POLLUTION WHEN THEY VISIT THE WILDERNESS...
BUT I SAY: LET 'EM COME...
LET 'EM DRINK IN THE BEAUTY...
...TOUCH THE GRANDEUR...
NED RULEZ
...AND HEAR THE SONG OF THE FOREST...
...THEN RETURN HOME, TO SHARE THAT SONG WITH THEIR CITY-SHACKLED FELLOWS...
...AFTER ALL, THE GLORY'S NOT IN WHAT THEY BRING TO THE WILDERNESS EXPERIENCE...
...BUT WHAT THEY TAKE AWAY.

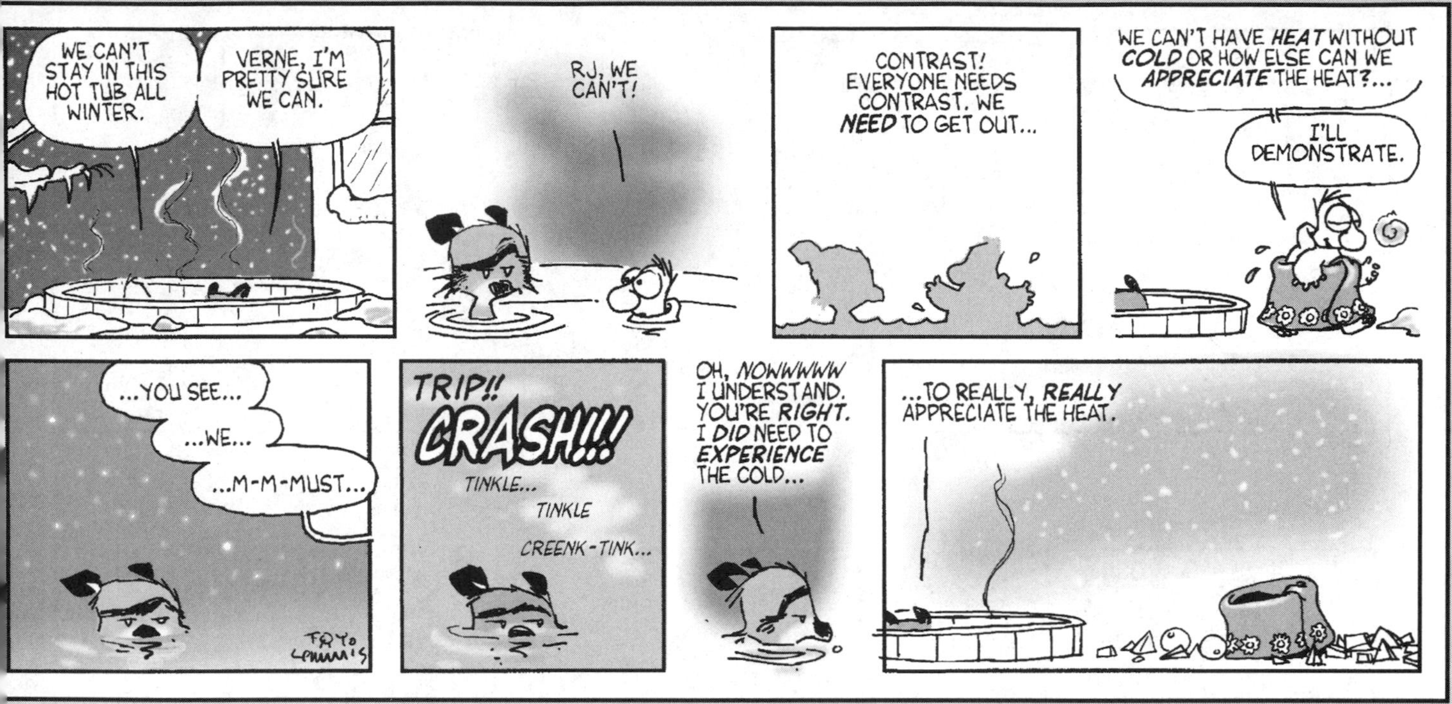
WE CAN'T STAY IN THIS HOT TUB ALL WINTER.
VERNE, I'M PRETTY SURE WE CAN.
RJ, WE CAN'T!
CONTRAST! EVERYONE NEEDS CONTRAST. WE NEED TO GET OUT...
WE CAN'T HAVE HEAT WITHOUT COLD OR HOW ELSE CAN WE APPRECIATE THE HEAT?...
I'LL DEMONSTRATE.
...YOU SEE...
...WE...
...M-M-MUST...
TRIP!!
CRASH!!!
TINKLE...
TINKLE
CREENK-TINK...
OH, NOWWWWW I UNDERSTAND. YOU'RE RIGHT. I DID NEED TO EXPERIENCE THE COLD...
...TO REALLY, REALLY APPRECIATE THE HEAT.

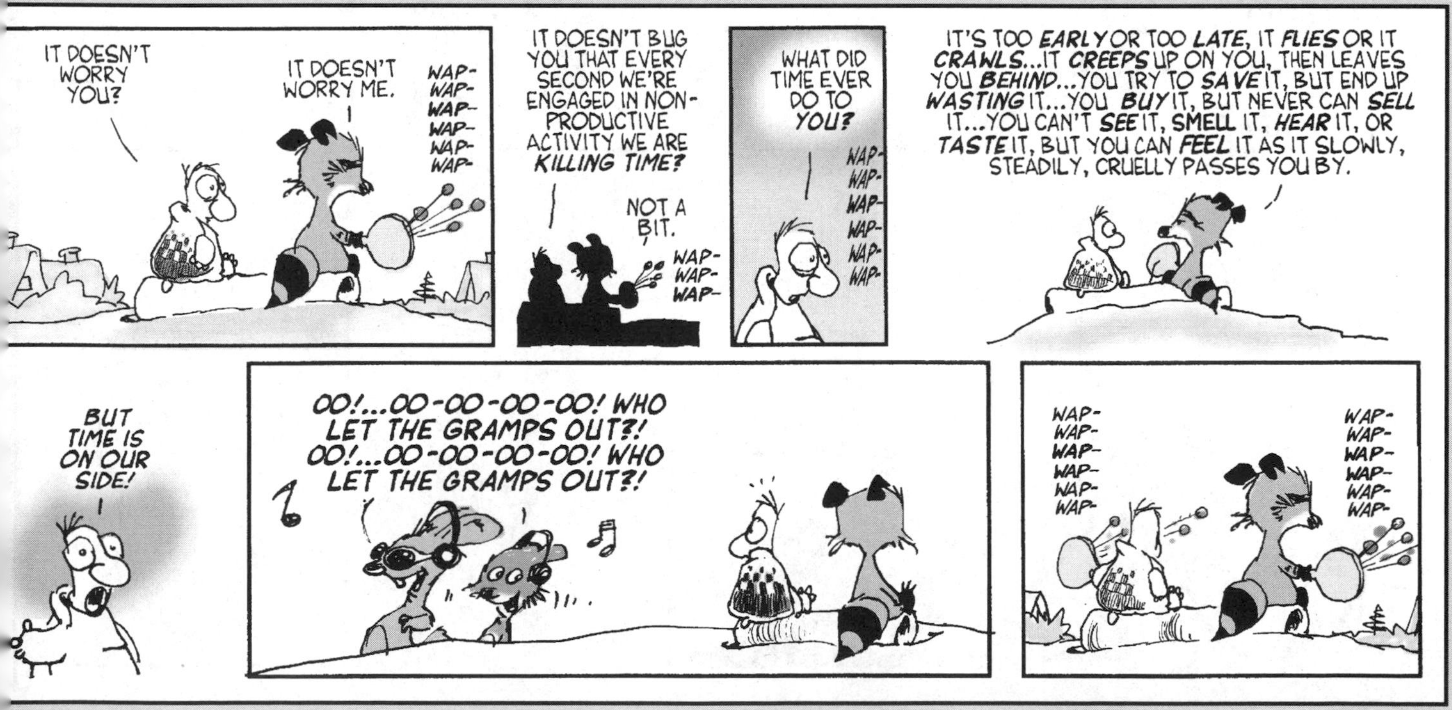
IT DOESN'T WORRY YOU?
IT DOESN'T WORRY ME.
WAP-WAP-WAP-WAP-WAP-WAP-
IT DOESN'T BUG YOU THAT EVERY SECOND WE'RE ENGAGED IN NON-PRODUCTIVE ACTIVITY WE ARE KILLING TIME?
NOT A BIT.
WAP-WAP-WAP-
WHAT DID TIME EVER DO TO YOU?
WAP-WAP-WAP-WAP-WAP-WAP-
IT'S TOO EARLY OR TOO LATE, IT FLIES OR IT CRAWLS...IT CREEPS UP ON YOU, THEN LEAVES YOU BEHIND...YOU TRY TO SAVE IT, BUT END UP WASTING IT...YOU BUY IT, BUT NEVER CAN SELL IT...YOU CAN'T SEE IT, SMELL IT, HEAR IT, OR TASTE IT, BUT YOU CAN FEEL IT AS IT SLOWLY, STEADILY, CRUELLY PASSES YOU BY.
BUT TIME IS ON OUR SIDE!
OO!...OO-OO-OO-OO! WHO LET THE GRAMPS OUT?!
OO!...OO-OO-OO-OO! WHO LET THE GRAMPS OUT?!
WAP-WAP-WAP-WAP-WAP-WAP-
WAP-WAP-WAP-WAP-WAP-WAP-

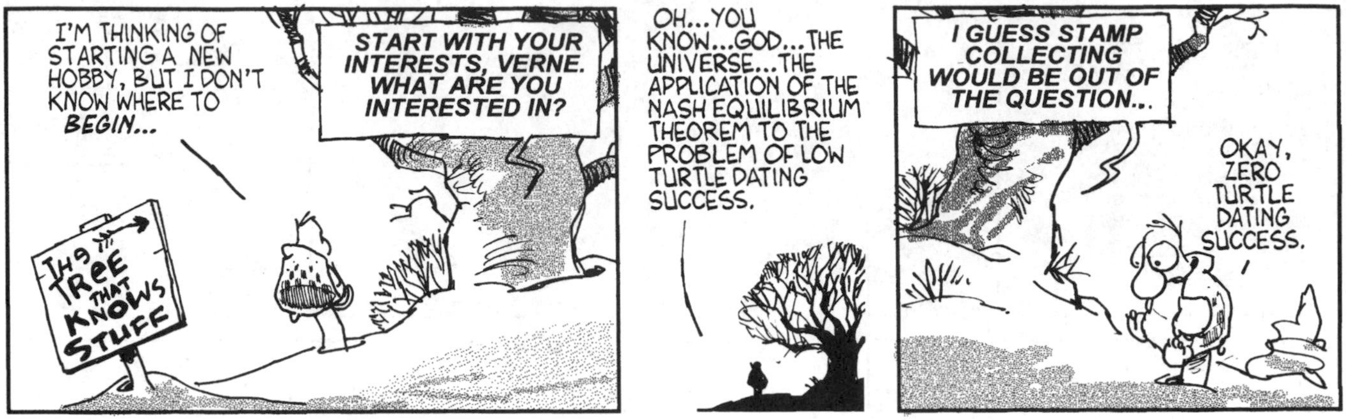
I'M THINKING OF STARTING A NEW HOBBY, BUT I DON'T KNOW WHERE TO *BEGIN...*
THE TREE THAT KNOWS STUFF
START WITH YOUR INTERESTS, VERNE. WHAT ARE YOU INTERESTED IN?
OH...YOU KNOW...GOD...THE UNIVERSE...THE APPLICATION OF THE NASH EQUILIBRIUM THEOREM TO THE PROBLEM OF LOW TURTLE DATING SUCCESS.
I GUESS STAMP COLLECTING WOULD BE OUT OF THE QUESTION...
OKAY, ZERO TURTLE DATING SUCCESS.

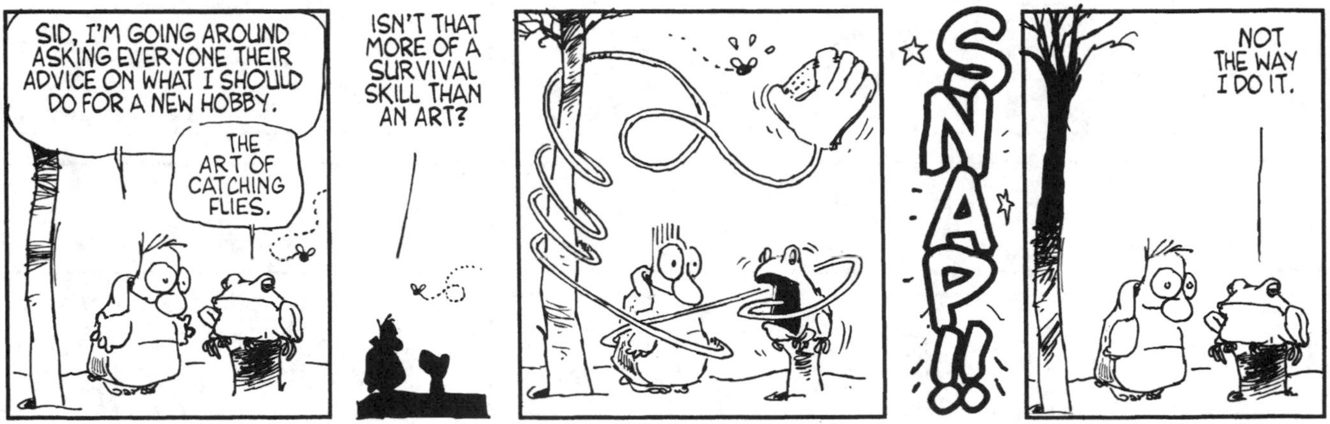
SID, I'M GOING AROUND ASKING EVERYONE THEIR ADVICE ON WHAT I SHOULD DO FOR A NEW HOBBY.
THE ART OF CATCHING FLIES.
ISN'T THAT MORE OF A SURVIVAL SKILL THAN AN ART?
SNAP!!
NOT THE WAY I DO IT.

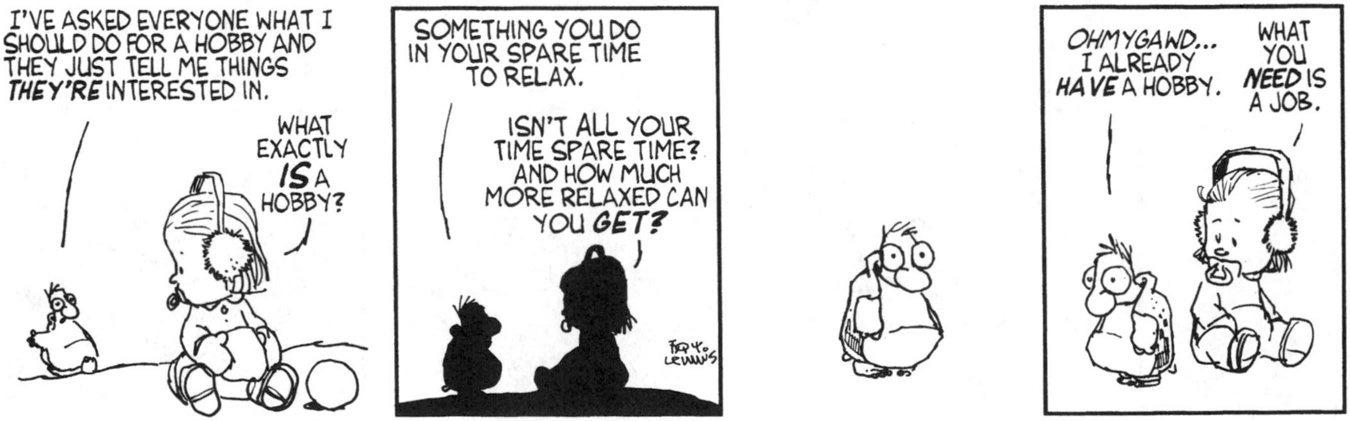
I'VE ASKED EVERYONE WHAT I SHOULD DO FOR A HOBBY AND THEY JUST TELL ME THINGS ***THEY'RE*** INTERESTED IN.
WHAT EXACTLY ***IS*** A HOBBY?
SOMETHING YOU DO IN YOUR SPARE TIME TO RELAX.
ISN'T ALL YOUR TIME SPARE TIME? AND HOW MUCH MORE RELAXED CAN YOU ***GET?***
OHMYGAWD... I ALREADY ***HAVE*** A HOBBY.
WHAT YOU ***NEED*** IS A JOB.

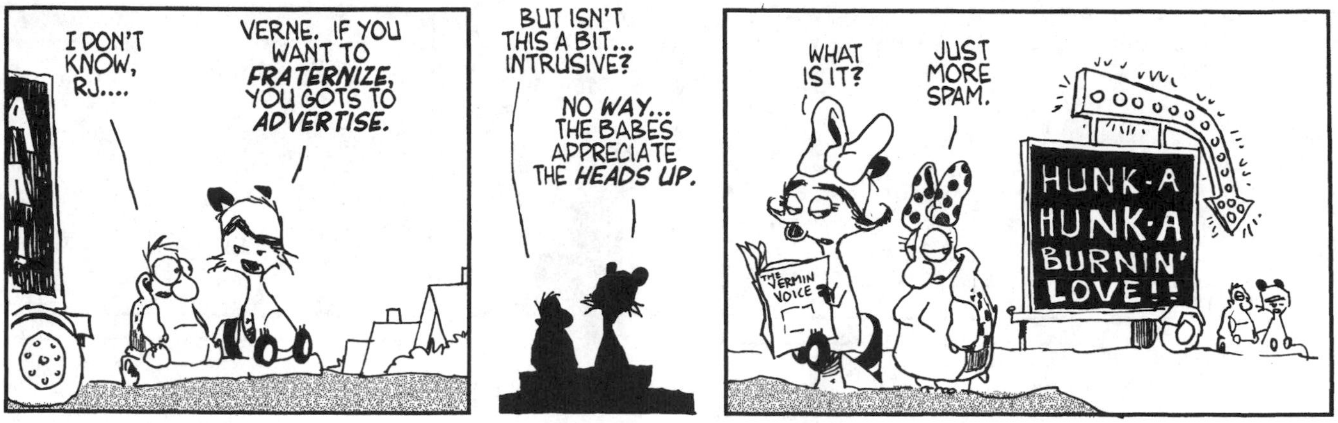
I DON'T KNOW, RJ....
VERNE. IF YOU WANT TO *FRATERNIZE,* YOU GOTS TO *ADVERTISE.*
BUT ISN'T THIS A BIT... INTRUSIVE?
NO *WAY*... THE BABES APPRECIATE THE *HEADS UP.*
WHAT IS IT?
JUST MORE SPAM.
THE VERMIN VOICE
HUNK-A HUNK-A BURNIN' LOVE!!

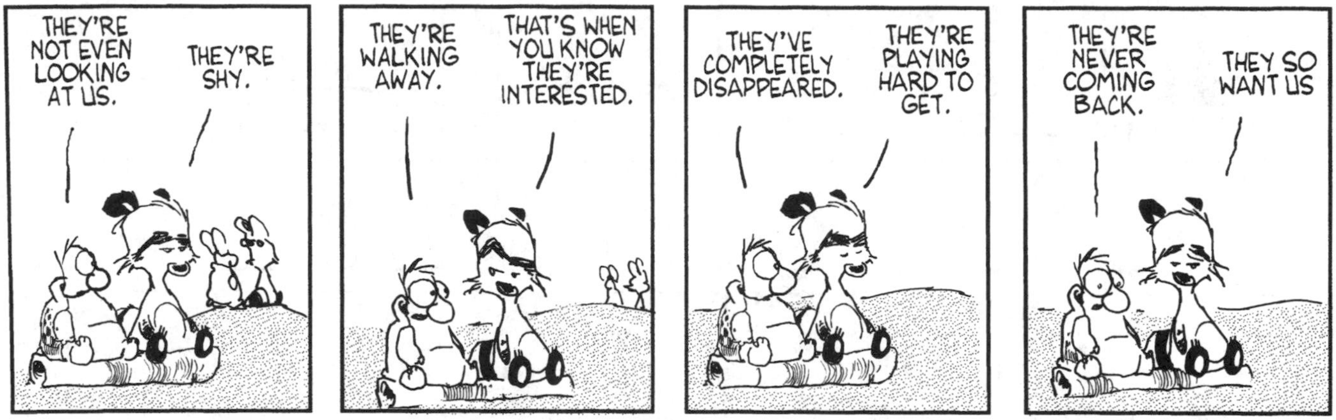
THEY'RE NOT EVEN LOOKING AT US.
THEY'RE SHY.
THEY'RE WALKING AWAY.
THAT'S WHEN YOU KNOW THEY'RE INTERESTED.
THEY'VE COMPLETELY DISAPPEARED.
THEY'RE PLAYING HARD TO GET.
THEY'RE NEVER COMING BACK.
THEY SO WANT US

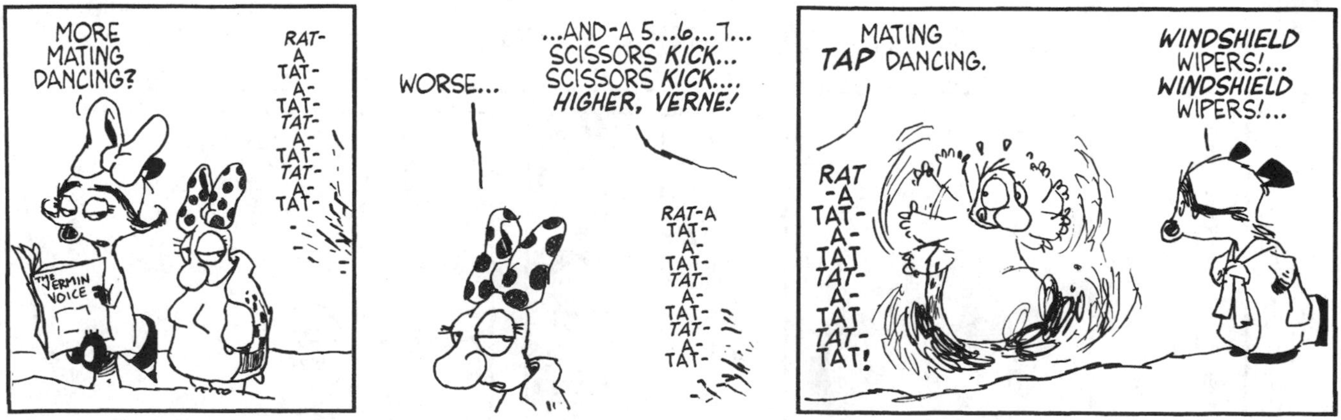
MORE MATING DANCING?
RAT-A-TAT-A-TAT-TAT-A-TAT-TAT-A-TAT-
THE VERMIN VOICE
WORSE...
...AND-A 5...6...7... SCISSORS *KICK*... SCISSORS *KICK*.... *HIGHER, VERNE!*
RAT-A TAT-A-TAT-TAT-A-TAT-TAT-A-TAT-
MATING *TAP* DANCING.
WINDSHIELD WIPERS!... *WINDSHIELD* WIPERS!...
RAT-A-TAT-A-TAT TAT-A-TAT TAT-TAT!

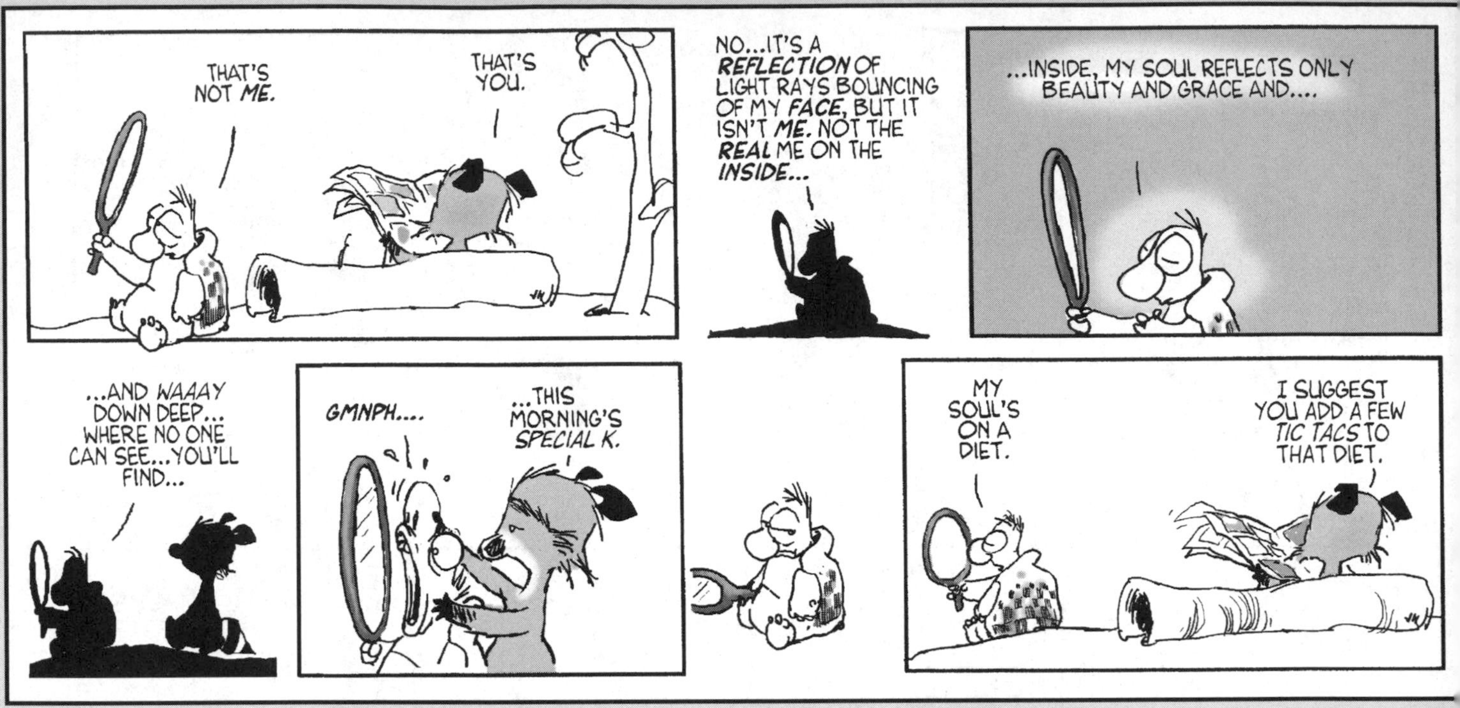
THAT'S NOT *ME.*
THAT'S YOU.
NO...IT'S A *REFLECTION* OF LIGHT RAYS BOUNCING OF MY *FACE*, BUT IT ISN'T *ME.* NOT THE *REAL* ME ON THE *INSIDE*...
...INSIDE, MY SOUL REFLECTS ONLY BEAUTY AND GRACE AND....
...AND *WAAAY* DOWN DEEP... WHERE NO ONE CAN SEE...YOU'LL FIND...
GMNPH....
...THIS MORNING'S *SPECIAL K.*
MY SOUL'S ON A DIET.
I SUGGEST YOU ADD A FEW *TIC TACS* TO THAT DIET.

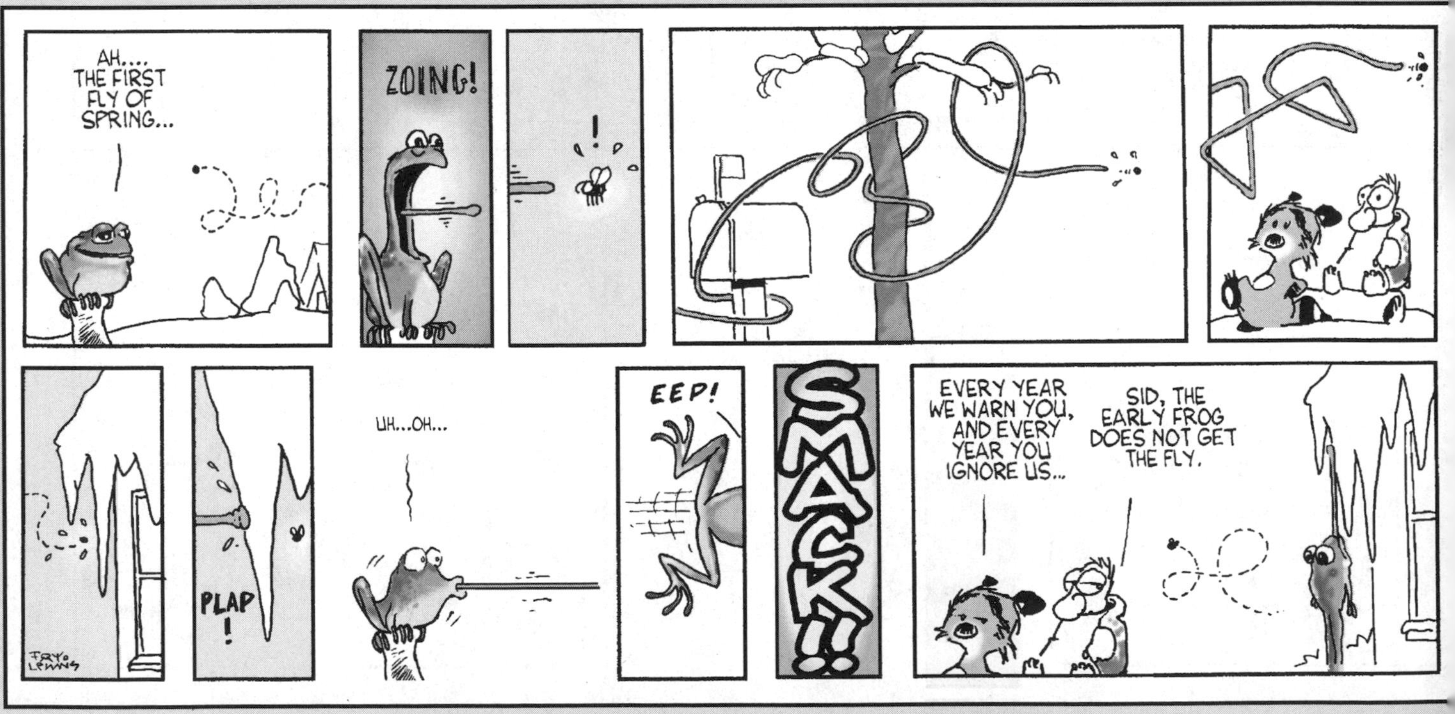
AH.... THE FIRST FLY OF SPRING...
ZOING!
!
PLAP !
UH...OH...
EEP!
SMACK!!
EVERY YEAR WE WARN YOU, AND EVERY YEAR YOU IGNORE US...
SID, THE EARLY FROG DOES NOT GET THE FLY.

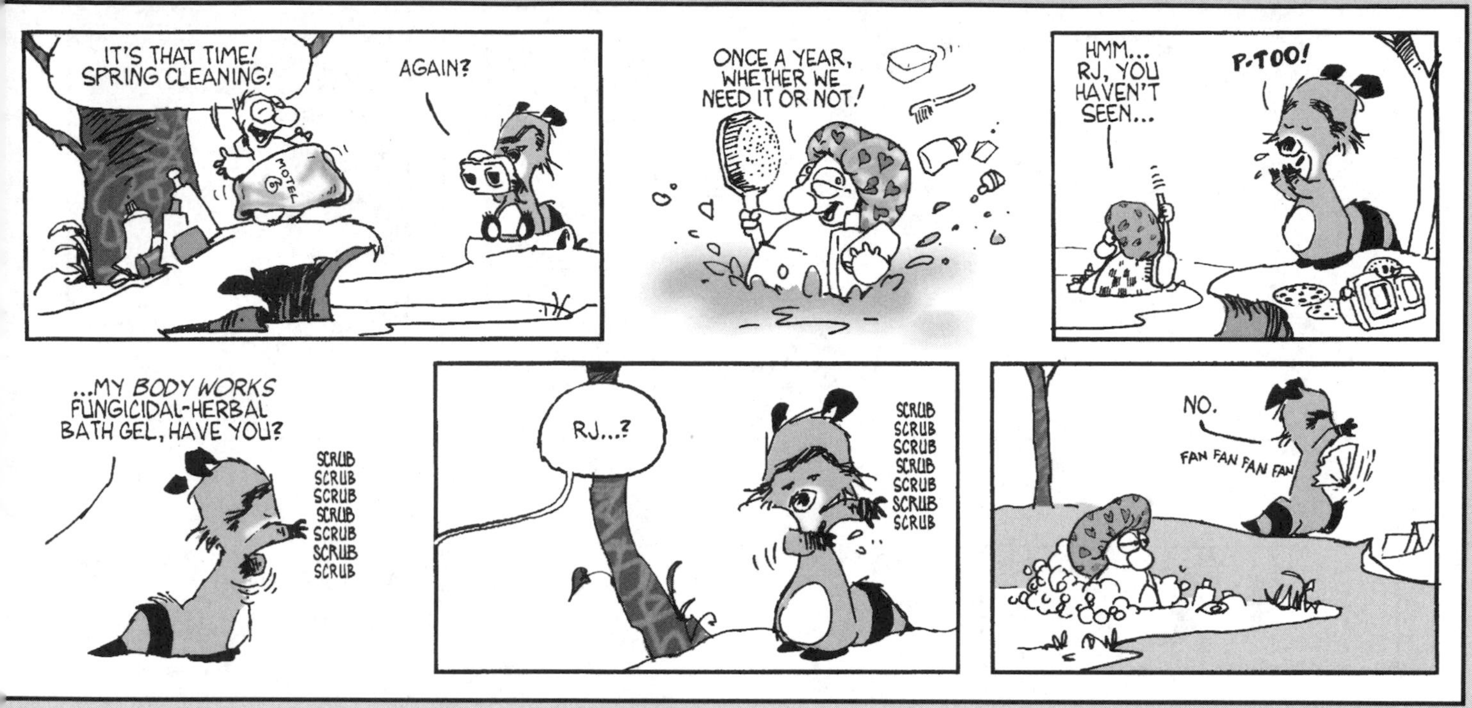
IT'S THAT TIME! SPRING CLEANING!
MOTEL 6
AGAIN?
ONCE A YEAR, WHETHER WE NEED IT OR NOT!
HMM... RJ, YOU HAVEN'T SEEN...
P-TOO!
...MY BODY WORKS FUNGICIDAL-HERBAL BATH GEL, HAVE YOU?
SCRUB SCRUB SCRUB SCRUB SCRUB SCRUB SCRUB
RJ...?
SCRUB SCRUB SCRUB SCRUB SCRUB SCRUB SCRUB
NO.
FAN FAN FAN FAN

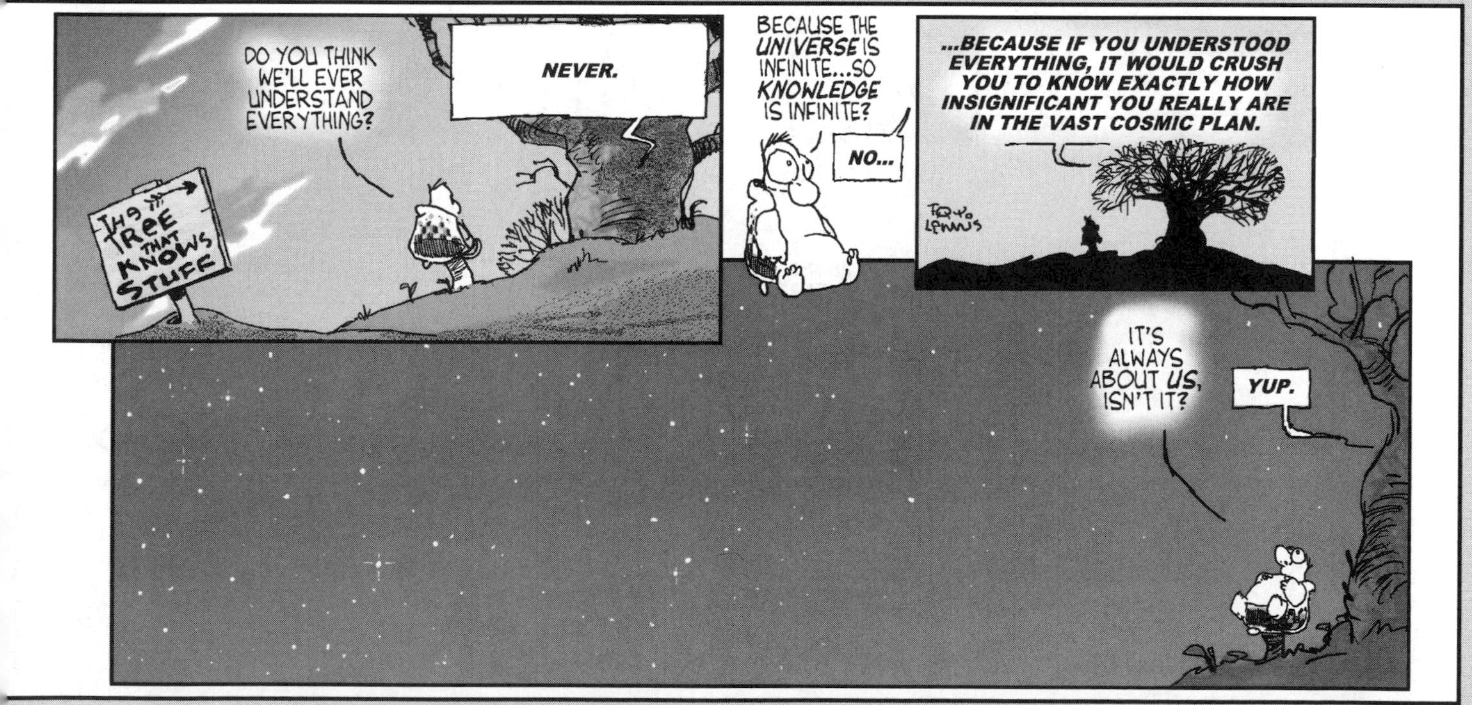
THE TREE THAT KNOWS STUFF
DO YOU THINK WE'LL EVER UNDERSTAND EVERYTHING?
NEVER.
BECAUSE THE UNIVERSE IS INFINITE...SO KNOWLEDGE IS INFINITE?
NO...
...BECAUSE IF YOU UNDERSTOOD EVERYTHING, IT WOULD CRUSH YOU TO KNOW EXACTLY HOW INSIGNIFICANT YOU REALLY ARE IN THE VAST COSMIC PLAN.
IT'S ALWAYS ABOUT US, ISN'T IT?
YUP.

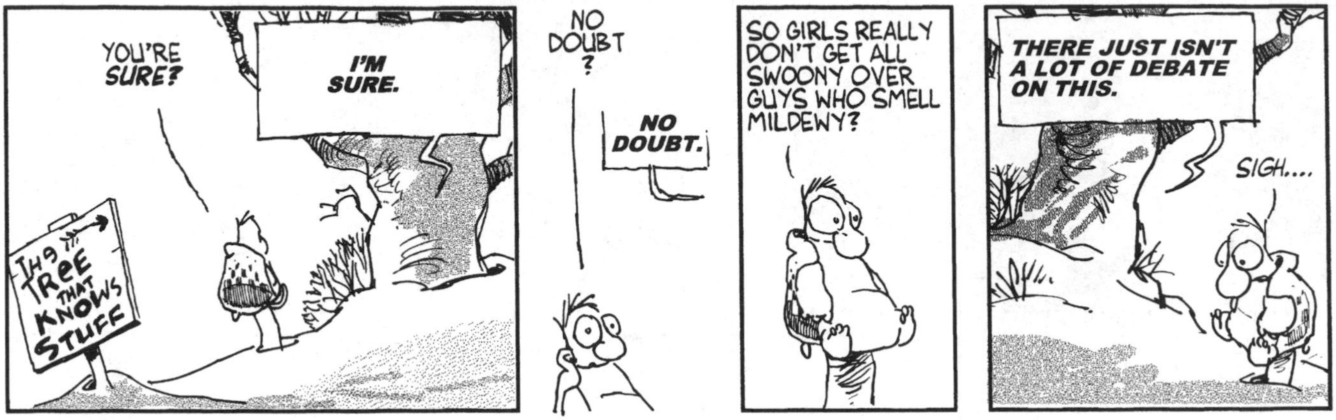
The TREE THAT KNOWS STUFF
YOU'RE SURE?
I'M SURE.
NO DOUBT?
NO DOUBT.
SO GIRLS REALLY DON'T GET ALL SWOONY OVER GUYS WHO SMELL MILDEWY?
THERE JUST ISN'T A LOT OF DEBATE ON THIS.
SIGH....

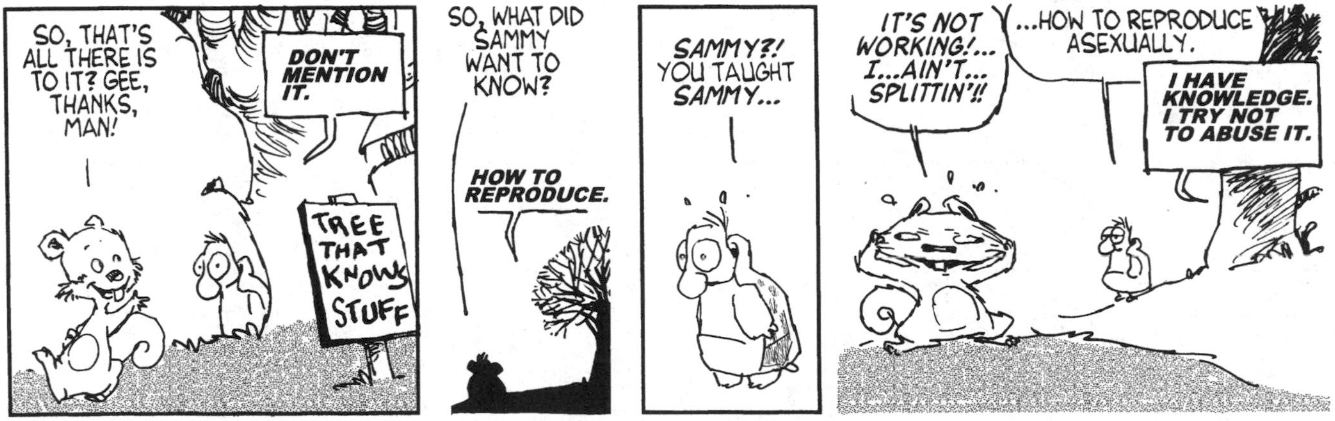
SO, THAT'S ALL THERE IS TO IT? GEE, THANKS, MAN!
DON'T MENTION IT.
TREE THAT KNOWS STUFF
SO, WHAT DID SAMMY WANT TO KNOW?
HOW TO REPRODUCE.
SAMMY?! YOU TAUGHT SAMMY...
IT'S NOT WORKING!... I...AIN'T... SPLITTIN'!!
...HOW TO REPRODUCE ASEXUALLY.
I HAVE KNOWLEDGE. I TRY NOT TO ABUSE IT.

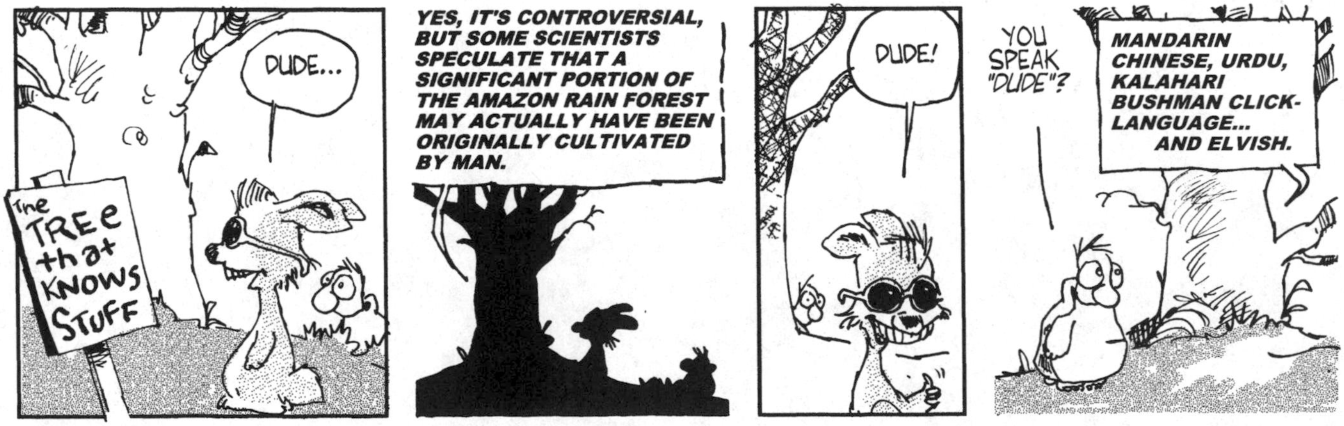
The TREE that KNOWS STUFF
DUDE...
YES, IT'S CONTROVERSIAL, BUT SOME SCIENTISTS SPECULATE THAT A SIGNIFICANT PORTION OF THE AMAZON RAIN FOREST MAY ACTUALLY HAVE BEEN ORIGINALLY CULTIVATED BY MAN.
DUDE!
YOU SPEAK "DUDE"?
MANDARIN CHINESE, URDU, KALAHARI BUSHMAN CLICK-LANGUAGE... AND ELVISH.

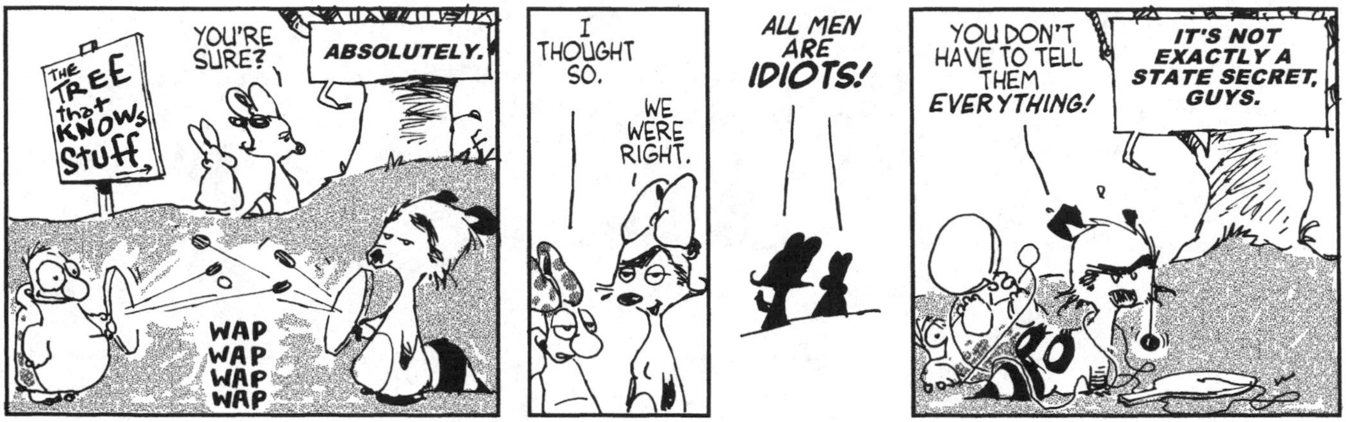
THE TREE that KNOWS Stuff
YOU'RE SURE?
ABSOLUTELY.
WAP WAP WAP WAP
I THOUGHT SO.
WE WERE RIGHT.
ALL MEN ARE IDIOTS!
YOU DON'T HAVE TO TELL THEM EVERYTHING!
IT'S NOT EXACTLY A STATE SECRET, GUYS.

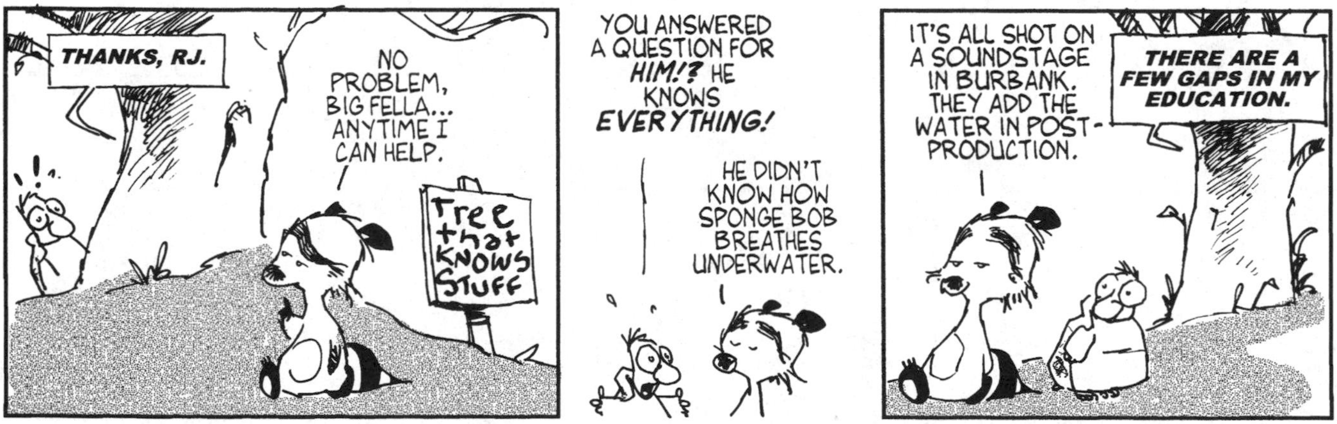
THANKS, RJ.
NO PROBLEM, BIG FELLA... ANYTIME I CAN HELP.
Tree that KNOWS Stuff
YOU ANSWERED A QUESTION FOR HIM!? HE KNOWS EVERYTHING!
HE DIDN'T KNOW HOW SPONGE BOB BREATHES UNDERWATER.
IT'S ALL SHOT ON A SOUNDSTAGE IN BURBANK. THEY ADD THE WATER IN POST-PRODUCTION.
THERE ARE A FEW GAPS IN MY EDUCATION.

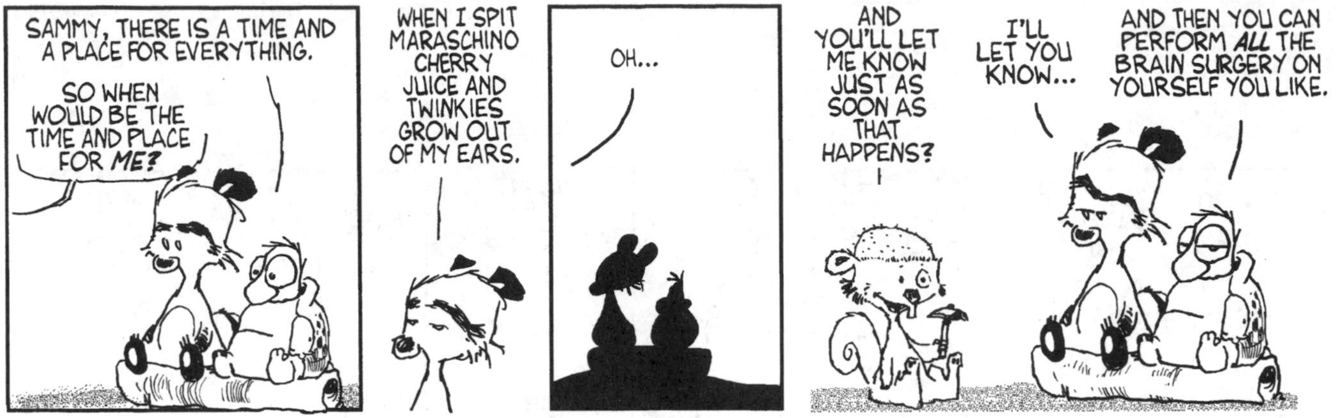
SAMMY, THERE IS A TIME AND A PLACE FOR EVERYTHING.
SO WHEN WOULD BE THE TIME AND PLACE FOR *ME?*
WHEN I SPIT MARASCHINO CHERRY JUICE AND TWINKIES GROW OUT OF MY EARS.
OH...
AND YOU'LL LET ME KNOW JUST AS SOON AS THAT HAPPENS?
I'LL LET YOU KNOW...
AND THEN YOU CAN PERFORM *ALL* THE BRAIN SURGERY ON YOURSELF YOU LIKE.

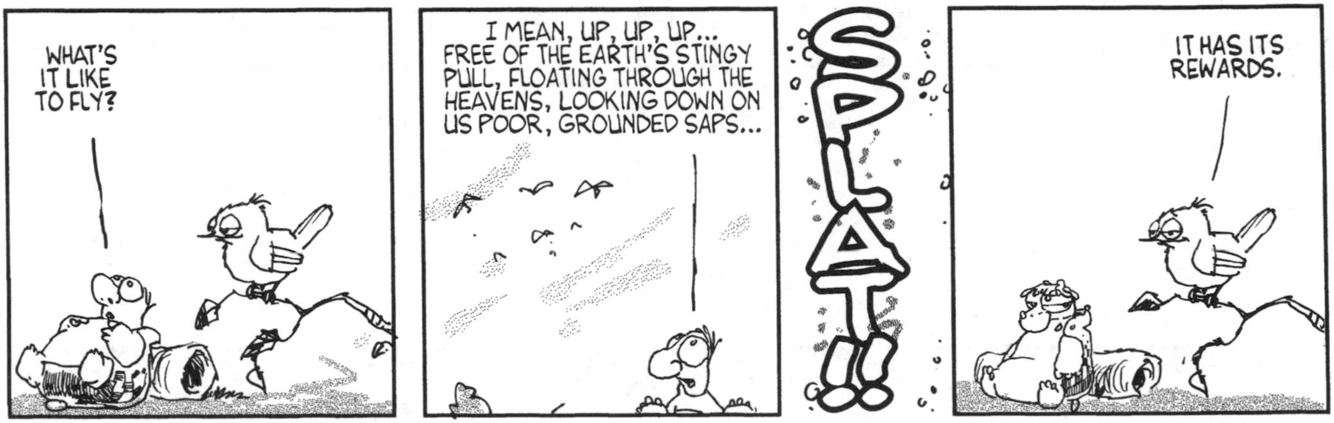
WHAT'S IT LIKE TO FLY?
I MEAN, UP, UP, UP... FREE OF THE EARTH'S STINGY PULL, FLOATING THROUGH THE HEAVENS, LOOKING DOWN ON US POOR, GROUNDED SAPS...
SPLAT!!
IT HAS ITS REWARDS.

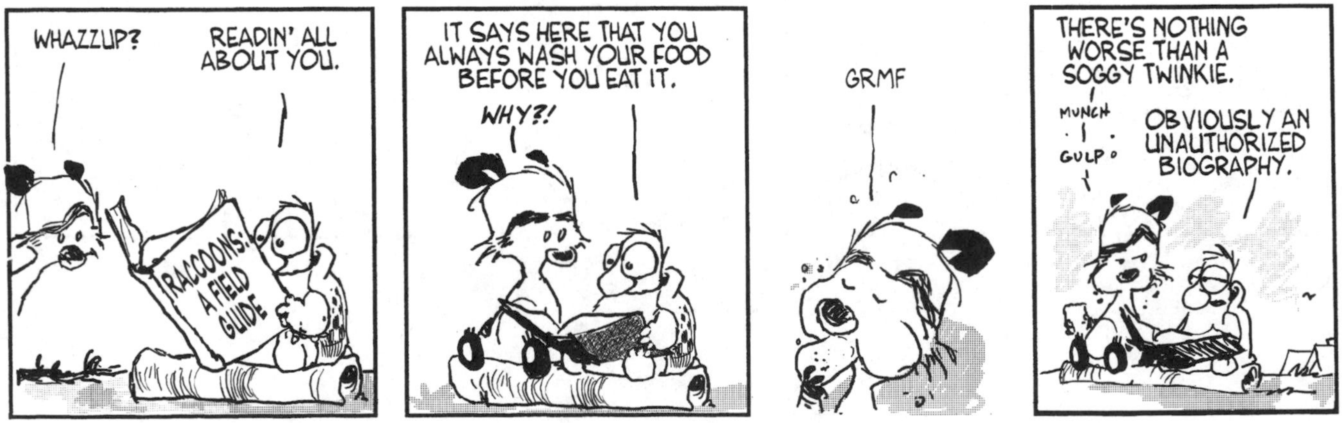
WHAZZUP?
READIN' ALL ABOUT YOU.
RACCOONS: A FIELD GUIDE
IT SAYS HERE THAT YOU ALWAYS WASH YOUR FOOD BEFORE YOU EAT IT.
WHY?!
GRMF
THERE'S NOTHING WORSE THAN A SOGGY TWINKIE.
MUNCH
GULP
OBVIOUSLY AN UNAUTHORIZED BIOGRAPHY.

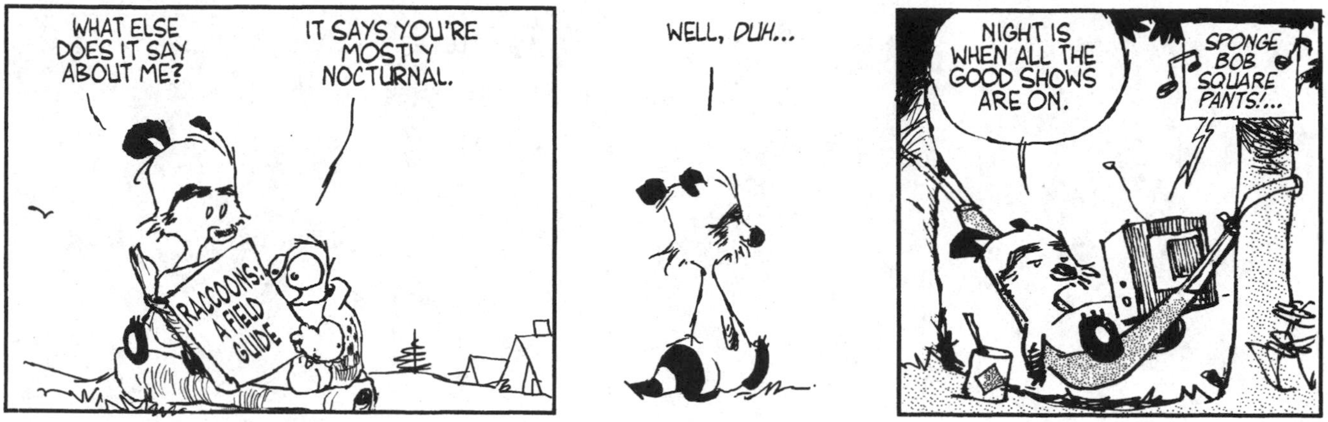
WHAT ELSE DOES IT SAY ABOUT ME?
IT SAYS YOU'RE MOSTLY NOCTURNAL.
RACCOONS: A FIELD GUIDE
WELL, *DUH*...
NIGHT IS WHEN ALL THE GOOD SHOWS ARE ON.
SPONGE BOB SQUARE PANTS!...

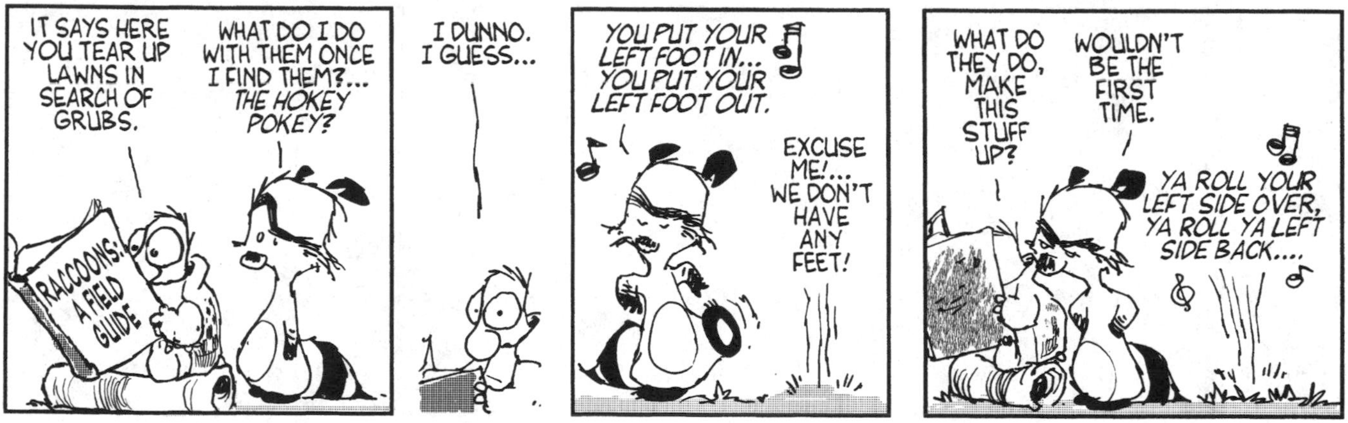
IT SAYS HERE YOU TEAR UP LAWNS IN SEARCH OF GRUBS.
WHAT DO I DO WITH THEM ONCE I FIND THEM?... *THE HOKEY POKEY?*
RACCOONS: A FIELD GUIDE
I DUNNO. I GUESS...
YOU PUT YOUR LEFT FOOT IN... YOU PUT YOUR LEFT FOOT OUT.
EXCUSE ME!... WE DON'T HAVE ANY FEET!
WHAT DO THEY DO, MAKE THIS STUFF UP?
WOULDN'T BE THE FIRST TIME.
YA ROLL YOUR LEFT SIDE OVER, YA ROLL YA LEFT SIDE BACK....

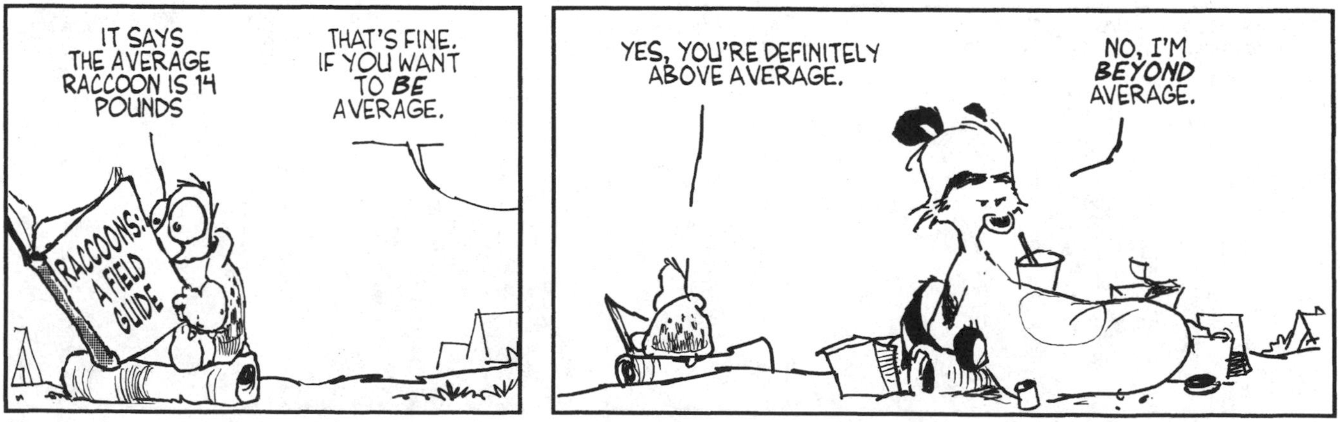
IT SAYS THE AVERAGE RACCOON IS 14 POUNDS
THAT'S FINE. IF YOU WANT TO ***BE*** AVERAGE.
RACCOONS: A FIELD GUIDE
YES, YOU'RE DEFINITELY ABOVE AVERAGE.
NO, I'M ***BEYOND*** AVERAGE.

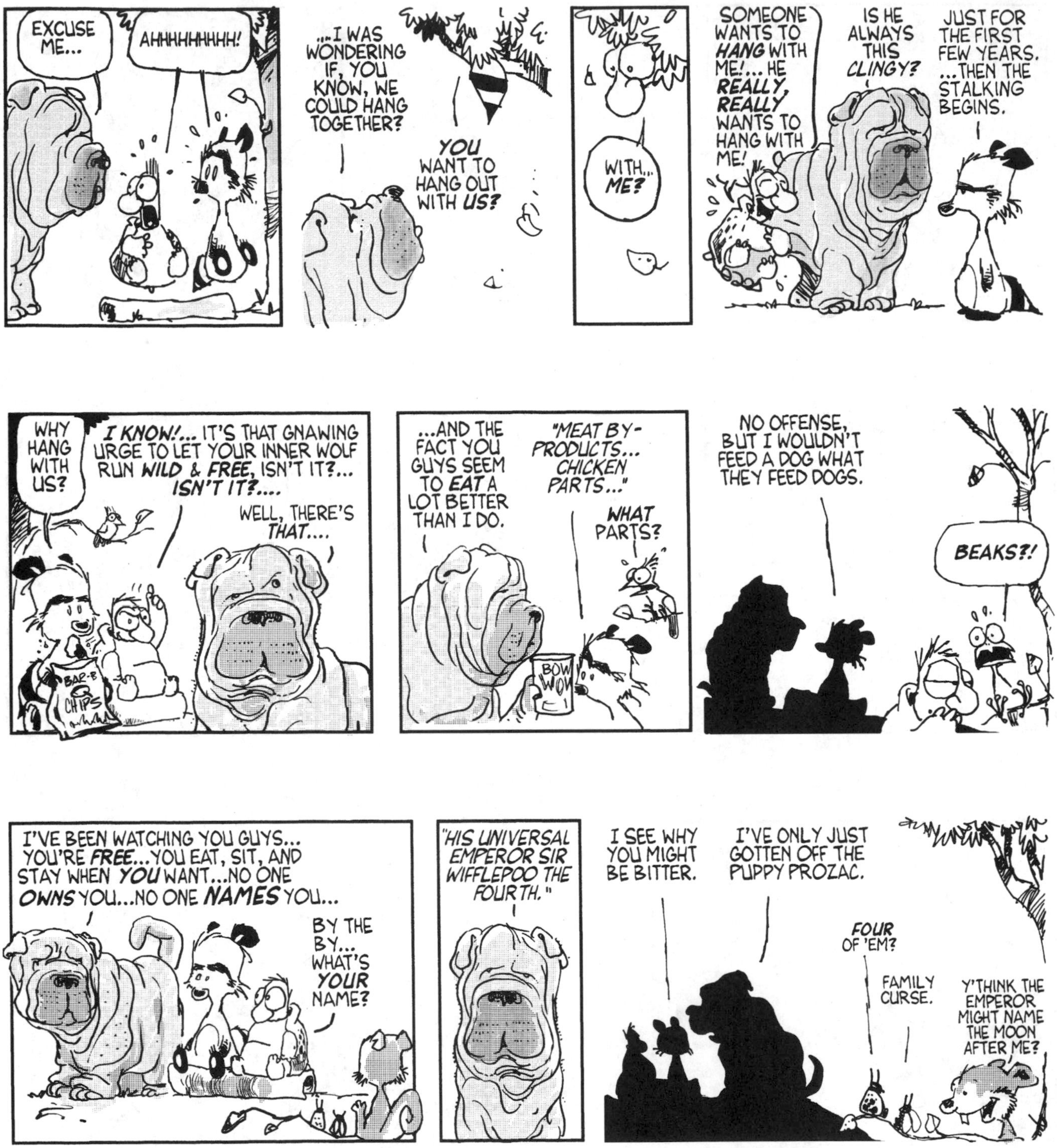
EXCUSE ME...
AHHHHHHHHH!
...I WAS WONDERING IF, YOU KNOW, WE COULD HANG TOGETHER?
YOU WANT TO HANG OUT WITH US?
WITH... ME?
SOMEONE WANTS TO HANG WITH ME!... HE REALLY, REALLY WANTS TO HANG WITH ME!
IS HE ALWAYS THIS CLINGY?
JUST FOR THE FIRST FEW YEARS. ...THEN THE STALKING BEGINS.
WHY HANG WITH US?
I KNOW!... IT'S THAT GNAWING URGE TO LET YOUR INNER WOLF RUN WILD & FREE, ISN'T IT?... ISN'T IT?....
WELL, THERE'S THAT....
BAR-B-Q CHIPS
...AND THE FACT YOU GUYS SEEM TO EAT A LOT BETTER THAN I DO.
"MEAT BY-PRODUCTS... CHICKEN PARTS..."
WHAT PARTS?
BOW WOW
NO OFFENSE, BUT I WOULDN'T FEED A DOG WHAT THEY FEED DOGS.
BEAKS?!
I'VE BEEN WATCHING YOU GUYS... YOU'RE FREE...YOU EAT, SIT, AND STAY WHEN YOU WANT...NO ONE OWNS YOU...NO ONE NAMES YOU...
BY THE BY... WHAT'S YOUR NAME?
"HIS UNIVERSAL EMPEROR SIR WIFFLEPOO THE FOURTH."
I SEE WHY YOU MIGHT BE BITTER.
I'VE ONLY JUST GOTTEN OFF THE PUPPY PROZAC.
FOUR OF 'EM?
FAMILY CURSE.
Y'THINK THE EMPEROR MIGHT NAME THE MOON AFTER ME?

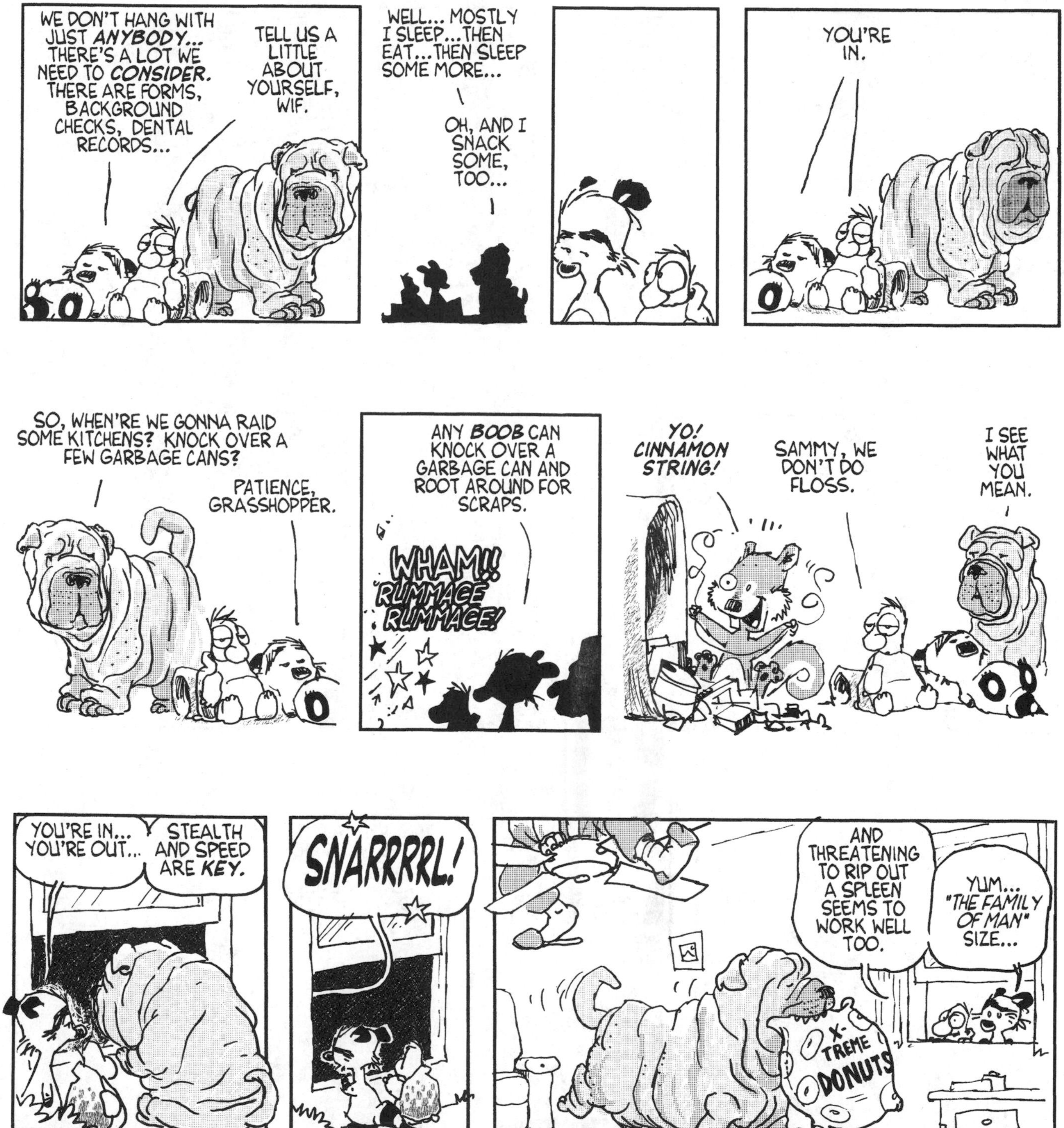
WE DON'T HANG WITH JUST ANYBODY... THERE'S A LOT WE NEED TO CONSIDER. THERE ARE FORMS, BACKGROUND CHECKS, DENTAL RECORDS...
TELL US A LITTLE ABOUT YOURSELF, WIF.
WELL... MOSTLY I SLEEP...THEN EAT...THEN SLEEP SOME MORE...
OH, AND I SNACK SOME, TOO...
YOU'RE IN.
SO, WHEN'RE WE GONNA RAID SOME KITCHENS? KNOCK OVER A FEW GARBAGE CANS?
PATIENCE, GRASSHOPPER.
ANY BOOB CAN KNOCK OVER A GARBAGE CAN AND ROOT AROUND FOR SCRAPS.
WHAM!!
RUMMAGE RUMMAGE!
YO! CINNAMON STRING!
SAMMY, WE DON'T DO FLOSS.
I SEE WHAT YOU MEAN.
YOU'RE IN... YOU'RE OUT...
STEALTH AND SPEED ARE KEY.
SNARRRRL!
AND THREATENING TO RIP OUT A SPLEEN SEEMS TO WORK WELL TOO.
YUM... "THE FAMILY OF MAN" SIZE...
X-TREME DONUTS

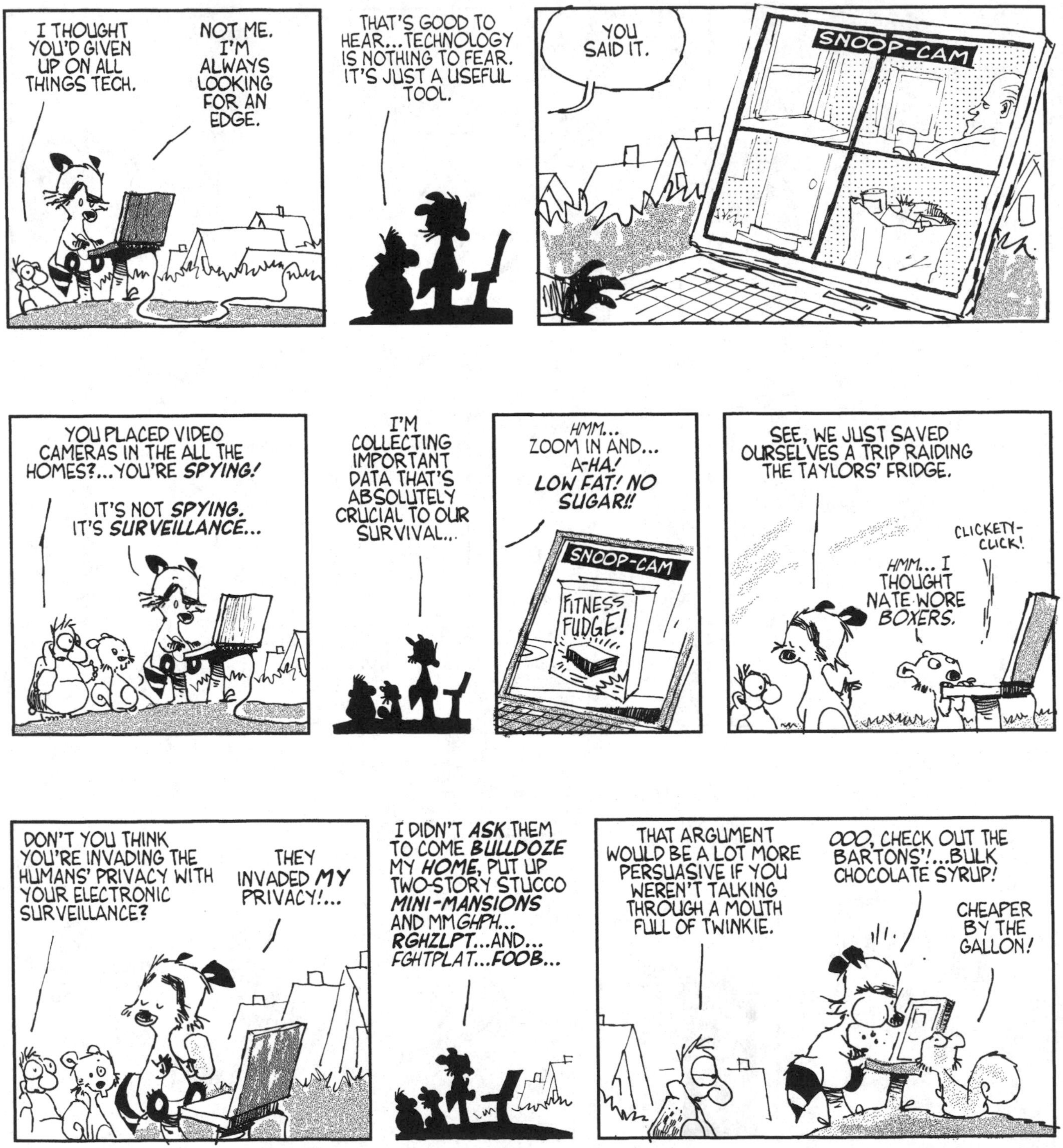
I THOUGHT YOU'D GIVEN UP ON ALL THINGS TECH.
NOT ME. I'M ALWAYS LOOKING FOR AN EDGE.
THAT'S GOOD TO HEAR... TECHNOLOGY IS NOTHING TO FEAR. IT'S JUST A USEFUL TOOL.
YOU SAID IT.
SNOOP-CAM
YOU PLACED VIDEO CAMERAS IN THE ALL THE HOMES?... YOU'RE SPYING!
IT'S NOT SPYING. IT'S SURVEILLANCE...
I'M COLLECTING IMPORTANT DATA THAT'S ABSOLUTELY CRUCIAL TO OUR SURVIVAL...
HMM... ZOOM IN AND... A-HA! LOW FAT! NO SUGAR!!
SNOOP-CAM
FITNESS FUDGE!
SEE, WE JUST SAVED OURSELVES A TRIP RAIDING THE TAYLORS' FRIDGE.
CLICKETY-CLICK!
HMM... I THOUGHT NATE WORE BOXERS.
DON'T YOU THINK YOU'RE INVADING THE HUMANS' PRIVACY WITH YOUR ELECTRONIC SURVEILLANCE?
THEY INVADED MY PRIVACY!...
I DIDN'T ASK THEM TO COME BULLDOZE MY HOME, PUT UP TWO-STORY STUCCO MINI-MANSIONS AND MMGHPH... RGHZLPT...AND... FGHTPLAT...FOOB...
THAT ARGUMENT WOULD BE A LOT MORE PERSUASIVE IF YOU WEREN'T TALKING THROUGH A MOUTH FULL OF TWINKIE.
OOO, CHECK OUT THE BARTONS'!...BULK CHOCOLATE SYRUP!
CHEAPER BY THE GALLON!

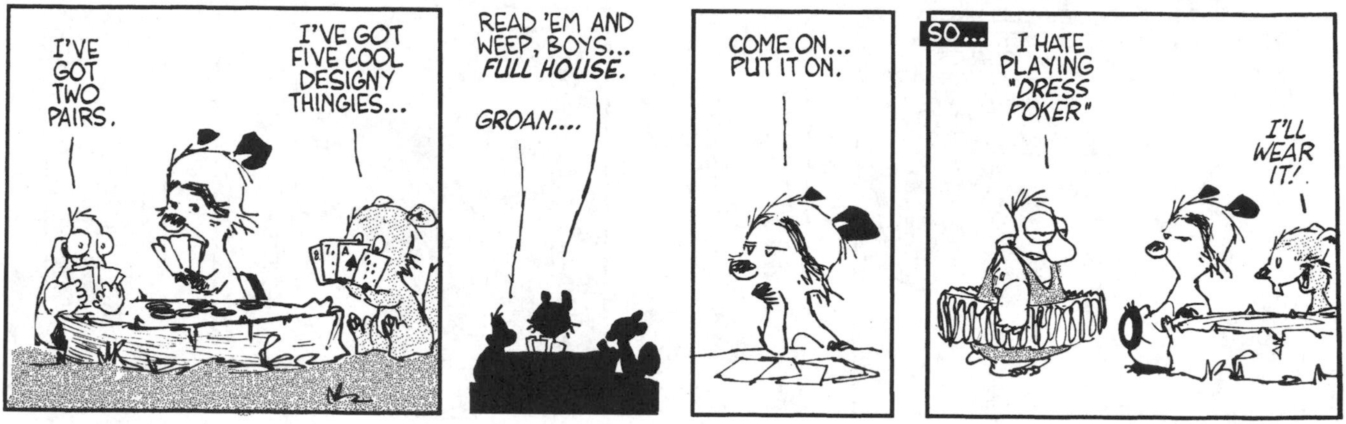
I'VE GOT TWO PAIRS.
I'VE GOT FIVE COOL DESIGNY THINGIES...
READ 'EM AND WEEP, BOYS... FULL HOUSE.
GROAN....
COME ON... PUT IT ON.
SO...
I HATE PLAYING "DRESS POKER"
I'LL WEAR IT!

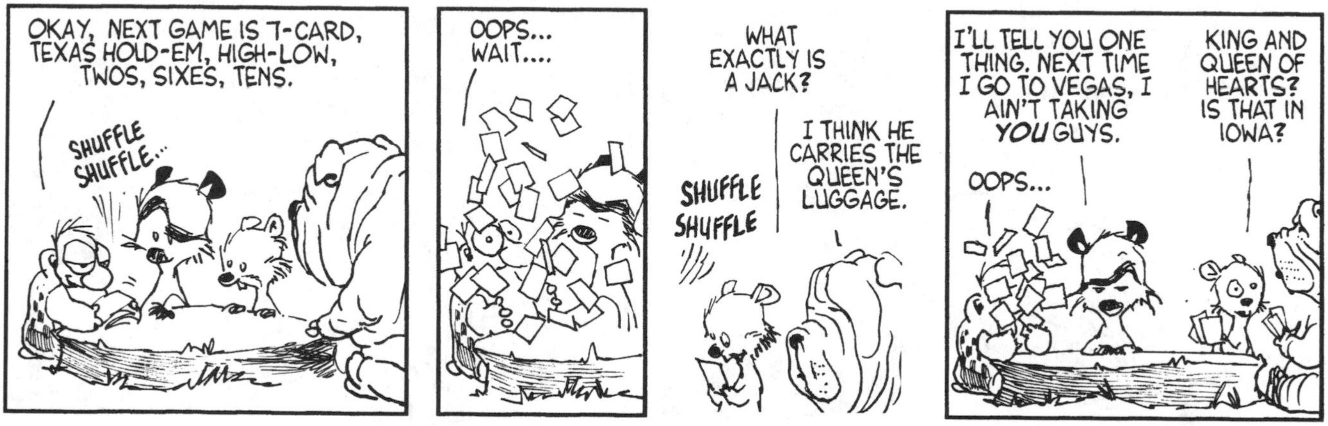
OKAY, NEXT GAME IS 7-CARD, TEXAS HOLD-EM, HIGH-LOW, TWOS, SIXES, TENS.
SHUFFLE SHUFFLE...
OOPS... WAIT....
WHAT EXACTLY IS A JACK?
I THINK HE CARRIES THE QUEEN'S LUGGAGE.
SHUFFLE SHUFFLE
I'LL TELL YOU ONE THING. NEXT TIME I GO TO VEGAS, I AIN'T TAKING YOU GUYS.
OOPS...
KING AND QUEEN OF HEARTS? IS THAT IN IOWA?

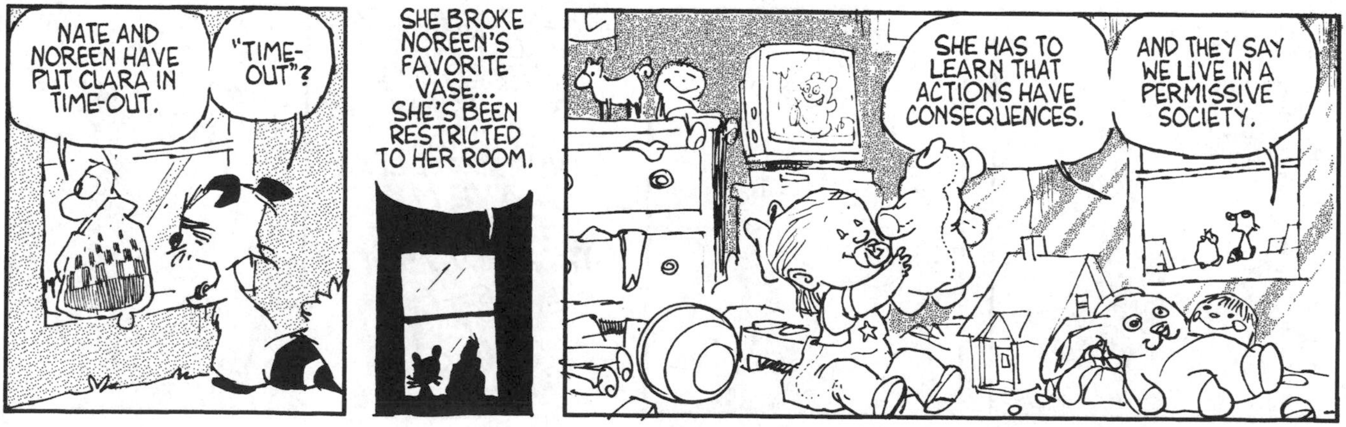
NATE AND NOREEN HAVE PUT CLARA IN TIME-OUT.
"TIME-OUT"?
SHE BROKE NOREEN'S FAVORITE VASE... SHE'S BEEN RESTRICTED TO HER ROOM.
SHE HAS TO LEARN THAT ACTIONS HAVE CONSEQUENCES.
AND THEY SAY WE LIVE IN A PERMISSIVE SOCIETY.

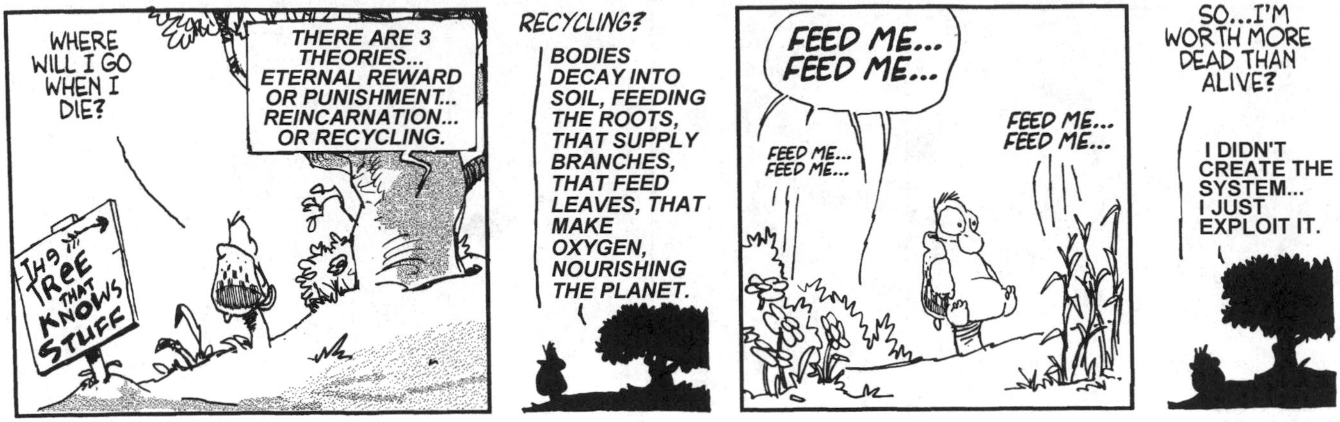
WHERE WILL I GO WHEN I DIE?
THERE ARE 3 THEORIES... ETERNAL REWARD OR PUNISHMENT... REINCARNATION... OR RECYCLING.
THE TREE THAT KNOWS STUFF
RECYCLING?
BODIES DECAY INTO SOIL, FEEDING THE ROOTS, THAT SUPPLY BRANCHES, THAT FEED LEAVES, THAT MAKE OXYGEN, NOURISHING THE PLANET.
FEED ME... FEED ME...
FEED ME... FEED ME...
FEED ME... FEED ME...
SO...I'M WORTH MORE DEAD THAN ALIVE?
I DIDN'T CREATE THE SYSTEM... I JUST EXPLOIT IT.

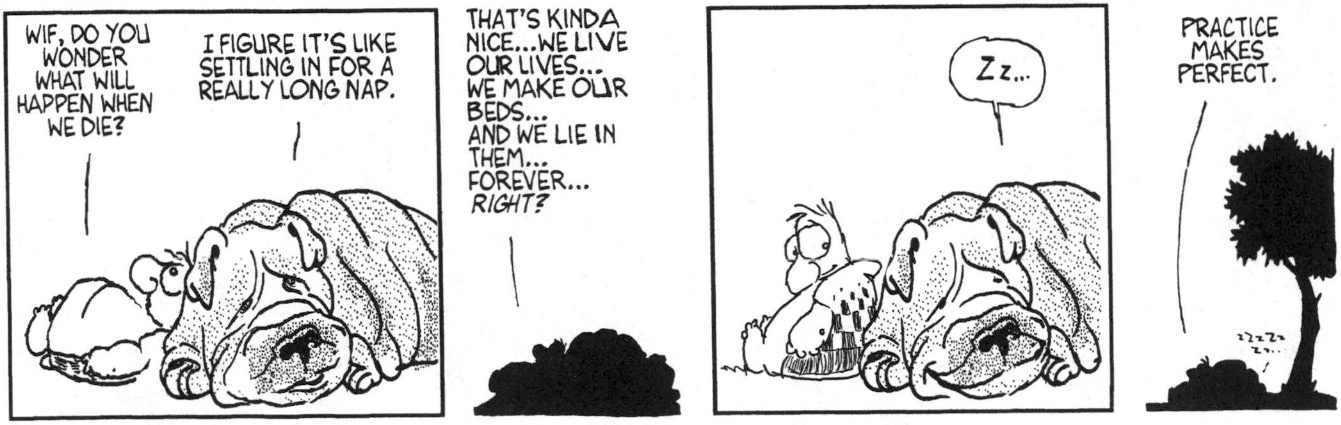
WIF, DO YOU WONDER WHAT WILL HAPPEN WHEN WE DIE?
I FIGURE IT'S LIKE SETTLING IN FOR A REALLY LONG NAP.
THAT'S KINDA NICE...WE LIVE OUR LIVES... WE MAKE OUR BEDS... AND WE LIE IN THEM... FOREVER... RIGHT?
Zz...
PRACTICE MAKES PERFECT.

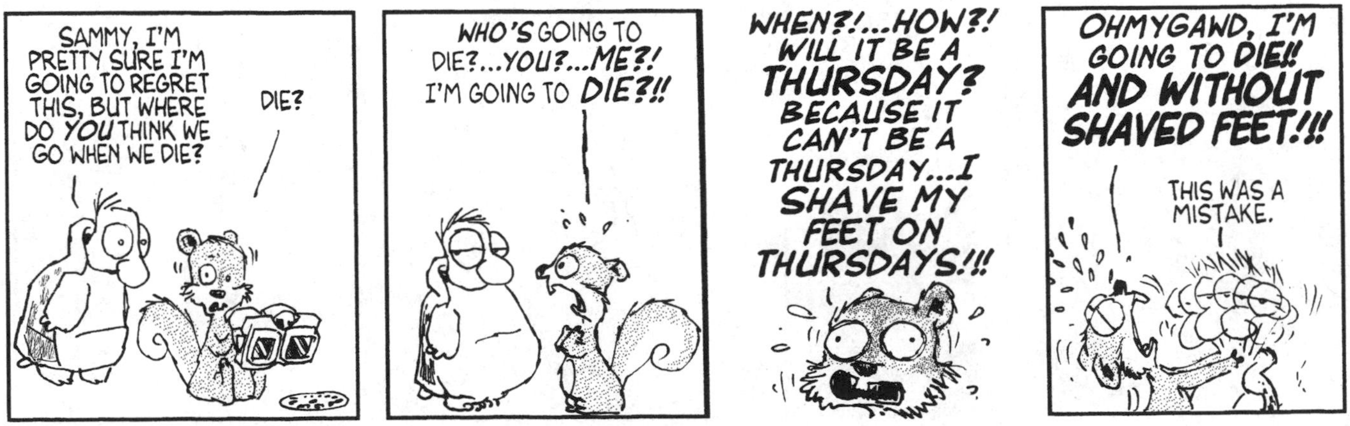
SAMMY, I'M PRETTY SURE I'M GOING TO REGRET THIS, BUT WHERE DO YOU THINK WE GO WHEN WE DIE?
DIE?
WHO'S GOING TO DIE?...YOU?...ME?! I'M GOING TO DIE?!!
WHEN?!...HOW?! WILL IT BE A THURSDAY? BECAUSE IT CAN'T BE A THURSDAY...I SHAVE MY FEET ON THURSDAYS!!!
OHMYGAND, I'M GOING TO DIE!! AND WITHOUT SHAVED FEET!!!
THIS WAS A MISTAKE.

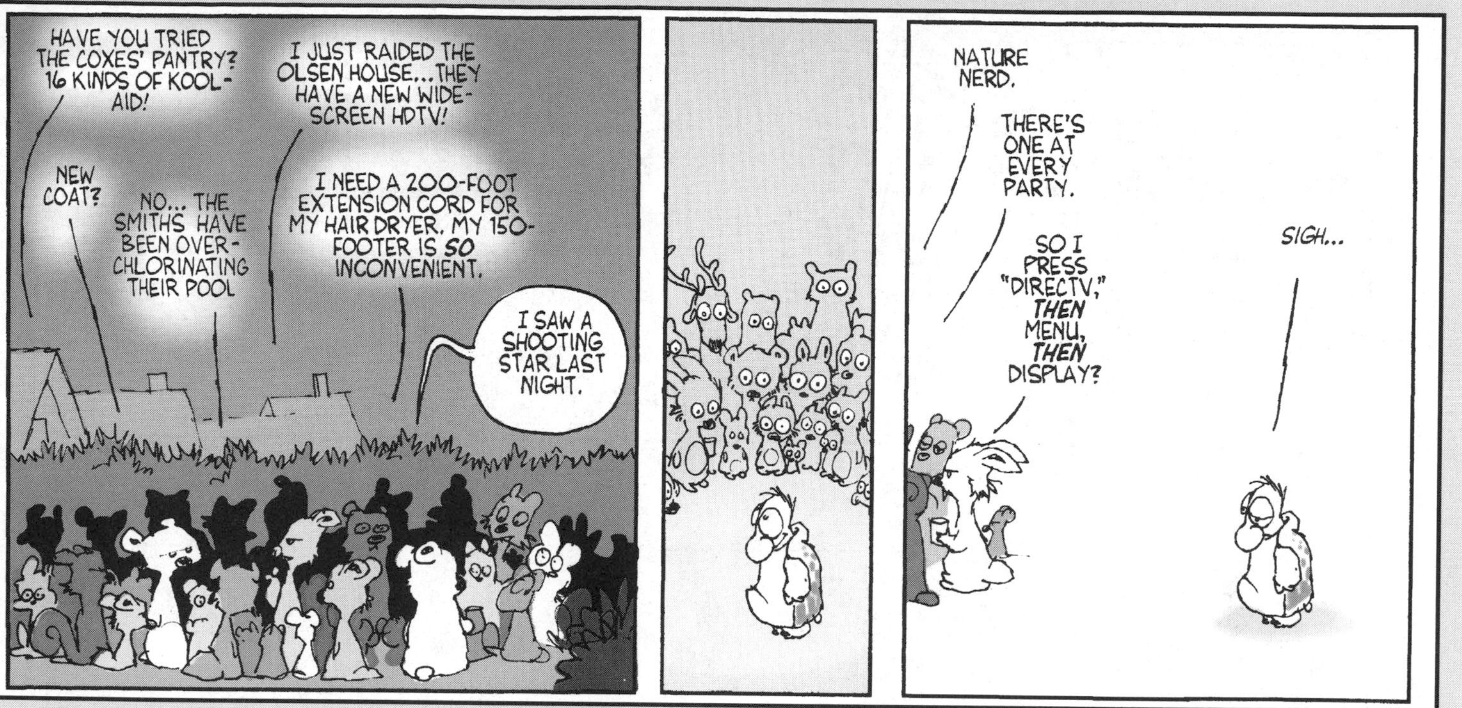
HAVE YOU TRIED THE COXES' PANTRY? 16 KINDS OF KOOL-AID!
I JUST RAIDED THE OLSEN HOUSE...THEY HAVE A NEW WIDE-SCREEN HDTV!
NEW COAT?
NO... THE SMITHS HAVE BEEN OVER-CHLORINATING THEIR POOL
I NEED A 200-FOOT EXTENSION CORD FOR MY HAIR DRYER. MY 150-FOOTER IS SO INCONVENIENT.
I SAW A SHOOTING STAR LAST NIGHT.
NATURE NERD.
THERE'S ONE AT EVERY PARTY.
SO I PRESS "DIRECTV," THEN MENU, THEN DISPLAY?
SIGH...

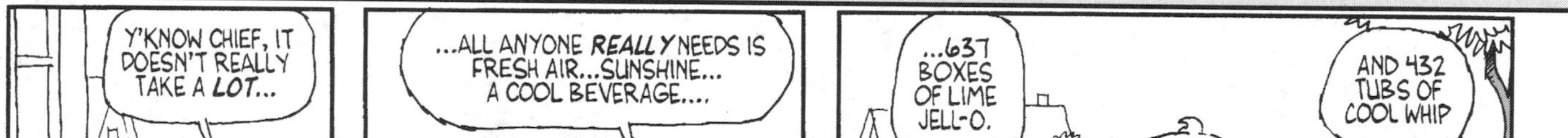
Y'KNOW CHIEF, IT DOESN'T REALLY TAKE A LOT...
...ALL ANYONE REALLY NEEDS IS FRESH AIR...SUNSHINE... A COOL BEVERAGE....
...637 BOXES OF LIME JELL-O.
AND 432 TUBS OF COOL WHIP
IT JUST DOESN'T GET ANY BETTER THAN...
HOLD IT...
GENTLE-MEN?
FOING!
I STAND CORRECTED.

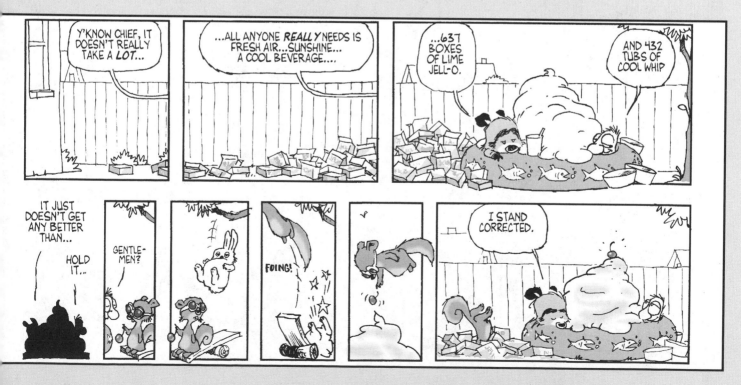

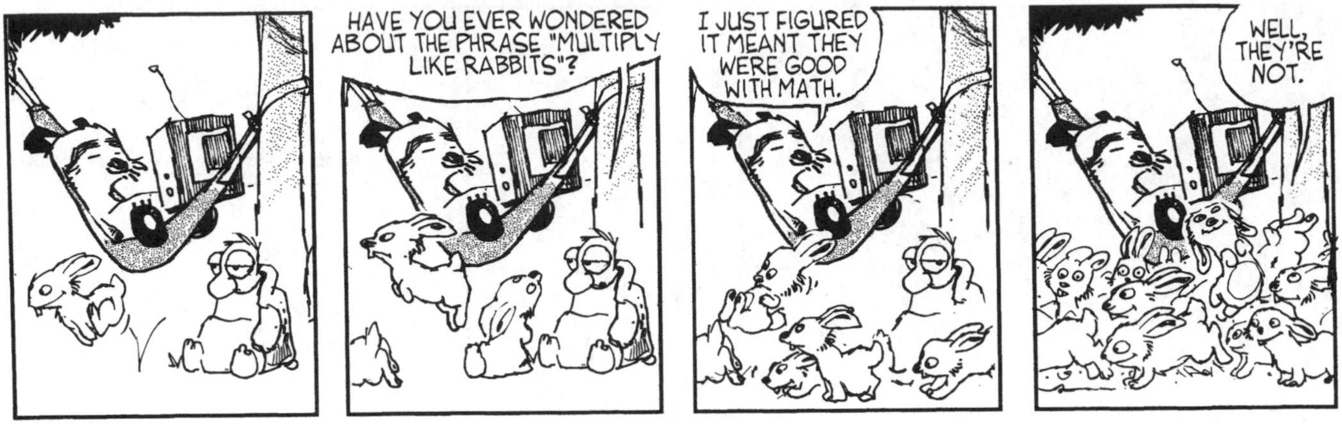
HAVE YOU EVER WONDERED ABOUT THE PHRASE "MULTIPLY LIKE RABBITS"?
I JUST FIGURED IT MEANT THEY WERE GOOD WITH MATH.
WELL, THEY'RE NOT.

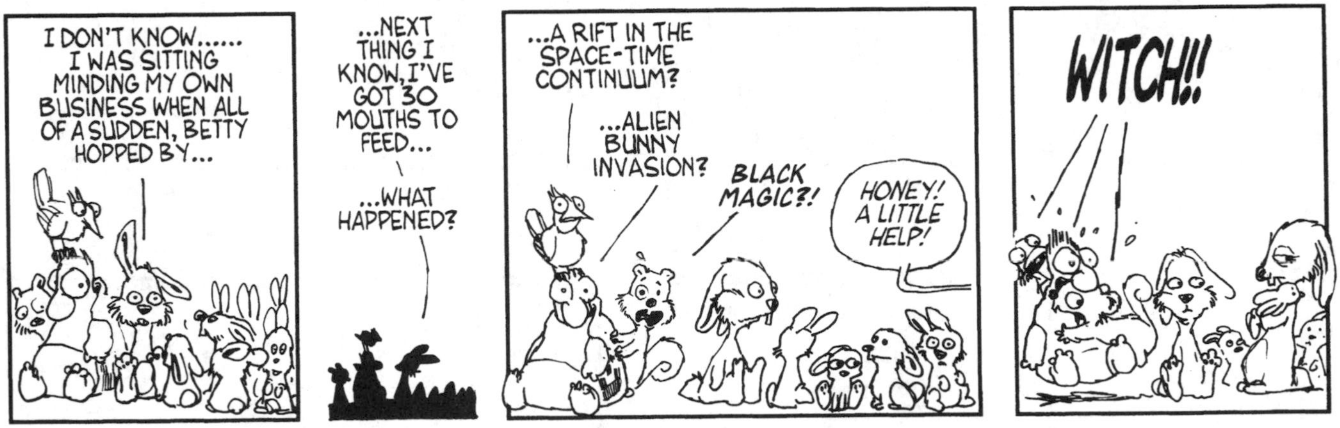
I DON'T KNOW...... I WAS SITTING MINDING MY OWN BUSINESS WHEN ALL OF A SUDDEN, BETTY HOPPED BY...
...NEXT THING I KNOW, I'VE GOT 30 MOUTHS TO FEED...
...WHAT HAPPENED?
...A RIFT IN THE SPACE-TIME CONTINUUM?
...ALIEN BUNNY INVASION?
BLACK MAGIC?!
HONEY! A LITTLE HELP!
WITCH!!

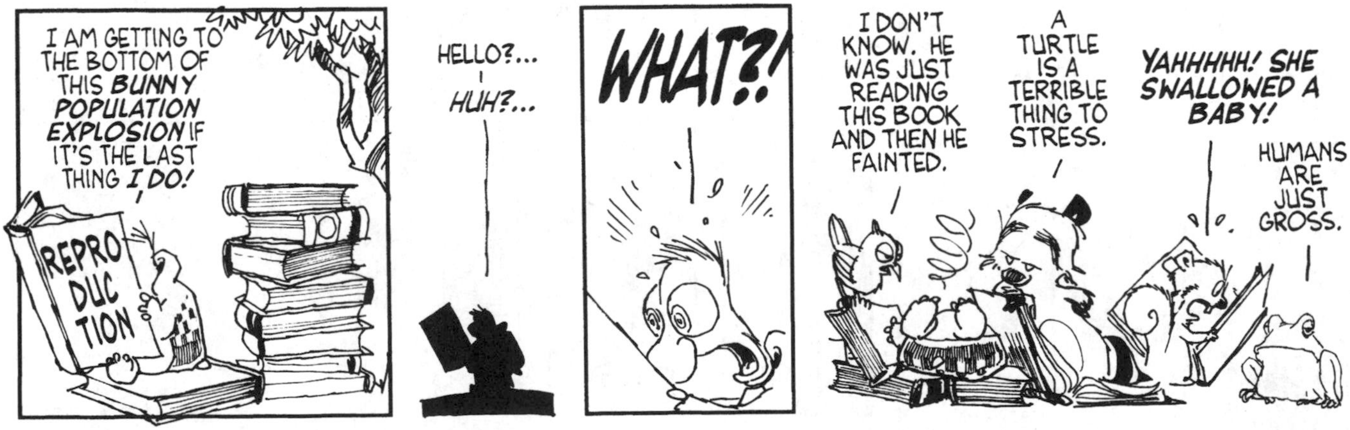
I AM GETTING TO THE BOTTOM OF THIS BUNNY POPULATION EXPLOSION IF IT'S THE LAST THING I DO!
REPRODUCTION
HELLO?...
HUH?...
WHAT?!
I DON'T KNOW. HE WAS JUST READING THIS BOOK AND THEN HE FAINTED.
A TURTLE IS A TERRIBLE THING TO STRESS.
YAHHHHH! SHE SWALLOWED A BABY!
HUMANS ARE JUST GROSS.

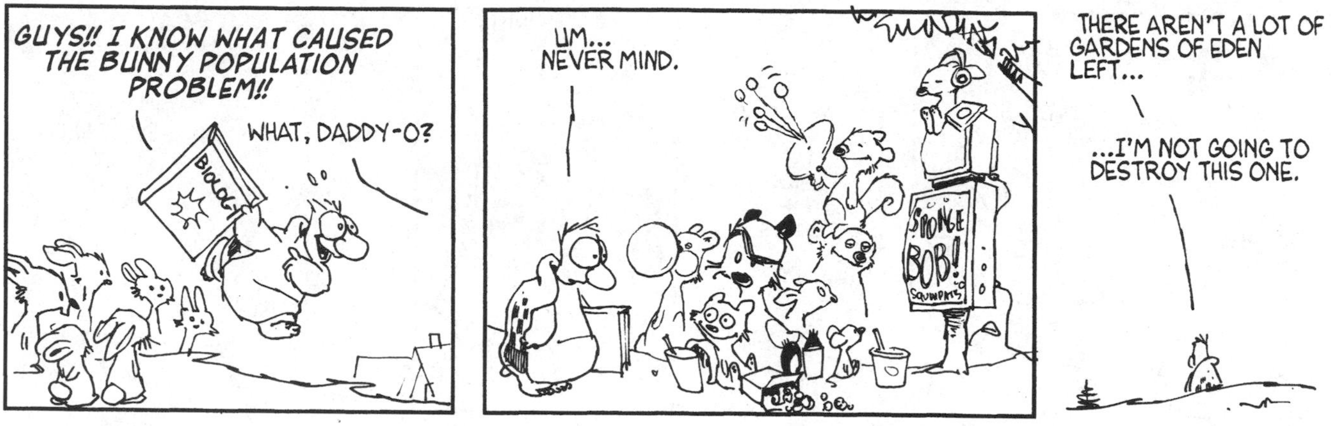
GUYS!! I KNOW WHAT CAUSED THE BUNNY POPULATION PROBLEM!!
WHAT, DADDY-O?
UM... NEVER MIND.
SPONGE BOB!
THERE AREN'T A LOT OF GARDENS OF EDEN LEFT...
...I'M NOT GOING TO DESTROY THIS ONE.

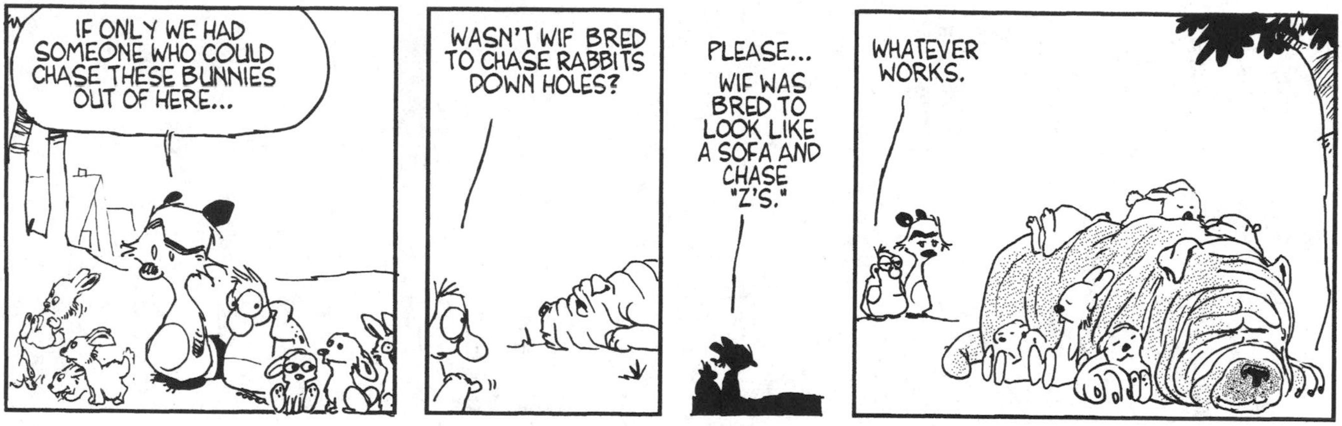
IF ONLY WE HAD SOMEONE WHO COULD CHASE THESE BUNNIES OUT OF HERE...
WASN'T WIF BRED TO CHASE RABBITS DOWN HOLES?
PLEASE... WIF WAS BRED TO LOOK LIKE A SOFA AND CHASE "Z'S."
WHATEVER WORKS.

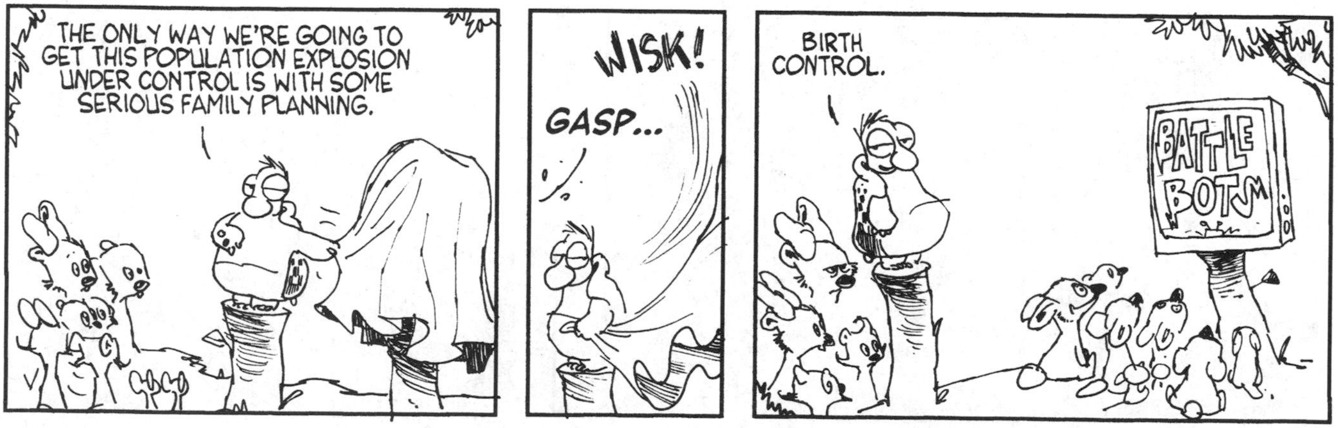
THE ONLY WAY WE'RE GOING TO GET THIS POPULATION EXPLOSION UNDER CONTROL IS WITH SOME SERIOUS FAMILY PLANNING.
WISK!
GASP...
BIRTH CONTROL.
BATTLE BOTS

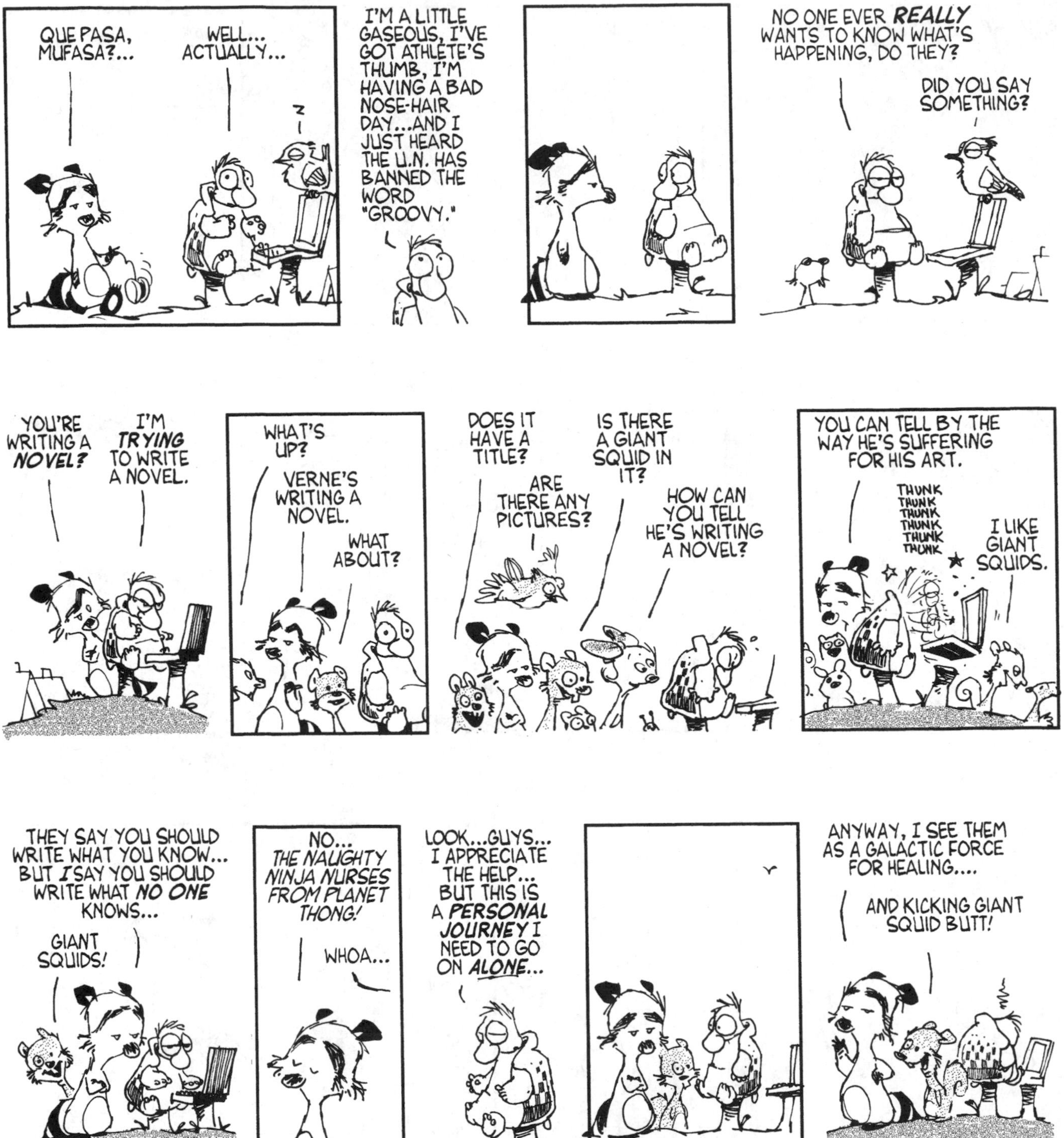
QUE PASA, MUFASA?...
WELL... ACTUALLY...
z
I'M A LITTLE GASEOUS, I'VE GOT ATHLETE'S THUMB, I'M HAVING A BAD NOSE-HAIR DAY...AND I JUST HEARD THE U.N. HAS BANNED THE WORD "GROOVY."
NO ONE EVER **REALLY** WANTS TO KNOW WHAT'S HAPPENING, DO THEY?
DID YOU SAY SOMETHING?
YOU'RE WRITING A ***NOVEL?***
I'M ***TRYING*** TO WRITE A NOVEL.
WHAT'S UP?
VERNE'S WRITING A NOVEL.
WHAT ABOUT?
DOES IT HAVE A TITLE?
ARE THERE ANY PICTURES?
IS THERE A GIANT SQUID IN IT?
HOW CAN YOU TELL HE'S WRITING A NOVEL?
YOU CAN TELL BY THE WAY HE'S SUFFERING FOR HIS ART.
THUNK THUNK THUNK THUNK THUNK THUNK
I LIKE GIANT SQUIDS.
THEY SAY YOU SHOULD WRITE WHAT YOU KNOW... BUT *I* SAY YOU SHOULD WRITE WHAT ***NO ONE*** KNOWS...
GIANT SQUIDS!
NO... *THE NAUGHTY NINJA NURSES FROM PLANET THONG!*
WHOA...
LOOK...GUYS... I APPRECIATE THE HELP... BUT THIS IS A ***PERSONAL JOURNEY*** I NEED TO GO ON ***ALONE***...
ANYWAY, I SEE THEM AS A GALACTIC FORCE FOR HEALING....
AND KICKING GIANT SQUID BUTT!

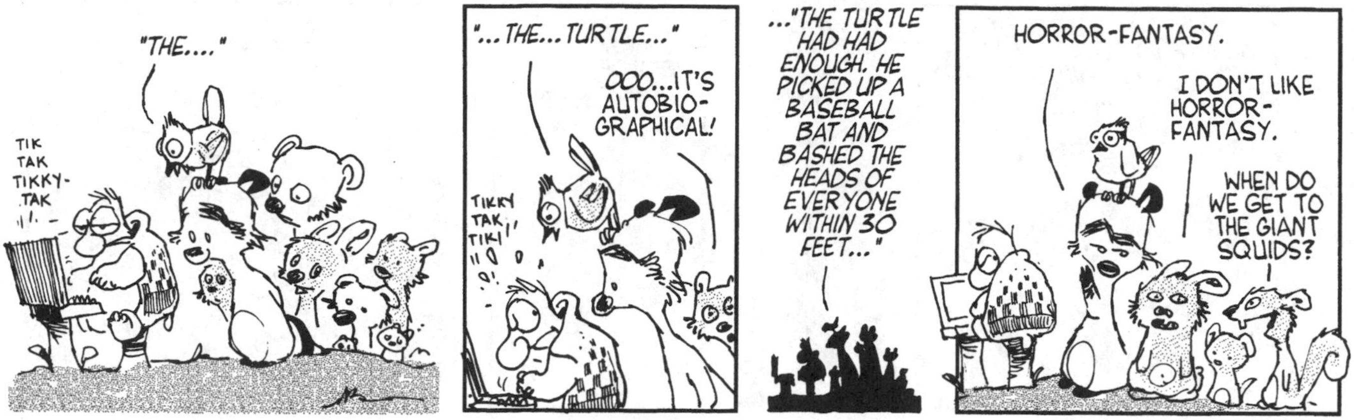
"THE...."
TIK TAK TIKKY-TAK
"...THE...TURTLE..."
TIKKY TAK TIKI
OOO...IT'S AUTOBIO-GRAPHICAL!
..."THE TURTLE HAD HAD ENOUGH. HE PICKED UP A BASEBALL BAT AND BASHED THE HEADS OF EVERYONE WITHIN 30 FEET..."
HORROR-FANTASY.
I DON'T LIKE HORROR-FANTASY.
WHEN DO WE GET TO THE GIANT SQUIDS?

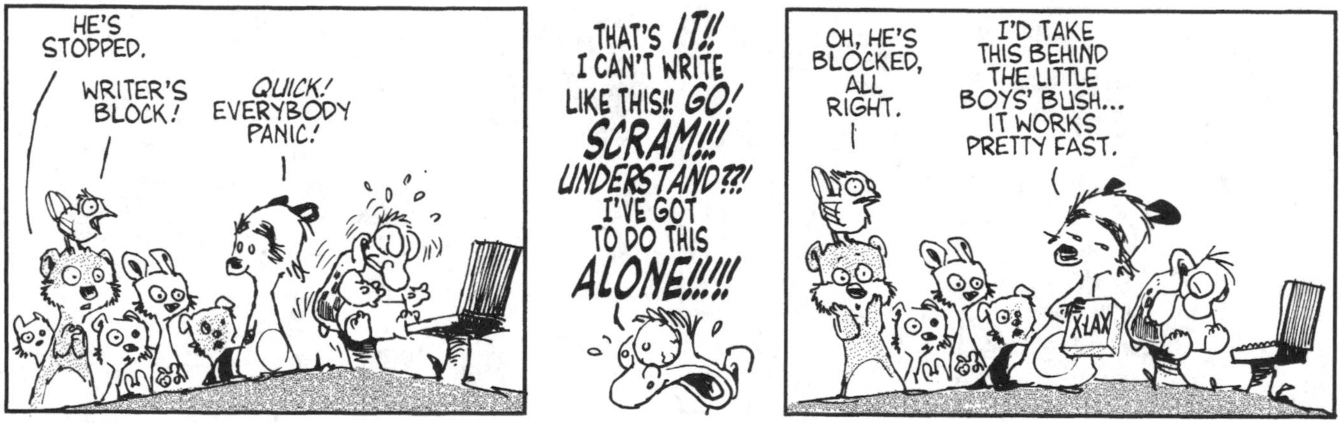
HE'S STOPPED.
WRITER'S BLOCK!
QUICK! EVERYBODY PANIC!
THAT'S IT!! I CAN'T WRITE LIKE THIS!! GO! SCRAM!!! UNDERSTAND??! I'VE GOT TO DO THIS ALONE!!!!!
OH, HE'S BLOCKED, ALL RIGHT.
I'D TAKE THIS BEHIND THE LITTLE BOYS' BUSH... IT WORKS PRETTY FAST.
X-LAX

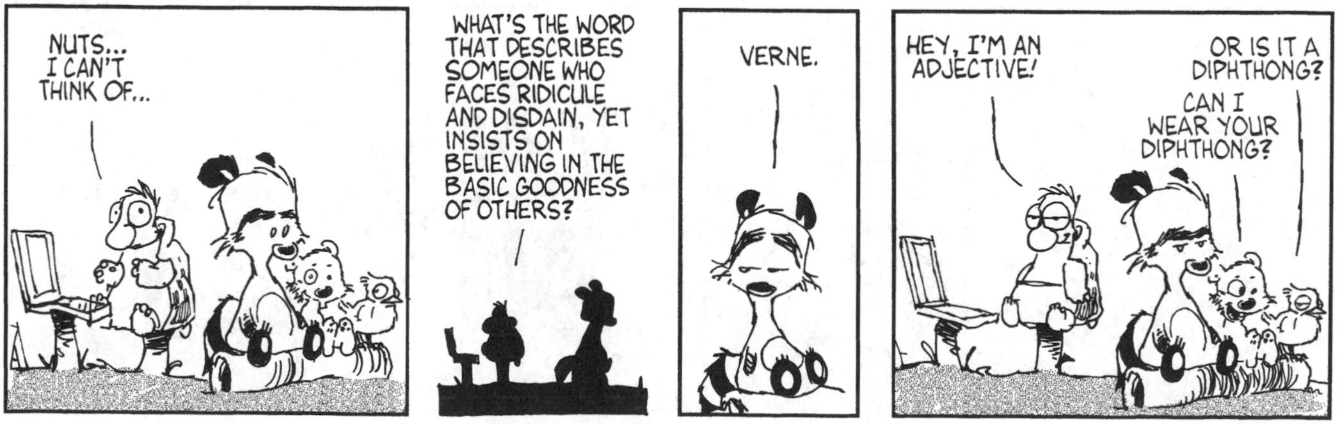
NUTS... I CAN'T THINK OF...
WHAT'S THE WORD THAT DESCRIBES SOMEONE WHO FACES RIDICULE AND DISDAIN, YET INSISTS ON BELIEVING IN THE BASIC GOODNESS OF OTHERS?
VERNE.
HEY, I'M AN ADJECTIVE!
OR IS IT A DIPHTHONG?
CAN I WEAR YOUR DIPHTHONG?

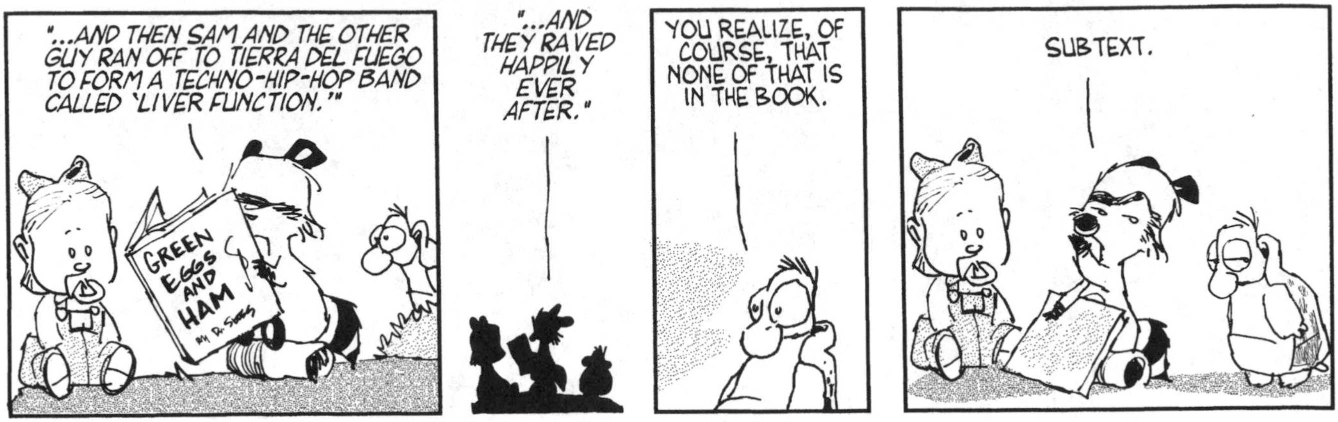
"...AND THEN SAM AND THE OTHER GUY RAN OFF TO TIERRA DEL FUEGO TO FORM A TECHNO-HIP-HOP BAND CALLED 'LIVER FUNCTION.'"
GREEN EGGS AND HAM
"...AND THEY RAVED HAPPILY EVER AFTER."
YOU REALIZE, OF COURSE, THAT NONE OF THAT IS IN THE BOOK.
SUBTEXT.

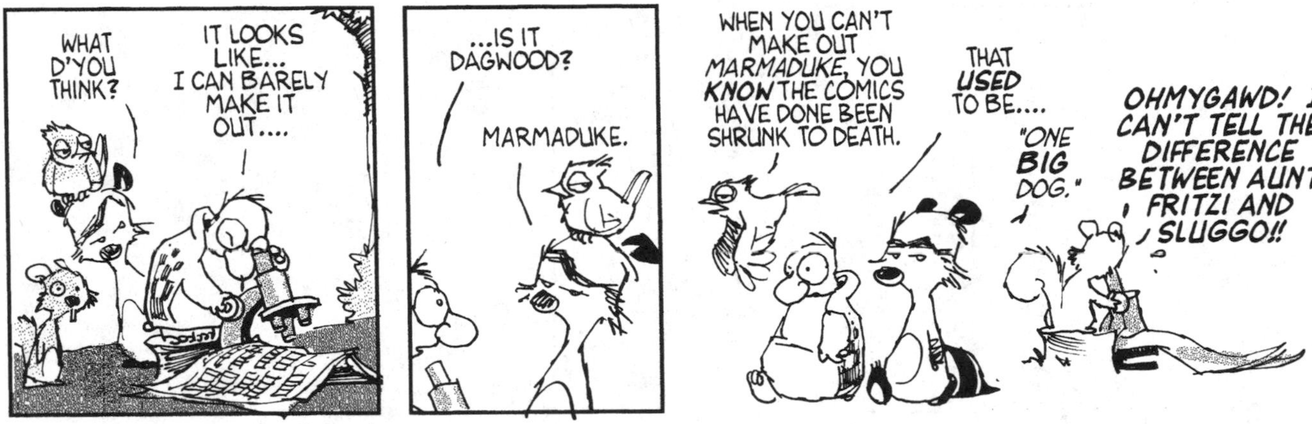
WHAT D'YOU THINK?
IT LOOKS LIKE... I CAN BARELY MAKE IT OUT....
...IS IT DAGWOOD?
MARMADUKE.
WHEN YOU CAN'T MAKE OUT MARMADUKE, YOU KNOW THE COMICS HAVE DONE BEEN SHRUNK TO DEATH.
THAT USED TO BE....
"ONE BIG DOG."
OHMYGAWD! I CAN'T TELL THE DIFFERENCE BETWEEN AUNT FRITZI AND SLUGGO!!

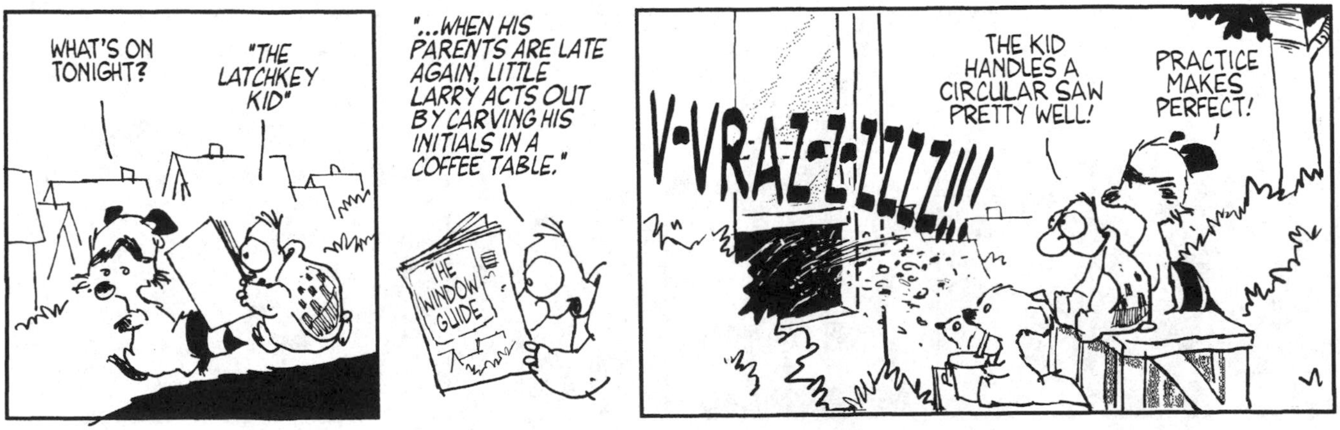
WHAT'S ON TONIGHT?
"THE LATCHKEY KID"
"...WHEN HIS PARENTS ARE LATE AGAIN, LITTLE LARRY ACTS OUT BY CARVING HIS INITIALS IN A COFFEE TABLE."
THE WINDOW GUIDE
V-VRAZ-Z-ZZZZ!!!
THE KID HANDLES A CIRCULAR SAW PRETTY WELL!
PRACTICE MAKES PERFECT!

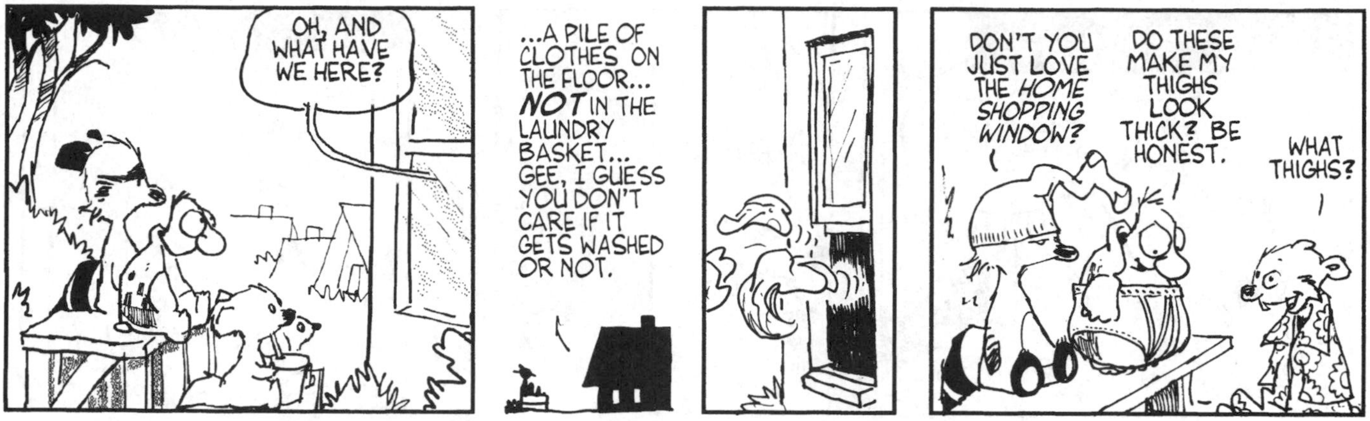

OH, AND WHAT HAVE WE HERE?
...A PILE OF CLOTHES ON THE FLOOR... *NOT* IN THE LAUNDRY BASKET... GEE, I GUESS YOU DON'T CARE IF IT GETS WASHED OR NOT.
DON'T YOU JUST LOVE THE *HOME SHOPPING WINDOW?*
DO THESE MAKE MY THIGHS LOOK THICK? BE HONEST.
WHAT THIGHS?

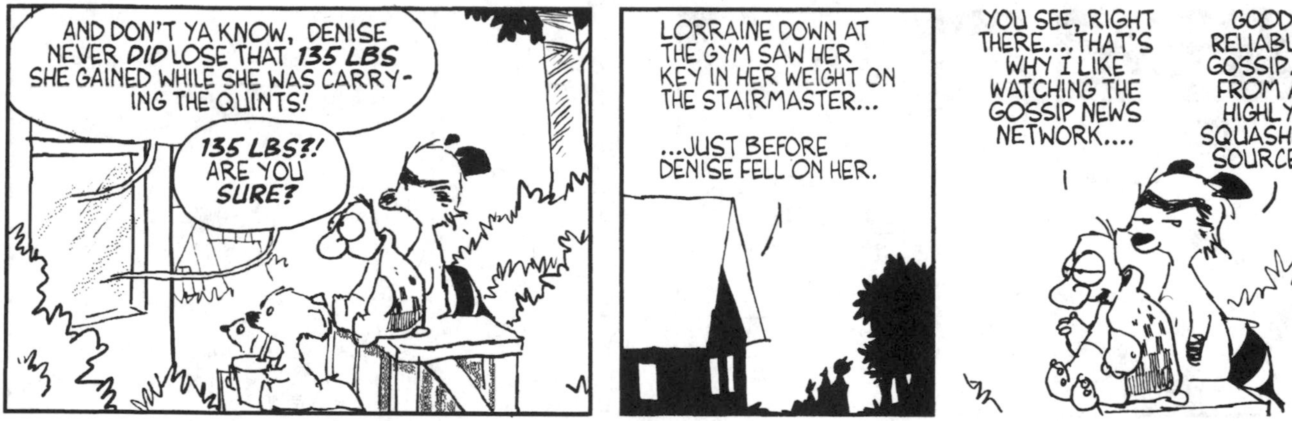

AND DON'T YA KNOW, DENISE NEVER *DID* LOSE THAT *135 LBS* SHE GAINED WHILE SHE WAS CARRYING THE QUINTS!
135 LBS?! ARE YOU *SURE?*
LORRAINE DOWN AT THE GYM SAW HER KEY IN HER WEIGHT ON THE STAIRMASTER...
...JUST BEFORE DENISE FELL ON HER.
YOU SEE, RIGHT THERE.... THAT'S WHY I LIKE WATCHING THE GOSSIP NEWS NETWORK....
GOOD, RELIABLE GOSSIP... FROM A HIGHLY SQUASHED SOURCE.

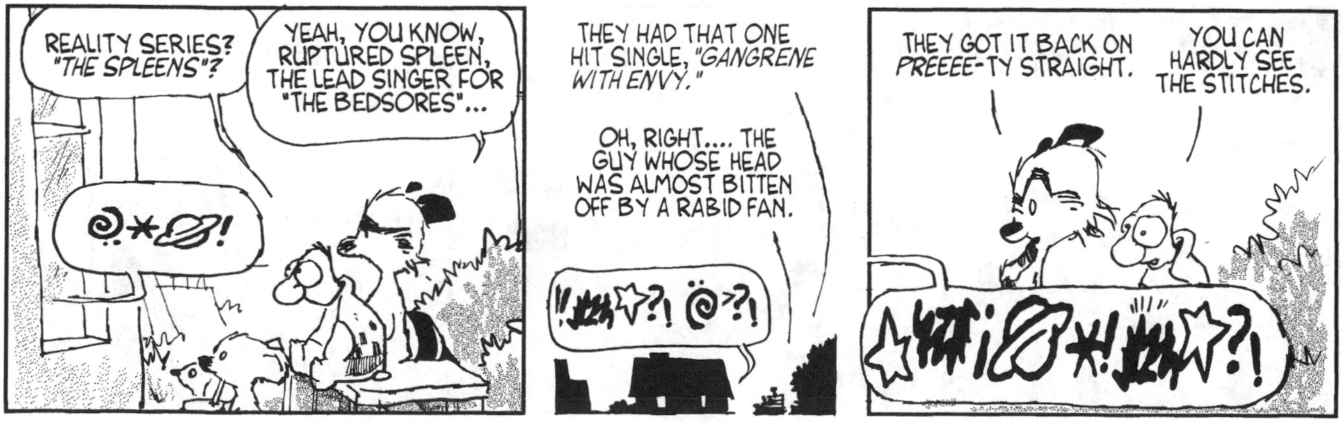

REALITY SERIES? *"THE SPLEENS"?*
YEAH, YOU KNOW, RUPTURED SPLEEN, THE LEAD SINGER FOR "THE BEDSORES"...
THEY HAD THAT ONE HIT SINGLE, *"GANGRENE WITH ENVY."*
OH, RIGHT.... THE GUY WHOSE HEAD WAS ALMOST BITTEN OFF BY A RABID FAN.
THEY GOT IT BACK ON *PREEEE*-TY STRAIGHT.
YOU CAN HARDLY SEE THE STITCHES.

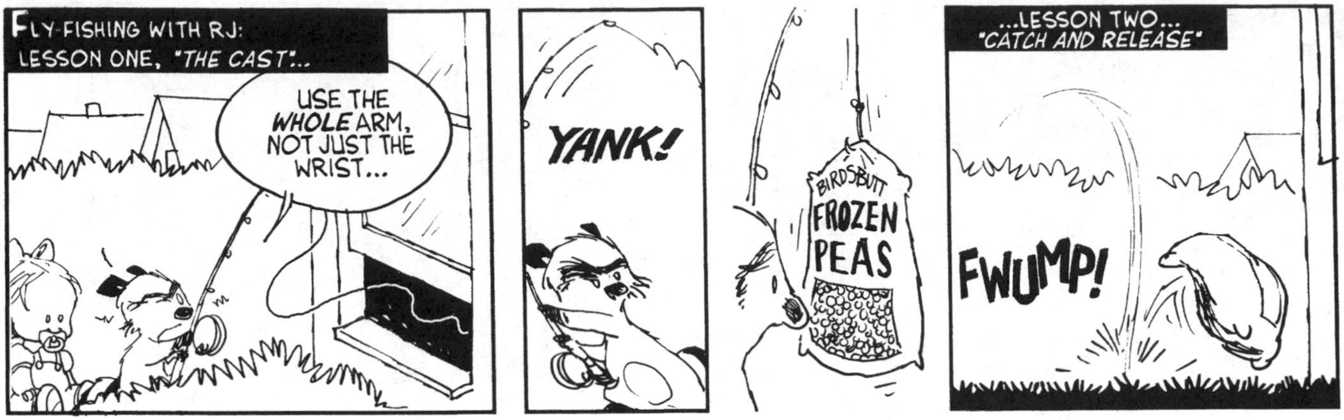
FLY-FISHING WITH RJ: LESSON ONE, "THE CAST"...
USE THE WHOLE ARM, NOT JUST THE WRIST...
YANK!
BIRDSBUTT FROZEN PEAS
...LESSON TWO... "CATCH AND RELEASE"
FWUMP!

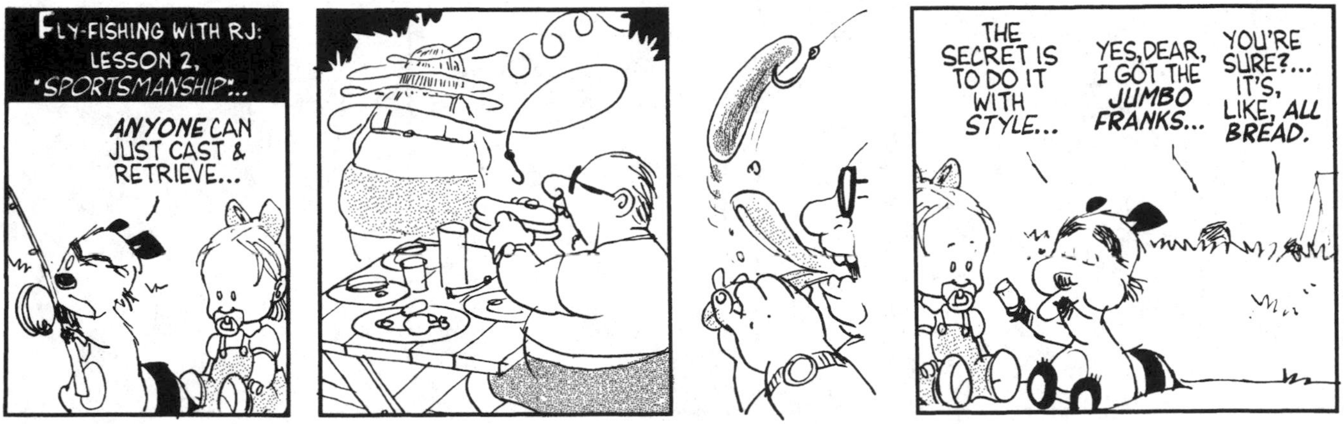
FLY-FISHING WITH RJ: LESSON 2, "SPORTSMANSHIP"...
ANYONE CAN JUST CAST & RETRIEVE...
THE SECRET IS TO DO IT WITH STYLE...
YES, DEAR, I GOT THE JUMBO FRANKS...
YOU'RE SURE?... IT'S, LIKE, ALL BREAD.

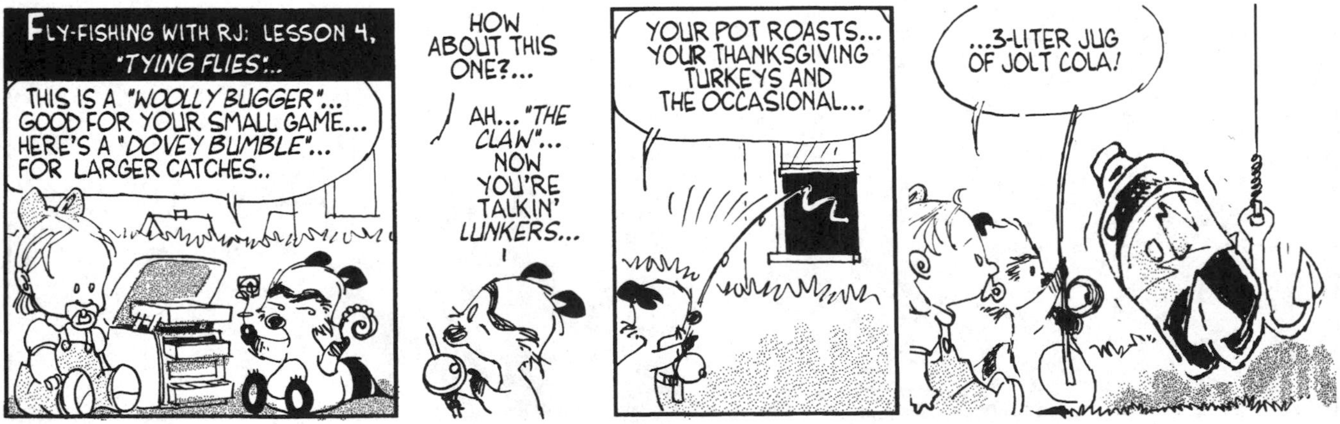
FLY-FISHING WITH RJ: LESSON 4, "TYING FLIES"...
THIS IS A "WOOLLY BUGGER"... GOOD FOR YOUR SMALL GAME... HERE'S A "DOVEY BUMBLE"... FOR LARGER CATCHES..
HOW ABOUT THIS ONE?...
AH... "THE CLAW"... NOW YOU'RE TALKIN' LUNKERS...
YOUR POT ROASTS... YOUR THANKSGIVING TURKEYS AND THE OCCASIONAL...
...3-LITER JUG OF JOLT COLA!

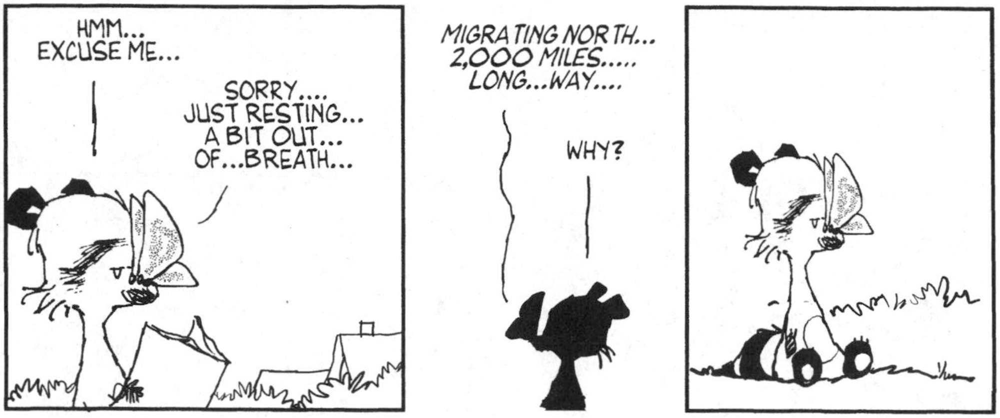
HMM... EXCUSE ME...
SORRY.... JUST RESTING... A BIT OUT... OF...BREATH...
MIGRATING NORTH... 2,000 MILES..... LONG...WAY....
WHY?
I DON'T HAVE THE SLIGHTEST IDEA.
BUMMER.

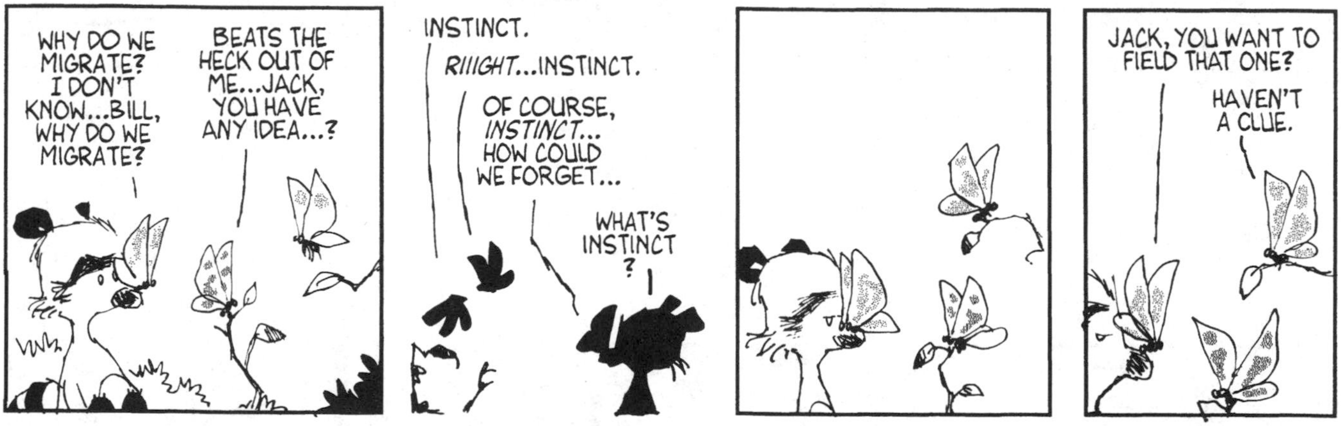
WHY DO WE MIGRATE? I DON'T KNOW...BILL, WHY DO WE MIGRATE?
BEATS THE HECK OUT OF ME...JACK, YOU HAVE ANY IDEA...?
INSTINCT.
RIIIGHT...INSTINCT.
OF COURSE, INSTINCT... HOW COULD WE FORGET...
WHAT'S INSTINCT ?
JACK, YOU WANT TO FIELD THAT ONE?
HAVEN'T A CLUE.

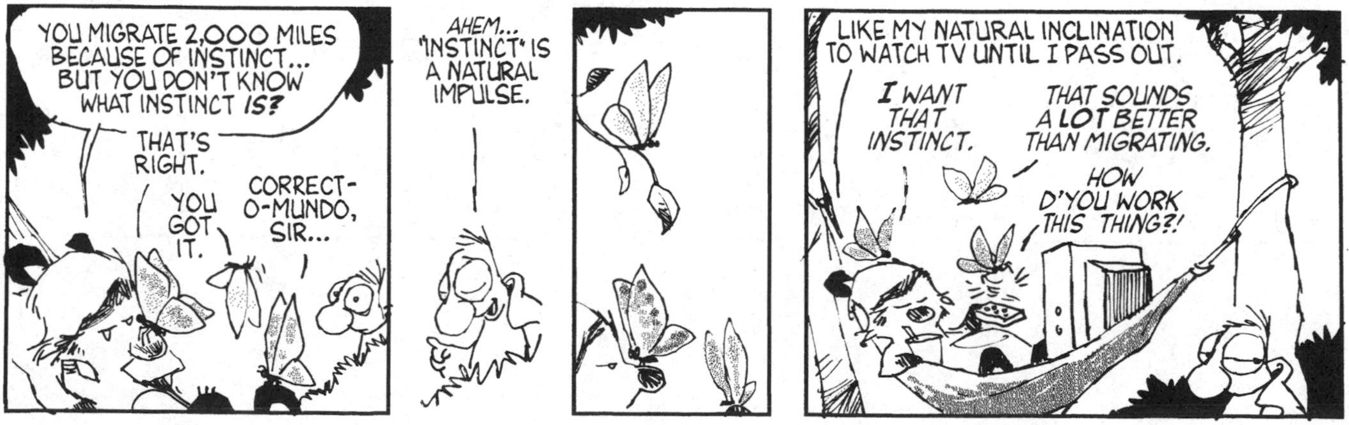
YOU MIGRATE 2,000 MILES BECAUSE OF INSTINCT... BUT YOU DON'T KNOW WHAT INSTINCT IS?
THAT'S RIGHT.
YOU GOT IT.
CORRECT-O-MUNDO, SIR...
AHEM... "INSTINCT" IS A NATURAL IMPULSE.
LIKE MY NATURAL INCLINATION TO WATCH TV UNTIL I PASS OUT.
I WANT THAT INSTINCT.
THAT SOUNDS A LOT BETTER THAN MIGRATING.
HOW D'YOU WORK THIS THING?!

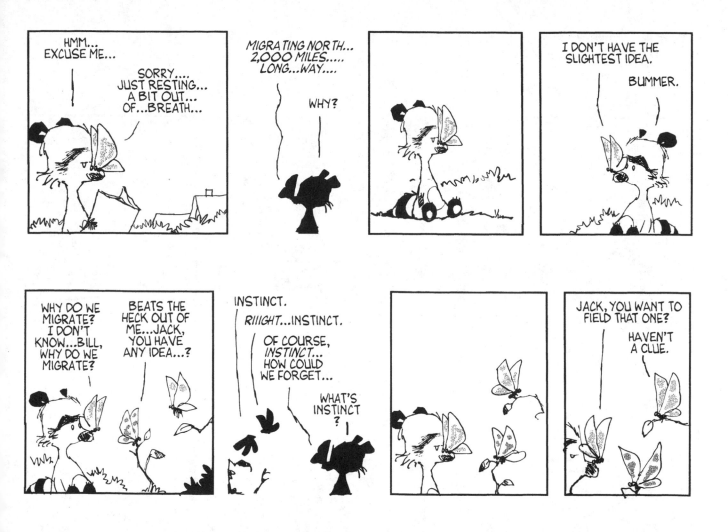

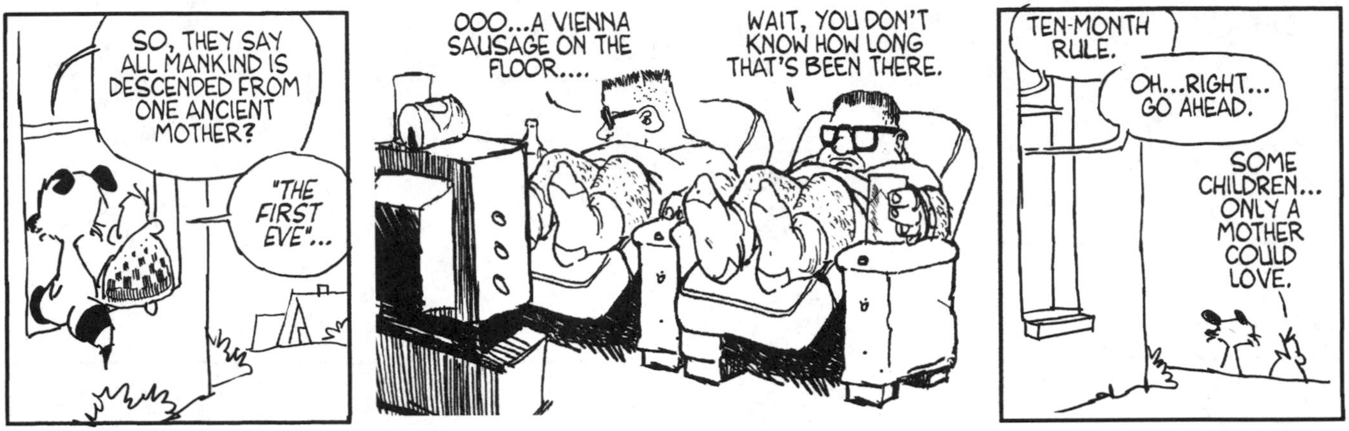
SO, THEY SAY ALL MANKIND IS DESCENDED FROM ONE ANCIENT MOTHER?
"THE FIRST EVE"...
OOO...A VIENNA SAUSAGE ON THE FLOOR....
WAIT, YOU DON'T KNOW HOW LONG THAT'S BEEN THERE.
TEN-MONTH RULE.
OH...RIGHT... GO AHEAD.
SOME CHILDREN... ONLY A MOTHER COULD LOVE.

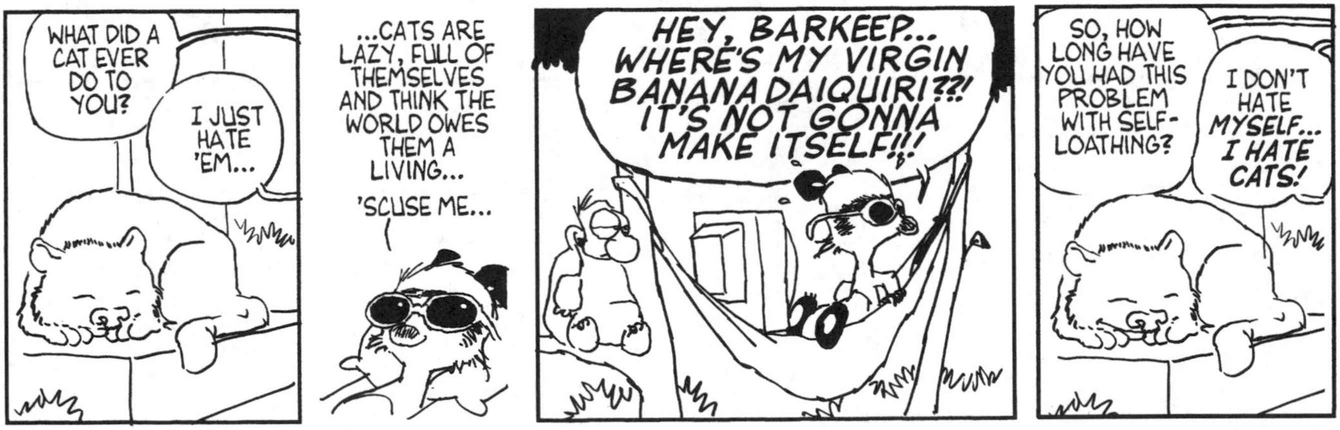
WHAT DID A CAT EVER DO TO YOU?
I JUST HATE 'EM...
...CATS ARE LAZY, FULL OF THEMSELVES AND THINK THE WORLD OWES THEM A LIVING...
'SCUSE ME...
HEY, BARKEEP... WHERE'S MY VIRGIN BANANA DAIQUIRI??! IT'S NOT GONNA MAKE ITSELF!!!
SO, HOW LONG HAVE YOU HAD THIS PROBLEM WITH SELF-LOATHING?
I DON'T HATE MYSELF... I HATE CATS!

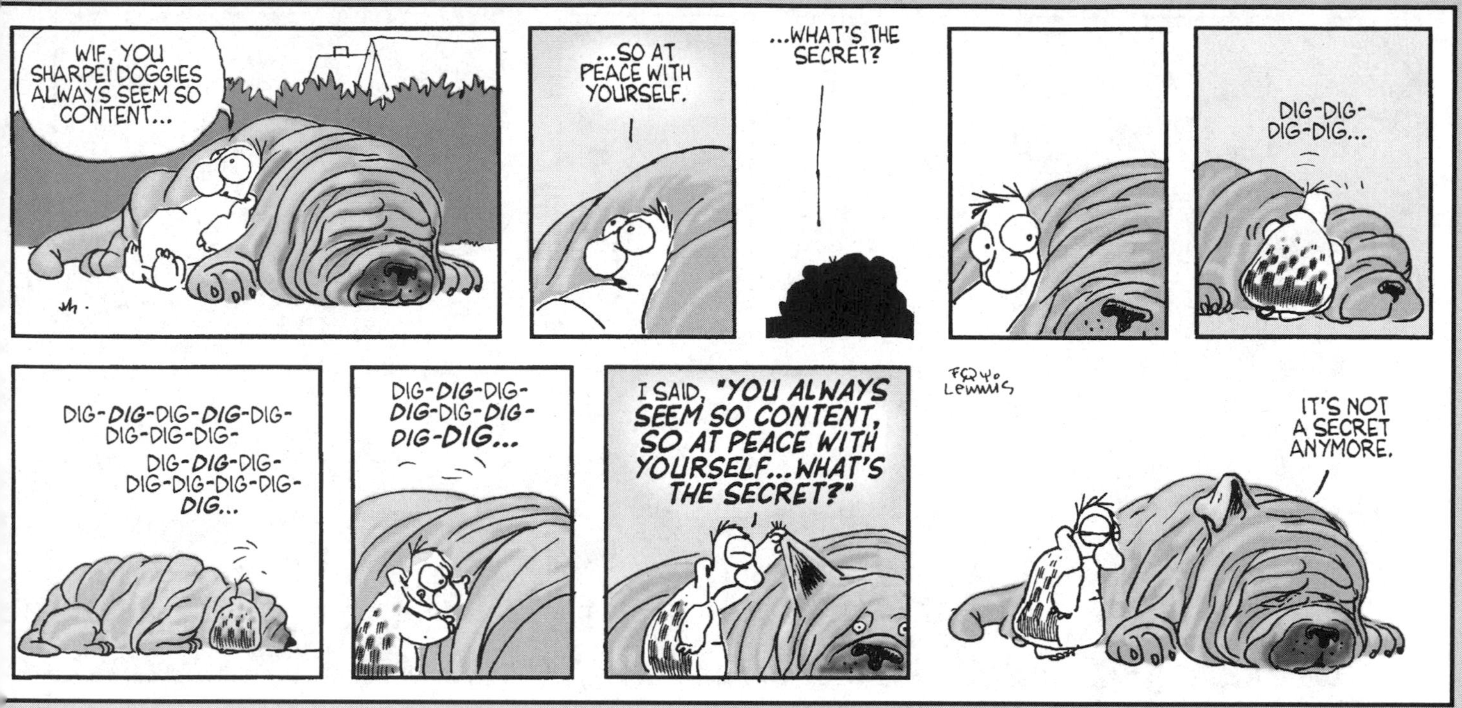
WIF, YOU SHARPEI DOGGIES ALWAYS SEEM SO CONTENT...
...SO AT PEACE WITH YOURSELF.
...WHAT'S THE SECRET?
DIG-DIG-DIG-DIG...
DIG-DIG-DIG-DIG-DIG-DIG-DIG-DIG-
DIG-DIG-DIG-DIG-DIG-DIG-DIG-DIG...
DIG-DIG-DIG-DIG-DIG-DIG-DIG-DIG...
I SAID, "YOU ALWAYS SEEM SO CONTENT, SO AT PEACE WITH YOURSELF...WHAT'S THE SECRET?"
IT'S NOT A SECRET ANYMORE.

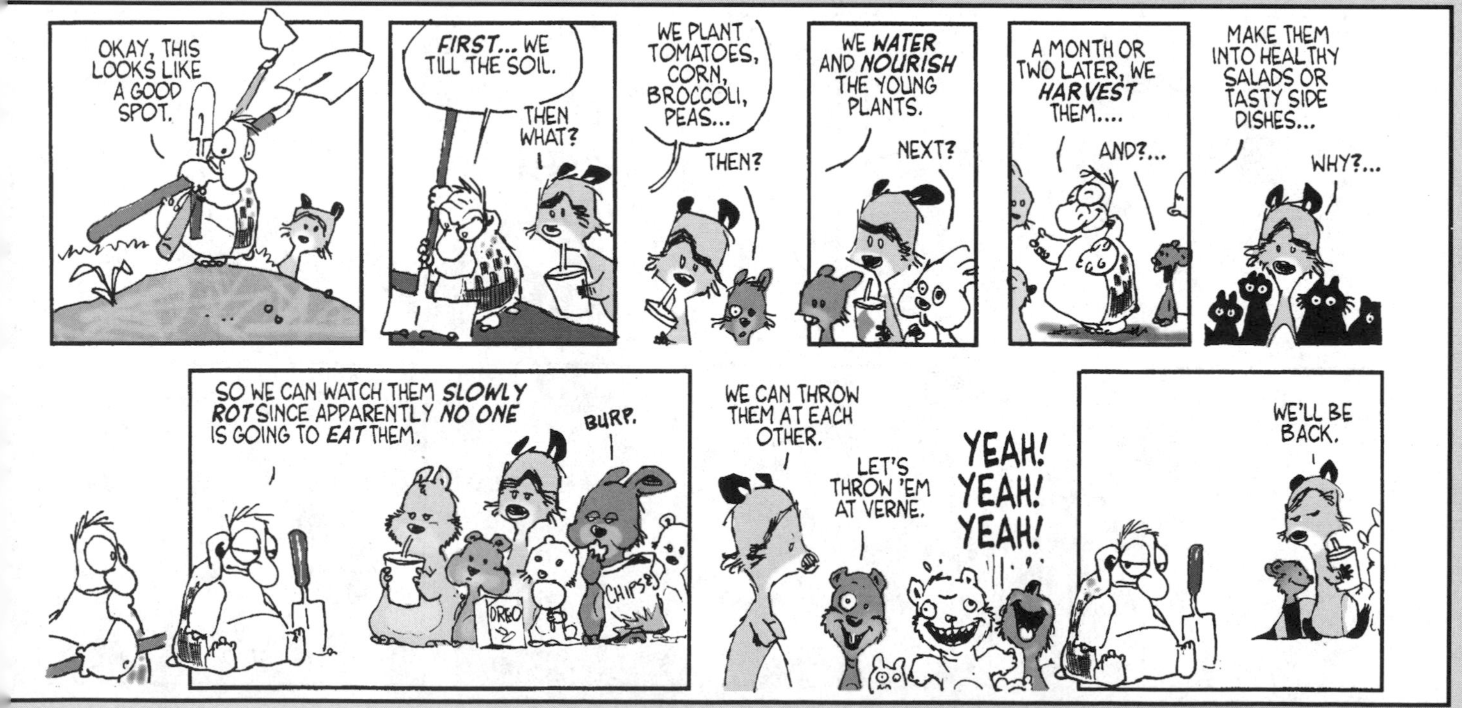
OKAY, THIS LOOKS LIKE A GOOD SPOT.
FIRST... WE TILL THE SOIL.
THEN WHAT?
WE PLANT TOMATOES, CORN, BROCCOLI, PEAS...
THEN?
WE WATER AND NOURISH THE YOUNG PLANTS.
NEXT?
A MONTH OR TWO LATER, WE HARVEST THEM....
AND?...
MAKE THEM INTO HEALTHY SALADS OR TASTY SIDE DISHES...
WHY?...
SO WE CAN WATCH THEM SLOWLY ROT SINCE APPARENTLY NO ONE IS GOING TO EAT THEM.
BURP.
OREO
CHIPS
WE CAN THROW THEM AT EACH OTHER.
LET'S THROW 'EM AT VERNE.
YEAH! YEAH! YEAH!
WE'LL BE BACK.

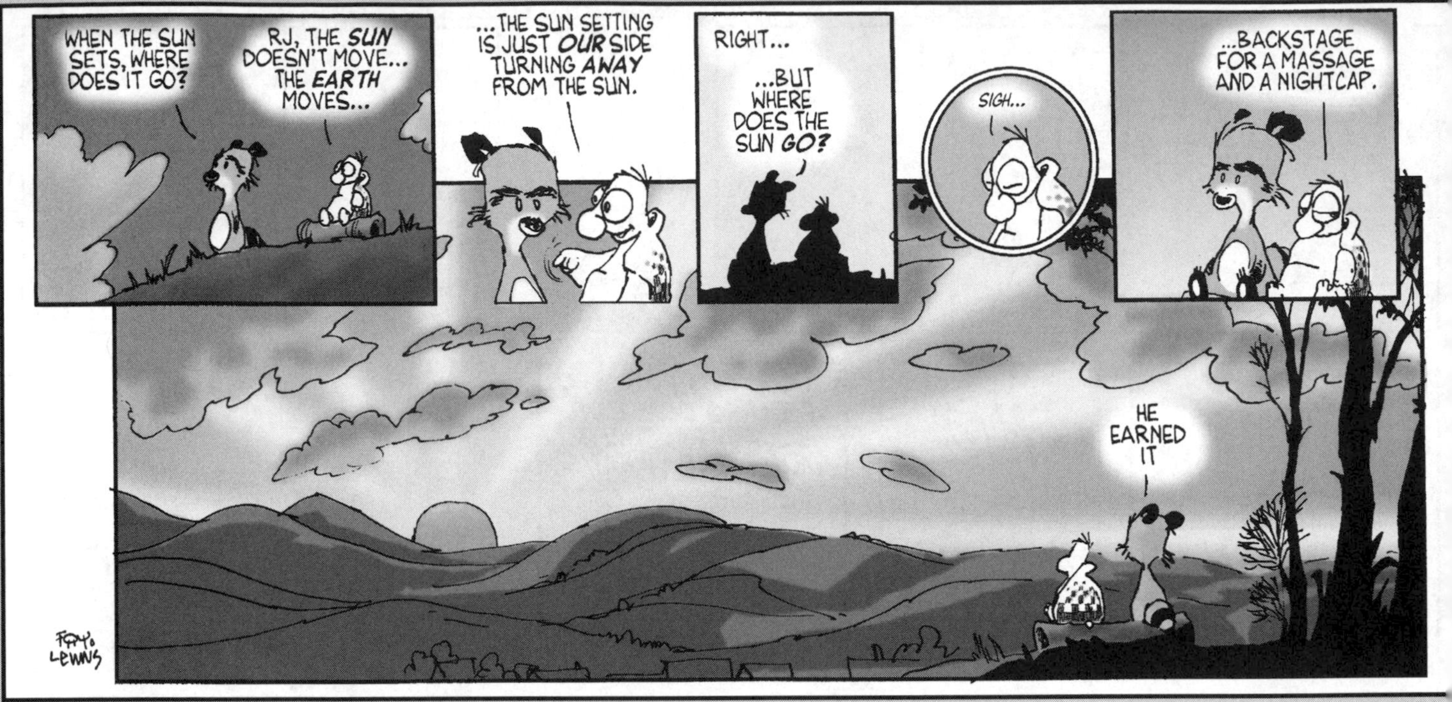
WHEN THE SUN SETS, WHERE DOES IT GO?
RJ, THE SUN DOESN'T MOVE... THE EARTH MOVES...
...THE SUN SETTING IS JUST OUR SIDE TURNING AWAY FROM THE SUN.
RIGHT...
...BUT WHERE DOES THE SUN GO?
SIGH...
...BACKSTAGE FOR A MASSAGE AND A NIGHTCAP.
HE EARNED IT

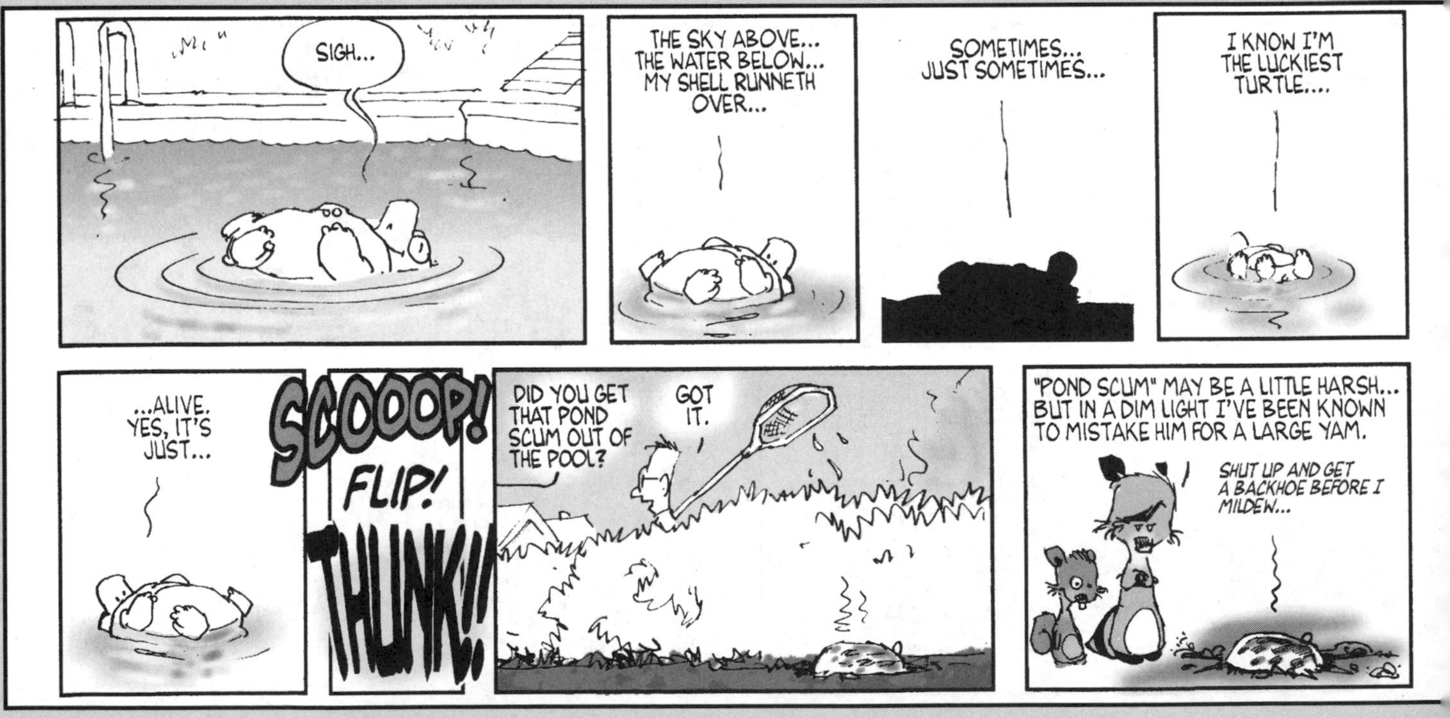
SIGH...
THE SKY ABOVE... THE WATER BELOW... MY SHELL RUNNETH OVER...
SOMETIMES... JUST SOMETIMES...
I KNOW I'M THE LUCKIEST TURTLE....
...ALIVE. YES, IT'S JUST...
SCOOOP!
FLIP!
THUNK!!
DID YOU GET THAT POND SCUM OUT OF THE POOL?
GOT IT.
"POND SCUM" MAY BE A LITTLE HARSH... BUT IN A DIM LIGHT I'VE BEEN KNOWN TO MISTAKE HIM FOR A LARGE YAM.
SHUT UP AND GET A BACKHOE BEFORE I MILDEW...

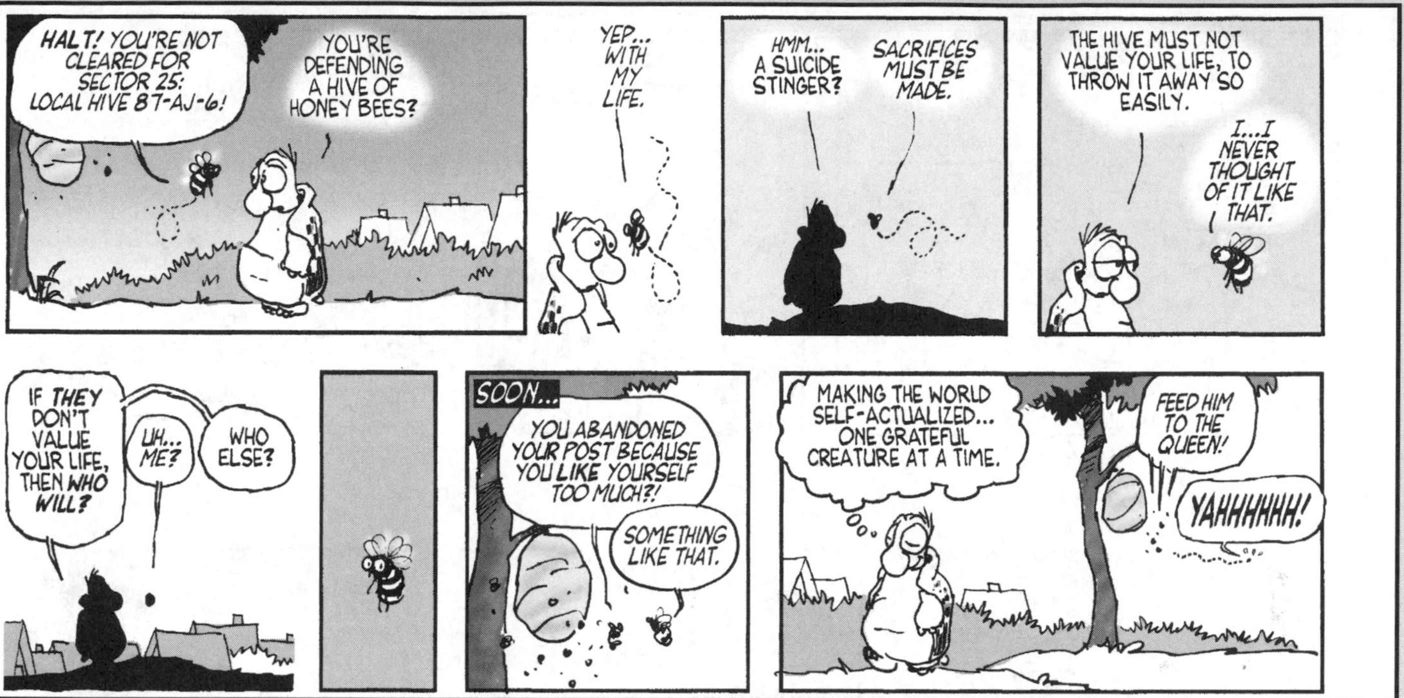

HALT! YOU'RE NOT CLEARED FOR SECTOR 25: LOCAL HIVE 87-AJ-6!
YOU'RE DEFENDING A HIVE OF HONEY BEES?
YEP... WITH MY LIFE.
HMM... A SUICIDE STINGER?
SACRIFICES MUST BE MADE.
THE HIVE MUST NOT VALUE YOUR LIFE, TO THROW IT AWAY SO EASILY.
I...I NEVER THOUGHT OF IT LIKE THAT.
IF THEY DON'T VALUE YOUR LIFE, THEN WHO WILL?
UH... ME?
WHO ELSE?
SOON...
YOU ABANDONED YOUR POST BECAUSE YOU LIKE YOURSELF TOO MUCH?!
SOMETHING LIKE THAT.
MAKING THE WORLD SELF-ACTUALIZED... ONE GRATEFUL CREATURE AT A TIME.
FEED HIM TO THE QUEEN!
YAHHHHHH!

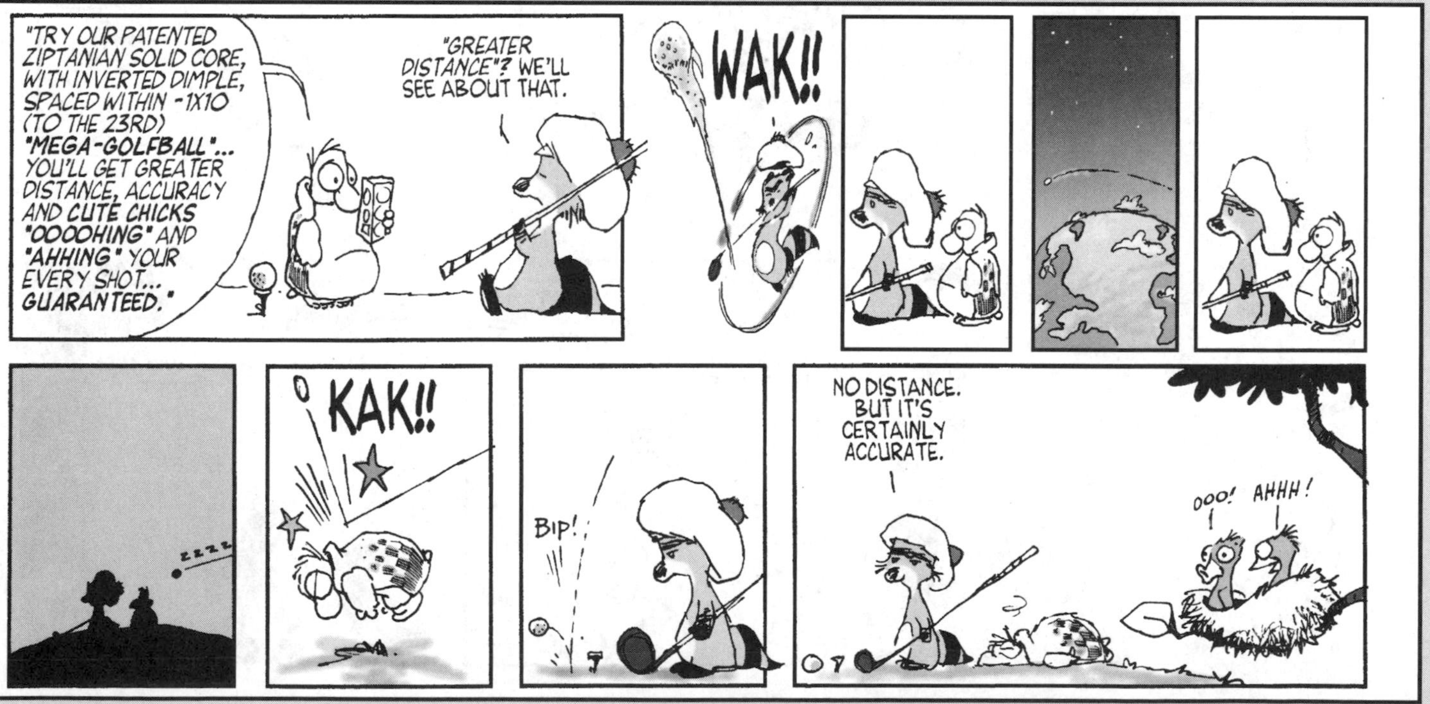

"TRY OUR PATENTED ZIPTANIAN SOLID CORE, WITH INVERTED DIMPLE, SPACED WITHIN -1X10 (TO THE 23RD) "MEGA-GOLFBALL"... YOU'LL GET GREATER DISTANCE, ACCURACY AND CUTE CHICKS "OOOOHING" AND "AHHING" YOUR EVERY SHOT... GUARANTEED."
"GREATER DISTANCE"? WE'LL SEE ABOUT THAT.
WAK!!
ZZZZ
KAK!!
BIP!
NO DISTANCE. BUT IT'S CERTAINLY ACCURATE.
OOO!
AHHH!

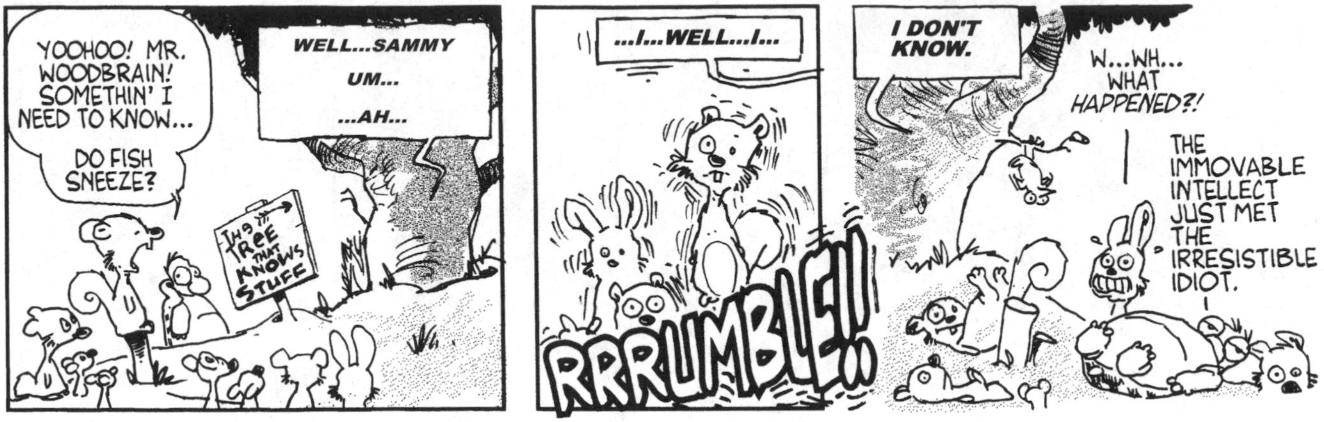
YOOHOO! MR. WOODBRAIN! SOMETHIN' I NEED TO KNOW...
DO FISH SNEEZE?
THE TREE THAT KNOWS STUFF
WELL...SAMMY
UM...
...AH...
...I...WELL...I...
RRRUMBLE!!
I DON'T KNOW.
W...WH... WHAT HAPPENED?!
THE IMMOVABLE INTELLECT JUST MET THE IRRESISTIBLE IDIOT.

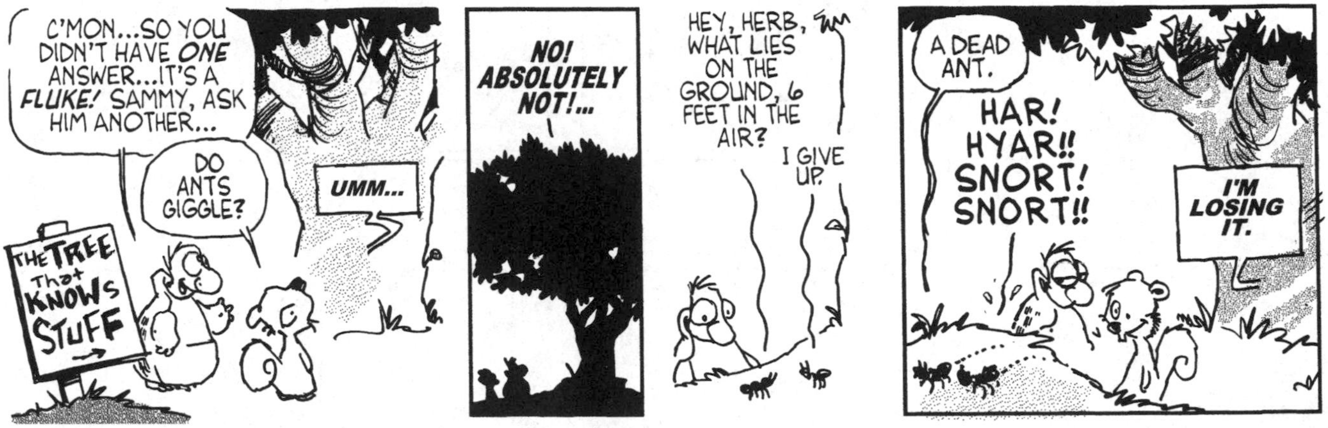
C'MON...SO YOU DIDN'T HAVE *ONE* ANSWER...IT'S A *FLUKE!* SAMMY, ASK HIM ANOTHER...
DO ANTS GIGGLE?
THE TREE That KNOWS STUFF
UMM...
NO! ABSOLUTELY NOT!...
HEY, HERB, WHAT LIES ON THE GROUND, 6 FEET IN THE AIR?
I GIVE UP.
A DEAD ANT.
HAR! HYAR!! SNORT! SNORT!!
I'M LOSING IT.

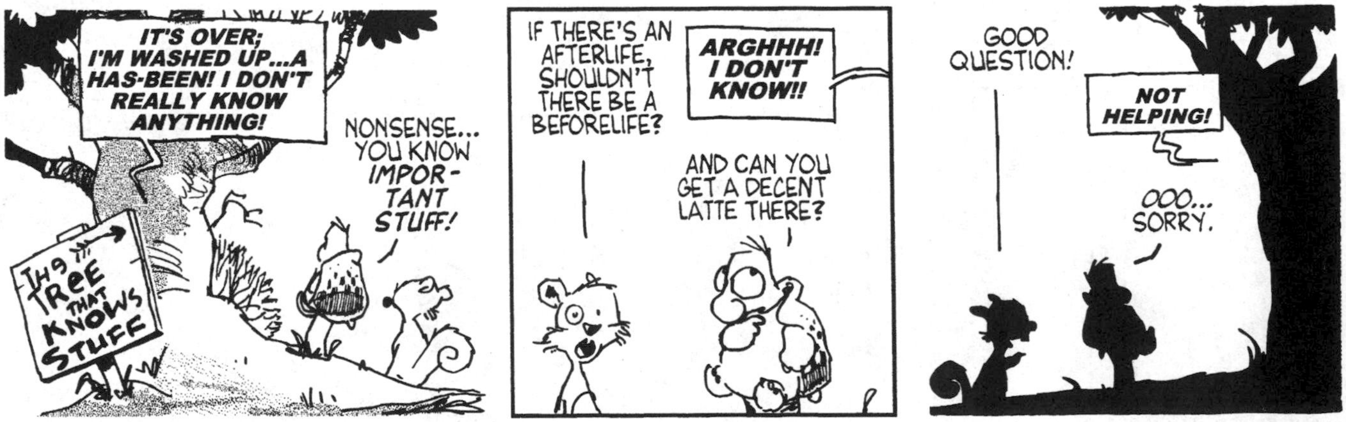
IT'S OVER; I'M WASHED UP...A HAS-BEEN! I DON'T REALLY KNOW ANYTHING!
NONSENSE... YOU KNOW *IMPOR-TANT STUFF!*
THE TREE THAT KNOWS STUFF
IF THERE'S AN AFTERLIFE, SHOULDN'T THERE BE A BEFORELIFE?
AND CAN YOU GET A DECENT LATTE THERE?
ARGHHH! I DON'T KNOW!!
GOOD QUESTION!
NOT HELPING!
OOO... SORRY.

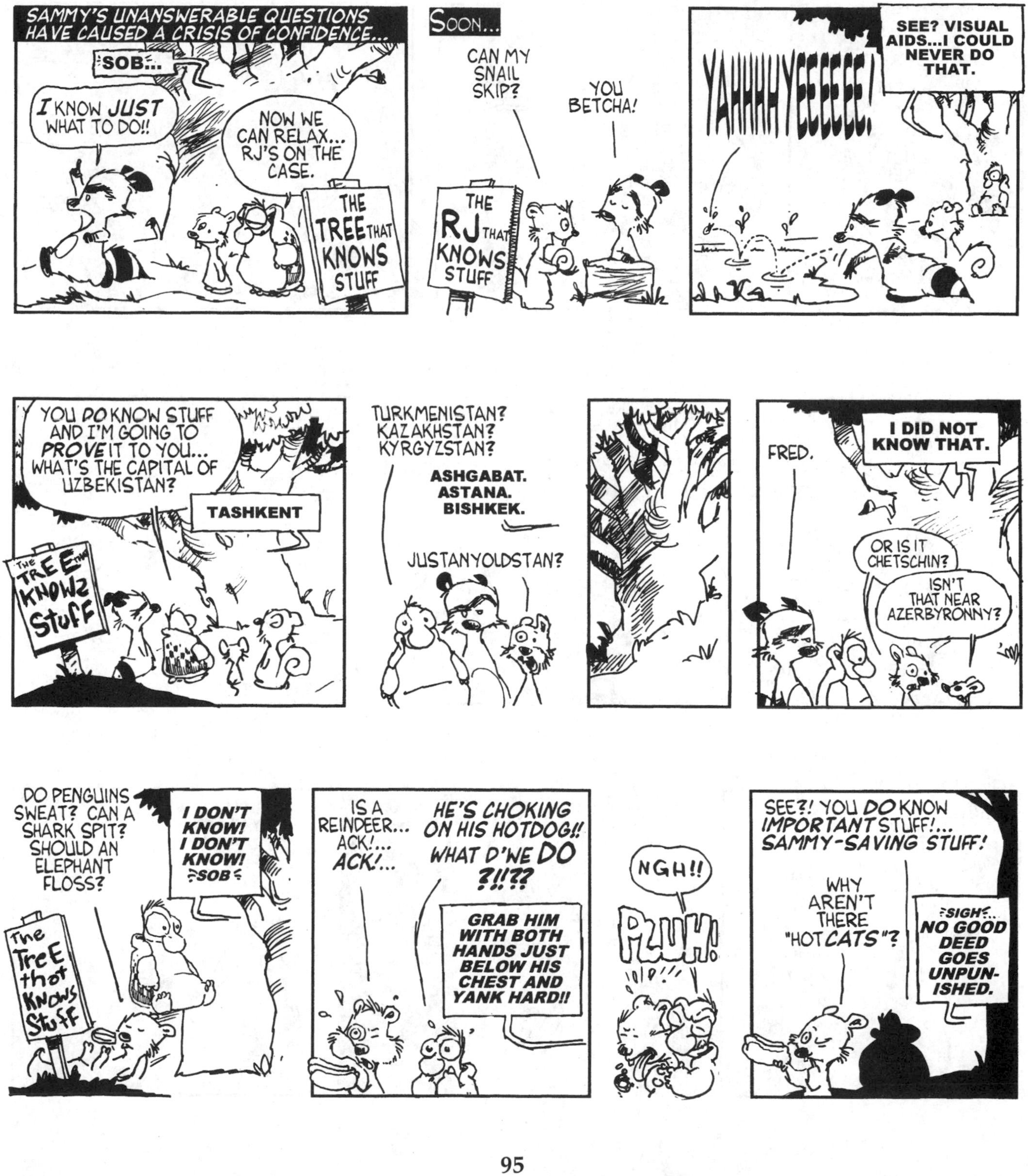
SAMMY'S UNANSWERABLE QUESTIONS HAVE CAUSED A CRISIS OF CONFIDENCE...
SOB...
I KNOW JUST WHAT TO DO!!
NOW WE CAN RELAX... RJ'S ON THE CASE.
THE TREE THAT KNOWS STUFF
SOON...
CAN MY SNAIL SKIP?
YOU BETCHA!
THE RJ THAT KNOWS STUFF
YAHHHHYEEEEEE!
SEE? VISUAL AIDS...I COULD NEVER DO THAT.
YOU DO KNOW STUFF AND I'M GOING TO PROVE IT TO YOU... WHAT'S THE CAPITAL OF UZBEKISTAN?
TASHKENT
THE TREE THAT KNOWZ STUFF
TURKMENISTAN? KAZAKHSTAN? KYRGYZSTAN?
ASHGABAT. ASTANA. BISHKEK.
JUSTANYOLDSTAN?
FRED.
I DID NOT KNOW THAT.
OR IS IT CHETSCHIN?
ISN'T THAT NEAR AZERBYRONNY?
DO PENGUINS SWEAT? CAN A SHARK SPIT? SHOULD AN ELEPHANT FLOSS?
I DON'T KNOW! I DON'T KNOW! SOB
The TreE that KNOWS Stuff
IS A REINDEER... ACK!... ACK!...
HE'S CHOKING ON HIS HOTDOG!! WHAT D'WE DO ?!!??
GRAB HIM WITH BOTH HANDS JUST BELOW HIS CHEST AND YANK HARD!!
NGH!!
PLUH!
SEE?! YOU DO KNOW IMPORTANT STUFF!... SAMMY-SAVING STUFF!
WHY AREN'T THERE "HOT CATS"?
SIGH... NO GOOD DEED GOES UNPUNISHED.

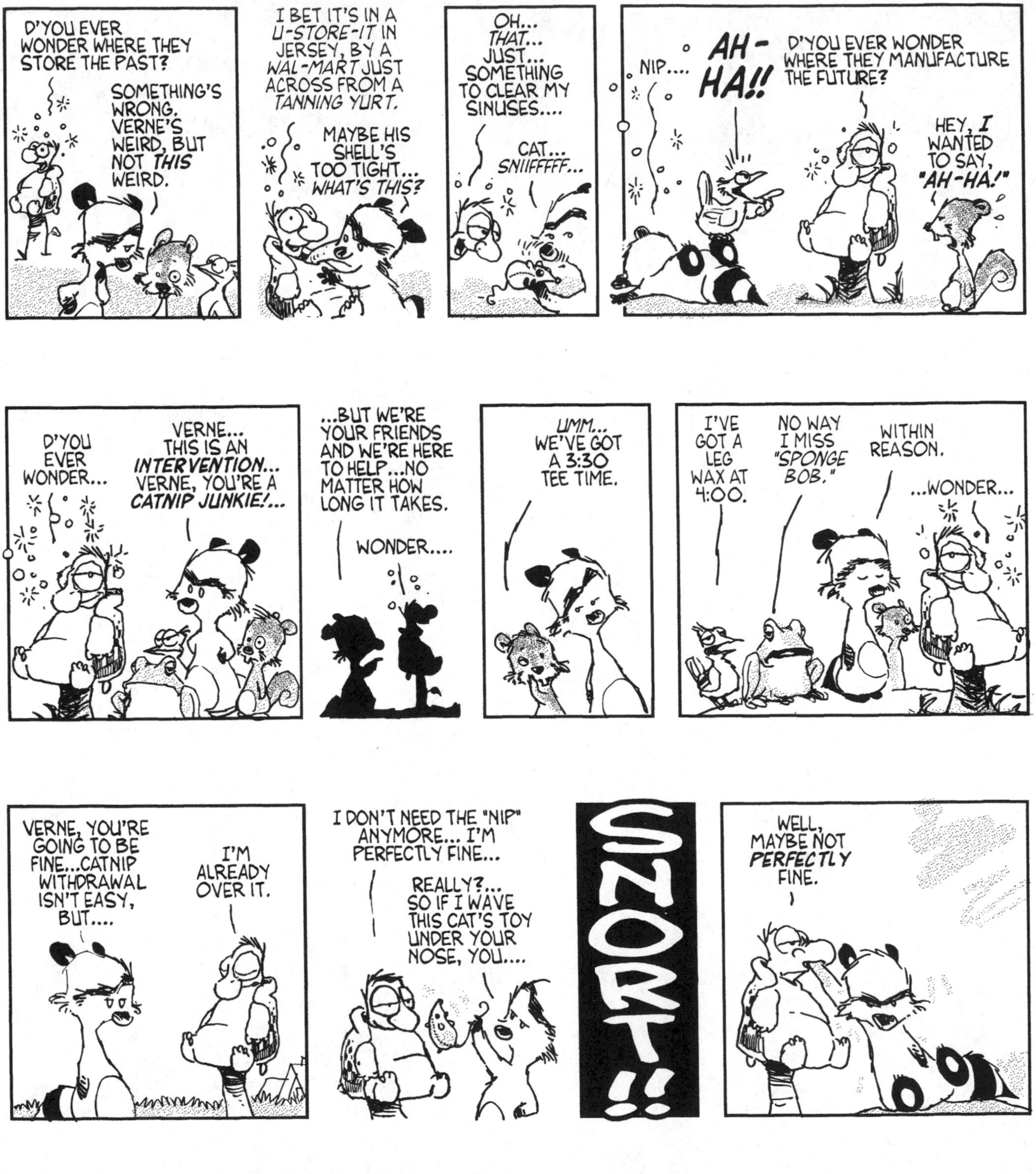
D'YOU EVER WONDER WHERE THEY STORE THE PAST?
SOMETHING'S WRONG. VERNE'S WEIRD, BUT NOT *THIS* WEIRD.
I BET IT'S IN A *U-STORE-IT* IN JERSEY, BY A *WAL-MART* JUST ACROSS FROM A *TANNING YURT.*
MAYBE HIS SHELL'S TOO TIGHT... *WHAT'S THIS?*
OH... *THAT*... JUST... SOMETHING TO CLEAR MY SINUSES....
CAT... *SNIIFFFFF*...
NIP....
AH-HA!!
D'YOU EVER WONDER WHERE THEY MANUFACTURE THE FUTURE?
HEY, *I* WANTED TO SAY, ***"AH-HA!"***
D'YOU EVER WONDER...
VERNE... THIS IS AN ***INTERVENTION...*** VERNE, YOU'RE A ***CATNIP JUNKIE!...***
...BUT WE'RE YOUR FRIENDS AND WE'RE HERE TO HELP...NO MATTER HOW LONG IT TAKES.
WONDER....
UMM... WE'VE GOT A 3:30 TEE TIME.
I'VE GOT A LEG WAX AT 4:00.
NO WAY I MISS *"SPONGE BOB."*
WITHIN REASON.
...WONDER...
VERNE, YOU'RE GOING TO BE FINE...CATNIP WITHDRAWAL ISN'T EASY, BUT....
I'M ALREADY OVER IT.
I DON'T NEED THE "NIP" ANYMORE... I'M PERFECTLY FINE...
REALLY?... SO IF I WAVE THIS CAT'S TOY UNDER YOUR NOSE, YOU....
SNORT!!
WELL, MAYBE NOT ***PERFECTLY*** FINE.

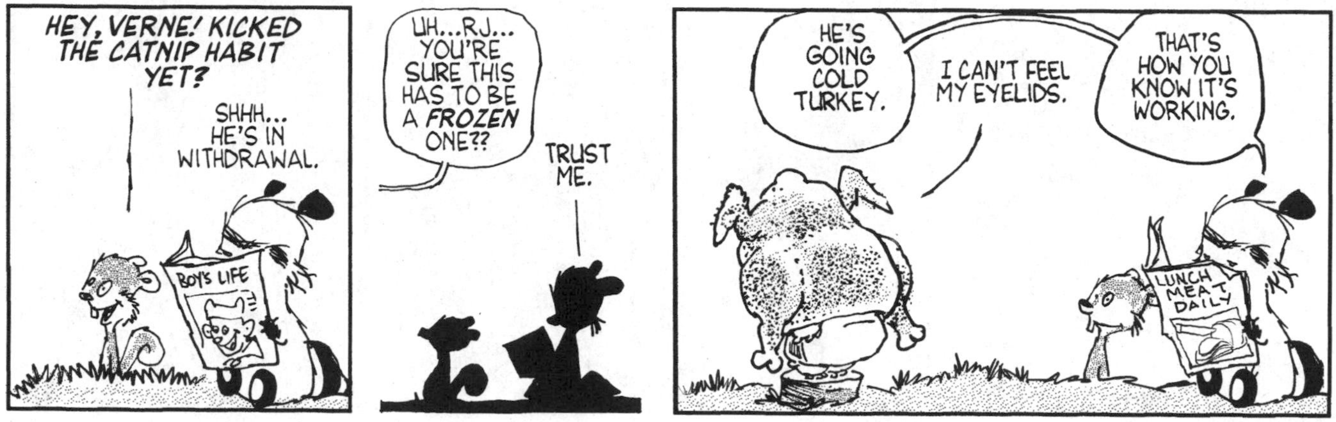
HEY, VERNE! KICKED THE CATNIP HABIT YET?
SHHH... HE'S IN WITHDRAWAL.
BOY'S LIFE
UH...RJ... YOU'RE SURE THIS HAS TO BE A FROZEN ONE??
TRUST ME.
HE'S GOING COLD TURKEY.
I CAN'T FEEL MY EYELIDS.
THAT'S HOW YOU KNOW IT'S WORKING.
LUNCH MEAT DAILY

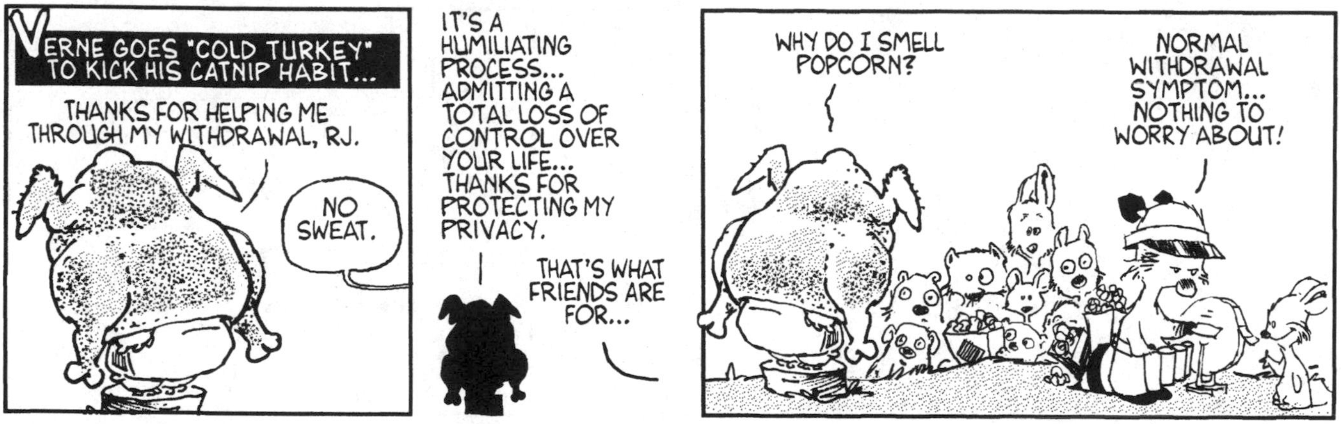
VERNE GOES "COLD TURKEY" TO KICK HIS CATNIP HABIT...
THANKS FOR HELPING ME THROUGH MY WITHDRAWAL, RJ.
NO SWEAT.
IT'S A HUMILIATING PROCESS... ADMITTING A TOTAL LOSS OF CONTROL OVER YOUR LIFE... THANKS FOR PROTECTING MY PRIVACY.
THAT'S WHAT FRIENDS ARE FOR...
WHY DO I SMELL POPCORN?
NORMAL WITHDRAWAL SYMPTOM... NOTHING TO WORRY ABOUT!

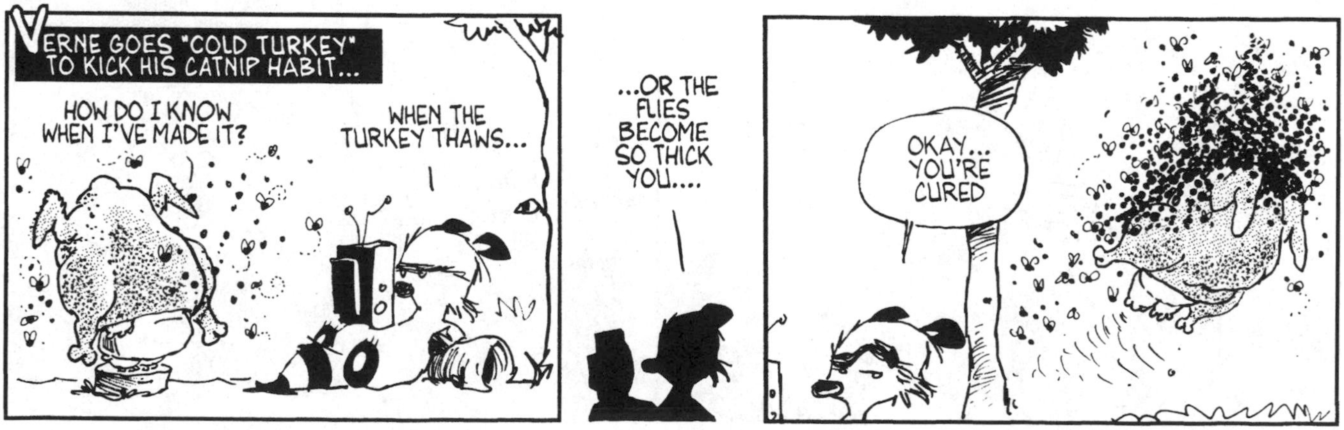
VERNE GOES "COLD TURKEY" TO KICK HIS CATNIP HABIT...
HOW DO I KNOW WHEN I'VE MADE IT?
WHEN THE TURKEY THAWS...
...OR THE FLIES BECOME SO THICK YOU....
OKAY... YOU'RE CURED

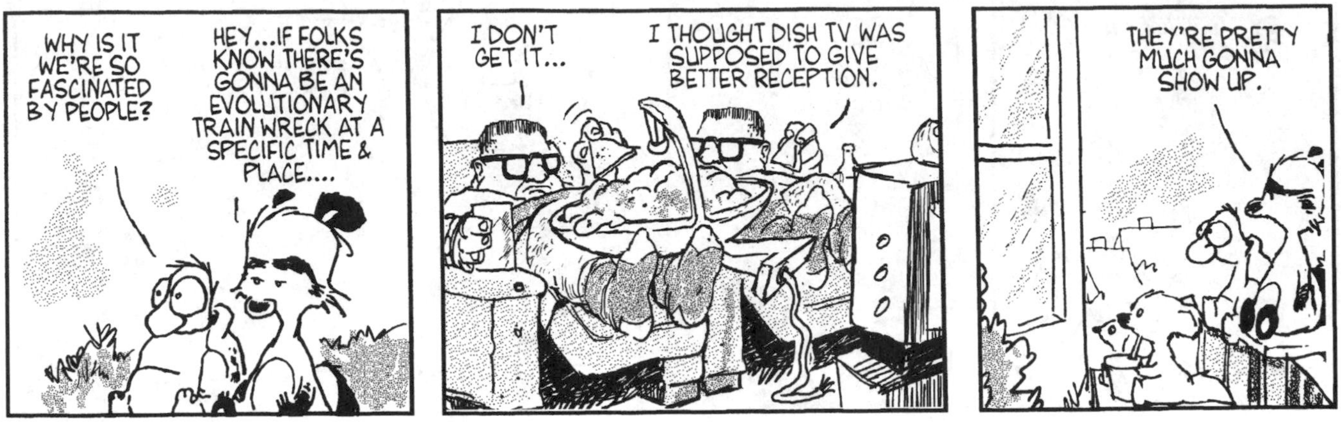
WHY IS IT WE'RE SO FASCINATED BY PEOPLE?
HEY...IF FOLKS KNOW THERE'S GONNA BE AN EVOLUTIONARY TRAIN WRECK AT A SPECIFIC TIME & PLACE....
I DON'T GET IT...
I THOUGHT DISH TV WAS SUPPOSED TO GIVE BETTER RECEPTION.
THEY'RE PRETTY MUCH GONNA SHOW UP.

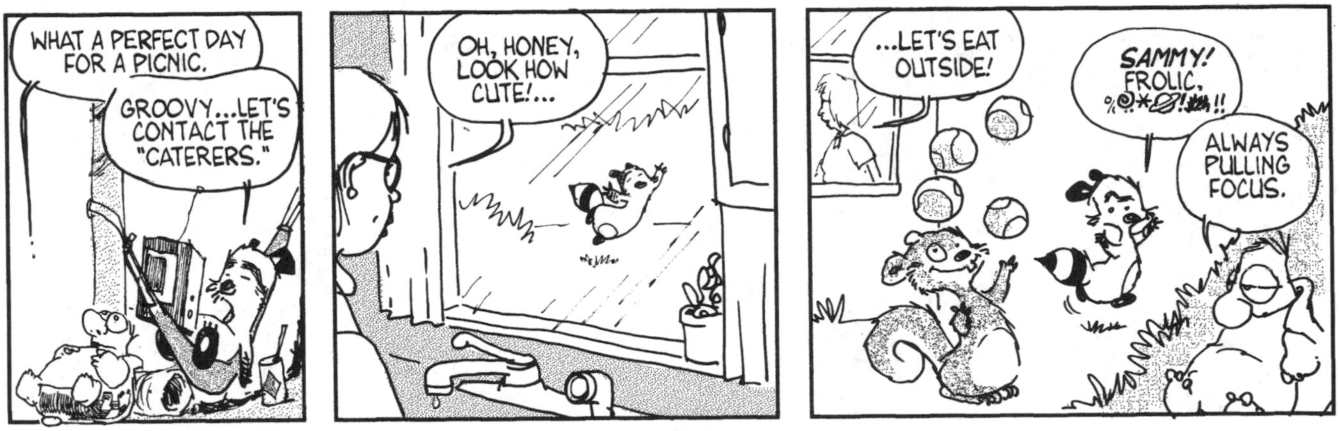
WHAT A PERFECT DAY FOR A PICNIC.
GROOVY...LET'S CONTACT THE "CATERERS."
OH, HONEY, LOOK HOW CUTE!...
...LET'S EAT OUTSIDE!
SAMMY! FROLIC, %@*@!##!!
ALWAYS PULLING FOCUS.

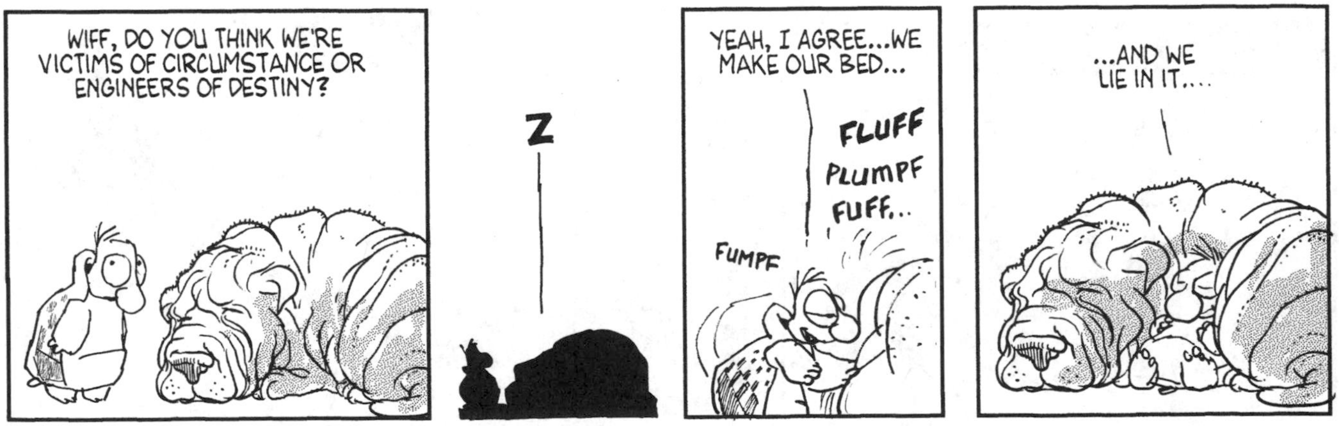
WIFF, DO YOU THINK WE'RE VICTIMS OF CIRCUMSTANCE OR ENGINEERS OF DESTINY?
Z
YEAH, I AGREE...WE MAKE OUR BED...
FLUFF
PLUMPF
FUFF...
FUMPF
...AND WE LIE IN IT....

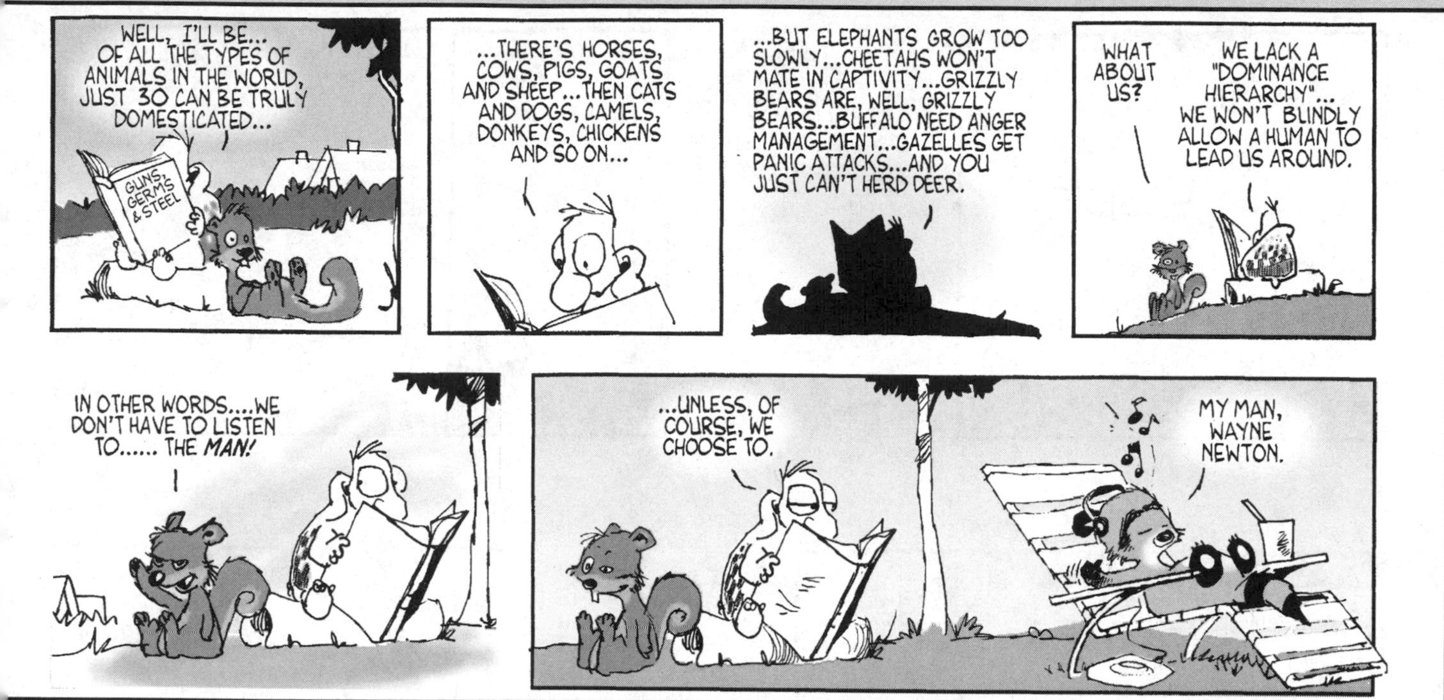
WELL, I'LL BE... OF ALL THE TYPES OF ANIMALS IN THE WORLD, JUST 30 CAN BE TRULY DOMESTICATED...
GUNS, GERMS & STEEL
...THERE'S HORSES, COWS, PIGS, GOATS AND SHEEP...THEN CATS AND DOGS, CAMELS, DONKEYS, CHICKENS AND SO ON...
...BUT ELEPHANTS GROW TOO SLOWLY...CHEETAHS WON'T MATE IN CAPTIVITY...GRIZZLY BEARS ARE, WELL, GRIZZLY BEARS...BUFFALO NEED ANGER MANAGEMENT...GAZELLES GET PANIC ATTACKS...AND YOU JUST CAN'T HERD DEER.
WHAT ABOUT US?
WE LACK A "DOMINANCE HIERARCHY"... WE WON'T BLINDLY ALLOW A HUMAN TO LEAD US AROUND.
IN OTHER WORDS....WE DON'T HAVE TO LISTEN TO...... THE MAN!
...UNLESS, OF COURSE, WE CHOOSE TO.
MY MAN, WAYNE NEWTON.

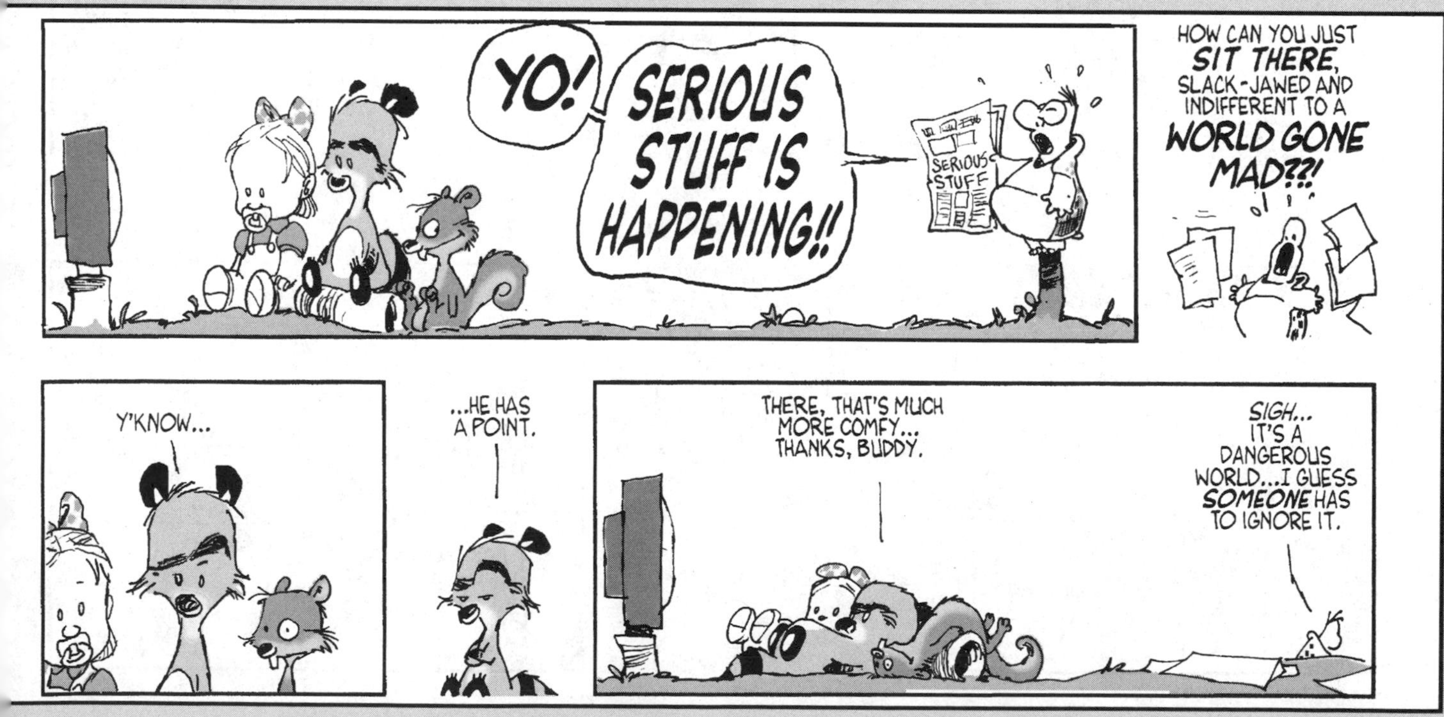
YO!
SERIOUS STUFF IS HAPPENING!!
SERIOUS STUFF
HOW CAN YOU JUST SIT THERE, SLACK-JAWED AND INDIFFERENT TO A WORLD GONE MAD??!
Y'KNOW...
...HE HAS A POINT.
THERE, THAT'S MUCH MORE COMFY... THANKS, BUDDY.
SIGH... IT'S A DANGEROUS WORLD...I GUESS SOMEONE HAS TO IGNORE IT.

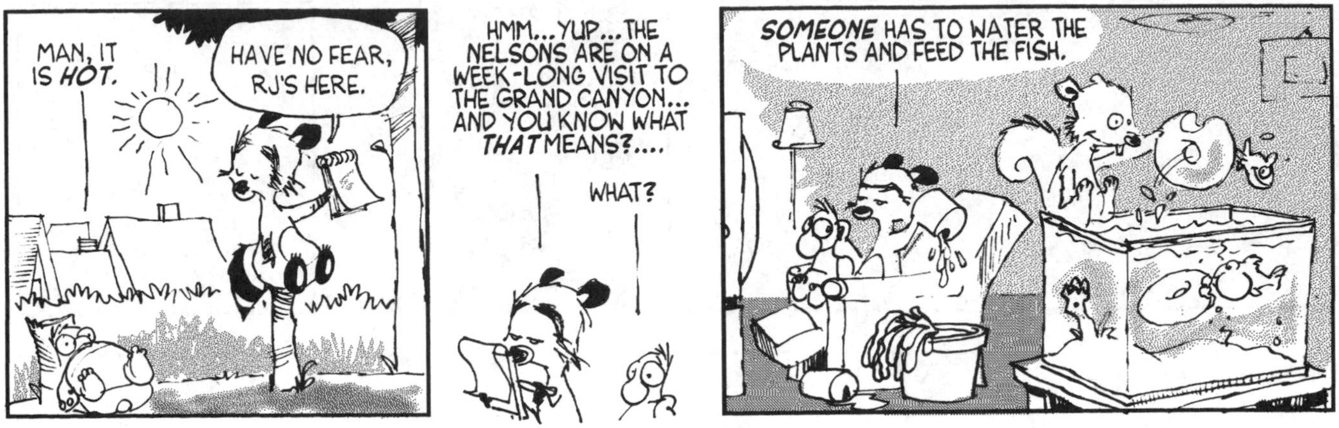
MAN, IT IS *HOT.*
HAVE NO FEAR, RJ'S HERE.
HMM...YUP...THE NELSONS ARE ON A WEEK-LONG VISIT TO THE GRAND CANYON... AND YOU KNOW WHAT *THAT* MEANS?....
WHAT?
SOMEONE HAS TO WATER THE PLANTS AND FEED THE FISH.

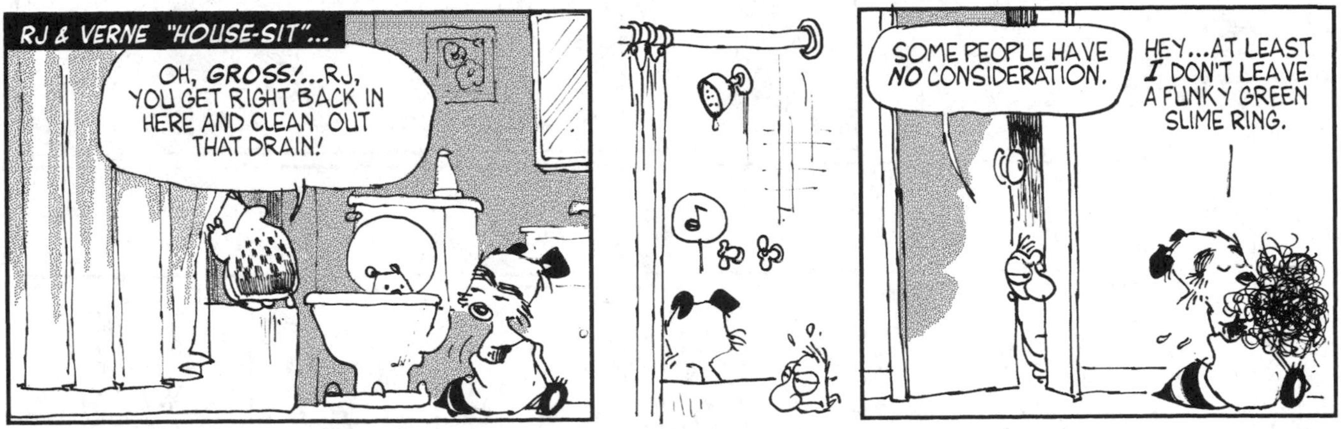
RJ & VERNE "HOUSE-SIT"...
OH, **GROSS!**...RJ, YOU GET RIGHT BACK IN HERE AND CLEAN OUT THAT DRAIN!
SOME PEOPLE HAVE *NO* CONSIDERATION.
HEY...AT LEAST *I* DON'T LEAVE A FUNKY GREEN SLIME RING.

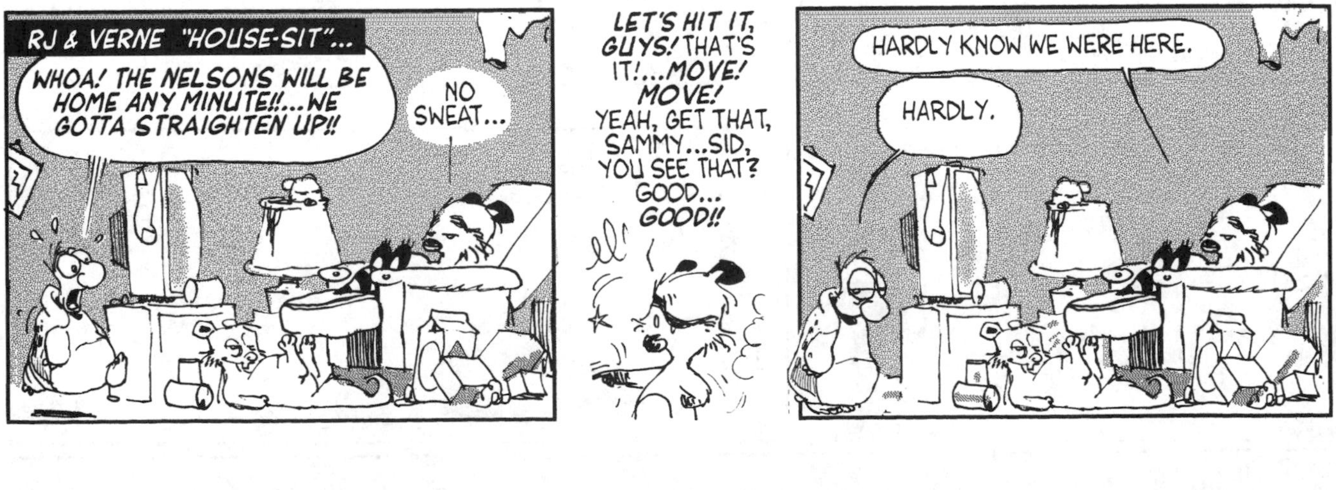
RJ & VERNE "HOUSE-SIT"...
WHOA! THE NELSONS WILL BE HOME ANY MINUTE!!...WE GOTTA STRAIGHTEN UP!!
NO SWEAT...
LET'S HIT IT, GUYS! THAT'S IT!...*MOVE! MOVE!* YEAH, GET THAT, SAMMY...SID, YOU SEE THAT? GOOD... *GOOD!!*
HARDLY KNOW WE WERE HERE.
HARDLY.

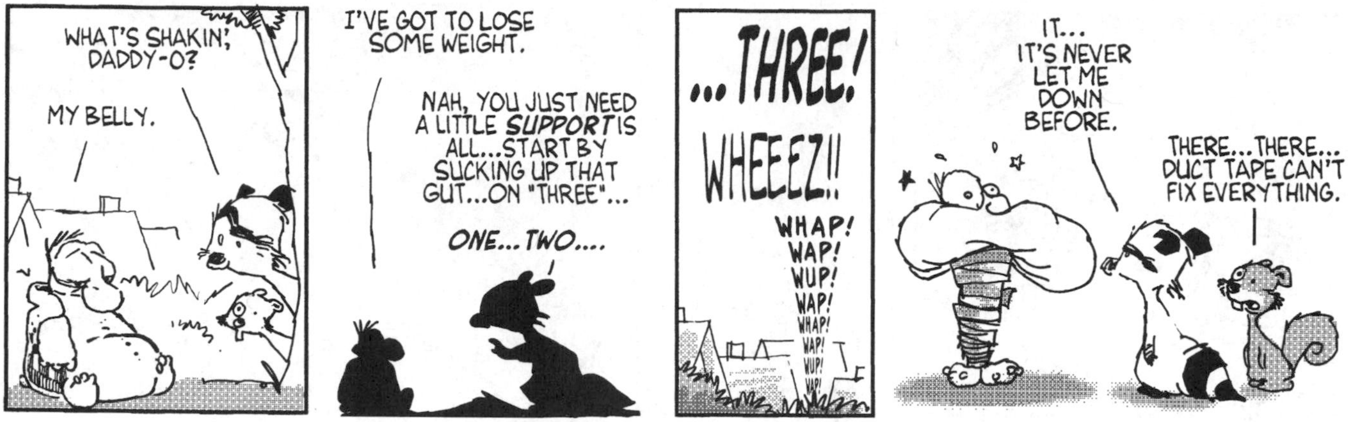
WHAT'S SHAKIN', DADDY-O?
MY BELLY.
I'VE GOT TO LOSE SOME WEIGHT.
NAH, YOU JUST NEED A LITTLE ***SUPPORT*** IS ALL...START BY SUCKING UP THAT GUT...ON "THREE"...
ONE...TWO....
...THREE!
WHEEEZ!!
WHAP! WAP! WUP! WAP! WHAP! WAP! WUP! WAP!
IT... IT'S NEVER LET ME DOWN BEFORE.
THERE...THERE... DUCT TAPE CAN'T FIX EVERYTHING.

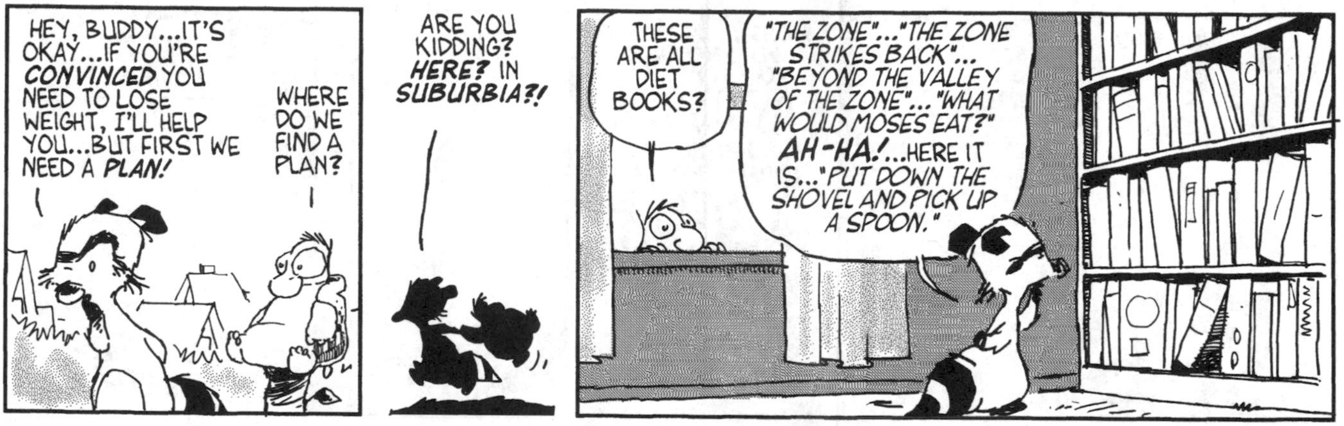
HEY, BUDDY...IT'S OKAY...IF YOU'RE ***CONVINCED*** YOU NEED TO LOSE WEIGHT, I'LL HELP YOU...BUT FIRST WE NEED A ***PLAN!***
WHERE DO WE FIND A PLAN?
ARE YOU KIDDING? ***HERE?*** IN ***SUBURBIA?!***
THESE ARE ALL DIET BOOKS?
"THE ZONE"..."THE ZONE STRIKES BACK"... "BEYOND THE VALLEY OF THE ZONE"..."WHAT WOULD MOSES EAT?" ***AH-HA!***...HERE IT IS...*"PUT DOWN THE SHOVEL AND PICK UP A SPOON."*

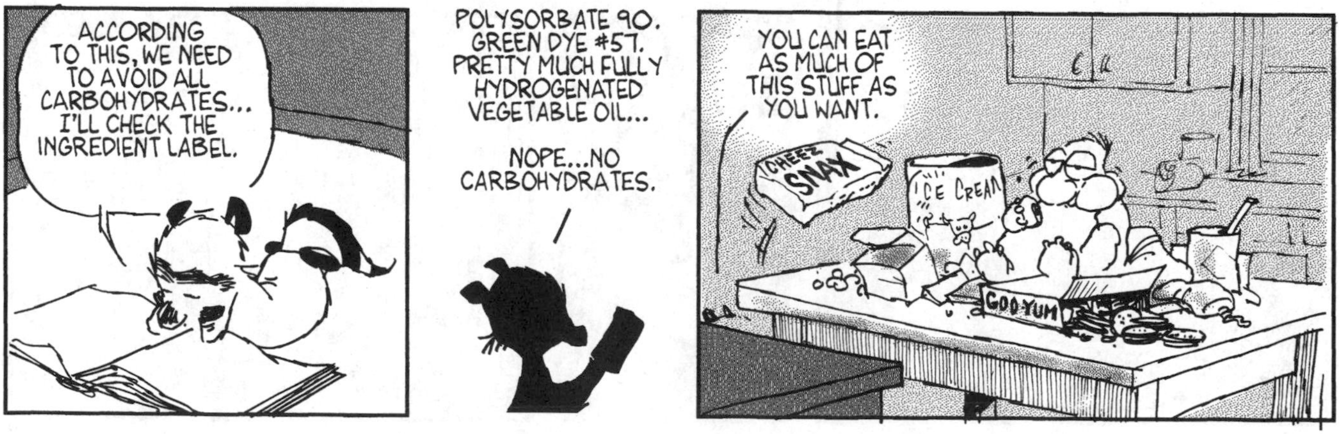
ACCORDING TO THIS, WE NEED TO AVOID ALL CARBOHYDRATES... I'LL CHECK THE INGREDIENT LABEL.
POLYSORBATE 90. GREEN DYE #57. PRETTY MUCH FULLY HYDROGENATED VEGETABLE OIL...
NOPE...NO CARBOHYDRATES.
YOU CAN EAT AS MUCH OF THIS STUFF AS YOU WANT.
CHEEZ SNAX
ICE CREAM
GOO-YUM

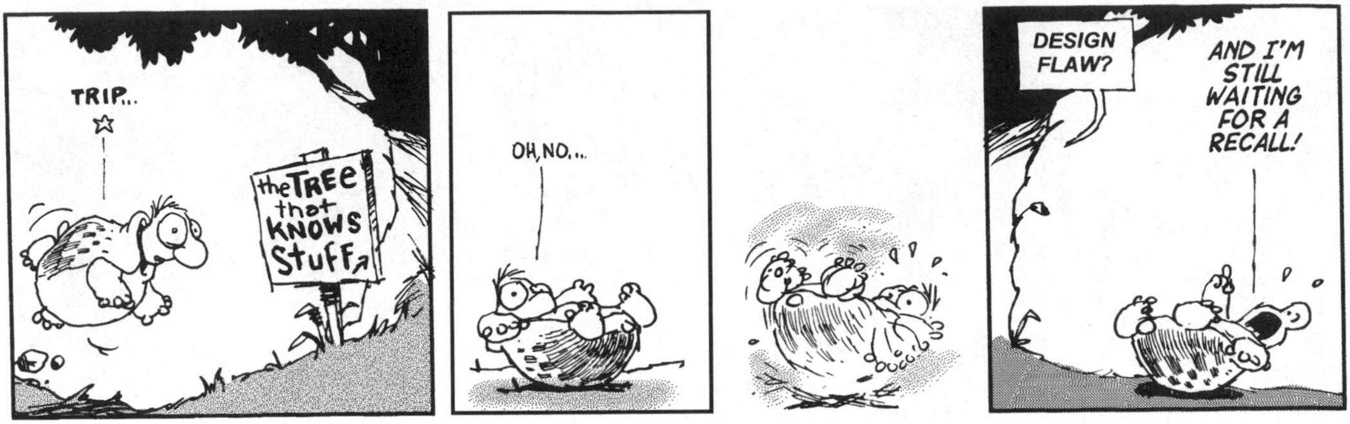
TRIP...
the TREE that KNOWS STUFF
OH, NO...
DESIGN FLAW?
AND I'M STILL WAITING FOR A RECALL!

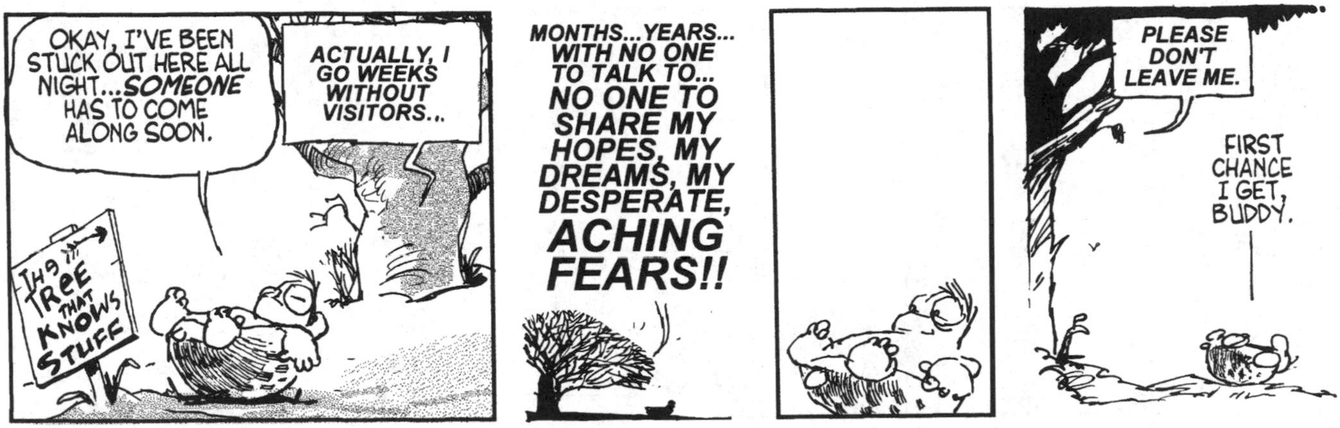
OKAY, I'VE BEEN STUCK OUT HERE ALL NIGHT...SOMEONE HAS TO COME ALONG SOON.
ACTUALLY, I GO WEEKS WITHOUT VISITORS...
THE TREE THAT KNOWS STUFF
MONTHS...YEARS... WITH NO ONE TO TALK TO... NO ONE TO SHARE MY HOPES, MY DREAMS, MY DESPERATE, ACHING FEARS!!
PLEASE DON'T LEAVE ME.
FIRST CHANCE I GET, BUDDY.

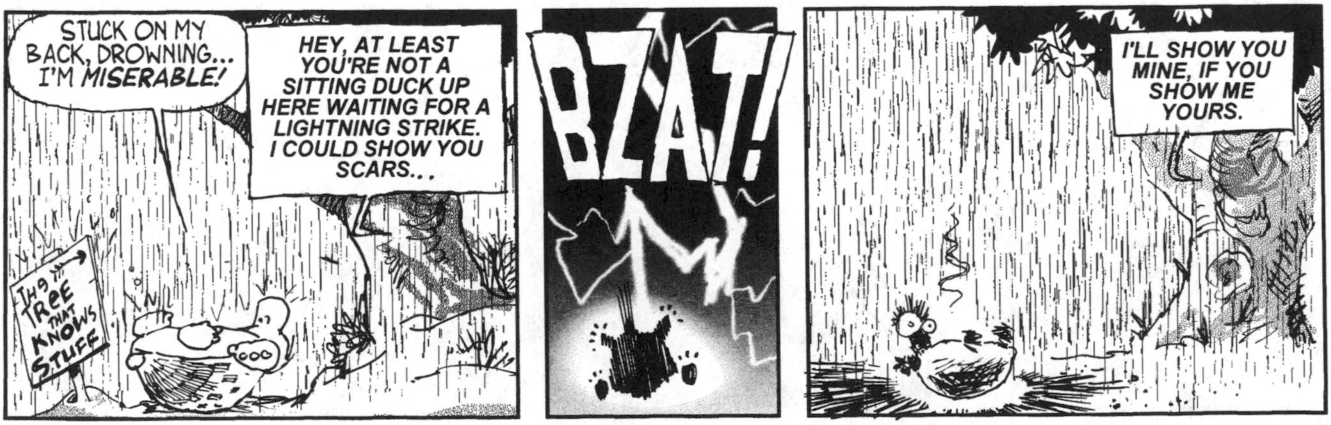
STUCK ON MY BACK, DROWNING... I'M MISERABLE!
HEY, AT LEAST YOU'RE NOT A SITTING DUCK UP HERE WAITING FOR A LIGHTNING STRIKE. I COULD SHOW YOU SCARS...
THE TREE THAT KNOWS STUFF
BZAT!
I'LL SHOW YOU MINE, IF YOU SHOW ME YOURS.

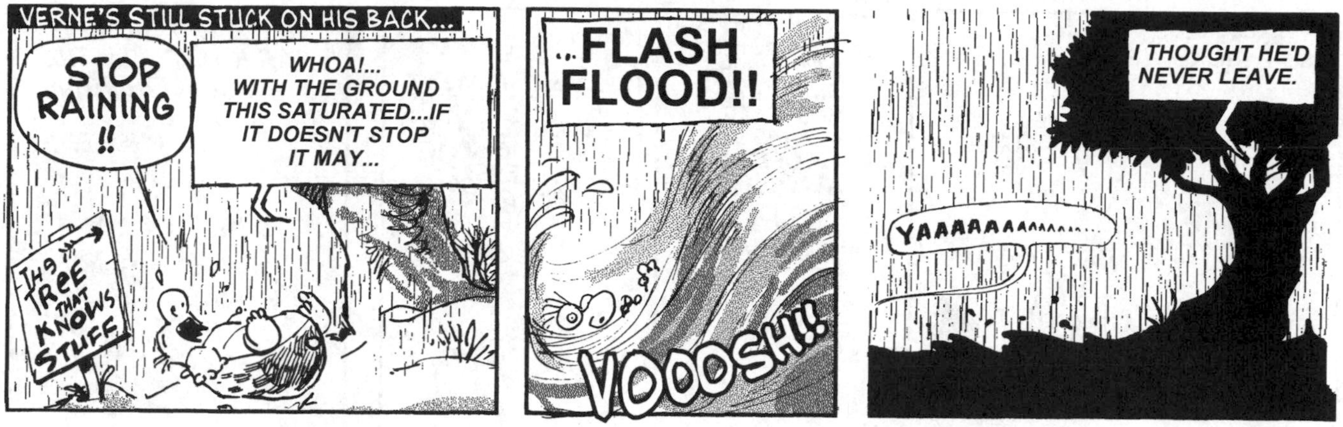

VERNE'S STILL STUCK ON HIS BACK...
STOP RAINING!!
WHOA!... WITH THE GROUND THIS SATURATED...IF IT DOESN'T STOP IT MAY...
THE TREE THAT KNOWS STUFF
...FLASH FLOOD!!
VOOOSH!!
YAAAAAAAAAAAA.....
I THOUGHT HE'D NEVER LEAVE.

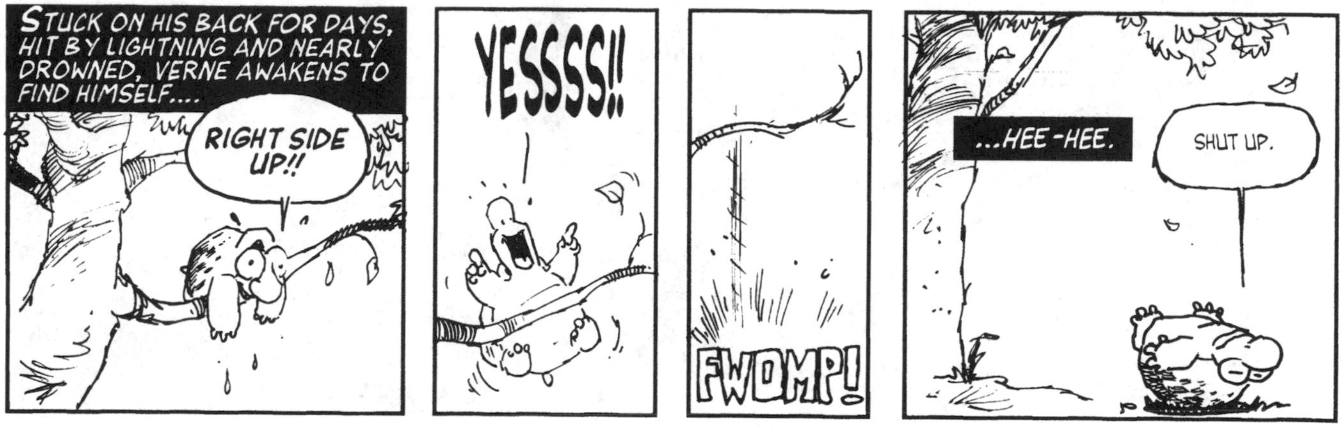

STUCK ON HIS BACK FOR DAYS, HIT BY LIGHTNING AND NEARLY DROWNED, VERNE AWAKENS TO FIND HIMSELF....
RIGHT SIDE UP!!
YESSSS!!
FWOMP!
...HEE-HEE.
SHUT UP.

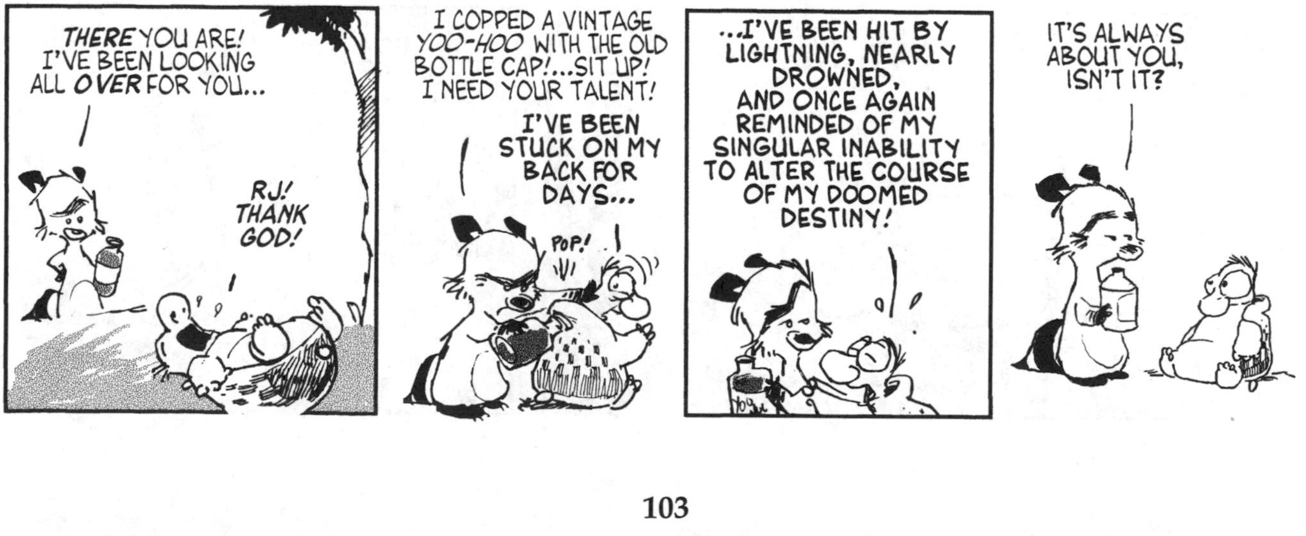

THERE YOU ARE! I'VE BEEN LOOKING ALL OVER FOR YOU...
RJ! THANK GOD!
I COPPED A VINTAGE YOO-HOO WITH THE OLD BOTTLE CAP!...SIT UP! I NEED YOUR TALENT!
I'VE BEEN STUCK ON MY BACK FOR DAYS...
POP!
...I'VE BEEN HIT BY LIGHTNING, NEARLY DROWNED, AND ONCE AGAIN REMINDED OF MY SINGULAR INABILITY TO ALTER THE COURSE OF MY DOOMED DESTINY!
IT'S ALWAYS ABOUT YOU, ISN'T IT?

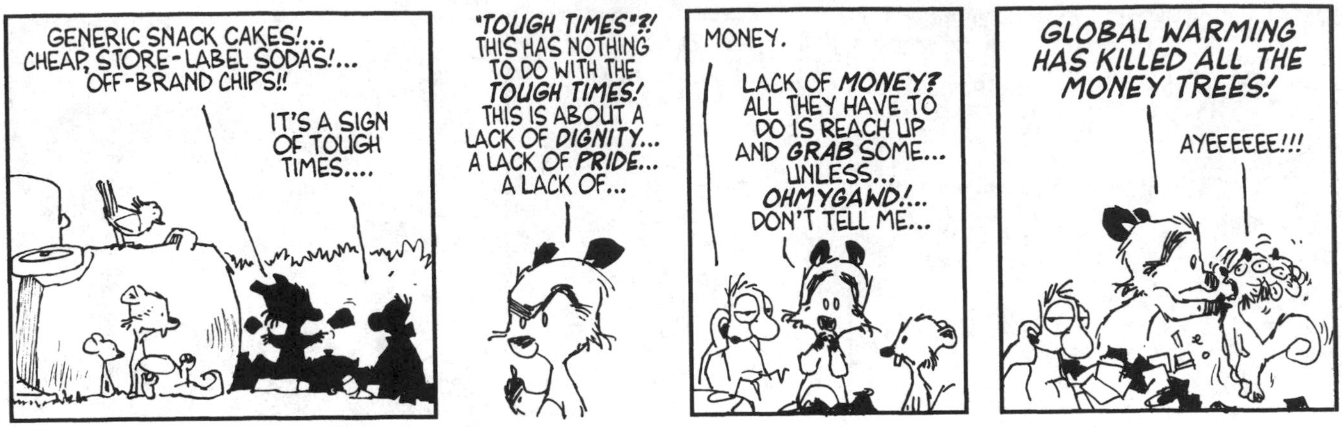
GENERIC SNACK CAKES!... CHEAP, STORE-LABEL SODAS!... OFF-BRAND CHIPS!!
IT'S A SIGN OF TOUGH TIMES....
"TOUGH TIMES"?! THIS HAS NOTHING TO DO WITH THE TOUGH TIMES! THIS IS ABOUT A LACK OF DIGNITY... A LACK OF PRIDE... A LACK OF...
MONEY.
LACK OF MONEY? ALL THEY HAVE TO DO IS REACH UP AND GRAB SOME... UNLESS... OHMYGAWD!... DON'T TELL ME...
GLOBAL WARMING HAS KILLED ALL THE MONEY TREES!
AYEEEEEE!!!

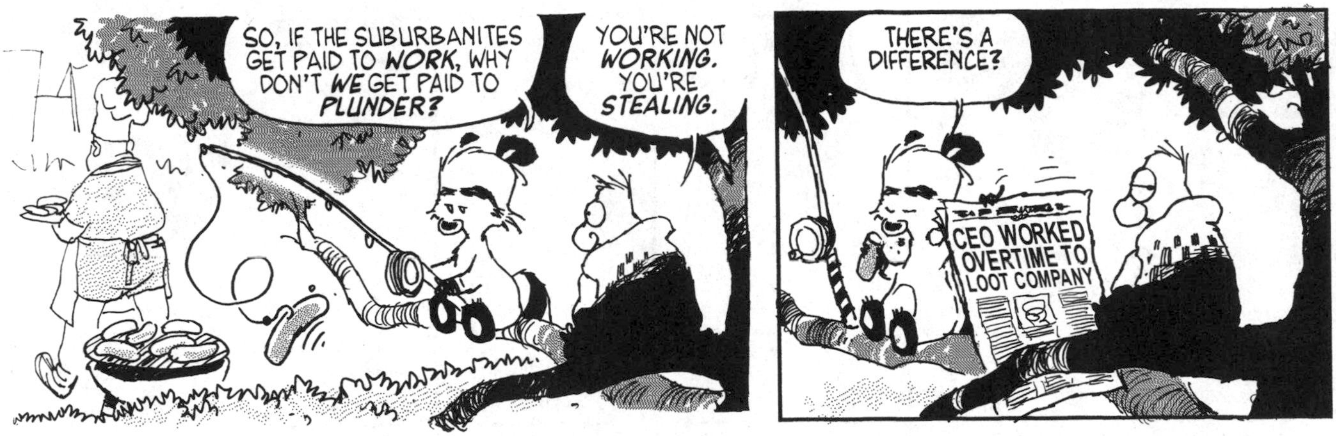
SO, IF THE SUBURBANITES GET PAID TO WORK, WHY DON'T WE GET PAID TO PLUNDER?
YOU'RE NOT WORKING. YOU'RE STEALING.
THERE'S A DIFFERENCE?
CEO WORKED OVERTIME TO LOOT COMPANY

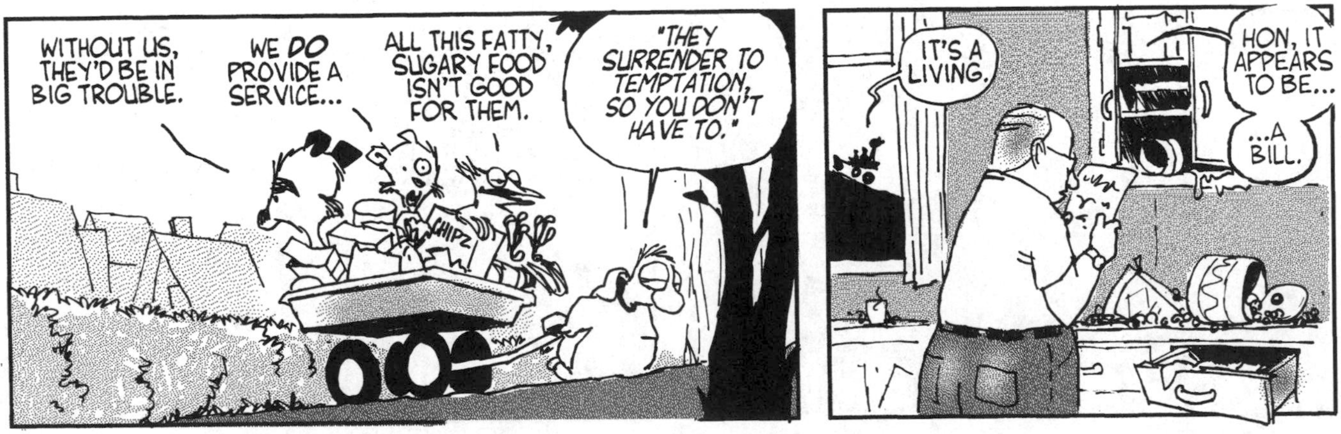
WITHOUT US, THEY'D BE IN BIG TROUBLE.
WE DO PROVIDE A SERVICE...
ALL THIS FATTY, SUGARY FOOD ISN'T GOOD FOR THEM.
"THEY SURRENDER TO TEMPTATION, SO YOU DON'T HAVE TO."
CHIPZ
IT'S A LIVING.
HON, IT APPEARS TO BE...
...A BILL.

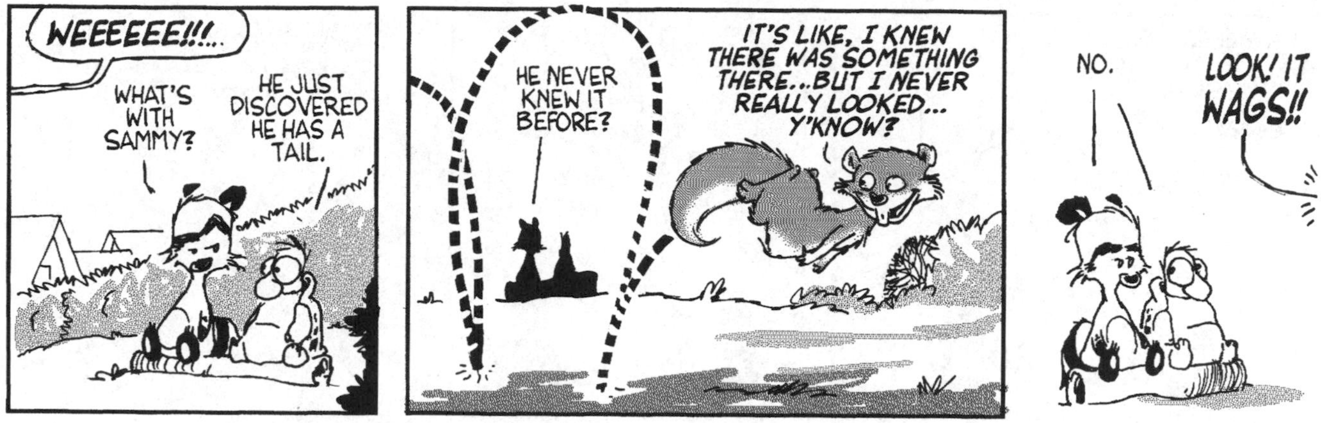
WEEEEEE!!!...
WHAT'S WITH SAMMY?
HE JUST DISCOVERED HE HAS A TAIL.
HE NEVER KNEW IT BEFORE?
IT'S LIKE, I KNEW THERE WAS SOMETHING THERE...BUT I NEVER REALLY LOOKED... Y'KNOW?
NO.
LOOK! IT WAGS!!

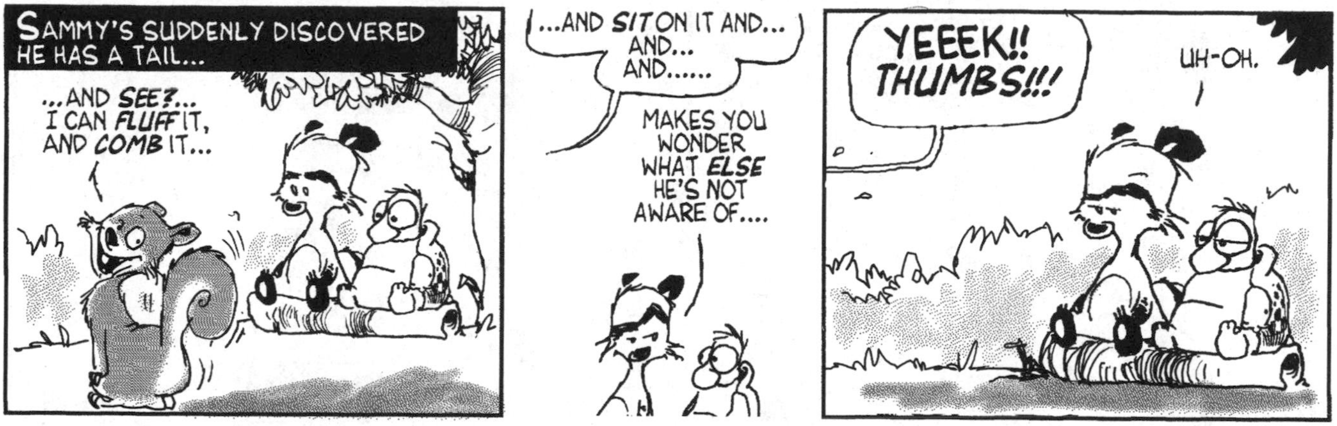
SAMMY'S SUDDENLY DISCOVERED HE HAS A TAIL...
...AND SEE?... I CAN FLUFF IT, AND COMB IT...
...AND SIT ON IT AND... AND... AND......
MAKES YOU WONDER WHAT ELSE HE'S NOT AWARE OF....
YEEEK!! THUMBS!!!
UH-OH.

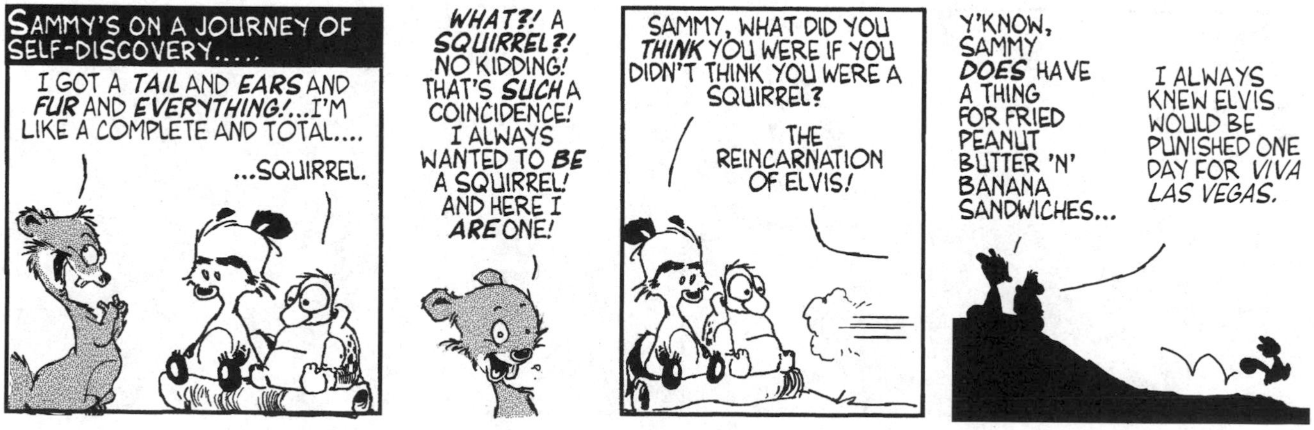
SAMMY'S ON A JOURNEY OF SELF-DISCOVERY.....
I GOT A TAIL AND EARS AND FUR AND EVERYTHING!...I'M LIKE A COMPLETE AND TOTAL....
...SQUIRREL.
WHAT?! A SQUIRREL?! NO KIDDING! THAT'S SUCH A COINCIDENCE! I ALWAYS WANTED TO BE A SQUIRREL! AND HERE I ARE ONE!
SAMMY, WHAT DID YOU THINK YOU WERE IF YOU DIDN'T THINK YOU WERE A SQUIRREL?
THE REINCARNATION OF ELVIS!
Y'KNOW, SAMMY DOES HAVE A THING FOR FRIED PEANUT BUTTER 'N' BANANA SANDWICHES...
I ALWAYS KNEW ELVIS WOULD BE PUNISHED ONE DAY FOR VIVA LAS VEGAS.

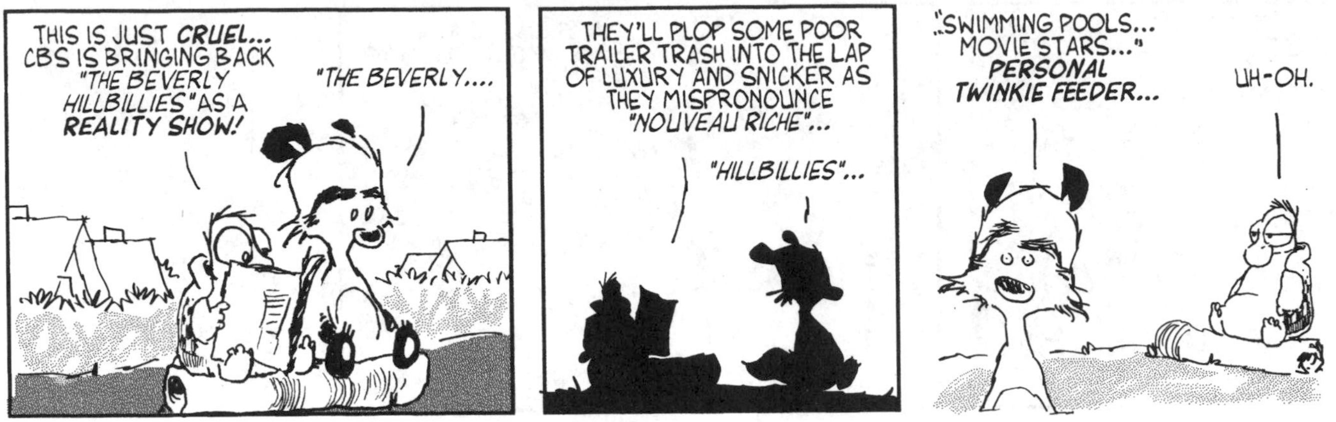
THIS IS JUST CRUEL... CBS IS BRINGING BACK "THE BEVERLY HILLBILLIES" AS A REALITY SHOW!
"THE BEVERLY....
THEY'LL PLOP SOME POOR TRAILER TRASH INTO THE LAP OF LUXURY AND SNICKER AS THEY MISPRONOUNCE "NOUVEAU RICHE"...
"HILLBILLIES"...
..."SWIMMING POOLS... MOVIE STARS..." PERSONAL TWINKIE FEEDER...
UH-OH.

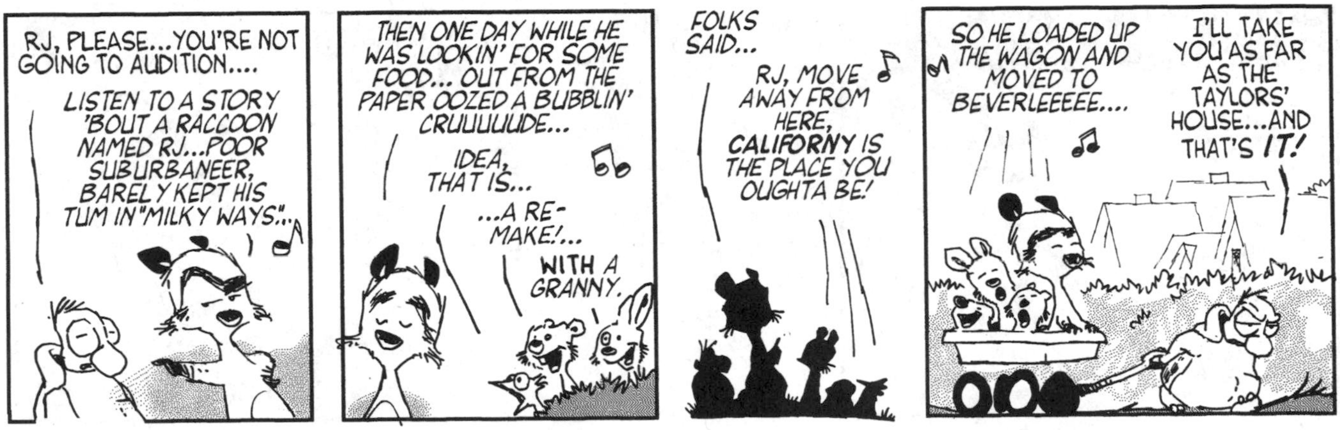
RJ, PLEASE....YOU'RE NOT GOING TO AUDITION....
LISTEN TO A STORY 'BOUT A RACCOON NAMED RJ...POOR SUBURBANEER, BARELY KEPT HIS TUM IN "MILKY WAYS"...
THEN ONE DAY WHILE HE WAS LOOKIN' FOR SOME FOOD... OUT FROM THE PAPER OOZED A BUBBLIN' CRUUUUUDE...
IDEA, THAT IS...
...A RE-MAKE!...
WITH A GRANNY.
FOLKS SAID...
RJ, MOVE AWAY FROM HERE, CALIFORNY IS THE PLACE YOU OUGHTA BE!
SO HE LOADED UP THE WAGON AND MOVED TO BEVERLEEEEE....
I'LL TAKE YOU AS FAR AS THE TAYLORS' HOUSE...AND THAT'S IT!

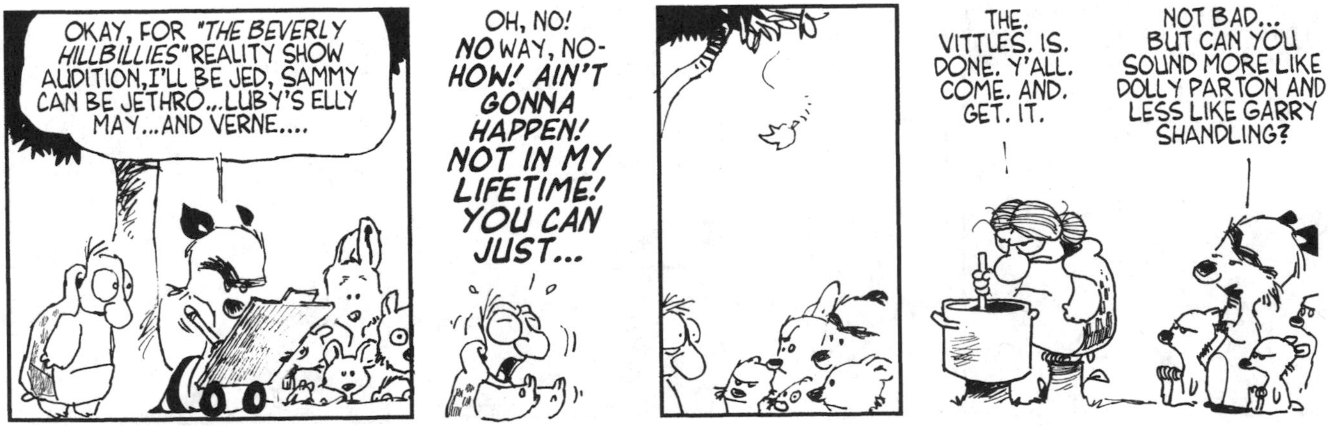
OKAY, FOR "THE BEVERLY HILLBILLIES" REALITY SHOW AUDITION, I'LL BE JED, SAMMY CAN BE JETHRO...LUBY'S ELLY MAY...AND VERNE....
OH, NO! NO WAY, NO-HOW! AIN'T GONNA HAPPEN! NOT IN MY LIFETIME! YOU CAN JUST...
THE. VITTLES. IS. DONE. Y'ALL. COME. AND. GET. IT.
NOT BAD... BUT CAN YOU SOUND MORE LIKE DOLLY PARTON AND LESS LIKE GARRY SHANDLING?

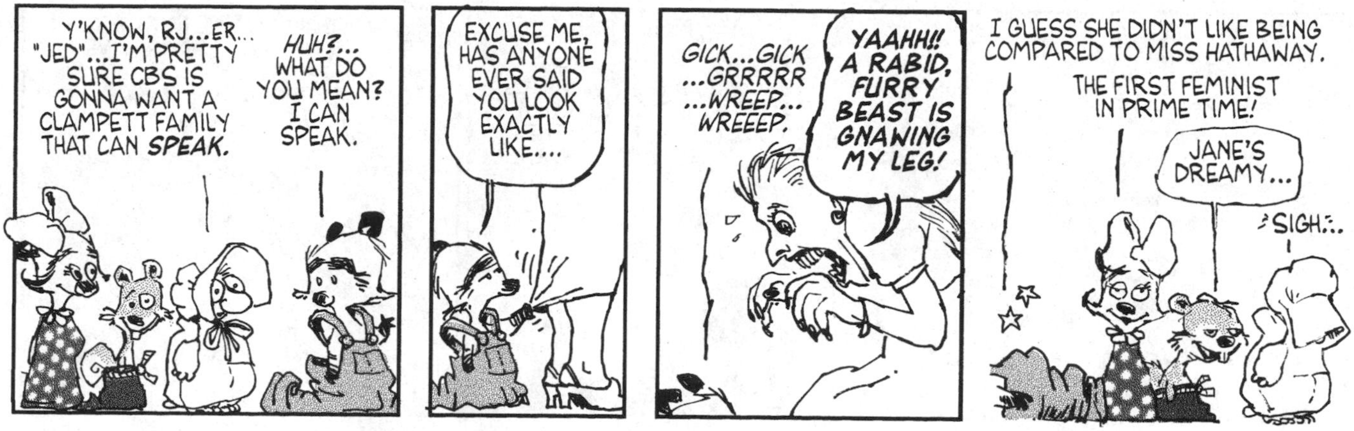

Y'KNOW, RJ...ER... "JED"...I'M PRETTY SURE CBS IS GONNA WANT A CLAMPETT FAMILY THAT CAN *SPEAK.*
HUH?... WHAT DO YOU MEAN? I CAN SPEAK.
EXCUSE ME, HAS ANYONE EVER SAID YOU LOOK EXACTLY LIKE....
GICK...GICK ...GRRRRR ...WREEP... WREEEP.
YAAHH!! A RABID, FURRY BEAST IS GNAWING MY LEG!
I GUESS SHE DIDN'T LIKE BEING COMPARED TO MISS HATHAWAY.
THE FIRST FEMINIST IN PRIME TIME!
JANE'S DREAMY...
SIGH...

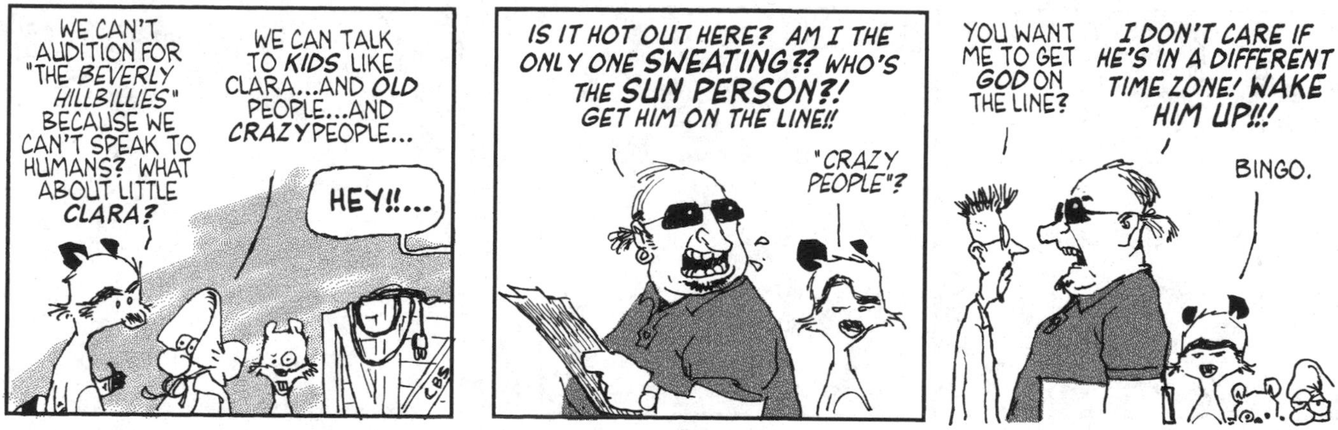

WE CAN'T AUDITION FOR "THE *BEVERLY HILLBILLIES*" BECAUSE WE CAN'T SPEAK TO HUMANS? WHAT ABOUT LITTLE *CLARA?*
WE CAN TALK TO *KIDS* LIKE CLARA...AND *OLD* PEOPLE...AND *CRAZY* PEOPLE...
HEY!!...
CBS
IS IT HOT OUT HERE? AM I THE ONLY ONE SWEATING?? WHO'S THE SUN PERSON?! GET HIM ON THE LINE!!
"CRAZY PEOPLE"?
YOU WANT ME TO GET *GOD* ON THE LINE?
I DON'T CARE IF HE'S IN A DIFFERENT TIME ZONE! WAKE HIM UP!!!
BINGO.

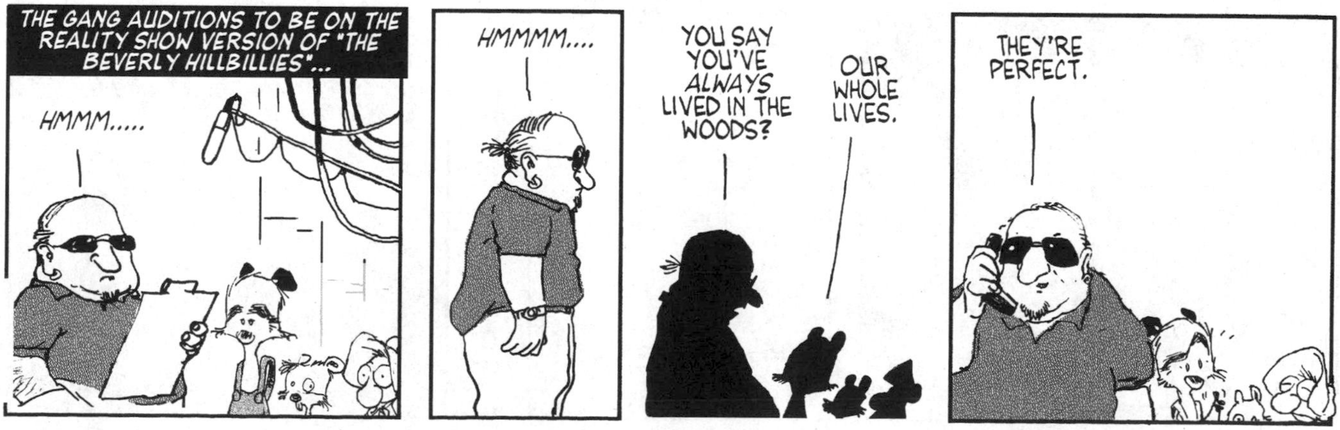

THE GANG AUDITIONS TO BE ON THE REALITY SHOW VERSION OF "THE BEVERLY HILLBILLIES"...
HMMM.....
HMMMM....
YOU SAY YOU'VE *ALWAYS* LIVED IN THE WOODS?
OUR WHOLE LIVES.
THEY'RE PERFECT.

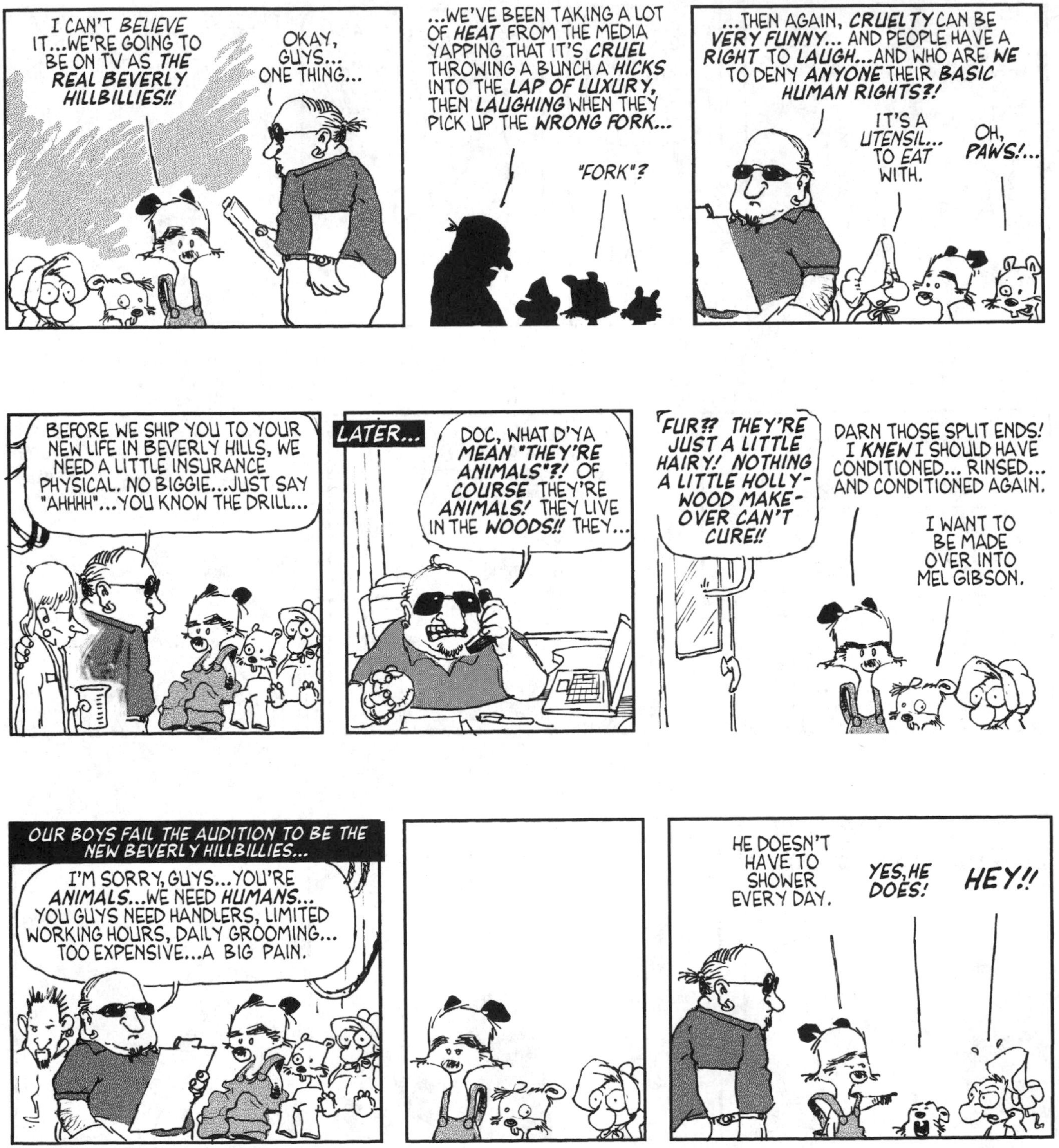
I CAN'T BELIEVE IT...WE'RE GOING TO BE ON TV AS THE REAL BEVERLY HILLBILLIES!!
OKAY, GUYS... ONE THING...
...WE'VE BEEN TAKING A LOT OF HEAT FROM THE MEDIA YAPPING THAT IT'S CRUEL THROWING A BUNCH A HICKS INTO THE LAP OF LUXURY, THEN LAUGHING WHEN THEY PICK UP THE WRONG FORK...
"FORK"?
...THEN AGAIN, CRUELTY CAN BE VERY FUNNY... AND PEOPLE HAVE A RIGHT TO LAUGH...AND WHO ARE WE TO DENY ANYONE THEIR BASIC HUMAN RIGHTS?!
IT'S A UTENSIL... TO EAT WITH.
OH, PAWS!...
BEFORE WE SHIP YOU TO YOUR NEW LIFE IN BEVERLY HILLS, WE NEED A LITTLE INSURANCE PHYSICAL. NO BIGGIE...JUST SAY "AHHHH"...YOU KNOW THE DRILL...
LATER...
DOC, WHAT D'YA MEAN "THEY'RE ANIMALS"?! OF COURSE THEY'RE ANIMALS! THEY LIVE IN THE WOODS!! THEY...
FUR?? THEY'RE JUST A LITTLE HAIRY! NOTHING A LITTLE HOLLY-WOOD MAKE-OVER CAN'T CURE!!
DARN THOSE SPLIT ENDS! I KNEW I SHOULD HAVE CONDITIONED... RINSED... AND CONDITIONED AGAIN.
I WANT TO BE MADE OVER INTO MEL GIBSON.
OUR BOYS FAIL THE AUDITION TO BE THE NEW BEVERLY HILLBILLIES...
I'M SORRY, GUYS...YOU'RE ANIMALS...WE NEED HUMANS... YOU GUYS NEED HANDLERS, LIMITED WORKING HOURS, DAILY GROOMING... TOO EXPENSIVE...A BIG PAIN.
HE DOESN'T HAVE TO SHOWER EVERY DAY.
YES, HE DOES!
HEY!!

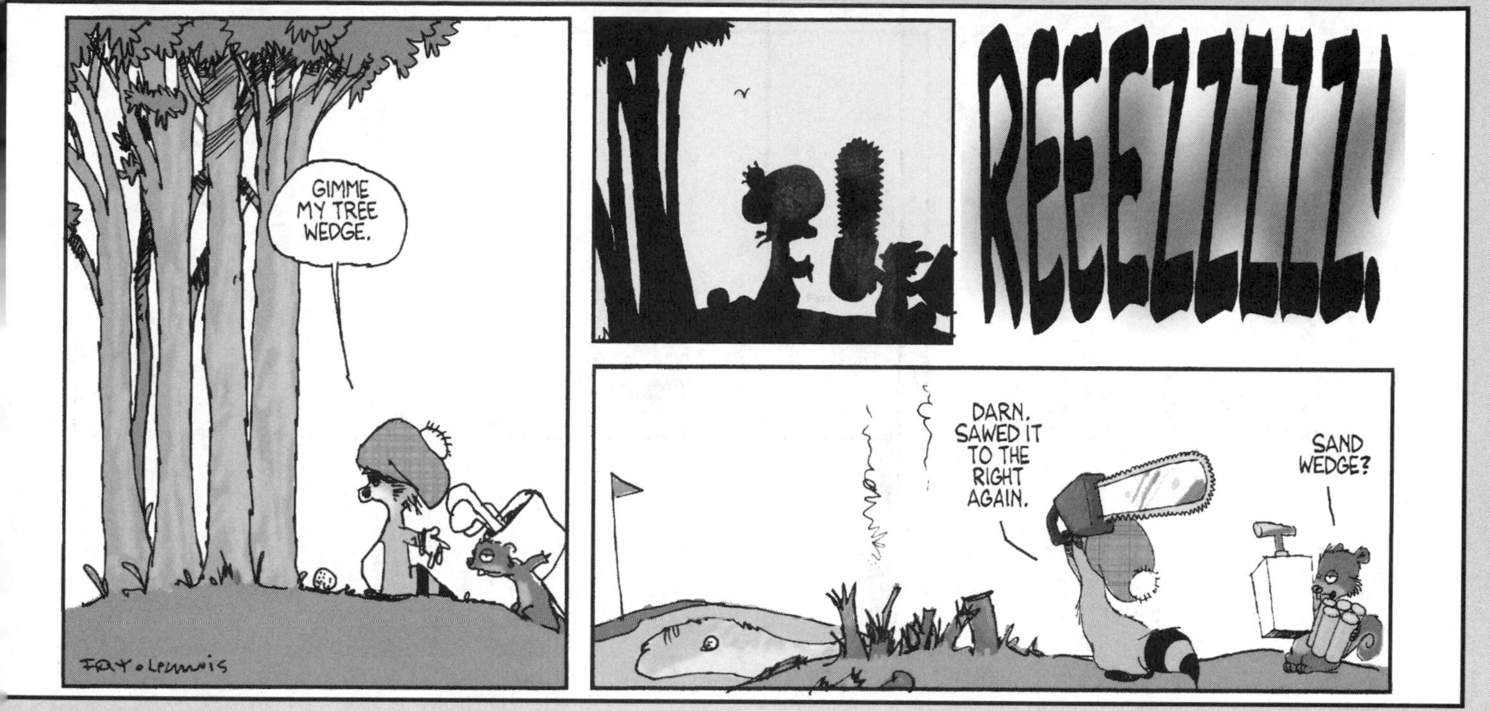
GIMME MY TREE WEDGE.
REEEZZZZZ!
DARN. SAWED IT TO THE RIGHT AGAIN.
SAND WEDGE?
FRYOLPLNNIS

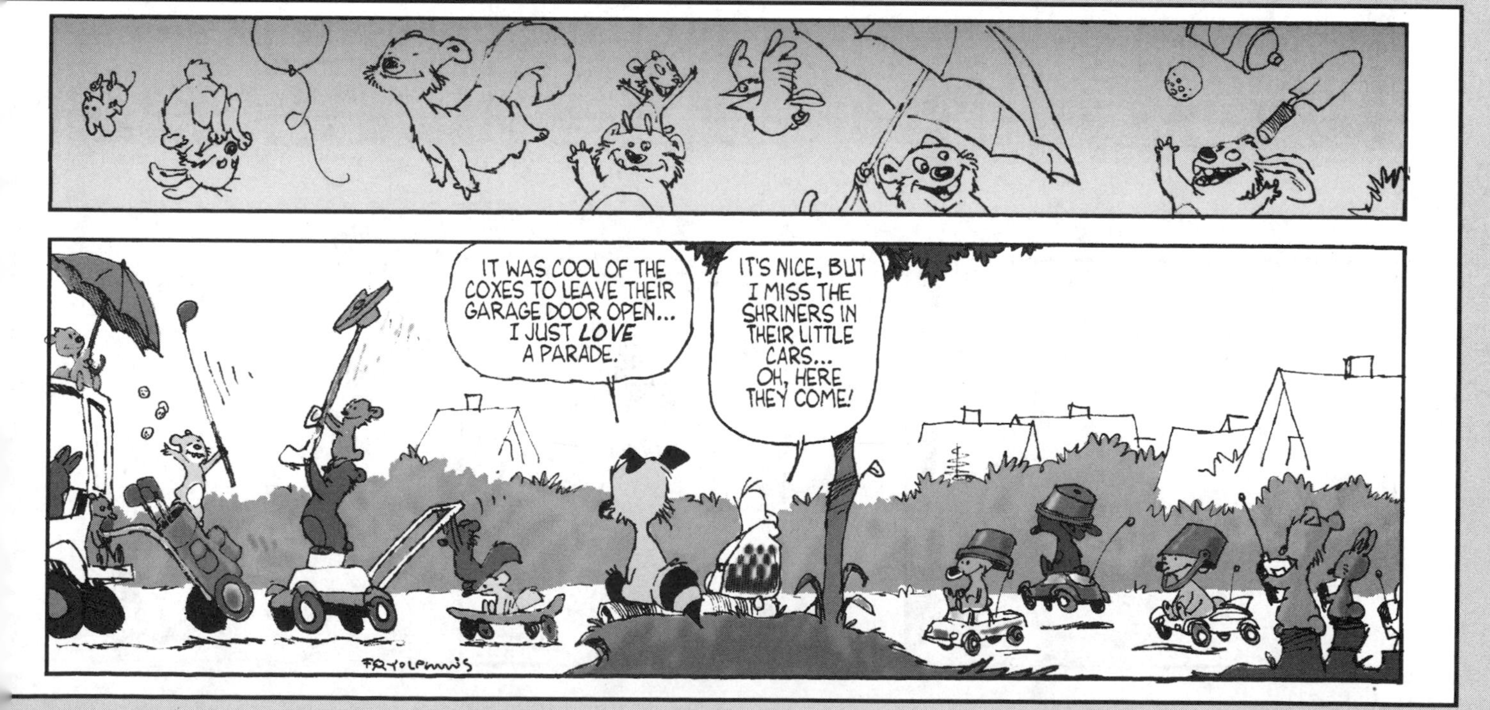
IT WAS COOL OF THE COXES TO LEAVE THEIR GARAGE DOOR OPEN... I JUST *LOVE* A PARADE.
IT'S NICE, BUT I MISS THE SHRINERS IN THEIR LITTLE CARS... OH, HERE THEY COME!
FRYOLPLNNIS

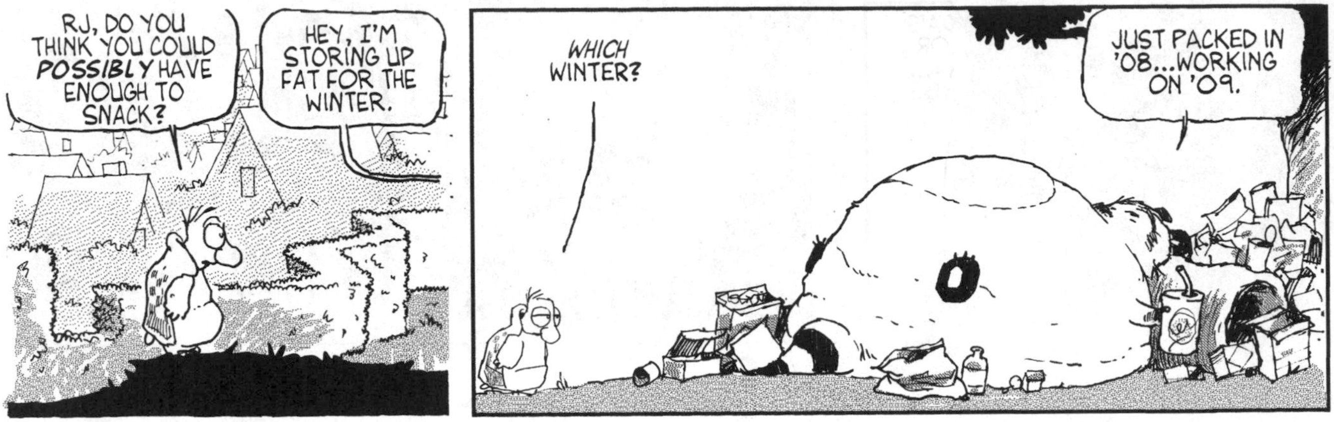
RJ, DO YOU THINK YOU COULD POSSIBLY HAVE ENOUGH TO SNACK?
HEY, I'M STORING UP FAT FOR THE WINTER.
WHICH WINTER?
JUST PACKED IN '08...WORKING ON '09.

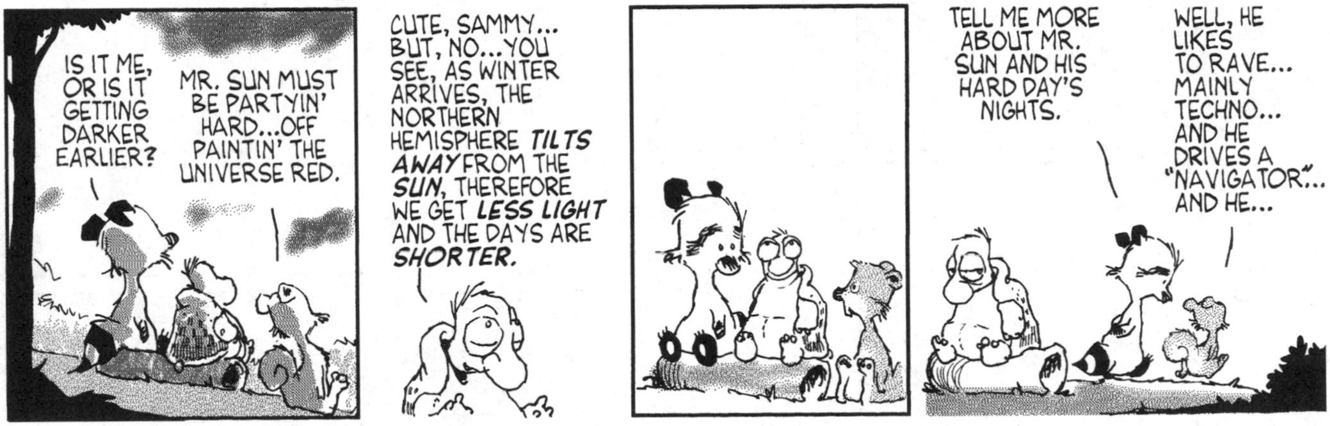
IS IT ME, OR IS IT GETTING DARKER EARLIER?
MR. SUN MUST BE PARTYIN' HARD...OFF PAINTIN' THE UNIVERSE RED.
CUTE, SAMMY... BUT, NO...YOU SEE, AS WINTER ARRIVES, THE NORTHERN HEMISPHERE TILTS AWAY FROM THE SUN, THEREFORE WE GET LESS LIGHT AND THE DAYS ARE SHORTER.
TELL ME MORE ABOUT MR. SUN AND HIS HARD DAY'S NIGHTS.
WELL, HE LIKES TO RAVE... MAINLY TECHNO... AND HE DRIVES A "NAVIGATOR"... AND HE...

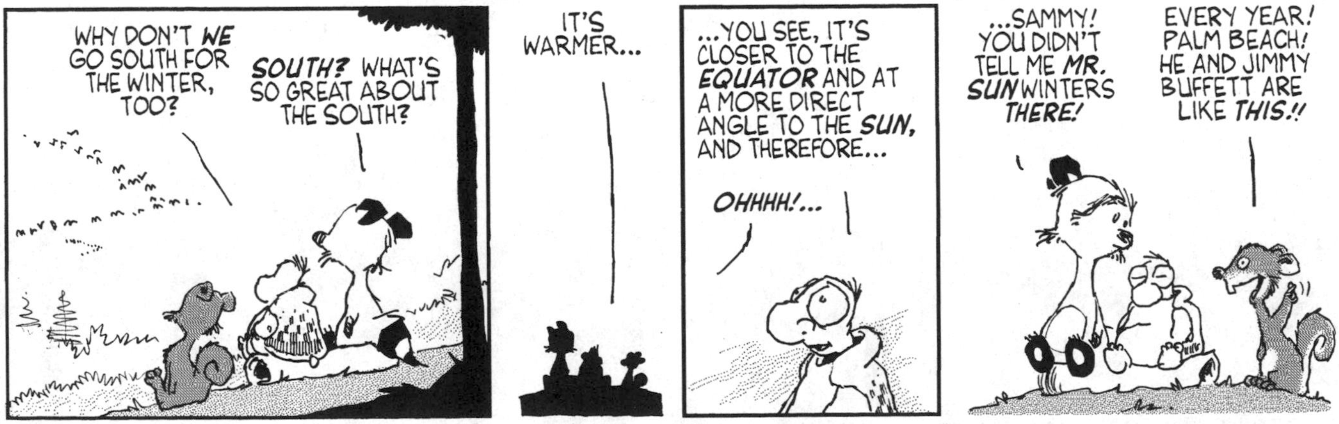
WHY DON'T WE GO SOUTH FOR THE WINTER, TOO?
SOUTH? WHAT'S SO GREAT ABOUT THE SOUTH?
IT'S WARMER...
...YOU SEE, IT'S CLOSER TO THE EQUATOR AND AT A MORE DIRECT ANGLE TO THE SUN, AND THEREFORE...
OHHHH!...
...SAMMY! YOU DIDN'T TELL ME MR. SUN WINTERS THERE!
EVERY YEAR! PALM BEACH! HE AND JIMMY BUFFETT ARE LIKE THIS!!

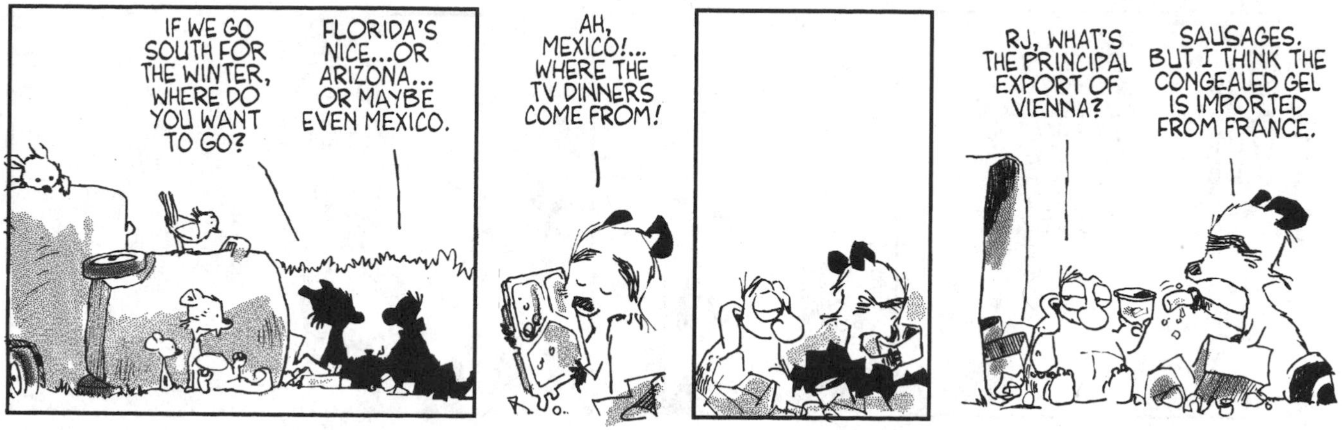
IF WE GO SOUTH FOR THE WINTER, WHERE DO YOU WANT TO GO?
FLORIDA'S NICE...OR ARIZONA... OR MAYBE EVEN MEXICO.
AH, MEXICO!... WHERE THE TV DINNERS COME FROM!
RJ, WHAT'S THE PRINCIPAL EXPORT OF VIENNA?
SAUSAGES. BUT I THINK THE CONGEALED GEL IS IMPORTED FROM FRANCE.

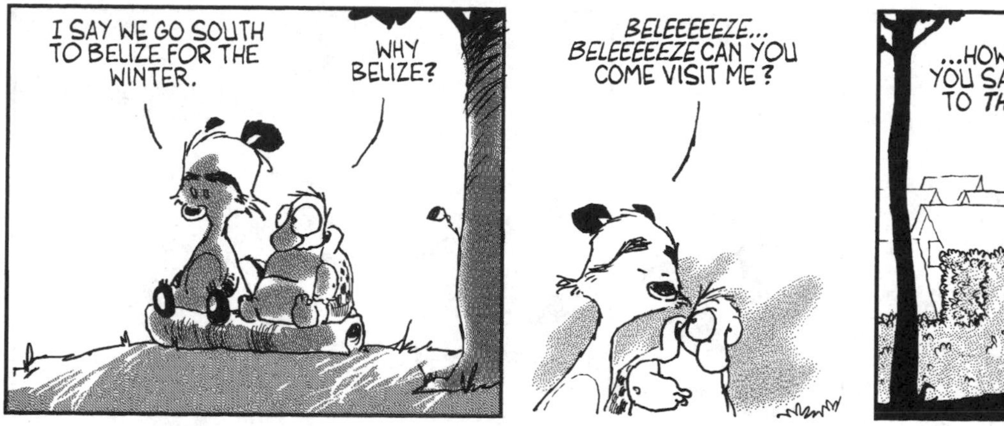
I SAY WE GO SOUTH TO BELIZE FOR THE WINTER.
WHY BELIZE?
BELEEEEEZE... BELEEEEEZE CAN YOU COME VISIT ME?
...HOW CAN YOU SAY NO TO THAT?
WILL YOU BELEEEEEZE SHUT UP?

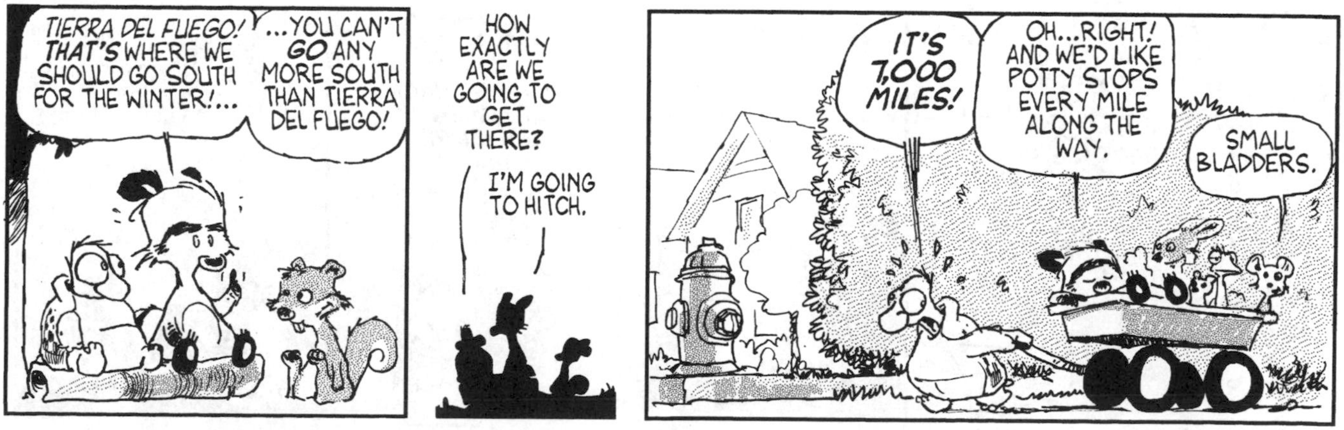
TIERRA DEL FUEGO! THAT'S WHERE WE SHOULD GO SOUTH FOR THE WINTER!...
...YOU CAN'T GO ANY MORE SOUTH THAN TIERRA DEL FUEGO!
HOW EXACTLY ARE WE GOING TO GET THERE?
I'M GOING TO HITCH.
IT'S 7,000 MILES!
OH...RIGHT! AND WE'D LIKE POTTY STOPS EVERY MILE ALONG THE WAY.
SMALL BLADDERS.

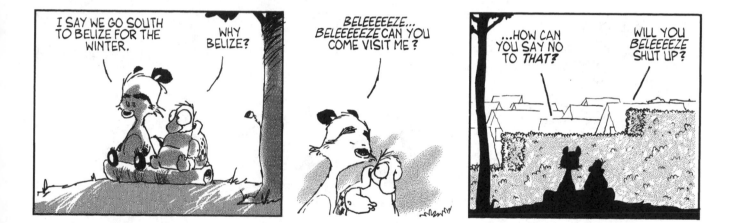

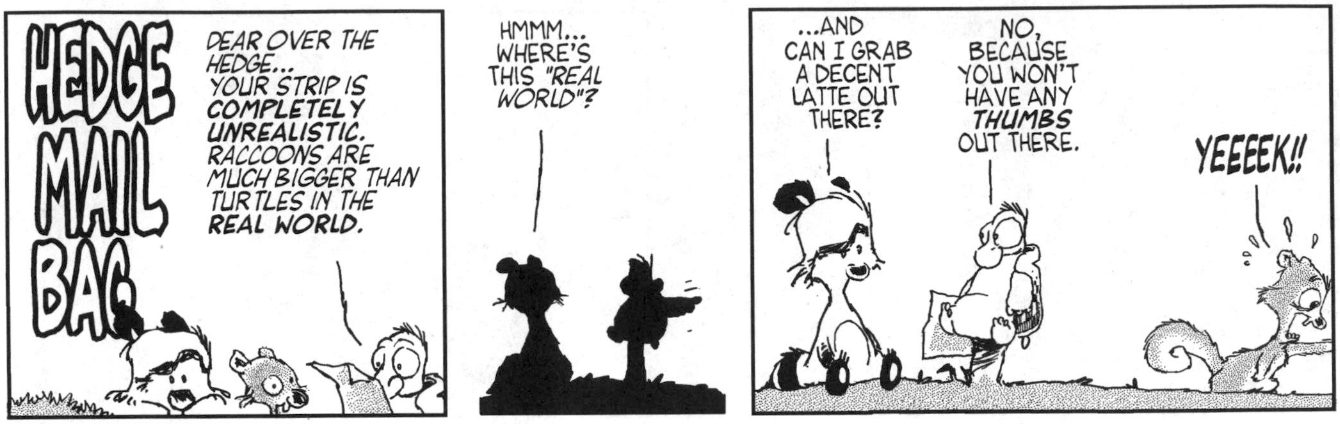
HEDGE MAIL BAG
DEAR OVER THE HEDGE... YOUR STRIP IS COMPLETELY UNREALISTIC. RACCOONS ARE MUCH BIGGER THAN TURTLES IN THE REAL WORLD.
HMMM... WHERE'S THIS "REAL WORLD"?
...AND CAN I GRAB A DECENT LATTE OUT THERE?
NO, BECAUSE YOU WON'T HAVE ANY THUMBS OUT THERE.
YEEEEK!!

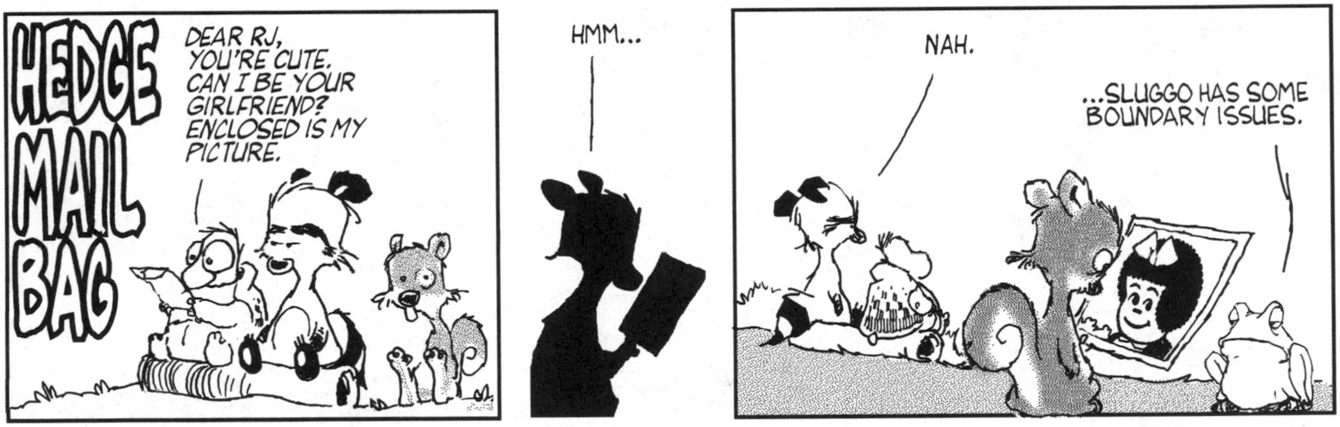
HEDGE MAIL BAG
DEAR RJ, YOU'RE CUTE. CAN I BE YOUR GIRLFRIEND? ENCLOSED IS MY PICTURE.
HMM...
NAH.
...SLUGGO HAS SOME BOUNDARY ISSUES.

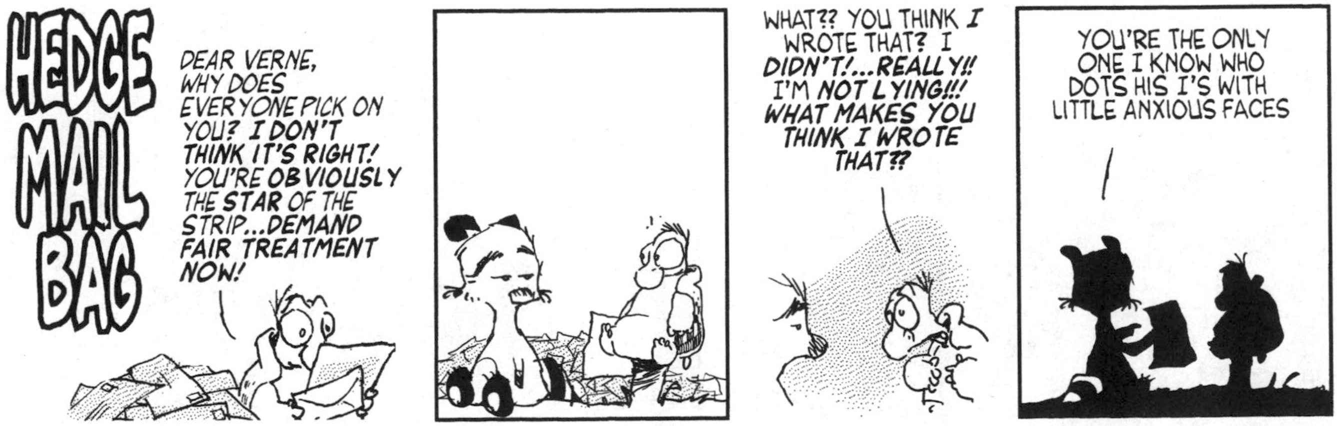
HEDGE MAIL BAG
DEAR VERNE, WHY DOES EVERYONE PICK ON YOU? I DON'T THINK IT'S RIGHT! YOU'RE OBVIOUSLY THE STAR OF THE STRIP...DEMAND FAIR TREATMENT NOW!
WHAT?? YOU THINK I WROTE THAT? I DIDN'T!...REALLY!! I'M NOT LYING!!! WHAT MAKES YOU THINK I WROTE THAT??
YOU'RE THE ONLY ONE I KNOW WHO DOTS HIS I'S WITH LITTLE ANXIOUS FACES

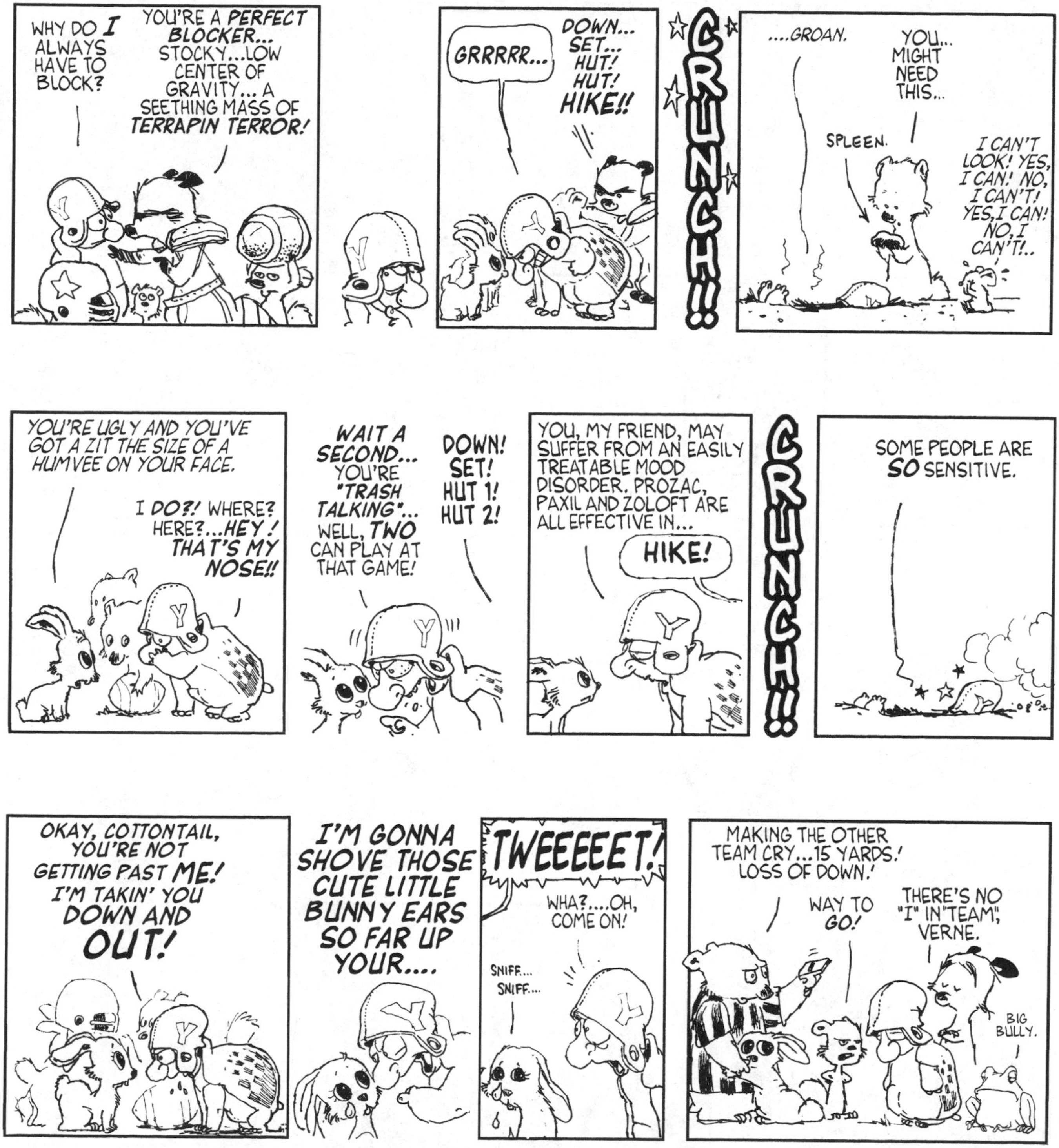
WHY DO I ALWAYS HAVE TO BLOCK?
YOU'RE A PERFECT BLOCKER... STOCKY...LOW CENTER OF GRAVITY... A SEETHING MASS OF TERRAPIN TERROR!
GRRRRR...
DOWN... SET... HUT! HUT! HIKE!!
CRUNCH!!
....GROAN.
YOU... MIGHT NEED THIS...
SPLEEN.
I CAN'T LOOK! YES, I CAN! NO, I CAN'T! YES, I CAN! NO, I CAN'T!..
YOU'RE UGLY AND YOU'VE GOT A ZIT THE SIZE OF A HUMVEE ON YOUR FACE.
I DO?! WHERE? HERE?...HEY! THAT'S MY NOSE!!
WAIT A SECOND... YOU'RE "TRASH TALKING"... WELL, TWO CAN PLAY AT THAT GAME!
DOWN! SET! HUT 1! HUT 2!
YOU, MY FRIEND, MAY SUFFER FROM AN EASILY TREATABLE MOOD DISORDER. PROZAC, PAXIL AND ZOLOFT ARE ALL EFFECTIVE IN...
HIKE!
CRUNCH!!
SOME PEOPLE ARE SO SENSITIVE.
OKAY, COTTONTAIL, YOU'RE NOT GETTING PAST ME! I'M TAKIN' YOU DOWN AND OUT!
I'M GONNA SHOVE THOSE CUTE LITTLE BUNNY EARS SO FAR UP YOUR....
TWEEEEEET!
WHA?....OH, COME ON!
SNIFF.... SNIFF....
MAKING THE OTHER TEAM CRY...15 YARDS! LOSS OF DOWN!
WAY TO GO!
THERE'S NO "I" IN "TEAM", VERNE.
BIG BULLY.

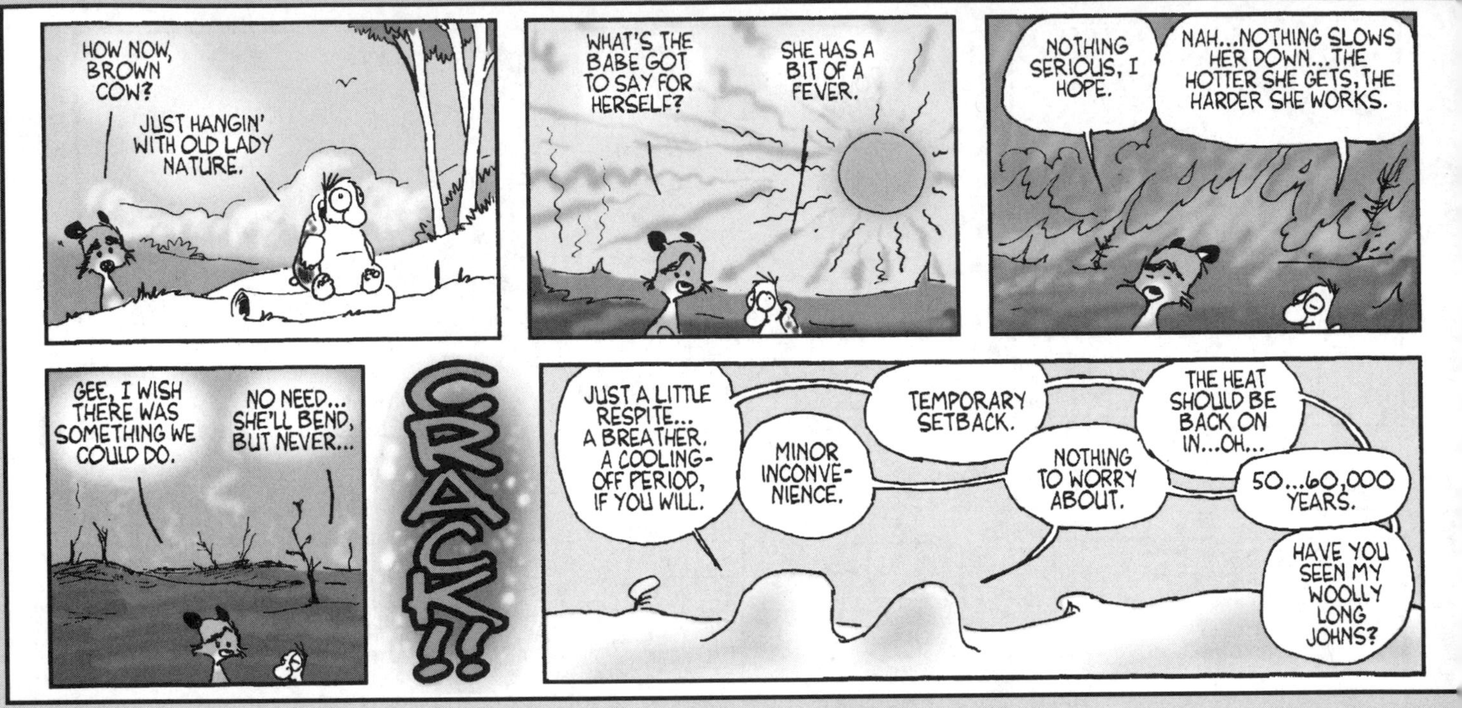
HOW NOW, BROWN COW?
JUST HANGIN' WITH OLD LADY NATURE.
WHAT'S THE BABE GOT TO SAY FOR HERSELF?
SHE HAS A BIT OF A FEVER.
NOTHING SERIOUS, I HOPE.
NAH...NOTHING SLOWS HER DOWN...THE HOTTER SHE GETS, THE HARDER SHE WORKS.
GEE, I WISH THERE WAS SOMETHING WE COULD DO.
NO NEED... SHE'LL BEND, BUT NEVER...
CRACK!!
JUST A LITTLE RESPITE... A BREATHER. A COOLING-OFF PERIOD, IF YOU WILL.
MINOR INCONVENIENCE.
TEMPORARY SETBACK.
NOTHING TO WORRY ABOUT.
THE HEAT SHOULD BE BACK ON IN...OH...
50...60,000 YEARS.
HAVE YOU SEEN MY WOOLLY LONG JOHNS?

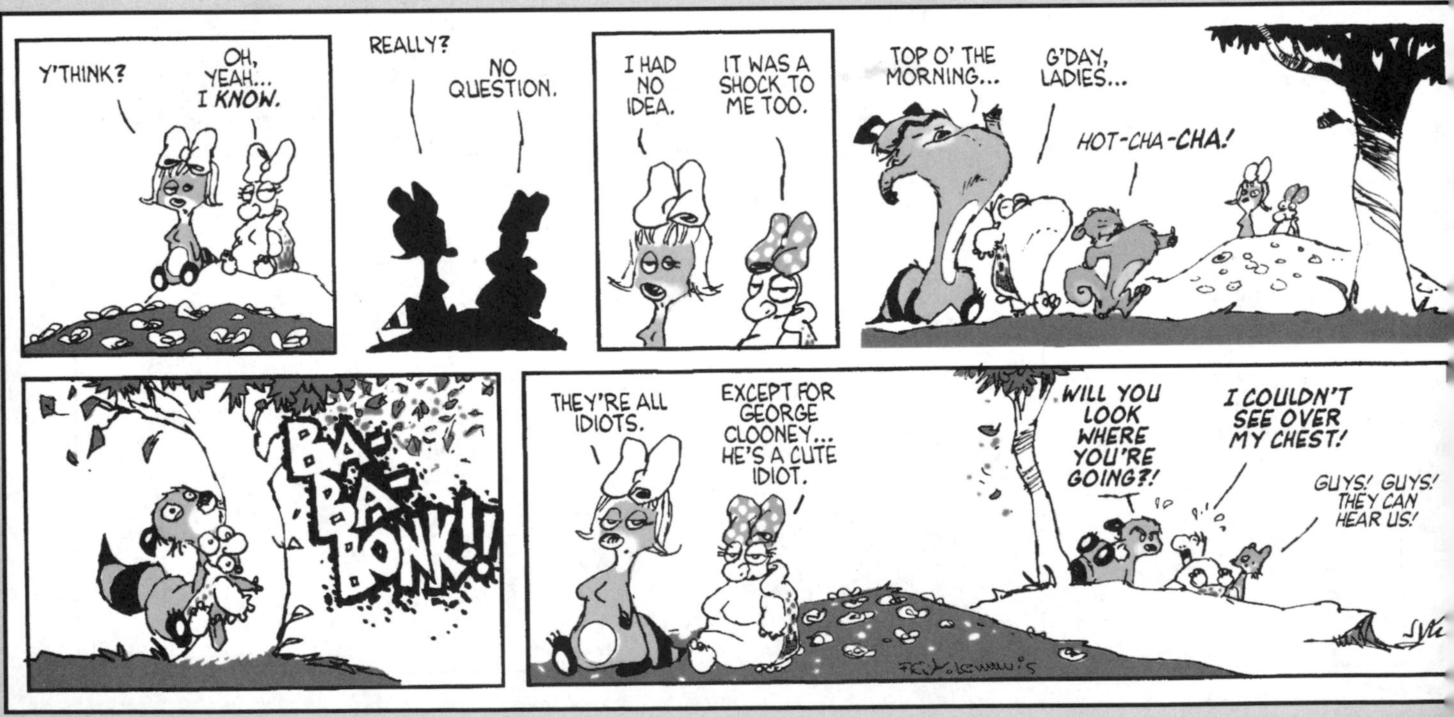
Y'THINK?
OH, YEAH... I KNOW.
REALLY?
NO QUESTION.
I HAD NO IDEA.
IT WAS A SHOCK TO ME TOO.
TOP O' THE MORNING...
G'DAY, LADIES...
HOT-CHA-CHA!
BA-BA-BONK!!
THEY'RE ALL IDIOTS.
EXCEPT FOR GEORGE CLOONEY... HE'S A CUTE IDIOT.
WILL YOU LOOK WHERE YOU'RE GOING?!
I COULDN'T SEE OVER MY CHEST!
GUYS! GUYS! THEY CAN HEAR US!

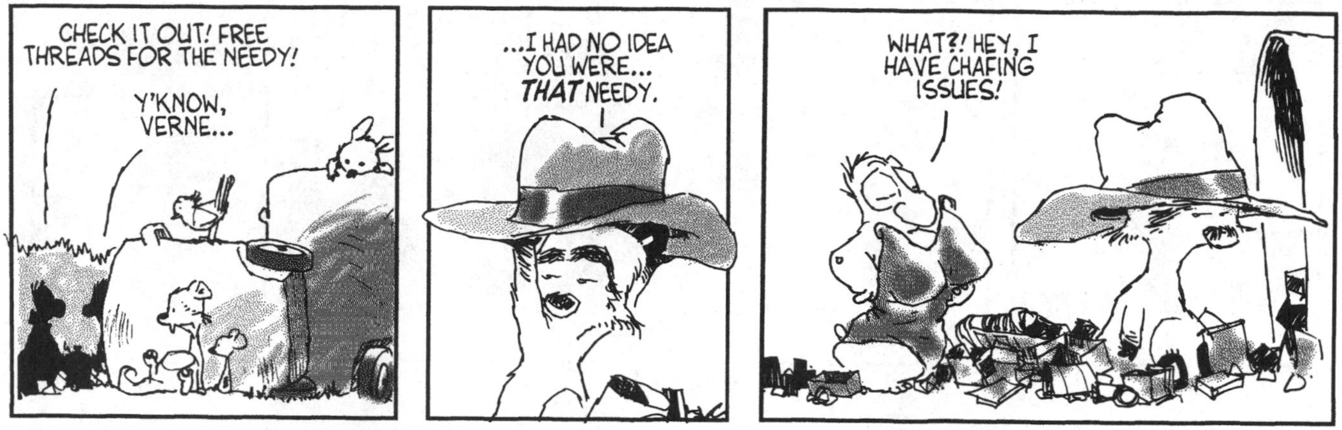
CHECK IT OUT! FREE THREADS FOR THE NEEDY!
Y'KNOW, VERNE...
...I HAD NO IDEA YOU WERE... THAT NEEDY.
WHAT?! HEY, I HAVE CHAFING ISSUES!

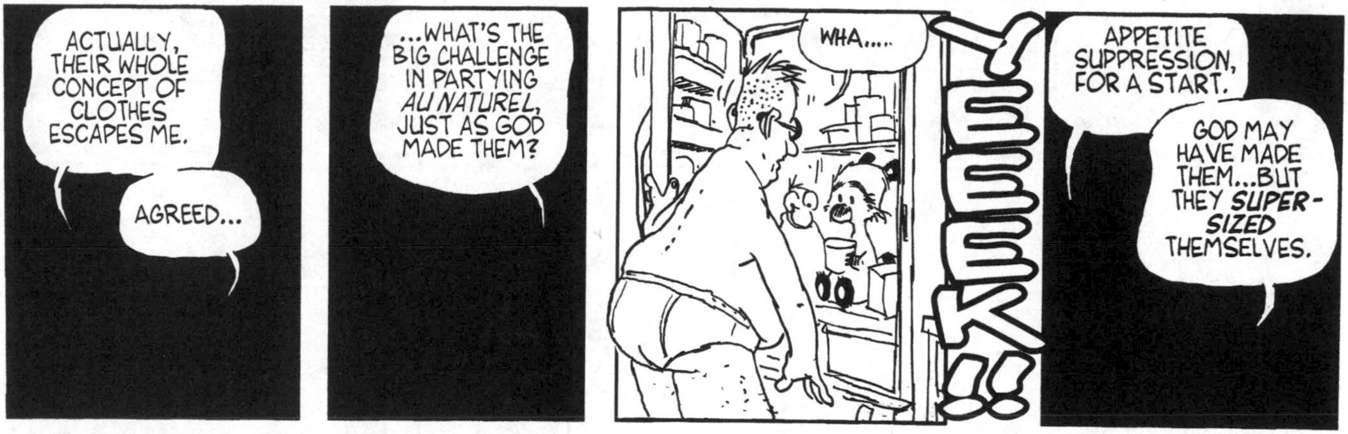
ACTUALLY, THEIR WHOLE CONCEPT OF CLOTHES ESCAPES ME.
AGREED...
...WHAT'S THE BIG CHALLENGE IN PARTYING AU NATUREL, JUST AS GOD MADE THEM?
WHA.....
YEEEEK!!
APPETITE SUPPRESSION, FOR A START.
GOD MAY HAVE MADE THEM...BUT THEY SUPER-SIZED THEMSELVES.

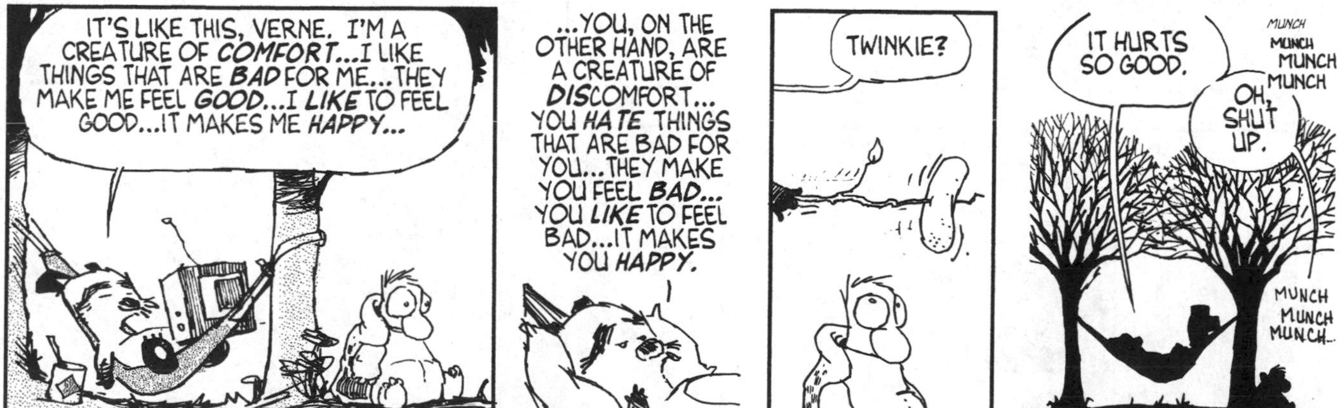
IT'S LIKE THIS, VERNE. I'M A CREATURE OF COMFORT...I LIKE THINGS THAT ARE BAD FOR ME...THEY MAKE ME FEEL GOOD...I LIKE TO FEEL GOOD...IT MAKES ME HAPPY...
...YOU, ON THE OTHER HAND, ARE A CREATURE OF DISCOMFORT... YOU HATE THINGS THAT ARE BAD FOR YOU...THEY MAKE YOU FEEL BAD... YOU LIKE TO FEEL BAD...IT MAKES YOU HAPPY.
TWINKIE?
IT HURTS SO GOOD.
MUNCH MUNCH MUNCH MUNCH
OH, SHUT UP.
MUNCH MUNCH MUNCH...

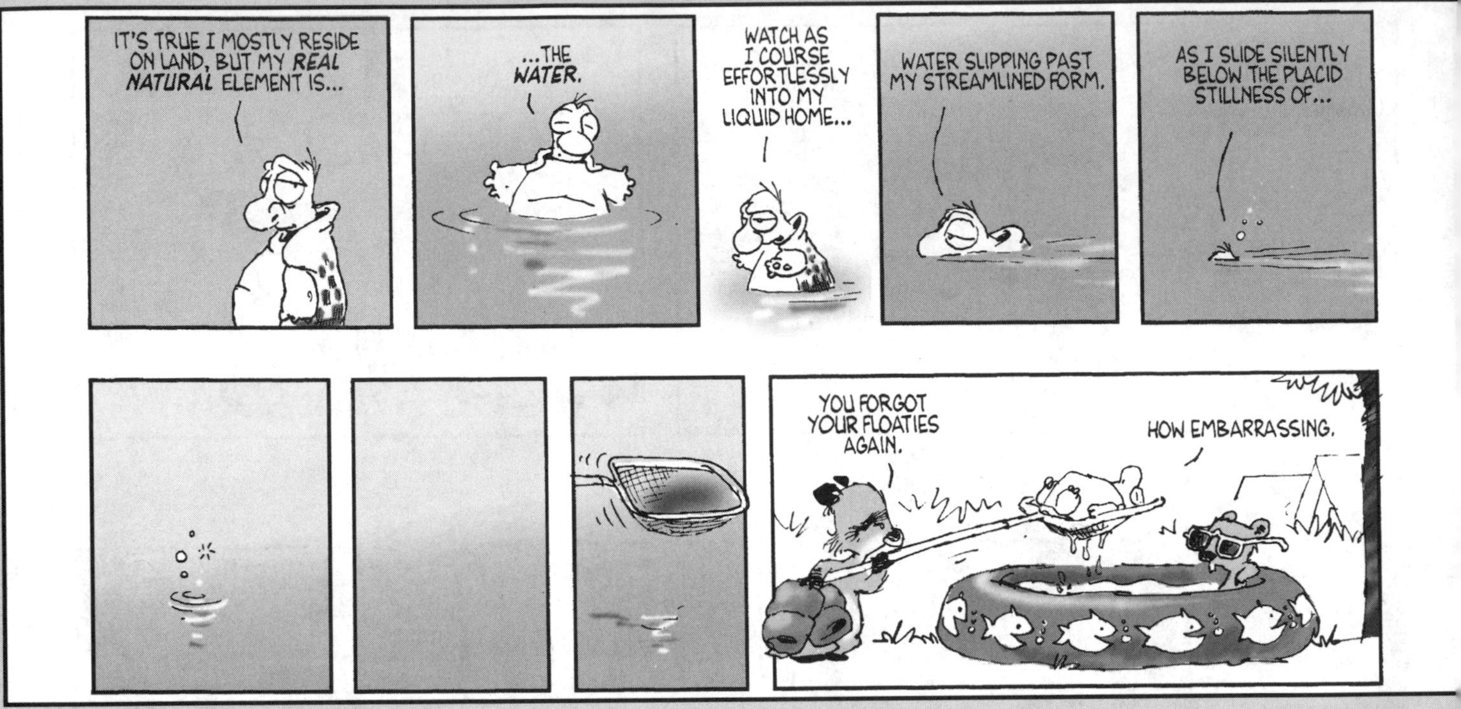
IT'S TRUE I MOSTLY RESIDE ON LAND, BUT MY *REAL NATURAL* ELEMENT IS...
...THE *WATER*.
WATCH AS I COURSE EFFORTLESSLY INTO MY LIQUID HOME...
WATER SLIPPING PAST MY STREAMLINED FORM.
AS I SLIDE SILENTLY BELOW THE PLACID STILLNESS OF...
YOU FORGOT YOUR FLOATIES AGAIN.
HOW EMBARRASSING.

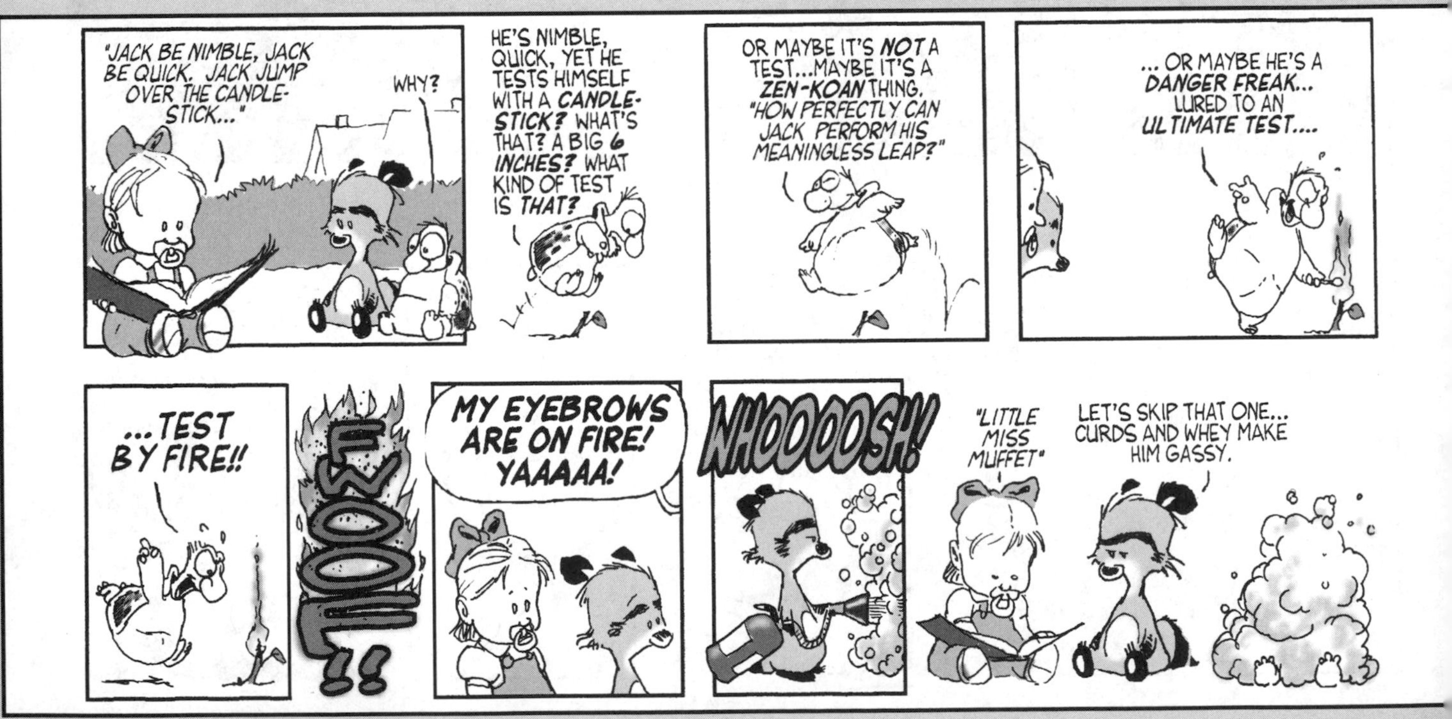
"JACK BE NIMBLE, JACK BE QUICK. JACK JUMP OVER THE CANDLE-STICK..."
WHY?
HE'S NIMBLE, QUICK, YET HE TESTS HIMSELF WITH A *CANDLE-STICK?* WHAT'S THAT? A BIG *6 INCHES?* WHAT KIND OF TEST IS *THAT?*
OR MAYBE IT'S *NOT* A TEST...MAYBE IT'S A *ZEN-KOAN* THING. "HOW PERFECTLY CAN JACK PERFORM HIS MEANINGLESS LEAP?"
...OR MAYBE HE'S A *DANGER FREAK...* LURED TO AN *ULTIMATE TEST....*
...TEST BY FIRE!!
FWOOSH!!
MY EYEBROWS ARE ON FIRE! YAAAAA!
WHOOOOSH!
"LITTLE MISS MUFFET"
LET'S SKIP THAT ONE... CURDS AND WHEY MAKE HIM GASSY.

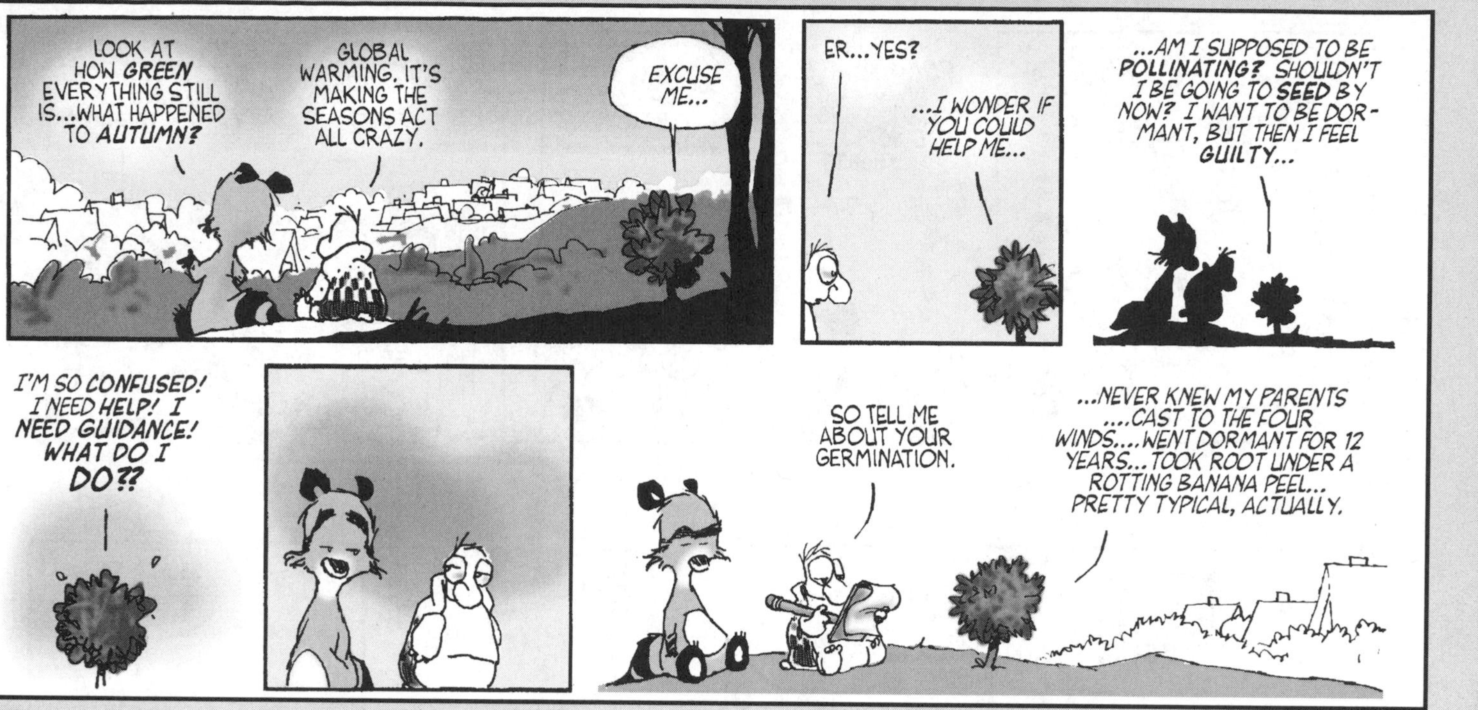
LOOK AT HOW GREEN EVERYTHING STILL IS...WHAT HAPPENED TO AUTUMN?
GLOBAL WARMING. IT'S MAKING THE SEASONS ACT ALL CRAZY.
EXCUSE ME...
ER...YES?
...I WONDER IF YOU COULD HELP ME...
...AM I SUPPOSED TO BE POLLINATING? SHOULDN'T I BE GOING TO SEED BY NOW? I WANT TO BE DORMANT, BUT THEN I FEEL GUILTY...
I'M SO CONFUSED! I NEED HELP! I NEED GUIDANCE! WHAT DO I DO??
SO TELL ME ABOUT YOUR GERMINATION.
...NEVER KNEW MY PARENTS ....CAST TO THE FOUR WINDS....WENT DORMANT FOR 12 YEARS...TOOK ROOT UNDER A ROTTING BANANA PEEL... PRETTY TYPICAL, ACTUALLY.

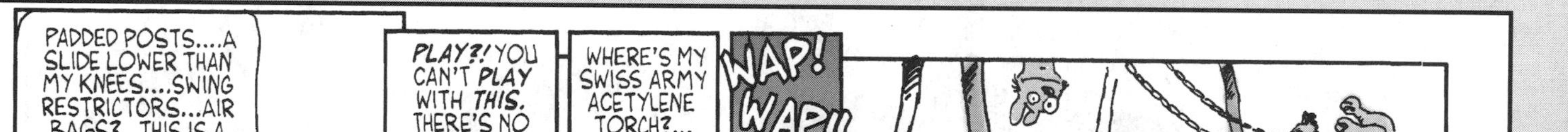
PADDED POSTS....A SLIDE LOWER THAN MY KNEES....SWING RESTRICTORS...AIR BAGS? THIS IS A DISGRACE! THIS IS A...
"PLAY ACTIVITY CENTER."
PLAY?! YOU CAN'T PLAY WITH THIS. THERE'S NO "PLAY" ALLOWED. WHERE'S THE RISK? WHERE'S THE FEAR? ...
WHERE'S MY SWISS ARMY ACETYLENE TORCH?...
WAP! WAP!!
FRZZZZZ
POUND!!
BANG!
NOW WE'RE HAVING FUN!!
PARACHUTES SOLD SEPARATELY.

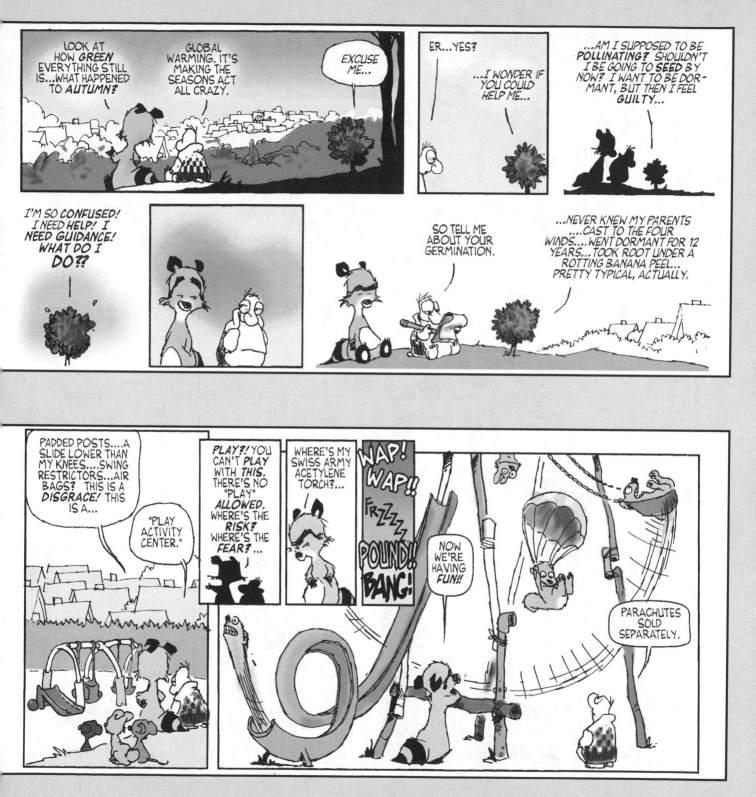

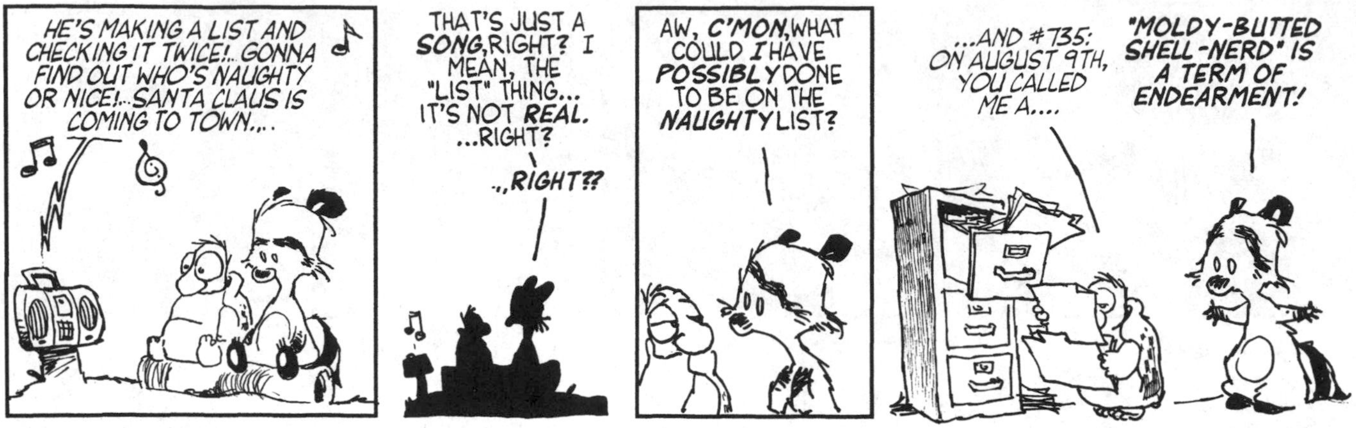
HE'S MAKING A LIST AND CHECKING IT TWICE!.. GONNA FIND OUT WHO'S NAUGHTY OR NICE!.. SANTA CLAUS IS COMING TO TOWN...
THAT'S JUST A SONG, RIGHT? I MEAN, THE "LIST" THING... IT'S NOT REAL. ...RIGHT?
..., RIGHT??
AW, C'MON, WHAT COULD I HAVE POSSIBLY DONE TO BE ON THE NAUGHTY LIST?
...AND #735: ON AUGUST 9TH, YOU CALLED ME A....
"MOLDY-BUTTED SHELL-NERD" IS A TERM OF ENDEARMENT!

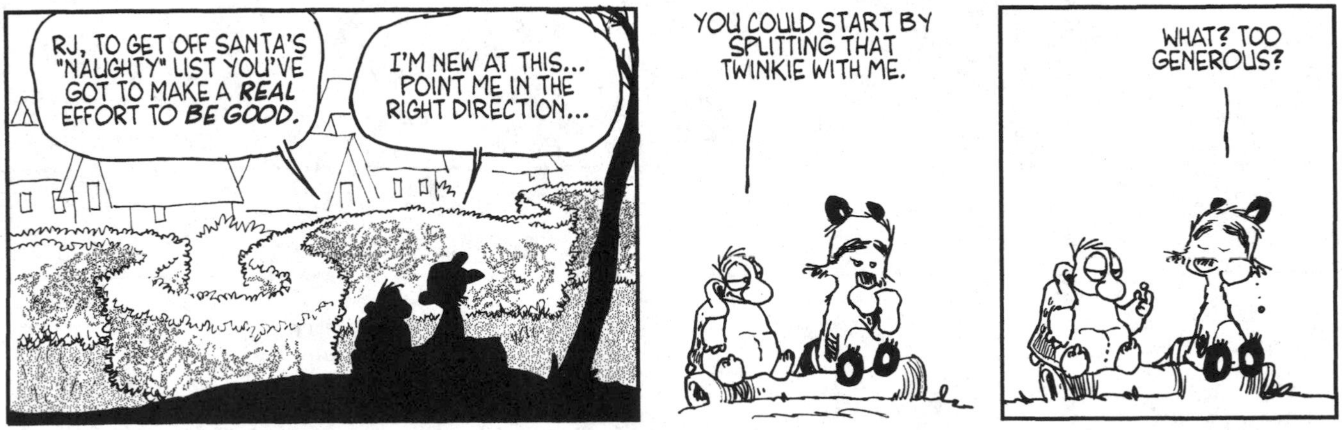
RJ, TO GET OFF SANTA'S "NAUGHTY" LIST YOU'VE GOT TO MAKE A REAL EFFORT TO BE GOOD.
I'M NEW AT THIS... POINT ME IN THE RIGHT DIRECTION...
YOU COULD START BY SPLITTING THAT TWINKIE WITH ME.
WHAT? TOO GENEROUS?

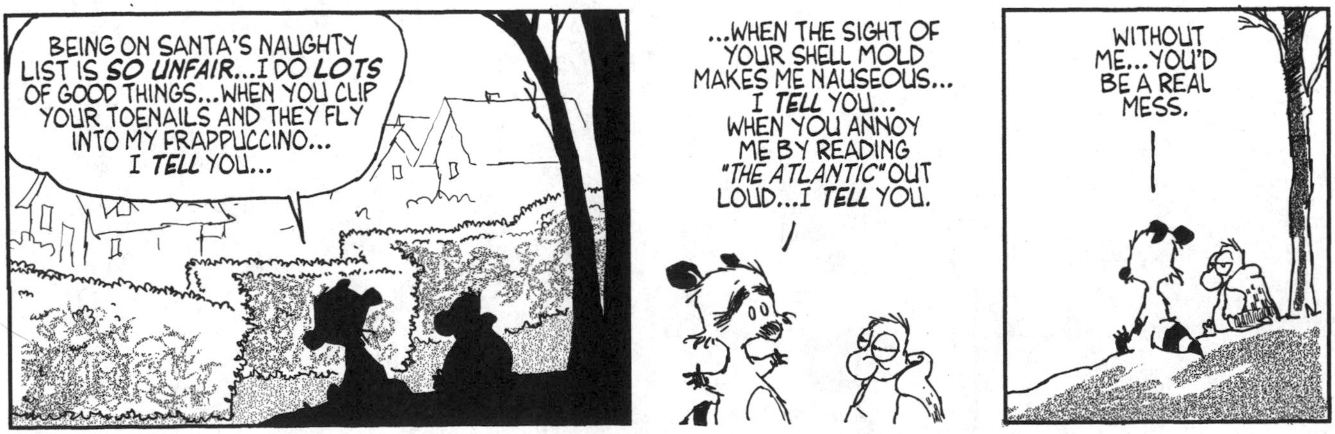
BEING ON SANTA'S NAUGHTY LIST IS SO UNFAIR...I DO LOTS OF GOOD THINGS...WHEN YOU CLIP YOUR TOENAILS AND THEY FLY INTO MY FRAPPUCCINO... I TELL YOU...
...WHEN THE SIGHT OF YOUR SHELL MOLD MAKES ME NAUSEOUS... I TELL YOU... WHEN YOU ANNOY ME BY READING "THE ATLANTIC" OUT LOUD...I TELL YOU.
WITHOUT ME...YOU'D BE A REAL MESS.

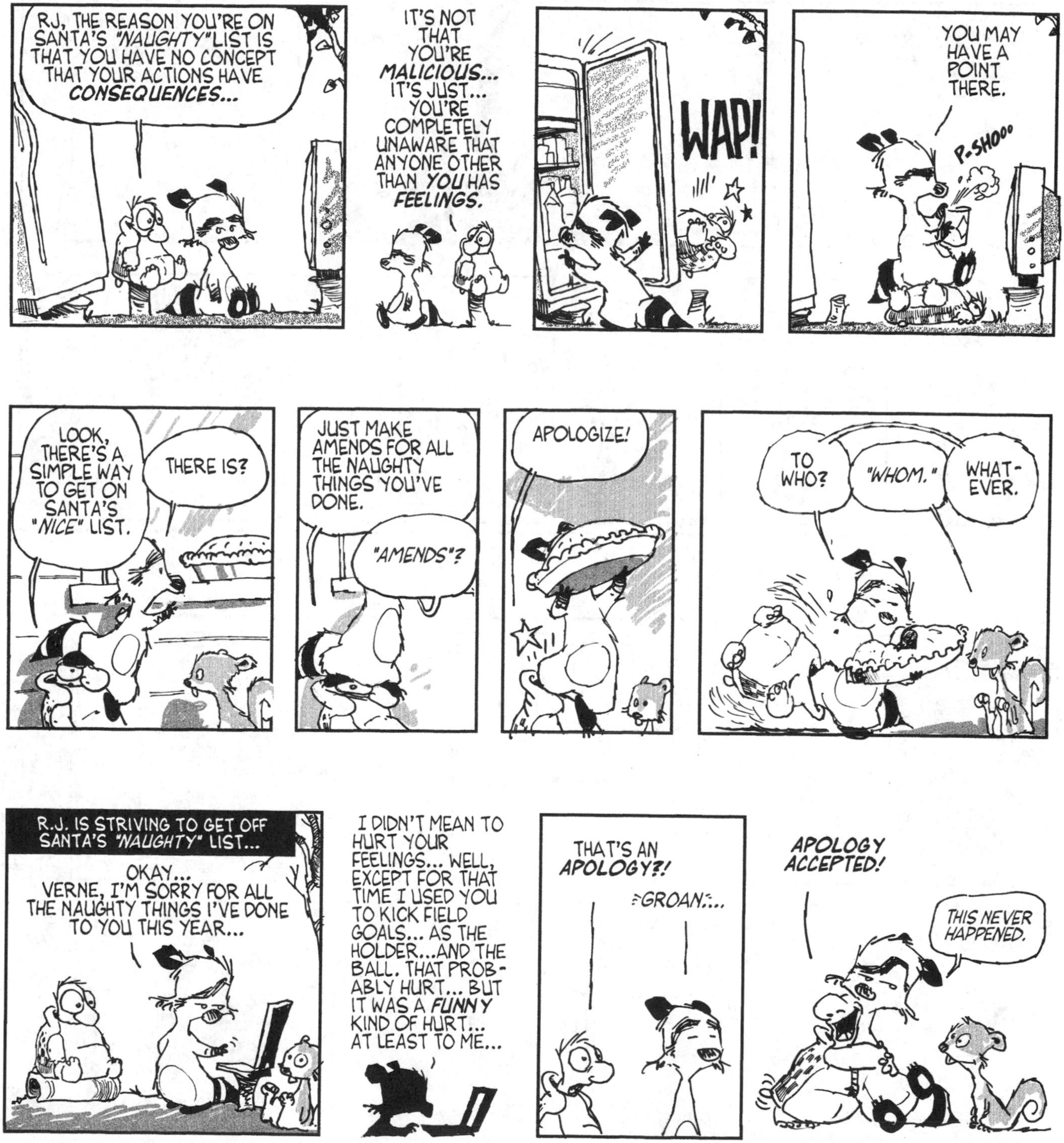
RJ, THE REASON YOU'RE ON SANTA'S "NAUGHTY" LIST IS THAT YOU HAVE NO CONCEPT THAT YOUR ACTIONS HAVE CONSEQUENCES...
IT'S NOT THAT YOU'RE MALICIOUS... IT'S JUST... YOU'RE COMPLETELY UNAWARE THAT ANYONE OTHER THAN YOU HAS FEELINGS.
WAP!
YOU MAY HAVE A POINT THERE.
P-SHOOO
LOOK, THERE'S A SIMPLE WAY TO GET ON SANTA'S "NICE" LIST.
THERE IS?
JUST MAKE AMENDS FOR ALL THE NAUGHTY THINGS YOU'VE DONE.
"AMENDS"?
APOLOGIZE!
TO WHO?
"WHOM."
WHAT-EVER.
R.J. IS STRIVING TO GET OFF SANTA'S "NAUGHTY" LIST...
OKAY... VERNE, I'M SORRY FOR ALL THE NAUGHTY THINGS I'VE DONE TO YOU THIS YEAR...
I DIDN'T MEAN TO HURT YOUR FEELINGS... WELL, EXCEPT FOR THAT TIME I USED YOU TO KICK FIELD GOALS... AS THE HOLDER...AND THE BALL. THAT PROBABLY HURT... BUT IT WAS A FUNNY KIND OF HURT... AT LEAST TO ME...
THAT'S AN APOLOGY?!
GROAN...
APOLOGY ACCEPTED!
THIS NEVER HAPPENED.

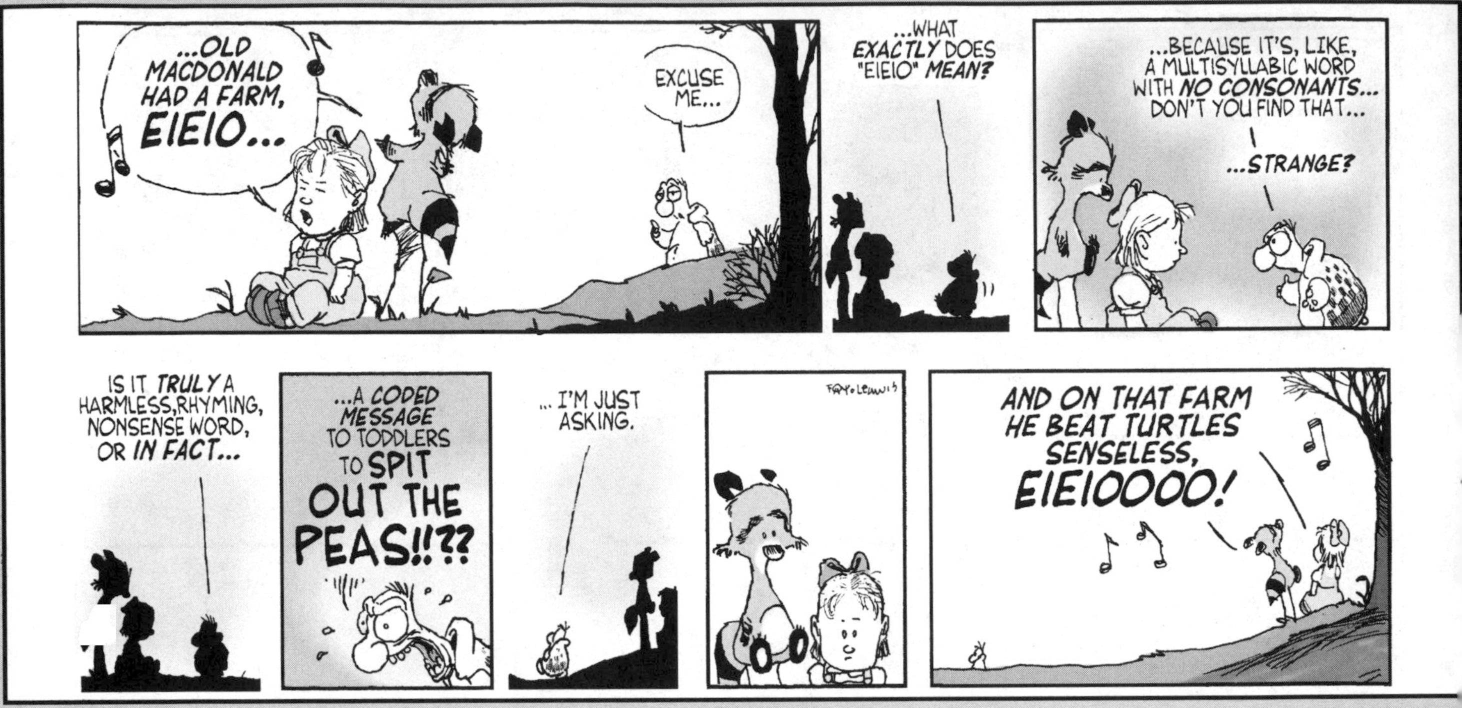

...OLD MACDONALD HAD A FARM, EIEIO...
EXCUSE ME...
...WHAT *EXACTLY* DOES "EIEIO" *MEAN?*
...BECAUSE IT'S, LIKE, A MULTISYLLABIC WORD WITH *NO CONSONANTS...* DON'T YOU FIND THAT...
...STRANGE?
IS IT *TRULY* A HARMLESS, RHYMING, NONSENSE WORD, OR *IN FACT...*
...A *CODED MESSAGE* TO TODDLERS TO SPIT OUT THE PEAS!!??
...I'M JUST ASKING.
AND ON THAT FARM HE BEAT TURTLES SENSELESS, EIEIOOOO!

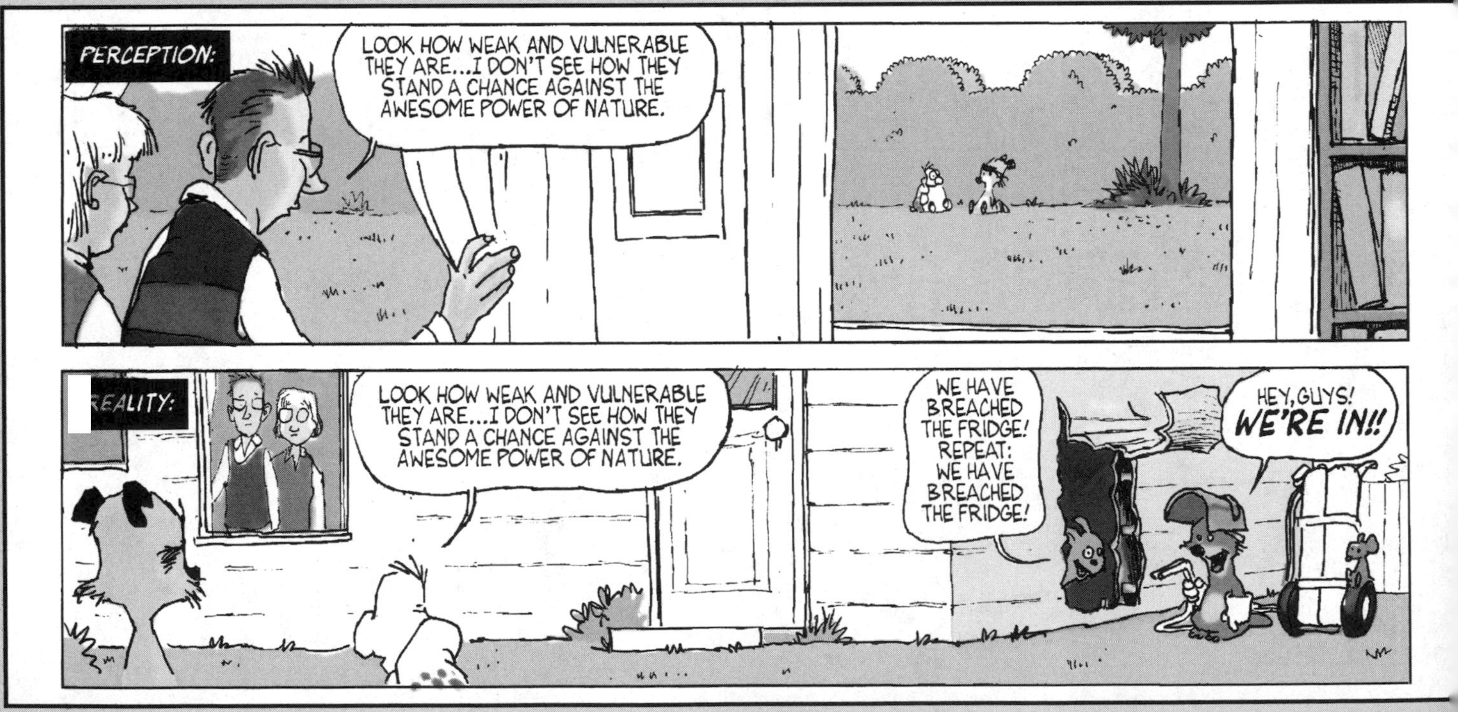

PERCEPTION:
LOOK HOW WEAK AND VULNERABLE THEY ARE...I DON'T SEE HOW THEY STAND A CHANCE AGAINST THE AWESOME POWER OF NATURE.
EALITY:
LOOK HOW WEAK AND VULNERABLE THEY ARE...I DON'T SEE HOW THEY STAND A CHANCE AGAINST THE AWESOME POWER OF NATURE.
WE HAVE BREACHED THE FRIDGE! REPEAT: WE HAVE BREACHED THE FRIDGE!
HEY, GUYS! WE'RE IN!!

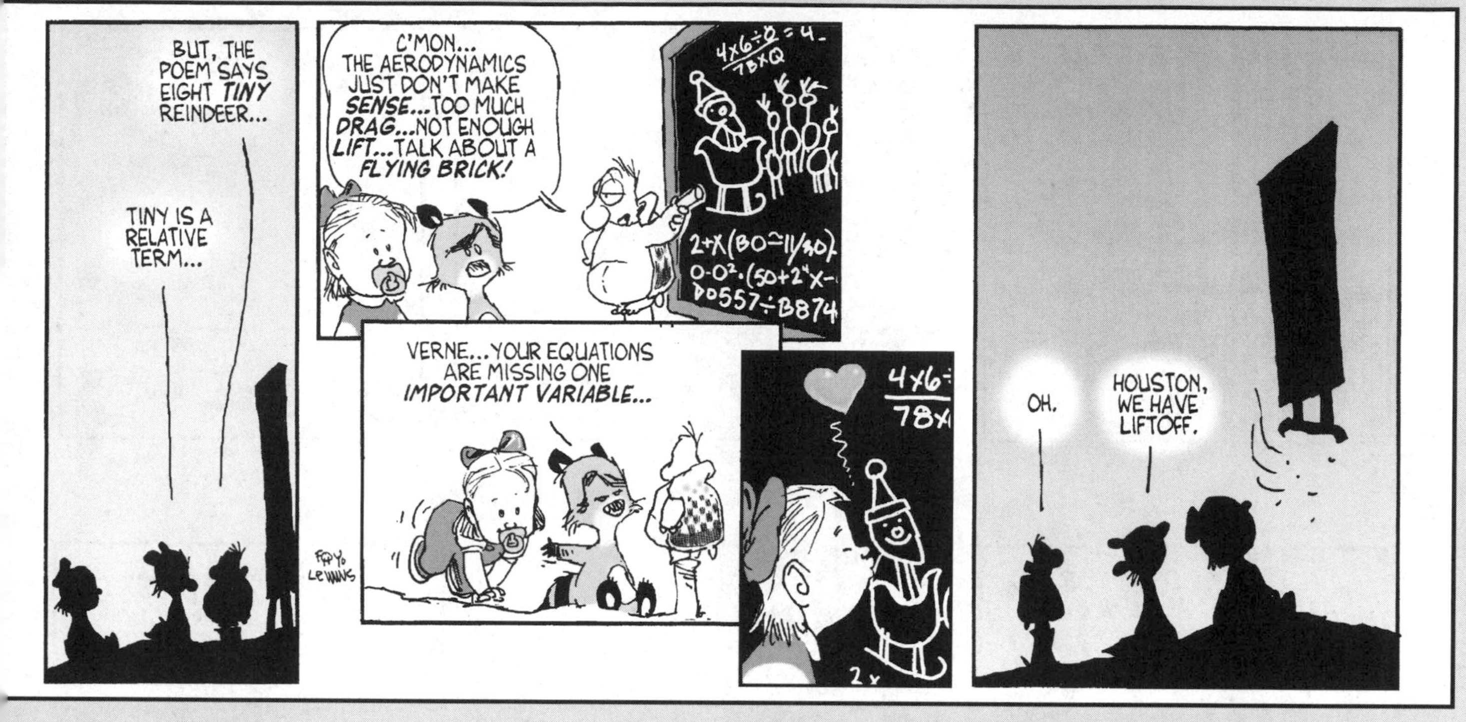
BUT, THE POEM SAYS EIGHT *TINY* REINDEER...
TINY IS A RELATIVE TERM...
C'MON... THE AERODYNAMICS JUST DON'T MAKE *SENSE*...TOO MUCH *DRAG*...NOT ENOUGH *LIFT*...TALK ABOUT A *FLYING BRICK!*
VERNE...YOUR EQUATIONS ARE MISSING ONE *IMPORTANT VARIABLE...*
OH.
HOUSTON, WE HAVE LIFTOFF.

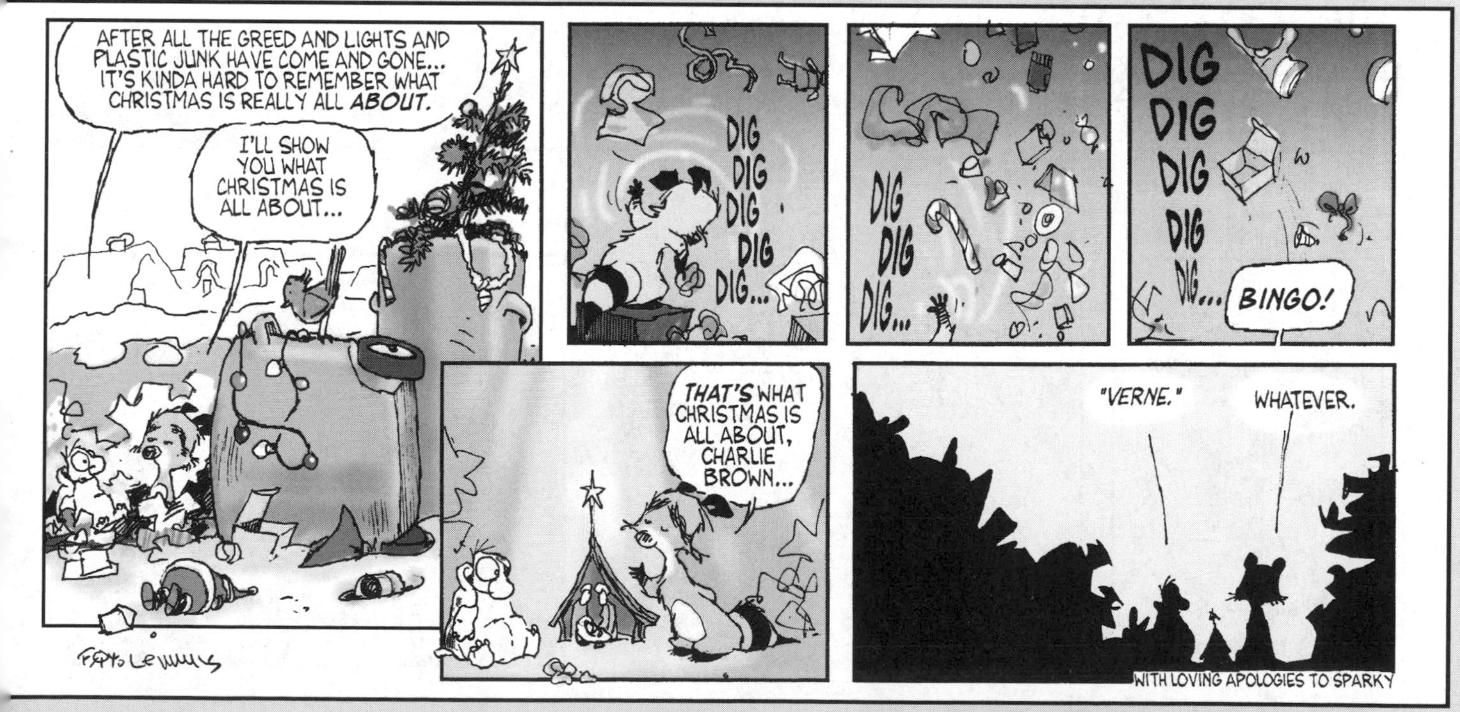
AFTER ALL THE GREED AND LIGHTS AND PLASTIC JUNK HAVE COME AND GONE... IT'S KINDA HARD TO REMEMBER WHAT CHRISTMAS IS REALLY ALL *ABOUT.*
I'LL SHOW YOU WHAT CHRISTMAS IS ALL ABOUT...
DIG DIG DIG DIG DIG...
DIG DIG DIG...
DIG DIG DIG DIG DIG...
BINGO!
THAT'S WHAT CHRISTMAS IS ALL ABOUT, CHARLIE BROWN...
"VERNE."
WHATEVER.
WITH LOVING APOLOGIES TO SPARKY

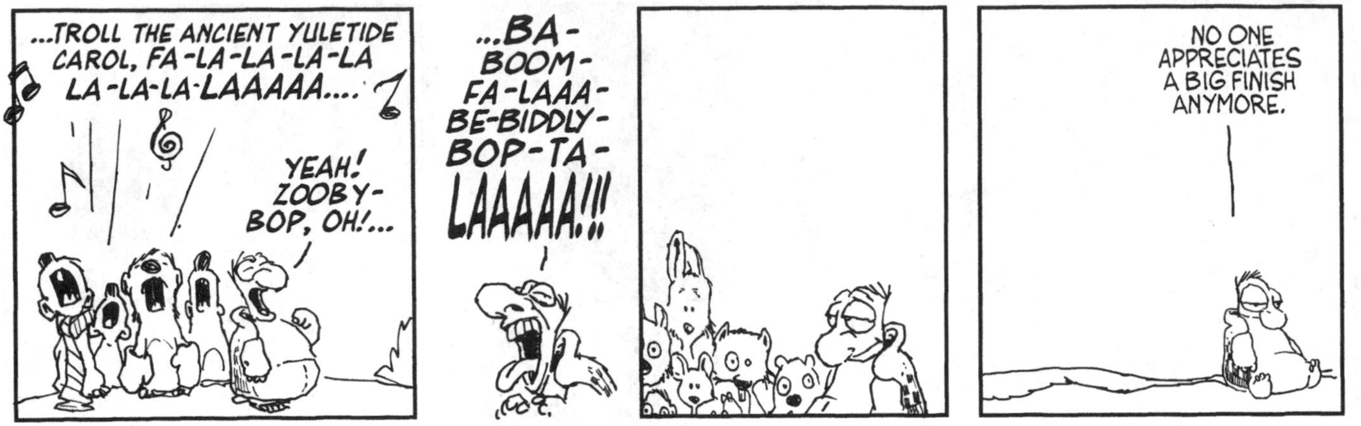
...TROLL THE ANCIENT YULETIDE CAROL, FA-LA-LA-LA-LA LA-LA-LA-LAAAAA....
YEAH! ZOOBY-BOP, OH!...
...BA-BOOM-FA-LAAA-BE-BIDDLY-BOP-TA-LAAAAA!!!
NO ONE APPRECIATES A BIG FINISH ANYMORE.

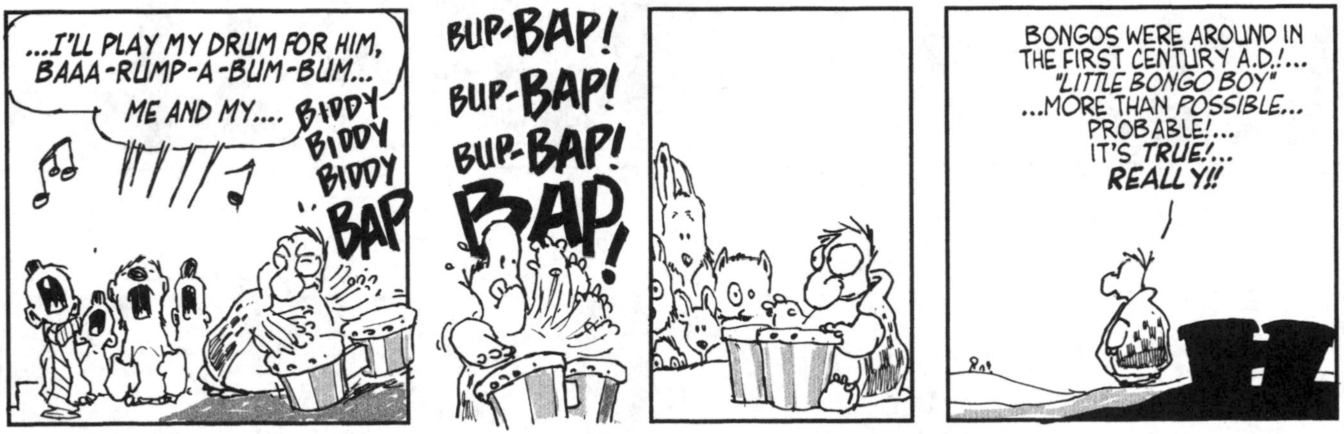
...I'LL PLAY MY DRUM FOR HIM, BAAA-RUMP-A-BUM-BUM... ME AND MY....
BIDDY BIDDY BIDDY BAP
BUP-BAP! BUP-BAP! BUP-BAP! BAP!
BONGOS WERE AROUND IN THE FIRST CENTURY A.D.!... "LITTLE BONGO BOY" ...MORE THAN POSSIBLE... PROBABLE!... IT'S TRUE!... REALLY!!

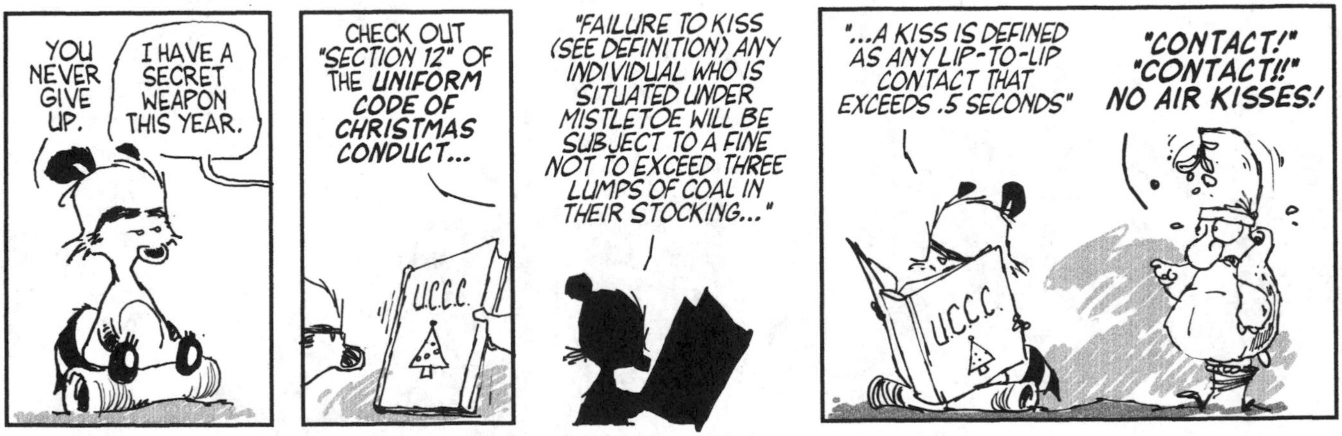
YOU NEVER GIVE UP.
I HAVE A SECRET WEAPON THIS YEAR.
CHECK OUT "SECTION 12" OF THE UNIFORM CODE OF CHRISTMAS CONDUCT...
U.C.C.C.
"FAILURE TO KISS (SEE DEFINITION) ANY INDIVIDUAL WHO IS SITUATED UNDER MISTLETOE WILL BE SUBJECT TO A FINE NOT TO EXCEED THREE LUMPS OF COAL IN THEIR STOCKING..."
"...A KISS IS DEFINED AS ANY LIP-TO-LIP CONTACT THAT EXCEEDS .5 SECONDS"
"CONTACT!" "CONTACT!!" NO AIR KISSES!
U.C.C.C.

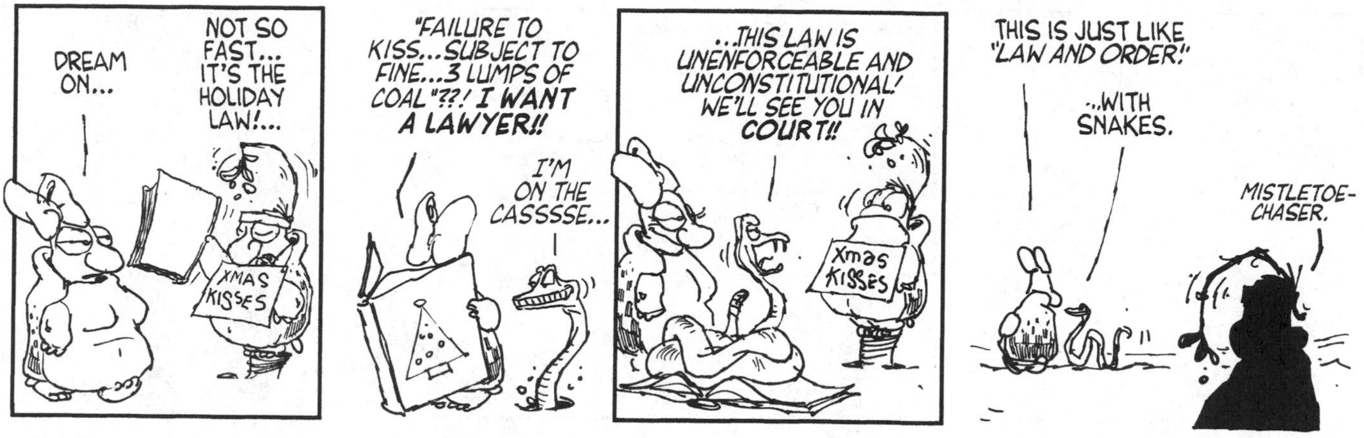
DREAM ON...
NOT SO FAST... IT'S THE HOLIDAY LAW!...
"FAILURE TO KISS...SUBJECT TO FINE...3 LUMPS OF COAL"??! I WANT A LAWYER!!
I'M ON THE CASSSSE...
XMAS KISSES
...THIS LAW IS UNENFORCEABLE AND UNCONSTITUTIONAL! WE'LL SEE YOU IN COURT!!
Xmas KISSES
THIS IS JUST LIKE "LAW AND ORDER!"
...WITH SNAKES.
MISTLETOE-CHASER.

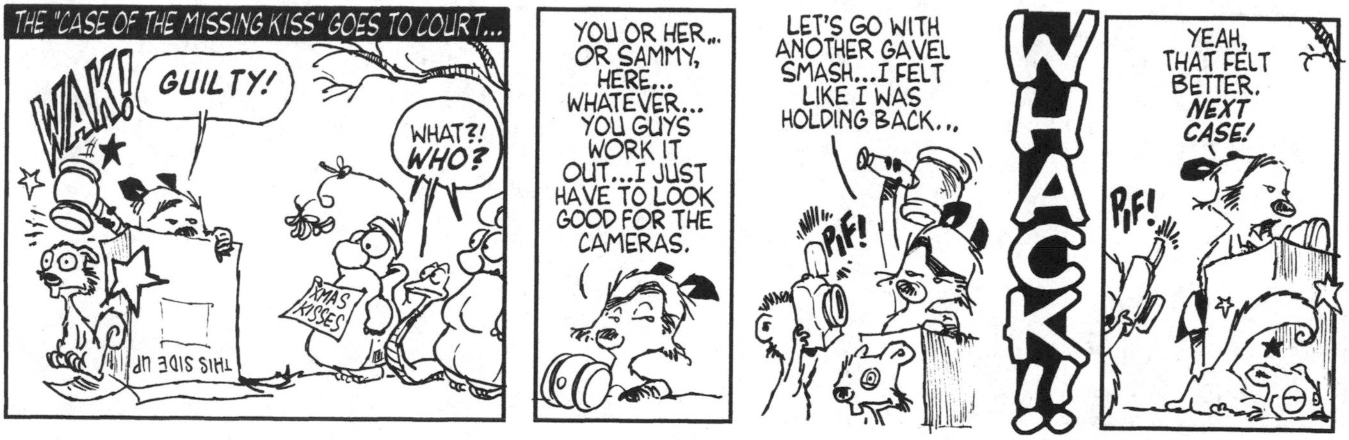
THE "CASE OF THE MISSING KISS" GOES TO COURT...
WAK!
GUILTY!
WHAT?! WHO?
XMAS KISSES
THIS SIDE UP
YOU OR HER... OR SAMMY, HERE... WHATEVER... YOU GUYS WORK IT OUT...I JUST HAVE TO LOOK GOOD FOR THE CAMERAS.
LET'S GO WITH ANOTHER GAVEL SMASH...I FELT LIKE I WAS HOLDING BACK...
PIF!
WHACK!!
PIF!
YEAH, THAT FELT BETTER. NEXT CASE!

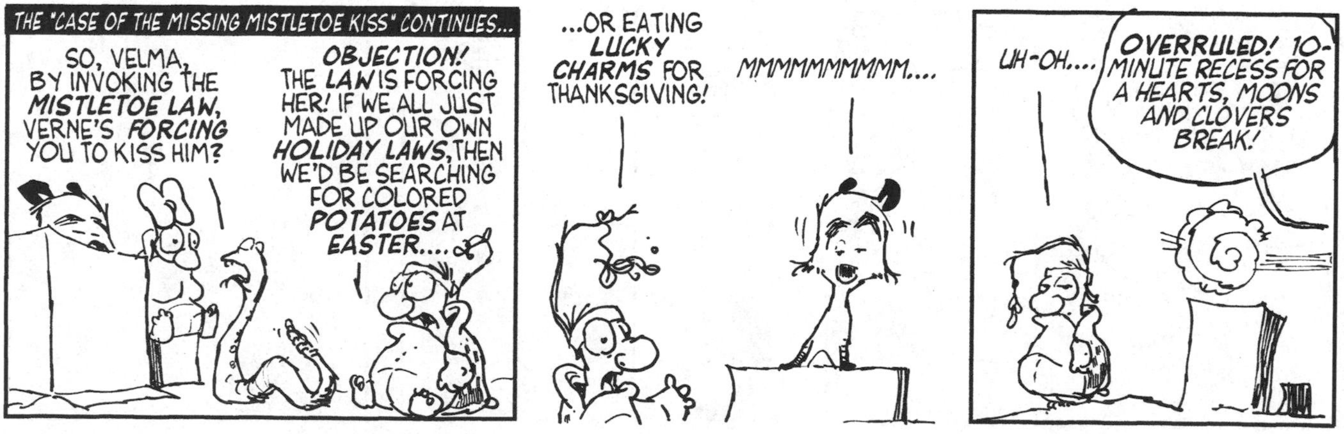
THE "CASE OF THE MISSING MISTLETOE KISS" CONTINUES...
SO, VELMA, BY INVOKING THE MISTLETOE LAW, VERNE'S FORCING YOU TO KISS HIM?
OBJECTION! THE LAW IS FORCING HER! IF WE ALL JUST MADE UP OUR OWN HOLIDAY LAWS, THEN WE'D BE SEARCHING FOR COLORED POTATOES AT EASTER....
...OR EATING LUCKY CHARMS FOR THANKSGIVING!
MMMMMMMMMM....
UH-OH....
OVERRULED! 10-MINUTE RECESS FOR A HEARTS, MOONS AND CLOVERS BREAK!

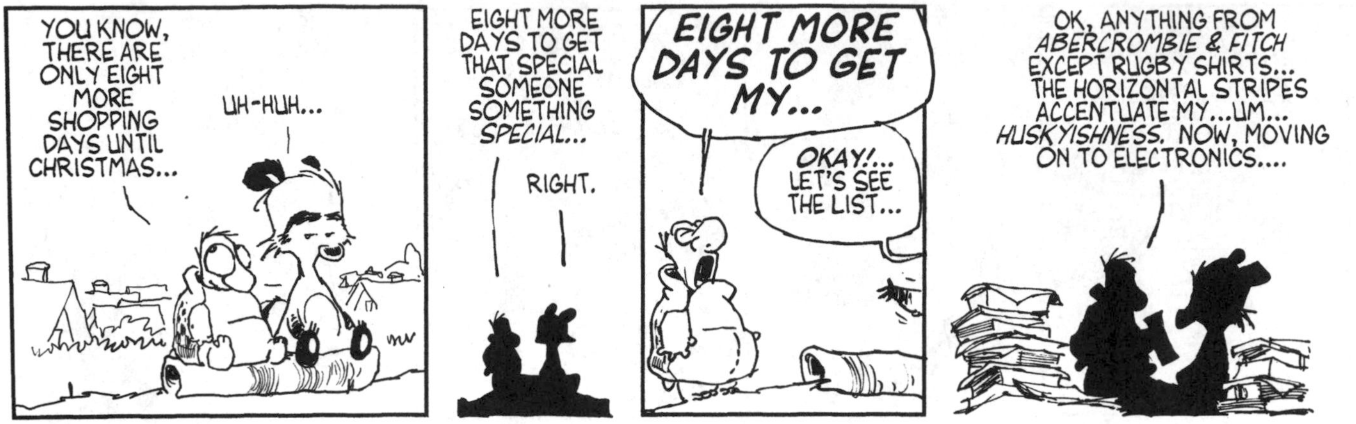
YOU KNOW, THERE ARE ONLY EIGHT MORE SHOPPING DAYS UNTIL CHRISTMAS...
UH-HUH...
EIGHT MORE DAYS TO GET THAT SPECIAL SOMEONE SOMETHING *SPECIAL*...
RIGHT.
EIGHT MORE DAYS TO GET MY...
OKAY!... LET'S SEE THE LIST...
OK, ANYTHING FROM *ABERCROMBIE & FITCH* EXCEPT RUGBY SHIRTS... THE HORIZONTAL STRIPES ACCENTUATE MY...UM... *HUSKYISHNESS.* NOW, MOVING ON TO ELECTRONICS....

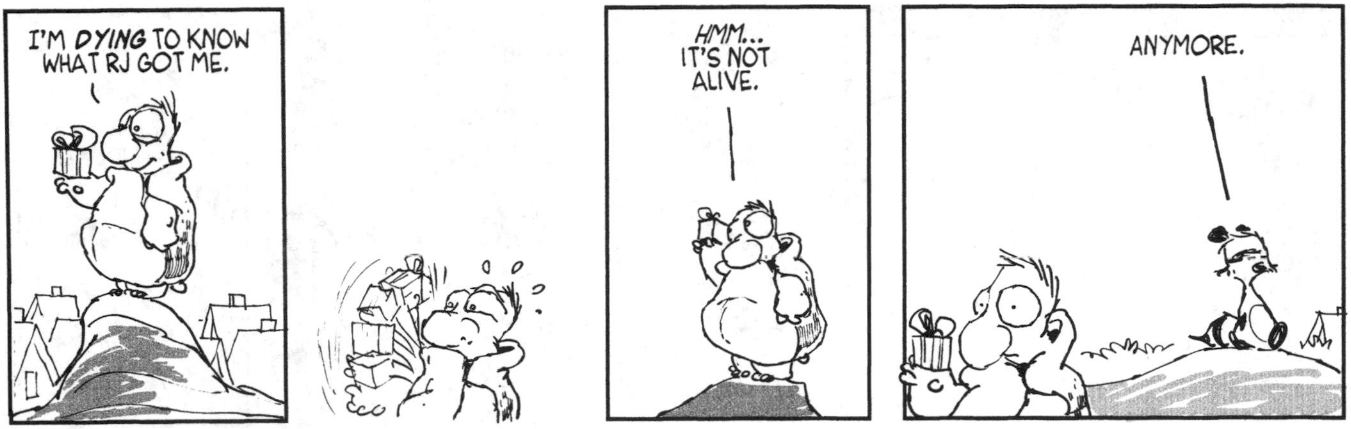
I'M **DYING** TO KNOW WHAT RJ GOT ME.
HMM... IT'S NOT ALIVE.
ANYMORE.

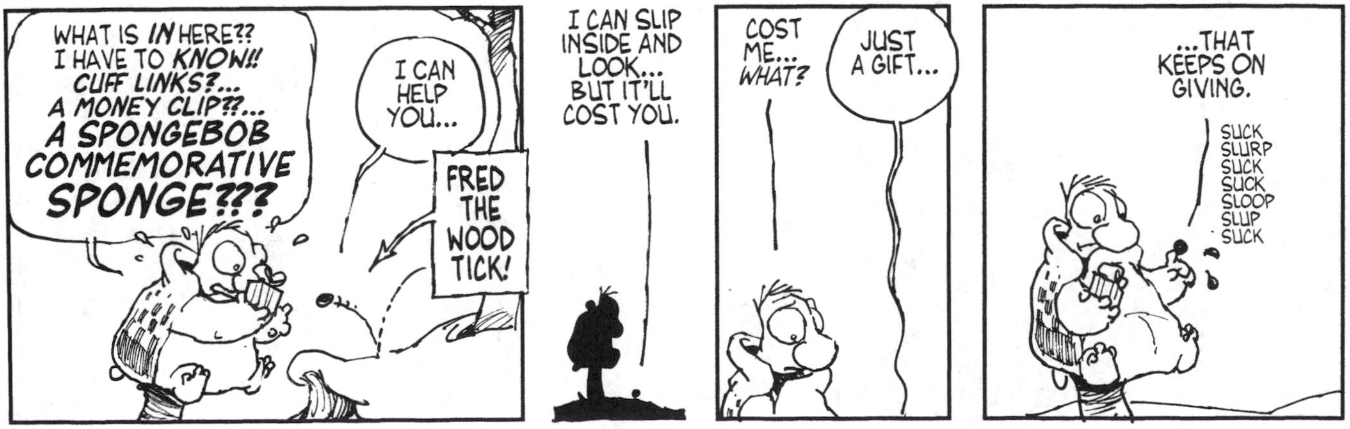
WHAT IS **IN** HERE?? I HAVE TO **KNOW!!** **CUFF LINKS?... A MONEY CLIP??... A SPONGEBOB COMMEMORATIVE SPONGE???**
I CAN HELP YOU...
FRED THE WOOD TICK!
I CAN SLIP INSIDE AND LOOK... BUT IT'LL COST YOU.
COST ME... *WHAT?*
JUST A GIFT...
...THAT KEEPS ON GIVING.
SUCK SLURP SUCK SUCK SLOOP SLUP SUCK

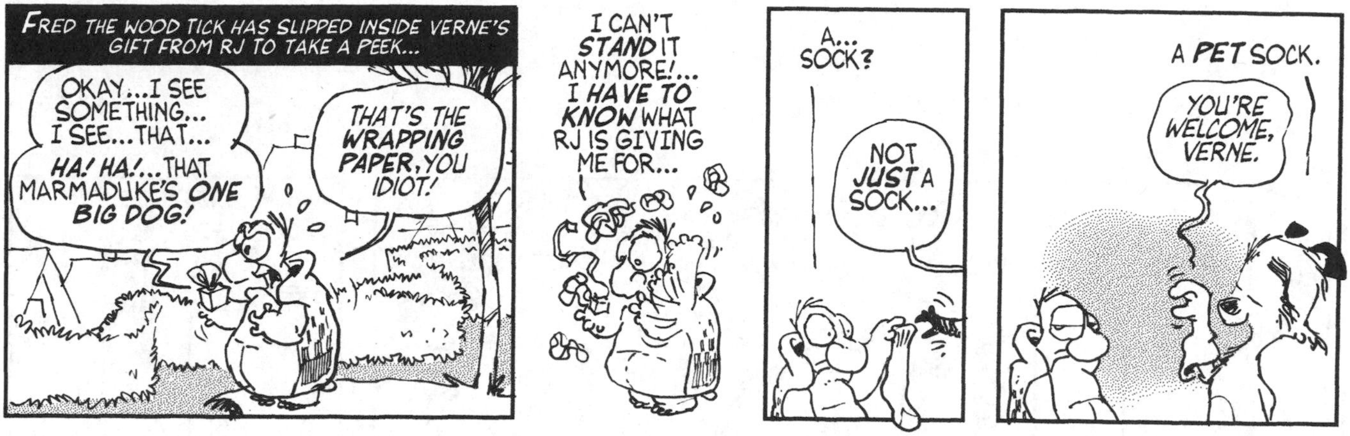
FRED THE WOOD TICK HAS SLIPPED INSIDE VERNE'S GIFT FROM RJ TO TAKE A PEEK...
OKAY...I SEE SOMETHING... I SEE...THAT... HA! HA!...THAT MARMADUKE'S ONE BIG DOG!
THAT'S THE WRAPPING PAPER, YOU IDIOT!
I CAN'T STAND IT ANYMORE!... I HAVE TO KNOW WHAT RJ IS GIVING ME FOR...
A... SOCK?
NOT JUST A SOCK...
A PET SOCK.
YOU'RE WELCOME, VERNE.

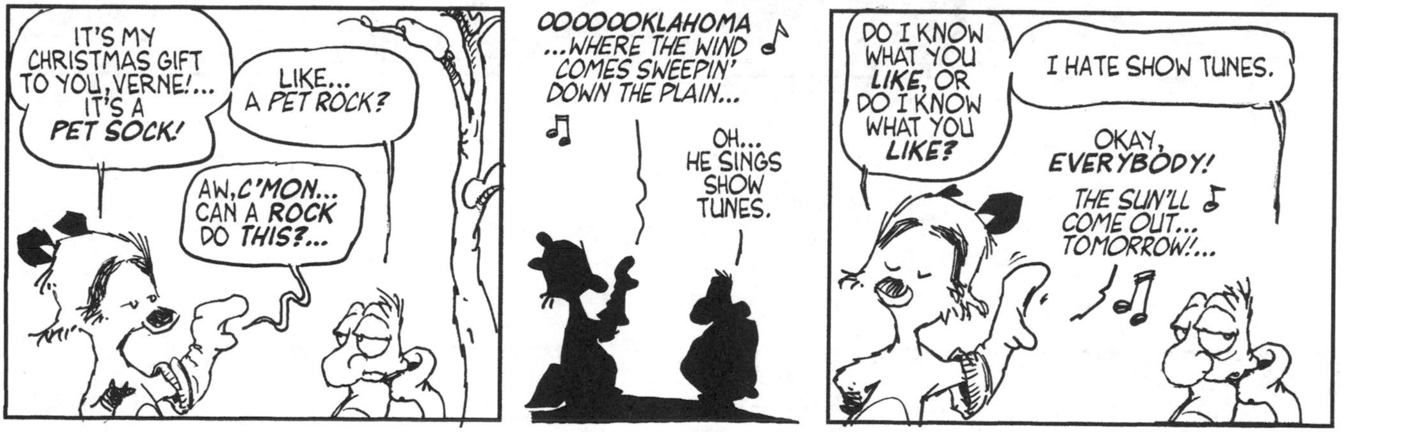
IT'S MY CHRISTMAS GIFT TO YOU, VERNE!... IT'S A PET SOCK!
LIKE... A PET ROCK?
AW, C'MON... CAN A ROCK DO THIS?...
OOOOOOKLAHOMA ...WHERE THE WIND COMES SWEEPIN' DOWN THE PLAIN...
OH... HE SINGS SHOW TUNES.
DO I KNOW WHAT YOU LIKE, OR DO I KNOW WHAT YOU LIKE?
I HATE SHOW TUNES.
OKAY, EVERYBODY! THE SUN'LL COME OUT... TOMORROW!...

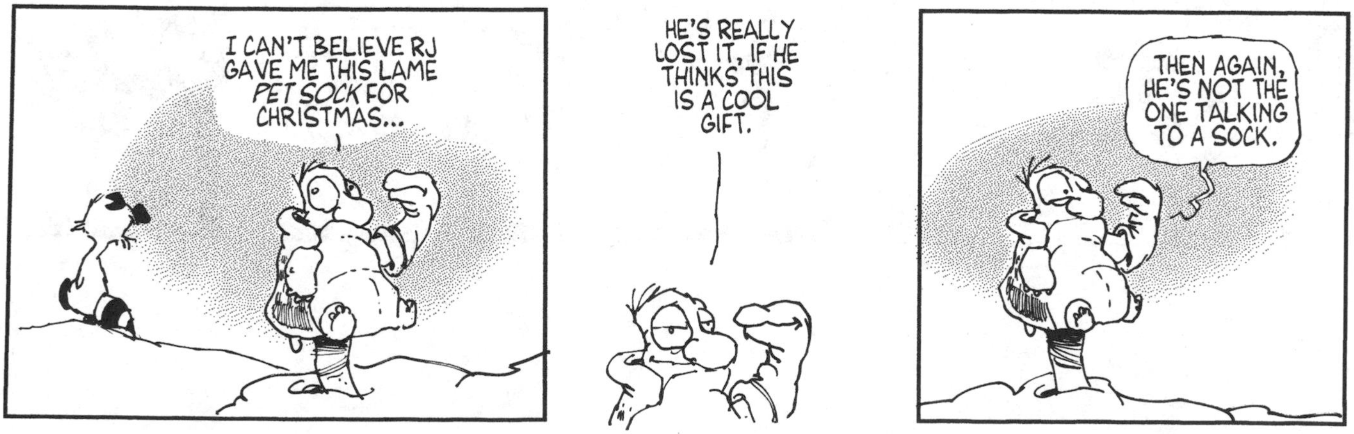
I CAN'T BELIEVE RJ GAVE ME THIS LAME PET SOCK FOR CHRISTMAS...
HE'S REALLY LOST IT, IF HE THINKS THIS IS A COOL GIFT.
THEN AGAIN, HE'S NOT THE ONE TALKING TO A SOCK.

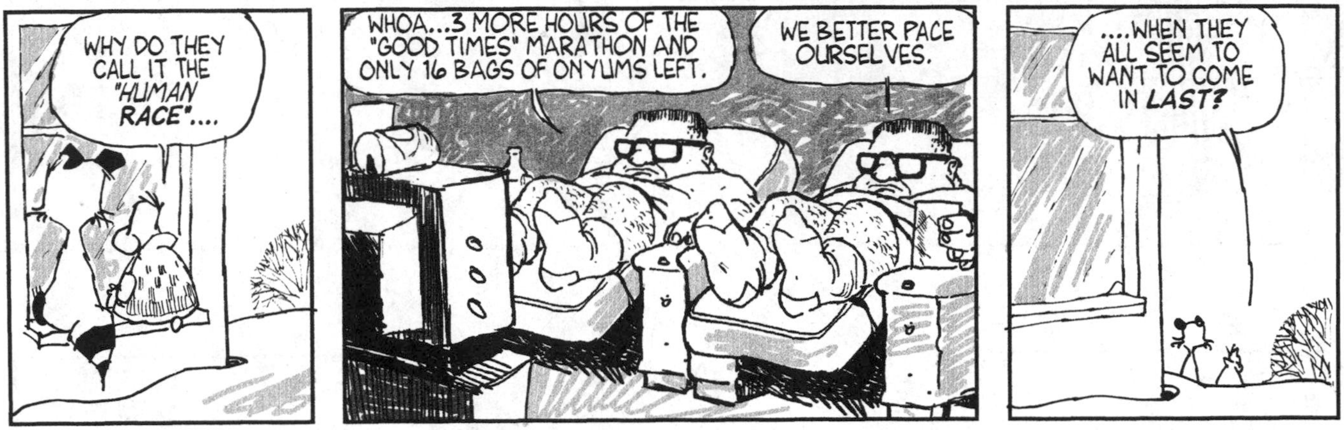
WHY DO THEY CALL IT THE "HUMAN RACE"....
WHOA...3 MORE HOURS OF THE "GOOD TIMES" MARATHON AND ONLY 16 BAGS OF ONYUMS LEFT.
WE BETTER PACE OURSELVES.
....WHEN THEY ALL SEEM TO WANT TO COME IN LAST?

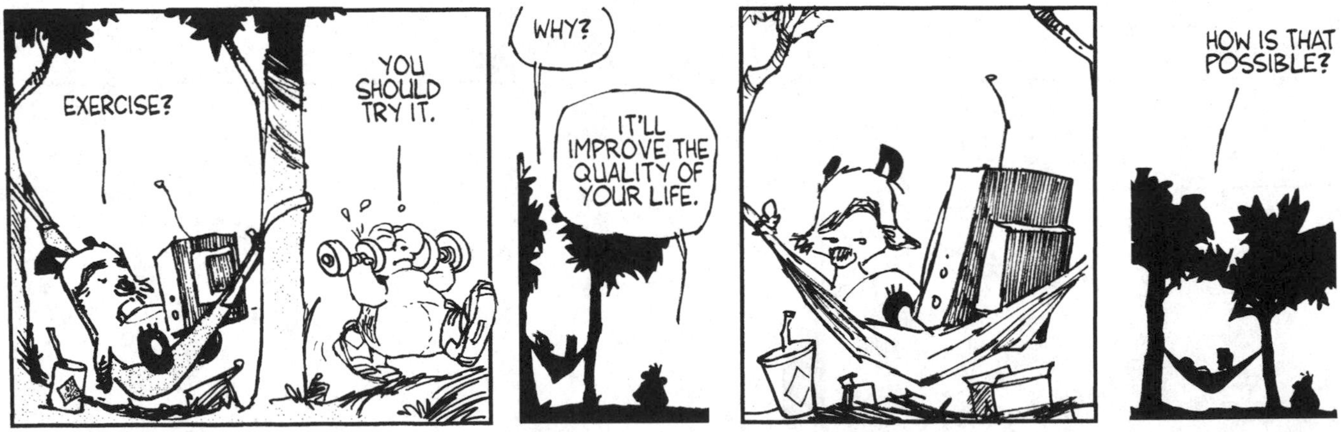
EXERCISE?
YOU SHOULD TRY IT.
WHY?
IT'LL IMPROVE THE QUALITY OF YOUR LIFE.
HOW IS THAT POSSIBLE?

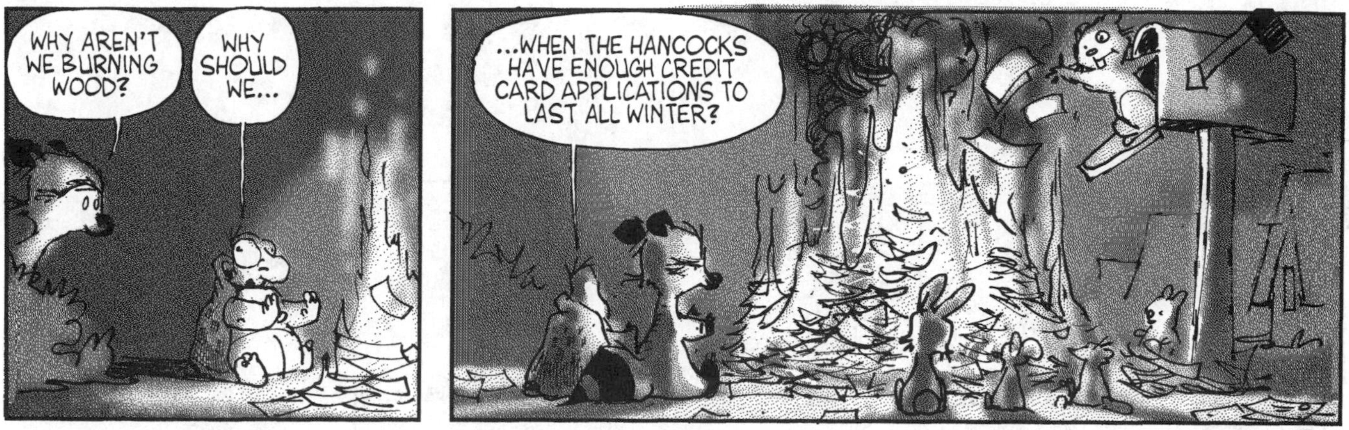
WHY AREN'T WE BURNING WOOD?
WHY SHOULD WE...
...WHEN THE HANCOCKS HAVE ENOUGH CREDIT CARD APPLICATIONS TO LAST ALL WINTER?

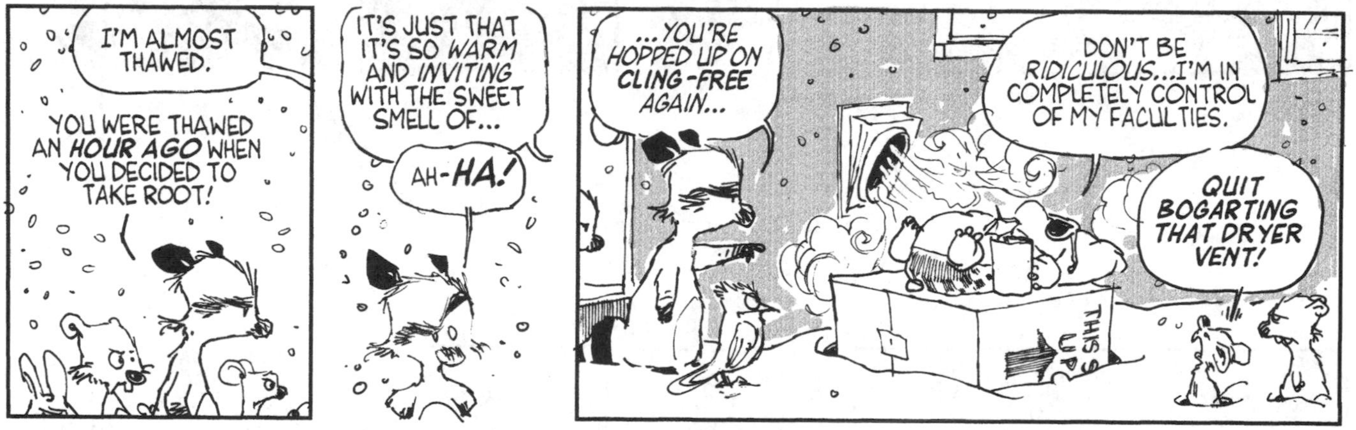
I'M ALMOST THAWED.
YOU WERE THAWED AN *HOUR AGO* WHEN YOU DECIDED TO TAKE ROOT!
IT'S JUST THAT IT'S SO *WARM* AND *INVITING* WITH THE SWEET SMELL OF...
AH-*HA!*
...*YOU'RE HOPPED UP ON* **CLING-FREE** *AGAIN...*
DON'T BE *RIDICULOUS*...I'M IN COMPLETELY CONTROL OF MY FACULTIES.
QUIT BOGARTING THAT DRYER VENT!
THIS SIDE UP

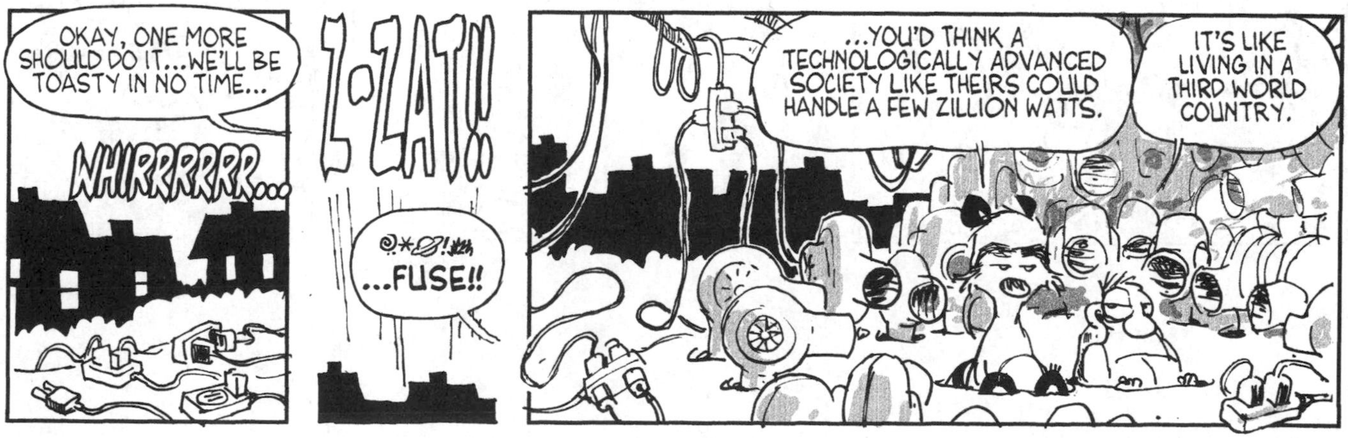
OKAY, ONE MORE SHOULD DO IT...WE'LL BE TOASTY IN NO TIME...
WHIRRRRRR...
Z-ZAT!!
...FUSE!!
...YOU'D THINK A TECHNOLOGICALLY ADVANCED SOCIETY LIKE THEIRS COULD HANDLE A FEW ZILLION WATTS.
IT'S LIKE LIVING IN A THIRD WORLD COUNTRY.

VERNE'S NEW WALLET...

WHO'S IN THE PHOTO?

OH, HER?... NOBODY... NOBODY IMPORTANT... OKAY, IF YOU *INSIST*...

PARIS...1993... IT WAS RAINING... SHE WAS SMILING... WE FELL IN LOVE... BUT WE WERE KIDDING OURSELVES... SHE SAID: *"CLAM-AA-TO"*... I SAID: *"CLAM-AW-TO"*...

SHE CAME WITH THE WALLET, DIDN'T SHE?

IT COULD HAPPEN!!

"...AND THEY LIVED HAPPILY EVER AFTER... THE END."

HOW CAN THEY LIVE HAPPILY *EVER AFTER* IF IT'S *THE END?*

IT'S THE END OF THE *BOOK,* BUT NOT THE END OF THE *STORY.*

HUH?

SIGH...

...THEY RETIRED... LIVING IN FLORIDA...THE PRINCESS TOOK UP YOGA. THE FROG PRINCE PLAYS A LOT OF GOLF... THEY SEEM HAPPY.

SEE? MIXED MARRIAGES *CAN* WORK.